THE MANUAL OF PSYCHEDELIC SUPPORT

GWYLLM LLWYDD • *The Chemist* (dedicated to Sasha Shulgin), 2013 • multimedia, digital collage
http://www.gwyllm-art.com

THE MANUAL OF PSYCHEDELIC SUPPORT

Second Edition
Multidisciplinary Association for Psychedelic Studies (MAPS)

Copies of this Manual may be downloaded freely from
http://www.psychsitter.com

Sales of this book will help fund psychedelic harm reduction.

The Manual of Psychedelic Support
Second Edition (2017) Multidisciplinary Association for Psychedelic Studies (MAPS)
Printed in China by Asia Pacific Offset
ISBN 978-0-9982765-1-9

LICENSING & COPYRIGHT

This work, *excluding all art and photos*, is licensed under a Creative Commons Attribution—Non-Commercial 4.0 International licence. You are free to Share (copy/redistribute in any medium) and Adapt (remix, transform, build upon) the text of this work, as long as you attribute its original source to *The Manual of Psychedelic Support* and provide a link to the CC BY-NC 4.0 licence https://creativecommons.org/licenses/by-nc/4.0/. Additionally, no part of this work may be used directly for commercial purposes. Art and photos in this work are copyright by their respective artists and photographers.

EDITORS

ANNIE OAK	Founder of the Women's Visionary Congress and the Full Circle Tea House
JON HANNA	Co-founder of Mind States
KAYA	
SVEA NIELSEN	Psychologist, Vision Board Coach, Nikken Consultant, and Mama of fine organic children
TWILIGHT	
ZEVIC MISHOR, PhD	

FOREWORDS

FIRE & EARTH EROWID	Co-founders of Erowid Center, Erowid.org, and EcstasyData.org
DIOGO RUIVO	Founder of Good Mood Productions and the Boom Festival
RICK DOBLIN, PhD	Founder & Executive Director of the Multidisciplinary Association for Psychedelic Studies (MAPS)
ALICIA DANFORTH, PhD	Clinical Psychedelics Researcher
SAM CUTLER	Former Tour Manager for the Rolling Stones and the Grateful Dead

AUTHORS

ALEXANDRE QUARANTA, PhD	Writer, Tantric Yoga Teacher, and Lucid Dreaming Trainer
ALICIA DANFORTH, PhD	Clinical Psychedelics Researcher
ANNIE OAK	Founder of the Women's Visionary Congress and the Full Circle Tea House
BEN ATKINSON	Critical Incident Debriefer/Crisis Care Worker
BEN HOLDEN	Board Member & Lead Volunteer for Kosmicare UK, and Harm Reduction Outreach Worker (Leeds, United Kingdom)
BERRY	
CHRISTOPHER J. WARD	
CONSTANCE RODRIGUES	Clinical Psychologist, Somatic-Psychotherapist, Pilot for KosmiCare Boom Festival (2010), Teacher & Co-founder of the Portuguese Center of Jungian Studies
CONSTANTINOS EFSTRATIOU	

DANIEL LEUENBERGER	Trance-lator, DJ Almacalma, and Daddy
ELISSA HARWOOD	Researcher
EMMA METCALF	
GASTONE ZANETTE (Gas), MD	Anaesthesiologist
GRACE LIEW	
IGOR DOMSAC	Psychonaut, Artist, Father, and Founder of Alter Consciens
ISLA CAMILLE DUPORGE	
JACK LIEBERMAN	
JACOB POTKONYAK	
JOAN OBIOLS-LLANDRICH, MD, PhD	Psychiatrist and Anthropologist
JOÃO GONÇALVES	
JON HANNA	Co-founder of Mind States
JONAS DI GREGORIO	
KAI SCHULZE	
KARIN SILENZI DE STAGNI	Coordinator of Kosmicare UK
KAYA	
KIM PENDERS	
LEVENTE MÓRÓ	Coordinator for DÁT2 Psy Help
LINNAE PONTÉ	Former Director of Harm Reduction (Zendo Project) for MAPS
MARC B. AIXALÀ	
MARIA CARMO CARVALHO	Lecturer at the Faculty of Education, Catholic University of Portugal at Porto, and Pilot & Research Coordinator for KosmiCare Boom Festival (2010)
MARIANA PINTO DE SOUSA	Researcher for KosmiCare Boom Festival
MIMI PELEG	Director of Large Scale Cannabis Training at MECHKAR Israel, and Clinical Research Associate for the MAPS
MINTY DE LA PLAYA	
NATACHA RIBEIRO	
RICK DOBLIN, PhD	Founder & Executive Director of MAPS
SNU VOOGELBREINDER	Ethnobotanical Author and Psychonaut
SVEA NIELSEN	Psychologist, Vision Board Coach, Nikken Consultant, and Mama of fine organic children
TIMOTHY BAKAS	
TOM SHUTTE	Psychotherapist
TRACY DUNNE	Secretary & Care Service Leader for Kosmicare UK
TWILIGHT	
XAVIER URQUIAGA A.	
VINCE CAKIC	
ZEVIC MISHOR, PhD	

ARTISTS

ALEX GREY	http://www.alexgrey.com
ALLYSON GREY	http://www.allysongrey.com

FRED TOMASELLI	http://www.jamescohan.com/artists/fred-tomaselli
GWYLLM LLWYDD	http://www.gwyllm-art.com
JON HANNA	http://www.mindstates.org
LUKE BROWN	http://www.spectraleyes.com
LUKE GRAY	http://www.lukegray.net
MARK HENSON	http://www.markhensonart.com
MARTINA HOFFMANN	http://www.martinahoffmann.com
NAOTO HATTORI	http://www.naotohattori.com
ROBERT VENOSA	http://www.venosa.com
SHANNON THERON	http://plus.google.com/+ShannonTheron/posts
SHANTIQ	http://www.saatchiart.com/shantiq
VIBRATA CHROMODORIS	http://www.vibrata.com
ZEVIC MISHOR, PhD	

PHOTOGRAPHERS

DAVID ARNSON	Founder of the Insect Surfers and the Raw Power Rangers
EROWID	http://www.erowid.org
GREG MANNING	
JEN ZARIAT	http://www.zariat.com
JOHN COCKTOASTEN	
JON HANNA	Co-founder of Mind States
LEANDRO REINALDO	Anaesthesiologist, Medical Doctor
MADDIE RADNAN	Co-founder of Yo! Mad Dreadlocks, BSc. (Hons) Student, and Psychonaut
SUSANA SANTOS	Social Worker
VIBRATA CHROMODORIS	http://www.vibrata.com
ZEVIC MISHOR, PhD	

DESIGN TEAM

BLAKE HANNA	**Proofreader** • Educator and Cat Whisperer
DAVE KING	**Web Design** • Co-director of Breaking Convention
JON HANNA	**Art & Photography Editor** • Co-founder of Mind States
LUKE GRAY	**Cover Artwork** • http://www.lukegray.net
MARK PLUMMER	**Book & Cover Design**
SARAH JORDAN	**Production**

CONTRIBUTORS

ANA PAULA SILVA COSTA	
D.J. SIMMS	
DAVE KING	Co-director of Breaking Convention
GWYLLM LLWYDD	http://www.gwyllm-art.com
IKER PUENTE	
JOANNA TARNAVA	

NAMES within this Manual are generally arranged alphabetically by first name. Specific authors for each chapter are listed under that chapter's heading, with **bold type** indicating the chapter leads—those who were responsible for coordinating the writing of that chapter.

DISCLAIMER

This book is designed to present helpful information and motivation to our readers on the subjects addressed. It is provided with the understanding that its editors and its authors are not offering any type of psychological, medical, legal, or any other kind of professional advice. The content of each chapter is the sole expression and opinion of its authors, and not necessarily that of the editors.

This book is not meant to be used, nor should it be used, to diagnose nor treat any medical, psychological, and/or physiological condition. For diagnosis or treatment of any medical, psychological, or physiological problem, consult a licensed physician. The editors and authors are not responsible for any specific health needs that may require medical supervision and shall not be held liable for any damages or negative consequences from any treatment, action, application, or preparation undertaken by and/or provided to any person reading or following the information in this book.

References are provided for informational purposes only and do not constitute endorsement of any websites or other sources. Readers should be aware that the URLs listed in this book and/or the contents of their web sites may change at any time.

Every situation is different. The advice and strategies contained in this Manual may not be suitable for your situation. The editors and authors make no representations or warranties of any kind and specifically disclaim any implied warranties of merchantability or fitness of use for a particular purpose. Neither the editors nor the authors shall be held liable to any person or entity for any loss, or for physical, psychological, emotional, financial, and/or commercial damages, including, but not limited to, special, incidental, consequential or other damages caused, or alleged to have been caused, directly or indirectly by the information contained herein. The authors and editors retain their own views and rights. Readers are responsible for their own choices and results.

FEEDBACK

This Manual is an ongoing work, and we appreciate any comments or suggestions regarding its content. Feedback may be given at http://www.psychsitter.com.

DEDICATED...

with deep respect to **Dr. Andrew Sewell,** a courageous healer and researcher who helped develop the principles presented in this Manual and applied them with great compassion;

with love to **David K. Lord,** a precious friend on the Path who chose to go his own way. Travel well, dear Dave;

and in gratitude to **Alexander T. Shulgin,** pioneering chemist and pharmacologist who created numerous valuable psychedelic tools.

1. Drs. Albert Hofmann and Andrew Sewell displaying the Polish edition of *LSD—My Problem Child*. Photo by Jon Hanna, 2008.
2. David K. Lord. Photographer unknown.
3. Sasha Shulgin on the playa in Black Rock City, Nevada, at the Burning Man Festival. Photo by Greg Manning, 2007.
4. David Best's *Temple of Honor*, Black Rock City, Nevada, at the Burning Man Festival. Photo by Jon Hanna, 2003.

Contents

Forewords 1

Introduction 13

1. A History of Psychedelic Care Services 19
2. The Principles and Ethics of Psychedelic Support ... 37
3. Legal Considerations 49
4. Planning and First Steps for a New Project 59
5. Recruiting a Team 67
6. Supporting Roles 79
7. Building and Training a Team 87
8. Logistics 105
9. The Care Space 133
10. Running the Service 147
11. Screening 157
12. Complementary Therapies 167
13. Team Welfare 185
14. Working With Other Organisations 191
15. Risk Management and Performance Improvement ... 199
16. Case Studies and Impressions 213
17. Online Resources and Obtaining Assistance 263

Final Words 275

Appendix A
Street Names for
Commonly Encountered Psychoactives 279

Appendix B
Monitoring, Evaluating and Researching—
Recommendations from an Academic Perspective
for an Evidence-Based Approach to Psychoactive
Crisis Intervention 303

Guide to Drug Effects and Interactions 331

About the Publisher 379

NAOTO HATTORI • *Mind Form 03, 2012* • acrylic on board
http://naotohattori.com

FOREWORDS

Fire Erowid

Earth Erowid

Co-founders

of:

Erowid Center

Erowid.org

EcstasyData.org

The psychedelic and empathogenic states engendered by psychoactive drugs are some of the most profound states of consciousness that humans experience. These substances can also trigger some of the most challenging, confusing, and stressful moments of a person's life.

Concerts, electronic dance music parties, and festivals offer rich aesthetic and social environments that some attendees choose to explore with psychoactive drugs. Those who take ecstasy, LSD, cannabis, or other recreational drugs at these events are generally hoping to have a fun time with a sense of connection, interest, and wonder. But a combination of factors—inexperienced users, novel substances, festival chaos, contaminated or misidentified drugs, et cetera—creates a context where some participants may have psychologically difficult or physically dangerous experiences.

Emergency medical services are present at most large events, but these are set up to handle physical health issues, not emotional or psycho-spiritual crises. Individuals who find themselves overwhelmed by a psychedelic or empathogen need a different kind of support: a service designed to help those in mental turmoil who need a quiet space, a friendly voice, or assistance in recovering from internal and/or external chaos. The presence of trained and prepared care givers can have a strong positive impact on delicate psychedelic mind states, whether those states be fearful or joyous.

The authors of *The Manual of Psychedelic Support* have created a practical guide for designing, organising, and implementing psychedelic/psychological care services. It covers topics ranging from interfacing with festival organisers to complex legal considerations, from checklists for assembling physical structures to therapeutic grounding techniques. Whilst framed primarily for producing formal services at larger events, many of the recommendations are useful for any size gathering where psychoactive drugs are likely to be consumed.

In 1998, when we wrote the "Psychedelic Crisis FAQ", there were few publicly available resources describing how to help people in the midst of a difficult psychedelic experience. At the time, psychedelic support spaces were not provided at Burning Man or many other large events, and medical tents were the default destination for people experiencing "bad trips". This Manual shows how much the art and engineering of psychedelic support services have evolved over the last twenty years, and sets a new high bar for the manner in which these services should be run and what they can accomplish.

Psychedelic care services at festivals are now even more important, as a wildly increasing variety of psychoactive drugs has become available. The presence of novel psychoactive substances complicates all aspects of medical and psychological care. According to the United Nations Office on Drugs and Crime, over 250 new drugs appeared on the international scene between 2000 and 2013. Large festivals are the front lines where users (many of them young) encounter new drugs.

Regardless of the exact identity of the drugs, some use will result in challenging, dark experiences. Crisis care organisers are there to help transform stressful sessions into positive ones by offering a safe context and gentle support. Whilst it is hardly a new idea that set and setting are important, the last fifty years have taught us that the wisdom with which challenges are handled can make the difference between psychological casualties and enriched experimenters.

Although not the norm, difficult or "bad" trips also aren't rare. In a 2006 survey of visitors to Erowid.org who reported having tried LSD, 14.5% disclosed having had at least one experience they considered a "very" or "extremely" bad trip. An additional 20.8% reported a "mild" or "somewhat" bad trip. Even in research settings where psychedelics are administered under controlled conditions, extremely fearful experiences are fairly common. In research published in *Psychopharmacology* by Griffiths et al. in 2011, 39% of carefully screened, healthy adults given a strong dose of psilocybin experienced "extreme ratings of fear, fear of insanity, or feeling trapped" at some point during a session. Yet, despite these periods of intense fear, the comforting environment and trained sitter led to 90% of participants reporting increased well-being and life satisfaction.

Experienced users know that even fearful ordeals whilst under the influence of psychedelics, empathogens, or cannabis can ultimately lead to positive outcomes. When asked to look back on their lifetime of psychedelic use as part of Erowid's pilot "Wisdom Cycle" survey, over 80% of elders said that their difficult psychedelic experiences had also proven beneficial to some degree. Unfortunately, few young people are taught how to navigate psychedelic states by their more experienced elders.

The Manual of Psychedelic Support assembled here addresses the fact that festivals and large events are hubs for psychedelic and empathogen use, where challenging psychological states will inevitably occur. The authors argue that beyond simply providing basic medical care, festival producers and harm-reduction organisations need to offer psychological care as well. Avoiding physical harm at events can no longer be viewed as the only measure of health-related success. This book brings together experts in event planning, therapy, and crisis intervention to create a blueprint for producing psychedelic care services for large and small gatherings alike: improving outcomes, smoothing interactions with law enforcement, and easing the load on medical services. This Manual is an important next step in the sociocultural evolution towards healthier, happier festival attendees.

ANONYMOUS • *Guardian of the Light*, 2014 • watercolour and gouache

Holding Space for the Tribe

Diogo Ruivo
*Good Mood Productions
and Founder of the Boom Festival*

WHEN setting up a gathering with life transforming potential, the task of the promoters is far beyond that of providing a programme of art, culture, music, and the logistics to make it all run smoothly. As these events often offer the context for experiencing altered states of consciousness, the promoters cannot avoid dealing in a mature and responsible way with the potential "psychedelic emergencies" that may and do arise. In the perspective fostered by many researchers nowadays, which view gatherings involving "ecstatic practices" as a resurfacing of ancient tribal traditions, the promoters become those accountable for "holding the space for the tribe", and even more so when the event attracts many tens of thousands of people.

It is therefore mandatory to include in the event's production the construction of one or more spaces devoted to dealing responsibly with such "emergencies", regardless of the attitudes manifested by the hosting government. As a matter of fact, this would be a more sophisticated way for society as a whole to address the issue of practices leading to altered states of consciousness, which are well-known to occur and are too often (not to say always) dealt with through repressive strategies or utter negligence.

If the setting up of such dedicated spaces within events production (including the necessary training for the people offering the support service) had been a standard procedure since the emergence of music festivals and other large-scale events, the electronic and rock music scenes would probably not have the "bad name" that they have nowadays. If promoters had felt and accepted this responsibility on themselves—by taking care of the event, its participants, and the surrounding community as a whole—we could have avoided many young people hurting themselves and even dying because of mismanaged drug use.

During the years of event production, we at Good Mood have joined a fantastic team of multidisciplinary experts who trained hundreds of volunteers in providing psychedelic support, thus carrying out ground-breaking work in solving difficult cases, saving many lives, and keeping the "community body" harmonious.

Our experience with KosmiCare, Boom's pioneering harm-reduction project, allowed us to become aware of the need for gathering and sharing the information harvested by this and similar ground-breaking initiatives. We are therefore enthusiastic to see this Manual coming to life, as a cornerstone for the promotion and creation of similar projects all around the world. We are very thankful to the team of researchers and healers that has come together to make this happen!

May all states of consciousness be equally cared for, with dignity and respect, in a progressively maturing society!

An area at the 2009 Symbiosis Festival in Yosemite specifically designated to hold space for the sacred. Photo by Erowid.

An Encouraging Sign...

Rick Doblin, PhD
Founder and Executive Director,
Multidisciplinary Association for Psychedelic Studies (MAPS)

THE creation and publication of *The Manual of Psychedelic Support* is an encouraging sign of the maturation and compassion of the global community of psychedelic users. In the midst of the long-awaited but still early crumbling of the counterproductive system of Prohibition (with its explicit goal to increase harms and the perception of risk), this Manual provides essential information about psychedelic harm reduction in a self-regulatory voluntary context. Written by an experienced worldwide team, the Manual helps pave the way to a Post-Prohibition world respectful of people's basic human right to use psychedelics to explore their full range of consciousness—for personal growth, therapy, spirituality, celebration, and recreation—whilst simultaneously being mindful of the perils, pitfalls, and need for support.

The Manual of Psychedelic Support shares techniques that experience has shown can significantly reduce risks, making the transition to a Post-Prohibition world easier to envision.

Whilst Prohibition exacerbates the problems associated with the use of psychedelics, a Post-Prohibition world will not automatically eliminate those problems. Psychedelics are inherently challenging and risky by virtue of their mind-manifesting properties, which bring new ideas and emotions into awareness. Even when psychedelics are administered in clinical settings in which mentally healthy people are given pure substances of known quantities with support by trained facilitators, not all experiences are welcomed or well integrated. The risks of problematic outcomes are even greater when psychedelics of uncertain identity and potency are consumed in recreational settings by people who are not prepared for the full depth of what emerges from their own minds.

At present there are relatively few people who have the understanding to assist someone else through a difficult psychedelic experience. This Manual is a collection of the community's efforts to address the need for accurate information on how to provide such care, which will increase safety and decrease medical and psychiatric emergencies. The psychedelic community has created this Manual as one means of greater self-regulation. The writers of this Manual have put in lots of labour at festivals and have developed compassionate and skilled approaches in working with people who dove into their psyches more deeply than they anticipated.

The search for community, passion, and shared rites of passage are part of what makes us human, and are fundamentally healthy drives. For many people, especially young people, psychedelic festivals are vehicles for the attempted satisfaction of these drives. This Manual is a guide explaining how to create psychedelic support systems at festivals and other gatherings similar in nature to the medical support systems that respond to the inevitable physical injuries that can and do occur. The Manual's content is informed by the renaissance of psychedelic research taking place all over the world, as scientists seek a better understanding of the therapeutic, neuroscientific, and spiritual potentials of psychedelics, as well as their risks. Crises can often be de-escalated quickly with a safe space, compassionate listening, and affirmative guidance. Psychedelic harm reduction services also provide an opportunity through practical experience to train people who want to work in this area as therapists.

This Manual is an evolving document and will grow to include information from additional contributors in the future. Whilst helpful in assisting individuals with their difficult trips, on a larger scale this Manual is part of an effort to help society come into balance, to recover from the difficult trip of the 1960s. We seek by the publication of this Manual to contribute to our cultural evolution into a Post-Prohibition society in which we will all have legal access to ancient and modern technologies of transformation to help us address the existential challenges we face together as humans on a planet in crisis.

In 2001, Portugal mitigated Drug War damages by making personal possession an administrative infraction instead of a criminal offence. Boom Festival attendees can now more easily envision a peaceful Post-Prohibition society. Photo by Jen Zariat, 2008.

Participate

Alicia Danforth, PhD
Clinical Psychedelics Researcher

TEN years ago, a friend told me about an encounter that she had with a stranger at an art and music festival where psychedelics use for personal and collective transformation was common. In the midst of her own revelry, she noticed a young man who was tripping, alone, and frightened. I had never been to a festival or assisted someone who was having a difficult trip. If she tried to get help from law enforcement, I wondered, would he get into legal trouble? Would security or the police handle him roughly? If she sought emergency services, would medics restrain and tranquillise him? My friend stayed by his side, comforting him for hours, until he bolted like a nervous rabbit into the cold and chaos. I imagined better scenarios for both of them. What if there were safe and peaceful places where care providers who knew how to support the physical, mental, and emotional needs of folks experiencing challenging psychedelic voyages were waiting? The next year and every year since, I have volunteered in such places.

Care services for individuals in challenging altered states of consciousness related to psychedelics use are evolving concurrent with the resurgence of legal clinical research with classic hallucinogens. As long as I've been a volunteer at festivals and gatherings, I also have worked as a researcher on legal clinical trials with psychedelic medicines. Both settings inform each other. The intention for all psychedelic support is to create a secure container to attend to body, mind, and spirit for those who enter into vulnerable, sometimes even mystical, states, during which they need humane assistance. Researchers can consult protocols that have been published in peer-reviewed literature for safe and ethical psychedelic-assisted therapy in clinical settings. With the publication of *The Manual of Psychedelic Support*, now event organisers and volunteers have a best-practices guide for creating safe and ethical care services for the multitudes of individuals who are exploring with consciousness-expanding substances outside of Western medical research paradigms.

At the 2010 Boom Festival in Portugal, I met many of the editors and contributing authors of this Manual who volunteered on the KosmiCare team. Event organisers, physicians, drug policy activists, psychiatrists, therapists, scholars, body workers, first-responders, researchers, nurses, project managers, harm-reduction specialists, anthropologists, psychologists, chemists, peer-counsellors, sitters, legal

experts, and experienced psychedelic journeyers collaborated to create the best care service I had ever seen. Portugal decriminalised personal drug use in 2001, and the liberal drug laws there fostered a secure setting for free-flowing information-exchange on the historical, cross-cultural, safety, legal, medical, ethical, therapeutic, pragmatic, and spiritual aspects of running care services in diverse settings. As a result, this Manual covers a broad spectrum of ideological and practical considerations to assist organisers and team leaders in creating scalable services to protect and support their visitors.

The editors, along with multidisciplinary writers from around the world, have created a resource that is current, comprehensive, and compassionate. The contributors' wisdom and guidance is culled from diverse lineages: from the jungle to the desert; from stadiums to sweat lodges; from Grof to Goa, Shulgin to Shambhala. The result is a legacy reference source for event organisers and communities who honour and commit to the responsibility of providing psychedelic care services for individuals working through difficult experiences.

Emergency services volunteers at festivals who are unfamiliar with the psychedelic terrain sometimes whisper to me that someone in their care who was difficult to soothe took "some really bad acid". I know in these situations that, more likely than not, the individual took a *different* powerful psychedelic with effects and durations that they were not expecting, or clean LSD without preparing adequately for their trip. Some care service visitors arrive after getting dosed without their consent. It happens. However, issues most often arise from an improper setting or dose, problematic mindset, lack of ego strength, underlying mental illness, combining incompatible substances, or other unexpected disturbances. The time has come to stop blaming "bad" acid. Now, the focus is on spreading knowledge about how to support individuals who venture, knowingly or unwittingly, into challenging mind states and psycho-spiritual transitions on their psychedelic journeys.

The field of psychedelic support service is young enough for you, the reader, to contribute to the collation and dissemination of evolving care service practices. Read the Manual for what it contains and for what it lacks. Evaluate the content. Contact the editors with your suggestions if you identify areas for improvement. Provide a copy of the Manual to the organisers of the events you attend. If you are an event organiser, share it with your peers. Bring your skills to the volunteer space. Participate.

Psychoactive Drug Use and the Entertainment Industry

Sam Cutler
Former Tour Manager,
the Rolling Stones and the Grateful Dead

I **welcome wholeheartedly** *The Manual of Psychedelic Support* and congratulate those who have been involved in its production. It is a resource that the entertainment industry has needed for a long time, and I am sure its beneficial effects will go a long way to ameliorating the sometimes sad disturbances and unhappy results of the consumption of the more powerful of the illicit drugs.

The problems of drug consumption have been with the entertainment industry since the industry first existed, but for all practical purposes the experiences this Manual addresses date back to the sixties. It was during that decade that I first began working in the industry, and as is well known, it was during that decade that drug consumption slowly became the ubiquitous force that it is today. The problems of psychedelic drug consumption at rock and roll shows were (initially) not very well understood by either promoters, the police or the public, and matters were not helped by sections of the music community who proactively promoted the consumption of those drugs. Overdoses and psychotic behaviour became commonplace and the response was at best sporadic. Medical services at shows were rudimentary, if not nonexistent, and anyone with a "problem" was simply arrested.

Thankfully, in subsequent decades, the approach to these problems has changed, although it could still be improved. Promoters now accept that they have a legal "duty of care" to their customers at shows and that they are expected to provide emergency services. Large festivals are equipped with medical teams, evacuation helicopters, and various support mechanisms for those who find themselves physically in trouble. That having been said, a coherent and well-thought-out approach to the challenges that sometimes result from psychoactive drug consumption—particularly those of a psychological nature—has unfortunately still been lacking. *The Manual of Psychedelic Support* will go a long way towards filling the gaps in understanding. It will also, most importantly, act as a much needed guide for intervention on the "front lines" of shows, where all too frequently people get into difficulties and need help.

People who get into trouble after having ingested psychoactive substances are in need of sensitive and specialised assistance. They are in a fragile and vulnerable condition and cannot be brutalised into submission nor conveniently given antidotes (which in any case do not exist). There is a substantial body of specialist knowledge that needs to be brought to bear when dealing with such people, and it needs to be spread across all the stakeholders at shows and festivals, from concert-goers, to promoters, and the police.

The problem of drugs—of people having unfortunate reactions to the ingestion of drugs—will simply not go away. It cannot be ignored any longer. Put bluntly, people's lives and psychological well-being are often seriously at risk. I welcome any and all initiatives that seek to address this problem. We have a long way to go, but through education and a coherent approach I feel confident that progress will be made.

Participants take a two-wheeled trip at the 1st Annual Bicycle Day Parade, April 19, 2014, in Golden Gate Park, to celebrate Albert Hofmann's 1943 discovery of the psychoactive effects of LSD. Photo by Jon Hanna.

MARTINA HOFFMANN • *Lysergic Summer Dream*, 2006 • oil on canvas
http://shop.martinahoffmannfineart.com

INTRODUCTION

Following over four years of work since its inception, and involving the collaboration of more than fifty people from several countries around the world, we are delighted to bring you *The Manual of Psychedelic Support*. It is our hope that the material contained herein will be put to good use in helping people in some of their darkest hours of need. Those with experience in providing such care will know that describing a psychedelic crisis at a music festival or similar event as someone's "darkest hour of need" is often no exaggeration. The power of the psychoactive drugs commonly found in those settings to radically modify consciousness is immense, and the experiences of an individual in such states can be confrontational and very challenging. Whilst presenting valuable opportunities for profound insights and personal transformation, encounters with psychoactive substances can also be traumatic, and may destabilise deep psychological structures that have been laid down over many years. In other cases we find festival-goers who have mixed several psychoactive substances together, taken very high doses, and/or consumed alcohol with these materials, and are not having a difficult trip per se, but rather a "meltdown experience", in which they are simply in need of physical comfort and support. Finally, perhaps the most difficult cases of all are those in which some form of chronic mental illness is involved, often combined with an acute altered mental state induced from the consumption of psychoactive drugs.

In the absence of a care service, those undergoing any of the situations described above frequently find themselves alone in a tent, on the periphery of a dance floor or the festival grounds, or at the medical service. In the case of the latter, most medical staff, whilst clearly well intentioned, lack the knowledge, understanding, and experience necessary to help an individual through a psychologically difficult trip. The guest is immediately incorporated into a medical paradigm and turned into a "patient", who may be given a tranquilliser and/or evacuated to a hospital. Without legitimate medical necessity, this is precisely the scenario that a care service seeks to prevent, for it often results in the individual waking up with memories of a horrific experience that haunts them for a long time to come. We believe that in cases without medical complications, the ideal approach to a difficult drug experience (and certainly to a psychedelic one) is to let it run its course—with comforting support along the way—and find its own resolution. Usually (although not always) this resolution is a valuable and happy one, in which the guest experiences some kind of psycho-spiritual breakthrough or catharsis with concomitant healing. Precipitously halting the unfolding of such an experience through the administration of a tranquilliser, and turning the individual into a patient in a sterile and potentially frightening medical setting, can do more harm than good.

Having said that, we emphasise in no uncertain terms that in cases with *any indication whatsoever* of possible medical complications, or even doubt as to whether such a complication exists or not, a competent medic must assess the situation and determine whether medical aid is required. Underlying unknowns—including allergies, asthma, adverse drug reactions due to dosage, substance combinations, and/or prescription medication, cardiopulmonary disease, and many others—may be life-threatening, and must be dealt with by trained medical staff.

In a formalised manner since the 1960s, various care services have been helping people through difficult drug experiences at music festivals and similar events. There are many individuals in the community today who have accumulated a lot of knowledge in this domain, not only in terms of working with guests in need, but also in such areas as planning, legal considerations, budgeting, logistics, recruiting and training a care service team, and working with other event organisations. Up until now, however, this information has not been readily accessible in one place. The purpose of this Manual, then, is to serve as a repository of knowledge in all things related to establishing and facilitating care services at music festivals and other events. Its intended audience is anybody involved in such an undertaking—from the care service leader, through to team leads (if they exist), and ultimately (and importantly), to the care givers who are doing direct work with the guests themselves. This Manual contains material that may be used in the planning stages and lead-up to establishing a care service, resources directly applicable to training the care service team, and information that may be referenced during the actual running of the service. We also envisage it as a valuable document for anybody approaching an event organiser with the intent of setting up a care service for the first time; the scope, thoroughness, and quality of the material contained herein should help persuade organisers of the importance and seriousness of such an undertaking.

From the inception of this project, a key principle has been that this publication should be independent of any external organisation, freely available to all, its content open to adaptation (for example, to be used in training manuals for particular care services), and never to be used directly for commercial ends. We feel that this principle has been upheld, and invite you to make use of this material for any good and wholesome purpose. *The Manual of Psychedelic Support* project was conceived of following the 2010 Boom Festival in Portugal, and it grew out of the experiences of members of the care service there, called KosmiCare.

The main KosmiCare space at the 2010 Boom Festival. Photo by Leandro Reinaldo.

INTRODUCTION

Whilst completely independent of that organisation, we acknowledge the fertile ground that nurtured the roots of this work. Likewise, many of the key people who came on board in the early stages of the project have strong connections to Burning Man (United States) and its Green Dot Rangers, and we similarly acknowledge the deep knowledge and experience of individuals working with that organisation. Yet more people joined from additional walks of life—therapists, scholars, researchers, psychonauts, and others—all bound by a common passion for this field, and a recognition of the importance of helping others. Some became editors, others chapter leads or contributing authors. They formed the core of this project team, and without them it would not have been possible. We are most grateful for their participation and help along the sometimes smooth and sunny, yet at other times difficult and rocky, road. A special thanks to the design team, the artists, and the photographers, who turned the text draft of this Manual into a beautiful finished piece; and to our website designer, who in the final hours carefully constructed our virtual launch pad. Just like the majority of care services that we are familiar with, this project consisted entirely of volunteers (including ourselves, the editors); and so we are doubly grateful.

The result of all this work is the Manual you are now reading. We sincerely hope that it will be used to do good things in the world, and that it will strengthen our collective skills. May it be another small but significant drop in the ocean of work yet to be done in acknowledging and realising the immense power contained in psychoactive drugs for personal transformation, whilst remaining realistic and respectful of their potential dangers.

— The Editors
January 1, 2015

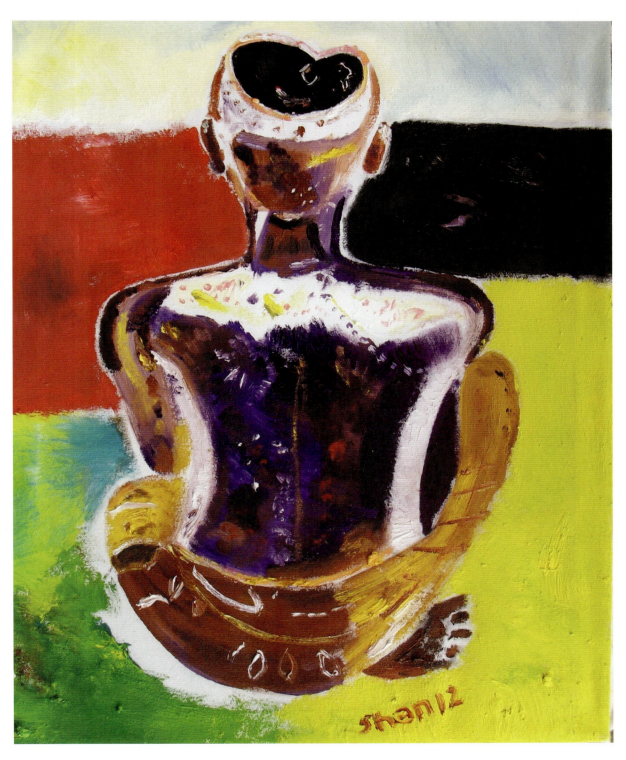

SHANTIQ • *l'ouverture*, 2011 • oil painting
http://www.saatchiart.com/shantiq

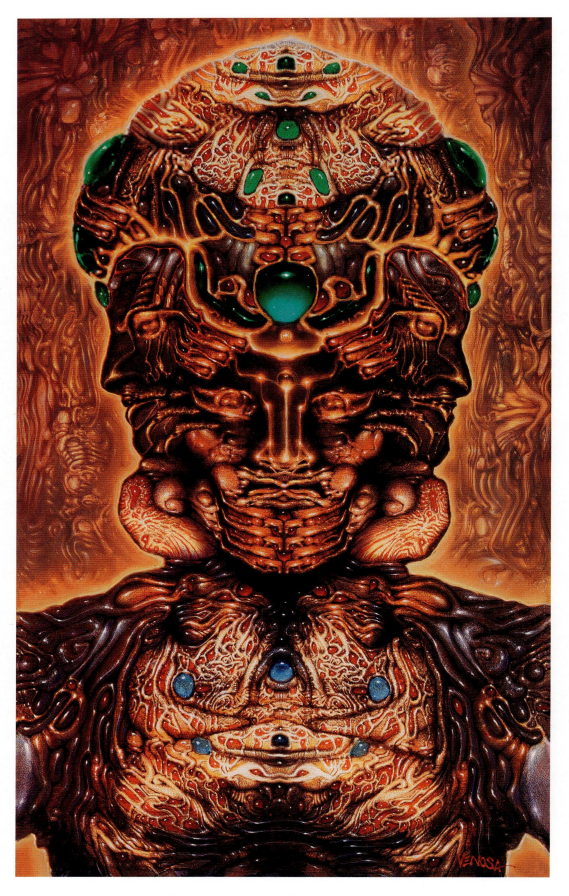

ROBERT VENOSA • *Hallucinatory Self-Portrait, 1997* • oil, montage
http://www.venosa.com

CHAPTER 1

A HISTORY OF PSYCHEDELIC CARE SERVICES

Annie Oak

Ben Holden

Elissa Harwood

João Gonçalves

Karin Silenzi de Stagni

Levente Móró

Linnae Ponté

Maria Carmo Carvalho

Svea Nielsen

Zevic Mishor

The modern history of psychedelic care services can be traced back to the mid-1960s, when young people began to consume mind-altering substances at concerts and events. Emergency medical services were not trained to provide compassionate support for participants in non-ordinary states of consciousness. In an effort to offer more effective and informed care, a number of groups created their own specialised teams to work with those who were having difficult experiences. This chapter takes a look at some of those early efforts in the United States, as well as a selection of more recent and current ones around the world, and how they developed specialised spaces and techniques as part of their on-site care services. Some of the first attempts at providing support for people who ingest psychedelics and other drugs were launched by the Hog Farmers, the CALM volunteers of the Rainbow Family, Rock Med, White Bird, and the innumerable parking lot medics who went on tour with the Grateful Dead. More recently created psychedelic care services have been developed by the Green Dot Rangers at Burning Man, by KosmiCare at Boom Festival, the Zendo Project, and the Full Circle Tea House. These groups are just a sample of the various services that exist around the world today. See Chapter 17, "Online Resources and Obtaining Assistance", for a more comprehensive list and links to further information. The groups profiled below represent almost fifty years of creative, compassionate care that has helped innumerable people.

Services Launched in the 1960s and 1970s

The Hog Farmers at Woodstock

In the mid-1960s a group of forty people associated with the Grateful Dead and the Merry Pranksters were offered a job feeding hogs in exchange for rent-free living on a Southern California mountaintop. The community, now known as the Hog Farm, is widely considered the longest running hippie commune in the United States. The Hog Farmers are best known for their services at the 1969 Woodstock Music & Art Fair, which attracted nearly half a million participants. Recruited by event organisers to build fire pits and trails on the festival grounds in Woodstock, New York, the Hog Farmers persuaded the promoters to let them set up a free kitchen. After flying into New York, the group was met by the press at the airport and informed that they had been assigned the job of providing security at the festival, which had been hastily relocated to a 600-acre dairy farm. Hog Farm co-founder and professional clown Wavy Gravy named this security team the "Please Force" (as in please don't do that, please do this instead) to reflect their non-intrusive approach. When asked by reporters what the group's strategy was for keeping order, Gravy replied, "Cream pies and seltzer bottles".

Wavy Gravy, still helping out on the festival circuit after all of these years; seen here at the 2010 Harmony Festival in California.
Photo by Jon Hanna.

After the perimeter fence was cut down by incoming crowds, the festival became a free event for hundreds of thousands of attendees. Whilst the county declared a state of emergency, the Hog Farmers valiantly fed, comforted, and looked after a flood of participants, effectively launching one of the first large-scale psychedelic care services. For three muddy, historic days, the Hog Farmers found creative ways to support attendees at the site, which lacked adequate sanitation and medical services. Standing on stage one rainy morning during the event, Gravy announced, "What we have in mind is breakfast in bed for 400,000!". The Woodstock Festival was remarkably peaceful considering the conditions and number of people involved. There were two recorded births during the three-day event and two fatalities, one from a suspected heroin overdose and another caused when a tractor accidently ran over an attendee sleeping in a nearby hay field. After Woodstock, the extended family of Hog Farmers bought a fleet of buses and hit the road to perform theatre shows. The activists and entertainers who made up the collective eventually settled in Northern California, and currently operate a 700-acre ranch where they host large music festivals, run a children's circus camp, and raise money for charitable work around the world.

Grateful Dead Parking Lot Medics

During the long concert tours of the Grateful Dead that began in the 1970s, many ardent fans, known as "Deadheads", followed the band and created lively, temporary communities that took up residence in parking lots near the music venues. After the shows were over, a group of volunteer medics remained behind to assist Deadheads who still roamed the lots. Rob Savoye, who served with one of these loosely organised medic teams from 1978 to 1986, is a founding member of the Ilchester Mountain Search and Rescue group, a collection of rock climbing buddies from West Virginia who provided parking lot services. Savoye says the medics tried to create a calm and secure space for people who were over-stimulated by psychedelic experiences or other psychological challenges. Savoye often brought a bus or truck to the lots—first a VW camper and later a 1964 Ford truck—and created a chill space inside the vehicle to care for guests. The medics, many of whom had formal medical training, also provided first aid for minor injuries. Frequently, says Savoye, law enforcement officers would try to chase the Deadheads from the parking lots, but he would let them hole-up in his parked vehicle for a day or two, often driving them to the next show to reconnect with their friends.

The CALM Volunteers of the Rainbow Gathering

Every year since 1972, a week-long Rainbow Gathering has been held on National Forest land somewhere in the United States. This temporary intentional community is coordinated by the Rainbow Family of Living Light, a loose affiliation of people committed to the principles of egalitarianism and non-violence. With deep roots in the counterculture of the 1960s, the Rainbow Family reaches decisions through consensus; they have no leaders, no structure, and no spokesperson, nor do they apply for permits for their gatherings. They once organised annual national events of up to 30,000 people (as well as international and regional gatherings). However, due to pressure from local authorities, including extensive roadblocks and illegal searches, most gatherings now attract about 5,000 people.

Health services at Rainbow Gatherings in the United States are provided by CALM, or the Center for Alternative Living Medicine, a volunteer, non-hierarchical group of about ten core members who assume responsibility for medical emergencies and sanitation. Embracing both conventional and alternative medical practices, CALM works closely with the Rainbow Gathering's Shanti Sena Peace Keepers, who provide transport for medical emergencies and create meet-up points with local ambulance services. CALM volunteers run an on-site medical tent and smaller first aid stations. As Rainbow Gatherings often take place in remote wilderness locations miles from the nearest trailhead, CALM relies on their radio-equipped stationary and roaming medical staff, rarely transporting patients off of the event site. The CALM unit does not dispense prescription pharmaceuticals but it does provide a wide variety of services, from campsite medical visits—"hippie house calls"—to birthing babies.

Psychedelic care services at Rainbow Gatherings are provided by Brew HaHa, a CALM subcamp run by a physician who is a long-time festival participant. Brew HaHa offers a quiet space bordered by tapestries hung from trees, serves herbal teas, and provides around-the-clock counselling to participants in need. Care givers who staff the space have no set shift schedule, but do have extensive personal experiences with psychedelic substances. Brew HaHa is also frequented by recovering drug addicts and alcoholics drawn to its quiet atmosphere. In rare cases where physical restraint is needed for an agitated guest, it is often combined with body massage at the incident scene. Since people at Rainbow Gatherings often lose track of time, the greatest challenge for the Brew HaHa crew is no longer adverse reactions to psychedelic substances, but participants who forget to take their prescription pharmaceutical medications and become self-destructive. For psychedelic care cases, the CALM and Brew HaHa staff are sensitive about protecting the anonymity of attendees. Guests are asked for information regarding what substance they took, what it looked like and where they got it from, but few formal records are kept. In a non-confrontational manner, care givers sometimes inform the source of the substance about adverse reactions, especially in cases involving "newer" drugs such as GHB and toad venom. According to care givers, suppliers sometimes volunteer information about treatment approaches and usually agree to stop distributing the substance(s) in question.

White Bird

White Bird is a non-profit human service agency based in Eugene, Oregon, that has been serving the people of Lane County and nearby festivals for more than forty years. A collective of largely volunteer care providers, White Bird was founded in 1969 by a Eugene-based community of care givers. The group provides direct service and education that helps people gain control of their social, emotional, and physical well-being. White Bird provides services at the annual Oregon Country Fair, where some participants visit the on-site White Bird clinic to receive their annual check up and primary heath care. White Bird also operates three permanent clinics that provide free health and dental care, mental health counselling, and other services to an estimated 12,000 homeless people in the Eugene area. CAHOOTS, or Crisis Assistance Helping Out On The Streets, is a department of White Bird funded by the City of Eugene. CAHOOTS fields a mobile, crisis intervention team—integrated into the city's public safety system—that responds to more than 85,000 service requests a year. The care givers of CAHOOTS receive 911 dispatch calls and provide services for cases involving severe intoxication, drug overdose, disorientation, mental illness, dispute resolution, non-emergency medical care, first aid, and transport to services. Pioneers in providing on-call psychedelic services and other care to marginalised communities, CAHOOTS operates a van that is staffed and managed by the White Bird Clinic.

Rock Med

For more than forty years, Rock Med volunteers have been providing medical care at large concerts and other events in the San Francisco Bay Area. The organisation was founded in 1972 when music promoter Bill Graham asked the Haight Ashbury Free Clinic, a medical service based in San Francisco's famous Haight-Ashbury neighbourhood, to staff a medical tent at outdoor concerts of the Grateful Dead and Led Zeppelin. Rock Med became a standalone organisation in 1973 and branched out to provide care at sporting events, marches, fairs, circuses, and other large gatherings, as well as concerts. The group now has about 1,200 volunteer doctors, nurses, and CPR-certified care givers, and serves at more than 700 events a year in Northern California.

Packing its supplies and equipment into "road boxes" modelled on those used by bands to transport music equipment, Rock Med runs urgent care medical tents, measuring their success on being non-judgemental and getting participants back to their families without involving the police or hospitals. In 2012 Rock Med merged with the Haight Ashbury Free Clinics and the Walden House drug rehabilitation service and formed HealthRight 360, in order to combine resources and raise funds through grants and donations. To assist people having difficult psychedelic experiences, Rock Med has an area in the medical tent equipped with mats that allow guests to lie down and receive compassionate care. In some cases medical volunteers also dispense the antipsychotic and muscle relaxant Haldol, and the anti-anxiety medicine Ativan. Rock Med has become a ubiquitous presence at San Francisco Bay Area music events and attracts seasoned care givers.

Services Launched from 1980 Onward

Green Dot Rangers and Sanctuary at Burning Man

The Burning Man Arts Festival began on a San Francisco beach in 1986. It is now a 70,000-person event in the Black Rock Desert, a dry lake bed in northern Nevada. Participants build a temporary community called Black Rock City, which contains theme camps, music performances, and many types of art. The event focuses on creating immediate experiences instead of commerce, and supports a gift economy that encourages radical self-reliance and the agreement to leave no trace at the end of the gathering. The highlight of the week-long festival is the burning of a large wooden effigy known as "The Man", and other fire art that creates an impressive spectacle on a high desert plateau ringed by distant mountains.

The Burning Man organisation that runs the event is structured to support the logistical challenges of creating an increasingly expanding gathering on a remote site. Organisers work with local law enforcement and the federal Bureau of Land Management to develop emergency protocols, environmental safeguards and safety plans. Burning Man's Emergency Services Department (ESD) provides Black Rock City with fire, medical, mental health, and communications services. ESD managers contract with a regional hospital to build a central field hospital and remote medical stations, providing on-site medical care. Burning Man also organises uniformed volunteers called the Black Rock Rangers who address safety issues and provide community mediation. Black Rock Rangers often hold a current certification in CPR and basic first aid (and this training is available on-site prior to the event). Care for participants undergoing challenging drug experiences is provided by psychiatric services from the ESD Mental Health Branch, and peer counselling comes from the Black Rock Ranger "Green Dots". The Green Dot Rangers also provide compassionate support for addressing interpersonal issues and offer mediation services throughout Black Rock City. They follow a FLAME model, which directs Green Dots to Find out, Listen, Analyse, Mediate, and Explain.

Together with members of the ESD Mental Health Branch, the Green Dots staff the Sanctuary space for non-medical, supportive care. Sanctuary offers a limited number of beds and provides a quiet location to help participants transform potentially difficult situations into positive experiences. Sanctuary is not advertised at the event, but Rangers, law enforcement, medical responders, and other Burning Man departments bring participants there for care. The space and its services are also available to the event's staff. As a safe haven for confidential care, the Burning Man Sanctuary space is open at all times during the event. The Green Dot Rangers and their ESD partners provide on-call counselling outside of Sanctuary—alongside warming fires contained in metal barrels and at other locations throughout the festival—during situations requiring emotional trauma support. Green Dot Rangers also work on-site as foot-, bicycle-, and vehicle-mobile Dirt Rangers. In addition to receiving training as Black Rock Rangers, they obtain instruction from the Green Dot Advanced Ranger Training Manual, a practical guide for compassionate care. The text Meeting the Divine Within is also used to train those working with psychedelic crises at Burning Man.

At the end of a long day-shift, a Sanctuary volunteer surprises her co-worker with a friendly kiss before venturing onto the playa to view art installations as the sun sets. Photo from the 2005 Burning Man Festival by Jon Hanna.

A HISTORY OF PSYCHEDELIC CARE SERVICES

KosmiCare at Boom Festival

Boom Festival is a week-long biennial event that takes place on the shores of a beautiful lake in Portugal. Launched in 1997 as a psytrance festival, Boom has evolved into a more inclusive event showcasing a variety of music styles and attracting some 30,000 people from 116 nationalities. Boom also features visionary art, sculptures made of natural or recycled materials, performances, fire dancing, and juggling. The Liminal Village hosts lectures, presentations, workshops, and documentaries on forward-thinking topics by international speakers. The Healing Area is devoted to therapeutic treatments including massage, meditation, and yoga. A Baby Boom area offers activities for children. In addition, Boom is an innovator and role model in the development and application of psychedelic care services and sustainability practices for large events.

In 2002 an area was set up in the Liminal Village where info on safer use practices for psychoactive substances was distributed and support was provided to those having challenging experiences. Calling itself Ground Central Station, this safe space was produced by Sandra Karpetas, facilitated by a volunteer crew of Canadian harm-reduction advocates from the Higher Knowledge Network, and sponsored by the Multidisciplinary Association for Psychedelic Studies (a U.S. non-profit organisation). In 2004 Boom organisers worked with Karpetas and MAPS to develop and expand effective care techniques by creating a dedicated care facility—a quiet space called CosmiKiva—that complemented the festival's medical services by offering professional attention to people undergoing "psychedelic emergencies". CosmiKiva was renamed KosmiCare in 2008, and relocated to a large geodesic dome run by thirty multilingual volunteers. Positioned between the three main music stages, the dome attracted many attendees seeking care and/or information. Representatives from Erowid and Check-In (a Portuguese risk-reduction group) provided computer access and printed materials, and answered questions about psychoactive substances.

Comprised of trained volunteers recruited from amongst Boomers—including medics, psychiatrists, psychologists, nurses, therapists, anthropologists, researchers, and others—KosmiCare's services are coordinated by team members, Boom organisers, on-site medical staff (paramedics), and event security services who assist with particularly difficult cases. The KosmiCare team uses a classic "sitting" method to provide peer counselling for attendees, but also offers additional kinds of care such as massage, homeopathy, and other alternative therapies. The KosmiCare dome stocks art materials for guests to draw and paint with, and provides information about assorted psychoactive drugs.

Official signs posted by the drug-testing service warn of dangers and deception related to drugs sold at the 2012 Boom Festival. Photo by Zevic Mishor.

A HISTORY OF PSYCHEDELIC CARE SERVICES

Also in 2008, KosmiCare collaborated with Energy Control, a Spanish drug-testing organisation that made its services available at Boom. Working out of a small, well-equipped laboratory, these professionals used thin-layer chromatography (TLC) to assay substances brought to them by festival-goers, or in some cases submitted by the KosmiCare team after the substances had been given to care givers by care space guests. The service provided information regarding the active compounds(s), as well as adulterants, present in the samples tested. This information was very useful not only for individual cases, but also in helping to build a general picture of the kinds of drugs that were being circulated at the festival, and indeed, of trends of disinformation and deception; for example, when one psychoactive was being sold under the guise of another. The photo on the pervious page, taken at Boom 2012 (which hosted a similar testing service), shows the level of honest concern and transparency possible under (and indeed, as part of its emphasis on harm reduction, largely supported by) current Portuguese law. These official signs, unthinkable at present under other jurisdictions in certain countries around the world, help to convey a sense of the atmosphere of openness, saneness, and support that has so far characterised Boom Festival. The article "Energy Control: TLC and Other Risk Reduction Approaches" by Sylvia Thyssen and Jon Hanna gives some background information on Energy Control, and presents an excellent depiction of their work at the 2008 Boom Festival.

In 2008 the Boom Festival worked closely with paramedics and security to maintain the KosmiCare psychedelic care space and provide effective medical care during a large-scale outbreak of a gastrointestinal illness that was dubbed the "Boom Bug". This phase of the project is documented in Svea Nielsen and Constance Bettencourt's essay, "KosmiCare: Creating Safe Spaces for Difficult Psychedelic Experiences".

In 2006 and 2008, CosmiKiva/KosmiCare launched a strategy to pursue a vision of expanded support and improved guest-outcomes for current and future care services. It consisted of a partnership between Boom organisers, the Faculty of Education and Psychology at the Catholic University of Porto (Portugal), and the Portuguese General-Directorate for Intervention on Addictive Behaviours and Dependencies (SICAD). The purpose of this partnership was to transform the existing care strategy into an *evidence-based crisis intervention model* that addressed the use of psychoactive substances in recreational settings.

The first results of these partnerships were delivered in 2011; psychedelic care resulted in very positive feedback from guests and staff, producing significant improvements in guests' short-term psychological and physical well-being as a result of treatment. Boom organisers continued to support research related to intervention, and more data was collected at KosmiCare in 2012. As results were made available during 2013, it was possible to verify that other, more quantitative measures of crisis resolution also prove equally positive, with mental state exam indicators increasing significantly between the periods of admission and departure of guests. Please see Appendix B, "Monitoring, Evaluating and Researching—Recommendations from an Academic Perspective for an Evidence-Based Approach to Psychoactive Crisis Intervention", for further discussion on this research.

At the 2012 Boom Festival the KosmiCare space was moved to a more central area of the event, compared to where it had been set up in 2010, making it easier for participants to locate. An increasingly experienced team of care givers, using tested-and-true methods, continued to provide and improve psychedelic care services, despite budget restrictions.

Kosmicare UK

Kosmicare UK is an organisation separate from the original KosmiCare project set up by Boom Festival, but owes much of its philosophy and ethos to that pioneering project. After a successful, challenging, and rewarding time as a volunteer with KosmiCare at the Boom Festival in 2008, Karin Silenzi de Stagni recognised the need for similar services at festivals in the United Kingdom. With support from the Multidisciplinary Association for Psychedelic Studies, Karin formed Kosmicare UK, using the framework for psychedelic emergency services that MAPS had developed with Diogo Ruivo, chief organiser of the Boom Festival.

Recognising the hard work and innovation of those involved with the original project, Kosmicare UK gratefully utilised their resources, building upon them to meet the challenges of working at festivals in the United Kingdom. The demands that Kosmicare UK faces include the harsh climate—often wet and cold even in the summer months—the logistics of attending a number of different festivals across the nation, and the lack of funding. Kosmicare UK is an independent community project that does not have sponsors, depending entirely on donations and voluntary work. In addition, many small festivals have a limited budget and are able to only just cover basic expenses; nevertheless, the Kosmicare UK team make every effort to have a presence at as many festivals as possible, because the team really believes in the importance of their project.

Since 2009, Kosmicare UK has provided care services at several festivals across England, Wales, and Scotland, including Sunrise Celebration, Eden Festival, Waveform,

Boomtown Fair, Glade, Magikana Festival, Alchemy Festival, and Sunset Collective. The project has made good connections with long-established and respected organisations in the United Kingdom festival scene and works closely on-site with event security, medical, and welfare services. Each year Kosmicare UK strives to improve operations through increased festival attendance, networking and sharing info with similar groups throughout Europe, and building a pool of experienced volunteers. Kosmicare UK also has the ongoing support of a diverse group of professionals whose guidance is invaluable and to whom they are grateful.

DanceSafe

DanceSafe was founded in the United States in 1998 by Emanuel Sferios to promote health and safety within the electronic music and nightlife community. The organisation provides peer-based educational programmes to reduce negative drug experiences. They pride themselves on providing unbiased information to help empower the young people who use drugs to make informed decisions about their health.

DanceSafe is a non-profit, harm-reduction organisation with local chapters throughout the United States and Canada. Regional chapters are run by individuals from within the dance culture. DanceSafe volunteers are trained to be health educators and drug abuse prevention counsellors, who use the principles and methods of harm reduction and popular education within their own communities.

A DanceSafe volunteer answers questions for attendees at the 2005 Mind States conference. Photo by Anonymous.

The volunteers staff harm-reduction booths at raves, nightclubs, and other dance events, providing information on drugs, safer sex, and assorted health and safety issues of concern to the electronic dance community. DanceSafe also provides adulterant-screening/pill-testing services for ecstasy (MDMA) users, an important harm-reduction service that may save lives and reduces medical emergencies by helping users avoid fake and/or tainted tablets that can contain substances far more dangerous than actual MDMA. In 2013, the Drug Policy Alliance acknowledged DanceSafe by honouring them with the Dr. Andrew Weil Award for Achievement in the Field of Drug Education.

The Psychedelic Nurses

The Psychedelic Nurses is a European organisation of health care providers that has offered psychedelic support services at parties and festivals in France and Switzerland since 2006. Members of the group base their care on natural healing and holistic therapies, including qigong, tai chi, Reiki, ayurvedic and Thai massage, and shiatsu. Whilst in recent years the Psychedelic Nurses have shifted their focus to offering natural health and exercise services at parties and festivals, they will still provide care for someone experiencing a psychedelic crisis if the need arises.

The Zendo Project

The Zendo Project was launched at the Burning Man Festival in 2012 as an outreach service sponsored by MAPS. Zendo operated from a circular structure near a popular music stage, and was staffed by trained volunteers. Since 2001, MAPS has brought together a diverse team of therapists, doctors, researchers, and experienced peer counsellors to provide compassionate care and psychedelic harm reduction at large gatherings. MAPS first provided volunteer recruitment and training for the Sanctuary space at Burning Man in 2003. The organisation later also joined production efforts to help develop a model for psychedelic harm reduction at the Boom Festival (see "KosmiCare at Boom Festival" above). Following these efforts, MAPS continued to expand its services to a circuit of international events.

The mission of the Zendo Project is to provide a supportive space to support those having difficult psychedelic experiences, reduce the number of psychedelic drug-related arrests and hospitalizations, and train volunteers to provide compassionate care. The Project strives to address the public stigma of psychedelics and encourage honest and responsible conversations about their use. The service clearly demonstrates that it is possible to mitigate the risks associated with the non-medical use of psychedelics at the community level, and that there is a strong interest within its community of volunteers to do so. Since its debut in 2012, Zendo volunteers have provided training and support at Burning Man (Black Rock City, Nevada), Envision Festival (Costa Rica), Bicycle Day (San Francisco), AfrikaBurn (Tankwa, South Africa), Lightning in a Bottle (California), Symbiosis (California), and a handful of smaller events in the United States.

During events where they provide services, the Zendo staff lead a public training for volunteers and the public, followed by a smaller private meeting with medical staff to discuss methods and techniques, and develop triage protocols. With Zendo and medical spaces situated directly beside one another, the collaboration is helpful for both teams. The Zendo has also led trainings for security and law enforcement professionals, sharing tools for deescalation and helping them understand the psychological effects of psychedelics.

Zendo volunteers provide care for participants who might otherwise have been arrested by police or unnecessarily hospitalized. The Zendo team collaborates with DanceSafe and other harm-reduction services at events. Whilst delivering service at AfrikaBurn, the largest regional Burning Man event with over 10,000 attendees, the Zendo team provides a supportive space, compassionate care, and drug education while working alongside medical staff and Rangers. Zendo volunteers helped relieve medical staff from caring for attendees who were primarily in need of psychological support, providing care as well as on-site thin-layer chromatography to screen drugs for adulterants.

By offering training to volunteers with different levels of experience, the Zendo creates an environment analogous to a teaching hospital, where volunteers share and compare techniques from their respective backgrounds and provide a context for helping train psychedelic therapists. Many Zendo volunteers are mental health or medical professionals. During the 2016 Burning Man Festival, the Zendo Project trained 180 volunteers. The Zendo service cared for more than 477 guests at the event, some of whom had ingested psychoactive substances and some who sought emotional support or information about psychedelics. From 2012 to 2016, the Zendo assisted over 1,986 guests and trained over 1,166 volunteers at events worldwide.

Full Circle Tea House

The Full Circle Tea House was launched by a group of California-based tea enthusiasts in 2011 to provide a safe place for festival participants to rest, hydrate, and integrate transformative experiences. Comprised of a large tent with a porch, bicycle parking, two tea bars, and a sleeping area, the Tea House deploys a staff that serves around the clock at events throughout the West Coast of the United States. Conceived as an alcohol-free social space, the Tea House provides free tea and water to guests and hosts occasional spoken word and acoustic musical performances. The tea service is intended as a calming ritual that helps participants ground and centre themselves during the often chaotic atmosphere found at music and arts festivals. The tea ritual is based on a contemporary interpretation of the traditional Chinese gongfu-style tea service, and uses small tea cups that are refilled whenever empty. Both herbal teas and pu-erh (a fermented black tea from the Yunnan province in China), are served at the Tea House.

Tea House organisers recruit volunteer tea servers who provide calm, compassionate support for guests through good listening skills and informal peer counselling. Some servers are mental health and medical professionals, whilst others have received training through the Zendo Project, the Green Dot Rangers, and/or the KosmiCare service at Boom. The Tea House trains servers to follow the emergency protocols established at festival sites and directs volunteers to be attentive to the possible medical and psychological needs of guests. The Tea House does not provide medical care, but is usually located close to festival medical facilities and sometimes guides guests to appropriate medical services. All tea servers are encouraged to receive certification in CPR and basic first aid.

The Full Circle Tea House is supported through donations and serves at many events in the United States, including Symbiosis, Occupy protests, Burning Man, the Psychedelic Science conferences, Earth Day celebrations, fundraisers, and private parties. It has developed mobile strategies for serving at large political demonstrations and helps other groups start satellite Tea Houses. At least four sister Tea Houses have now been organised: in Austin, Texas; Oakland, California; Philadelphia, Pennsylvania; and Paris, France. During the 2013 Burning Man Festival, the Full Circle Tea House worked together with the Zendo Project and the Rainbow Bridge mobile care unit to transport Tea House guests to the Zendo for focused psychedelic care. The Tea House, which served several thousand people during the week-long event, also provided a quiet space for those who received Zendo services to integrate their experiences and insights.

DÁT2 Psy Help

DÁT2 Psy Help is a team of volunteers associated with the Hungarian Psychedelic Community, a peer-help drug-user group focused primarily on harm reduction related to psychedelics. Embedded in the Goa/psy culture, volunteers of DÁT2 Psy Help have specialised in managing psychedelic emergencies and spiritual crises at dance events since 2004, including big international festivals in Hungary (O.Z.O.R.A. 2007, 2008, 2011, 2012, and S.U.N. 2013 in collaboration with NEWIP).

Safer Festival

Safer Festival was a European non-profit organisation founded in 2011 by Jonas Di Gregorio, a member of the Boom KosmiCare project in 2008 and 2010. According to its mission statement, the group was dedicated to "promoting well-being and safety at festivals in Europe". They offered a portfolio of services, including psychedelic care; cultural activities such as field libraries, documentary screenings, and visionary art exhibitions; food and catering; training for festival organisers and staff; and eco-consulting. One of its core offerings was "Universal Care", a care service with trained staff that could be established upon request at music festivals and similar events. Universal Care provided service at Sol Fest in Spain in 2011, and at O.Z.O.R.A. in Hungary in 2012 and 2013. Whilst Safer Festival is currently taking a hiatus, those interested in their services can email jonasdigregorio@gmail.com to see what might be arranged.

The frame grab above is from a video that describes The Haven, a care space established at O.Z.O.R.A. in 2012 by the European non-profit organisation Safer Festival, which helped to promote health, well-being, and safety at festivals. See https://www.youtube.com/watch?v=fdoPjsMct1k.

LUKE GRAY • *Peace Pipe*, 2012 • Staedtler Triplus Fineliner
http://www.lukegray.net

MARK HENSON • *Inner Voices*, 1983 • watercolour on paper
http://markhensonart.com/all-art-gallery-shop/inner-voices

The woman is about to enter into a state of communion
with the source of all beingness.
As she passes into the light,
voices of doubt and fear make one more attempt
to direct her thoughts elsewhere.
What if there is no love?
What if there is no caring?
Will I be left out?
As the light comes closer and closer,
the unresolved "Inner Voices" fade,
drawing her through the door of consciousness,
into the love that was there all the time.

— Commentary by Monti Moore

CHAPTER 2

THE PRINCIPLES AND ETHICS OF PSYCHEDELIC SUPPORT

Annie Oak

Snu Voogelbreinder

What is a Psychedelic Care Service?

A psychedelic care service assists people who are undergoing challenging experiences during altered states of consciousness or other forms of emotional or mental stress. This chapter reviews some basic principles for providing compassionate care that respects the needs of each person and helps them move from a place of difficulty to a more grounded, calm, and positive perspective. These principles are drawn from the authors' personal knowledge and experience, and from the wisdom of others before us who have found useful ways to support individuals in transition. Our intention is not to impose our beliefs on those in distress nor guide them to any particular outcome. Our intention is to be fully present whilst listening to and protecting those undergoing potentially transformative experiences. In order to provide a consistent level of compassionate care, care givers must act within a clearly defined code of conduct and ethical standards. This code of care should be taught in training sessions and agreed to by everyone who works at the care space.

Ethical Standards for Care Services

It is essential that care givers act within impeccable ethical standards whilst providing psychedelic support services. Individuals who request these services are often in a vulnerable state and must be treated with respect and dignity. It is important that care givers remain focused on the needs of guests, and act conscientiously whilst providing assistance. The care givers must agree to keep all discussions and events in confidence. They should refrain from sharing their own experiences and beliefs unless it is clear that this exchange is desired by the guest. Request permission from a guest before touching them in any way. Sexual advances from guests should be tactfully deflected. Clearly, sexual advances from a care giver towards a guest are forbidden.

Providing psychedelic support services can be intensely demanding work. The care givers must attentively monitor their own emotional responses and fatigue, recognising their personal limitations and asking for help if needed. Don't try to apply skills you do not possess. If you become ineffective in a given situation, ask another member of the team to replace you. Chapter 13, "Team Welfare", discusses the importance of taking care of yourself and your team members, for the effective and harmonious operation of the care service.

Seek medical services promptly for any guest who needs them. Antipsychotic medication should only be administered by licensed medical staff, and even then should be considered as a last resort; aborting a crisis experience pharmaceutically without resolving it psycho-spiritually can be detrimental to the guest in the long term, but care givers should not prevent a guest from receiving such intervention if the guest insists on it. Care givers have a duty to protect guests under their care, but do not have the right to make such decisions for them. However, it should be understood that licensed medical staff, when present, have the authority to provide whatever medical intervention they deem appropriate, regardless of the opinion of the guest or the care givers, and care givers must not obstruct them in their duty. Chapter 6, "Supporting Roles", contains more detailed information regarding working with medics, psychiatrists, and nurses in the care service team.

Request the permission of the guest before using any special techniques in your peer counselling, and avoid pressuring them into accepting. Be open to suggestions from your fellow care givers and mindful of your emotional state. Do not provide care whilst in an altered state of consciousness. Allow yourself to be the grounded energy that helps the guest transition towards their calm, untroubled self.

Once more, the care team must strive to take care of themselves and their fellow care givers. Respect the people you work with. Institute a dispute resolution process to negotiate disagreements and promote harmony among the staff. Encourage care givers to develop their skills and learn more about providing services. Provide training materials that can help care givers think on their feet. Care givers may want to read the *Code of Ethics for Spiritual Guides* (included at the end of this chapter), a set of principles established by the Council on Spiritual Practices (CSP) after extensive consultation with experienced therapists. Due to the nature of music festivals and similar events, it is usually not possible to obtain consent to assist whilst the guest is still in an "ordinary" state of consciousness, as suggested in Point 3 of the *Code of Ethics*. Since guests are often not in a position to actively consent to services, treat them with the care you would want for yourself or your own family. Act with integrity.

Create a Supportive Environment

A central principle of providing a care service is the creation of a safe, welcoming shelter that respects and protects the dignity of guests seeking assistance. The care space should ideally be located in a relatively quiet area and offer a comfortable, softly lit interior where guests can sit or lie down. Care should be taken to warm or cool the shelter depending on the prevailing weather conditions. The design and creation of a physical care space is discussed

*KosmiCare's yurt structure at the 2012 Boom Festival was for particularly challenging guests, or for those who felt a desire for solitude.
Photo by Susana Santos.*

in detail in Chapter 9, "The Care Space". The space should be staffed by calm, informed people who serve primarily as compassionate "sitters", not as "guides". It is important that the care givers address guests as equals and not talk down to them or make them feel inferior in any way. Organisers of the care space should identify and recruit care givers who are good natured, kind, present, grounded, and who refrain from imposing their own beliefs on guests. The process for assembling a care team is discussed in depth in Chapter 5, "Recruiting a Team".

The first goal of the care service is to address a guest's immediate need for fluids, shade, warmth, rest, or medical care. Taking steps to meet these simple needs often helps to quickly soothe individuals who arrive at the care space agitated or anxious. Upon arrival, each guest should be introduced to a care giver and offered a cup of water and/or other appropriate fluids. The care space can also offer simple snacks such as dried fruit, bread, crackers, or instant soup for guests who arrive hungry or with unsettled stomachs (see Chapters 9, "The Care Space" and 10, "Running the Service").

If guests need shade and respite from heat, they can be positioned in a cool area of the care space near fans or moving air. Guests who are cold should be offered blankets and warm clothes, which should be collected and cleaned in advance of the event. The care space should be positioned near toilet facilities, and the care givers should tell guests where these facilities are located when they arrive at the care space. Meeting the simple physical needs of guests helps to establish a rapport with those seeking assistance and signal to them that they will be cared for in a respectful manner.

Whilst providing for guests as they settle in to the space, the care team should be alert for medical and mental health issues that they may need to address. These may not be easy to distinguish from the effects of a psychoactive drug. If guests appear to have any immediate medical requirement involving their airway, breathing, heart, or circulation, they should be taken promptly to the nearest medical provider or a call should be made to summon these services (see Chapters 10, "Running the Service" and 11, "Screening"). If in doubt, summon a medical provider for an immediate physical assessment. Some events may also have an official crisis intervention team staffed by professional therapists. If a guest indicates that they may harm themselves or others, ask for immediate assistance from mental health professionals.

2.3 Provide Compassionate Listening

When providing support, care givers should remain calm and open to the needs of the guests without fussing over them. Guests should be treated as equals and care givers should speak to them without being condescending or patronising. Guests will often feel better simply by having a quiet conversation with someone who will truly listen to them talk about whatever it is they are going through. When we say "listen", we mean *really* listen to the guest; it is not sufficient or helpful to pretend to listen, or only give partial attention to what the guest is saying. Think carefully about what they tell you, and avoid any instinct towards being dismissive or belittling their experiences and concerns. A guest in an expanded state of consciousness is often exquisitely sensitive to the reactions of those caring for them; if they perceive that they are not being taken seriously, they may become even more anxious or upset and reject further assistance. *Guests are free to leave the care space at any time and for any reason.*

When interacting with guests, it is often useful to respond to what they are telling you. It is also important to let them know that you are listening and that you care about them. Guests will sometimes want to discuss sensitive or personal topics; the care givers should give guests permission to talk about these issues in confidence, whilst maintaining their own emotional and physical boundaries. You should encourage guests to explore their self-awareness and ask them to confirm or clarify your understanding of their situation. Try not to parrot back what they are saying (this could be annoying, or perceived as mocking), but respond in a way that shows that you understand, or are genuinely attempting to understand, what they are trying to communicate. Be honest about your feelings concerning their suggestions for resolution of their distress. If a guest informs you that they intend to do something that could have a drastic outcome, accept the comment seriously, but try to dissuade them from this course of action. Ask them to think about the consequences, not just for themselves, but for others. Suggest that they may want to wait until the next day to assess their decisions in a clearer light.

If guest make seemingly outlandish claims (for example: that they have special psychic powers; that there is a conspiracy against them; that they are royalty), do not argue or express your disbelief. If the claims appear that they may impact the guest's well-being and safety (such as the belief that someone is trying to kill them), invite the guest to explain the situation as clearly and calmly as possible. Giving guests the time to talk about their concerns will often help them feel less fearful. If there are logical holes in their story, gently pointing these out may help the guest realise that they are not under threat after all.

Encourage guests to discuss their own perceived emotional strengths and resources. Explore what they would consider a good outcome to their situation. You could also suggest that guests engage in forms of artistic self expression: writing, drawing, and so forth. If the guest feels anxious or tense, you might encourage them to take deep, slow breaths or engage in some form of movement that releases tightly wound energy. Guests should be given the opportunity to express themselves and/or release excess energy by any safe means that they feel is necessary, such as making noises, crying, singing, chanting, or moving around in whatever way is useful to them. Sometimes inviting the guest to take a walk with you outside the care space may be calming, especially if the space is crowded. Those providing care services should also be open to a variety of approaches that can help shift the guest's experience of distress towards a positive outcome. Some of the approaches mentioned above, along with others, are discussed in Chapter 12, "Complementary Therapies".

Care givers must take steps to care for themselves in order to be fully engaged listeners. Don't forget to drink water, eat occasionally, and stretch. If you feel that your calmness, patience, or positivity is slipping, take a break and ask another care giver to replace you; then introduce the new care giver to the guest before you depart. You cannot be fully present for others if you do not respect your own needs as well.

Accept and Work With Difficult Experiences

The so-called "bad trip" is poorly named. Care givers must understand that difficult experiences are not necessarily "bad", and know that they can be potentially transformative for the guest. Guests seeking assistance are often event participants who just wanted to have a good time. Most did not intend to embark on an extremely challenging journey or healing transformation. When their experience turns "bad" and they encounter emotional turbulence, they may seek a quick remedy that will allow them to return to happily partying after a short time. Unfortunately, if the guest is having an intense experience, the only non-pharmaceutical choices usually involve working through the experience as best they can, seeing the process though to its resolution. During this time, it's important to remind guests to breathe deeply and release tension.

Growth can be challenging and painful. Any difficult or powerful psychological experience—whether facilitated by drug ingestion or not—can be considered an opportunity for personal evolution. Not all experiences are easy, but the care giver can help guests remain calm and reassured. Emotional struggles and tension may be prompted by a mental effort to fight the experience in an attempt to maintain control. This resistance may arise when the guest is confronted with their fears or unresolved issues from the past. Some people may attempt to avoid this confrontation because it makes them feel afraid, threatened, and uncomfortable. For others, such states may simply be a case of "too much, too soon", and they may panic or become overwhelmed. Whilst there are other potential causes for distress, the important point is that these experiences are highly unsettling for the person undergoing them and frequently result in deep-seated fear of one kind or another. When unchecked, fear can quickly escalate, aggravating and magnifying the very thoughts and feelings that the guest is trying to avoid.

Removing or reducing resistance and fear helps shift the guest's mental perspective from "harrowing" to "healing". Such reassurance helps the guest focus on the personal growth that can be gained from these experiences and helps unknot mental blocks that may be encountered. It can be very beneficial for guests if you tell them this in your own way. Confirm with them that they are in a safe space where they will be treated with compassion and without judgement—somewhere they can unfurl and simply let it all happen. Attempting to outline and discuss the myriad varieties of strange things that people in strong altered states of consciousness may experience and/or believe could fill volumes, so we will avoid trying to over-simplify what care givers may encounter during their work. People differ greatly and are unpredictable; everyone's experiences are unique. Be kind, attentive, and reassuring.

It is often helpful to remind the guest that they feel the way they do because they have taken a drug (if they have) and that the experience is temporary and will not last forever; in all likelihood, they will feel fine within a matter of hours. This may be a small comfort to the guest, who could be experiencing minutes as hours, but it is important to provide reassurance that the experience *will* end. The same principle applies to guests who may believe that they have gone insane and will stay that way, or who believe that they are dying.

Guests who think they have gone insane may recognise that they have taken a drug, but see this as the trigger for permanent madness, rather than a temporary state. A small number of people are permanently negatively impacted by these states, but it is important to encourage guests to embrace the belief that they will regain their normal mental state. If the guest accepts this, their fear and anxiety may subside and they may be able to explore themselves with a safe and supportive demeanour, without worrying about getting lost forever in the forests of the mind. Some therapists believe that how a person "returns" from such experiences is at least partly a matter of choice and intent. However, some guests in such a state could have pre-existing mental disturbances that may remain when the impact of the drug experience has subsided. It is very difficult for care givers in such a situation to know what each guest's "baseline" state is like; it is therefore helpful if the care giver can talk with friends of the guest to get some sense of how the guest behaves under normal conditions.

In the case of guests who think they are dying, it is vitally important that this not be shrugged off as a psychiatric delusion, even though it often might be. Ask the guest what they have consumed (including drugs, food, and fluids), and have them describe their physical symptoms. If there is any doubt at all about their medical condition, have the guest checked out by medical services staff promptly, and accompany them to this care if you have already established a rapport. Guests who need additional medical help may be grateful to be accompanied by someone with whom they have spent time talking. If possible and appropriate, remain with the person whilst they are being cared for and continue to reassure them. In the case of a guest who is not actually dying, but believes that they are because of their present state of consciousness, receiving a basic check-up from a professional and the reassurance that their vital signs are normal, may be all that the guest needs to be able to relax and shrug it off as an illusory sensation.

Practical Considerations

Encourage guests to use the experience to explore themselves, but be aware that this expression may manifest in unexpected ways. Be ready to accept and work with anything that comes, as long as your personal safety or that of those around you is not in jeopardy. If a guest becomes physically aggressive, seek help immediately from fellow care givers and have a plan for calling in outside assistance. If a guest turns violent, the time for *sitting* is over, and intervention is clearly needed. If a guest is simply verbally aggressive, loud or obnoxious, remain calm and confident, whilst embracing any approach that may dissipate the situation peacefully and amicably. Ask the guest to lower their voice to avoid disturbing other people. It may sometimes be necessary to walk with an especially noisy guest out of the care space and allow them to express themselves outdoors. Some care spaces will have a separate space (for example, a dedicated hut or tepee) to house loud or aggressive guests.

2.5

Guests may experience a range of extreme emotions, from deep sadness to manic hysteria. This emotional outflowing or catharsis may also result in the guest soiling themselves or vomiting. If a guest does this, reassure them that it's okay and not a big deal. If there is time, accompany them to the toilet if they need help walking, or grab them a bucket if there is no time. Care givers should be prepared for any clean-ups that may be required in such an event. It should be understood that for much of their stay, guests may have difficulty attending to their physical needs, and it is the responsibility of care givers to keep an eye on guests and do their best to ensure that such needs are taken care of, with assistance offered when necessary. To reduce the possibility of choking, make sure that guests who are vomiting lie on one of their sides and not on their back.

Respect the dignity of each guest. Be alert for transitions in their state of perception or physical experience and consider the appropriate next step. Be prepared to attend to their ongoing physical needs over a number of shifts. If a guest lies down with their eyes shut, this is not a signal that they no longer need someone with them; there is a possibility they might stop breathing, or perhaps vomit and choke, in which case immediate assistance is mandatory. Some care givers with at least basic first aid training should be present in the care space at all times. Write down any information that could be useful for care givers who might assist a guest during the next shift—especially if it appears that the guest may have a long stay at the care space. Be patient. Psychedelic experiences often take many hours to resolve, and people who are cared for may come back for integration and reassurance after the immediate experience is over.

Code of Ethics for Spiritual Guides

Those organising and working at care services may wish to refer to the *Code of Ethics for Spiritual Guides* (see http://csp.org/code.html), a set of principles established by the Council on Spiritual Practices (CSP) after extensive consultation with experienced therapists. This document is partially reproduced below (with American English spelling preserved). The *Code of Ethics* is most relevant for sitting or guiding people undergoing *intentional* spiritual exploration with psychedelic substances. However, it is also useful as an ethical approach for care givers to take with someone who has ingested psychoactives in a recreational setting and unwittingly precipitated a "difficult trip", during which the individual ends up obtaining help from a stranger. In this context, again, care givers act as *sitters* and not as guides.

Code of Ethics for Spiritual Guides
by the Council on Spiritual Practices

1. [**Intention**] Spiritual guides are to practice and serve in ways that cultivate awareness, empathy, and wisdom.

2. [**Serving Society**] Spiritual practices are to be designed and conducted in ways that respect the common good, with due regard for public safety, health, and order. Because the increased awareness gained from spiritual practices can catalyze desire for personal and social change, guides shall use special care to help direct the energies of those they serve, as well as their own, in responsible ways that reflect a loving regard for all life.

3. [**Serving Individuals**] Spiritual guides shall respect and seek to preserve the autonomy and dignity of each person. Participation in any primary religious practice must be voluntary and based on prior disclosure and consent given individually by each participant whilst in an ordinary state of consciousness. Disclosure shall include, at a minimum, discussion of any elements of the practice that could reasonably be seen as presenting physical or psychological risks. In particular, participants must be warned that primary religious experience can be difficult and dramatically transformative.

Guides shall make reasonable preparations to protect each participant's health and safety during spiritual practices and in the periods of vulnerability that may follow. Limits on the behaviors of participants and facilitators are to be made clear and agreed upon in advance of any session. Appropriate customs of confidentiality are to be established and honored.

4. [**Competence**] Spiritual guides shall assist with only those practices for which they are qualified by personal experience and by training or education.

5. [**Integrity**] Spiritual guides shall strive to be aware of how their own belief systems, values, needs, and limitations affect their work. During primary religious practices, participants may be especially open to suggestion, manipulation, and exploitation; therefore, guides pledge to protect participants and not to allow anyone to use that vulnerability in ways that harm participants or others.

6. [**Quiet Presence**] To help safeguard against the harmful consequences of personal and organizational ambition, spiritual communities are usually better allowed to grow through attraction rather than active promotion.

7. [**Not for Profit**] Spiritual practices are to be conducted in the spirit of service. Spiritual guides shall strive to accommodate participants without regard to their ability to pay or make donations.

8. [**Tolerance**] Spiritual guides shall practice openness and respect towards people whose beliefs are in apparent contradiction to their own.

9. [**Peer Review**] Each guide shall seek the counsel of other guides to help ensure the wholesomeness of his or her practices and shall offer counsel when there is need.

**Further Reading
(see also Chapter 17, "Online Resources and Obtaining Assistance")**

MAPS (2014). *The Zendo Project Harm Reduction Manual.* http://www.zendoproject.org/wp-content/uploads/2016/03/zendo_052015.pdf

Erowid (2005). "Psychedelic Crisis FAQ: Helping Someone Through a Bad Trip, Psychic Crisis, or Spiritual Crisis". http://www.erowid.org/psychoactives/faqs/psychedelic_crisis_faq.shtml

Fadiman, J. (2011). *The Psychedelic Explorer's Guide—Safe, Therapeutic, and Sacred Journeys.* Vermont: Park Street Press. http://www.psychedelicexplorersguide.com

Goldsmith, N.M. (2011). *Psychedelic Healing: The Promise of Entheogens for Psychotherapy and Spiritual Development.* Vermont: Healing Arts Press. http://www.nealgoldsmith.com/psychedelics

Grof, S. (2008). "Crisis Intervention in Situations Related to Unsupervised Use of Psychedelics". *LSD Psychotherapy,* fourth edition (pages 308–319). California: Multidisciplinary Association for Psychedelic Studies. http://www.psychedelic-library.org/grof2.htm

Grof, S. and Grof, C. (1989). *Spiritual Emergency: When Personal Transformation Becomes a Crisis.* New York: Jeremy P. Tarcher/Putnam.

McCabe, O.L. (1977). "Psychedelic Drug Crises: Toxicity and Therapeutics". *Journal of Psychedelic Drugs* 9(2): 107–121.

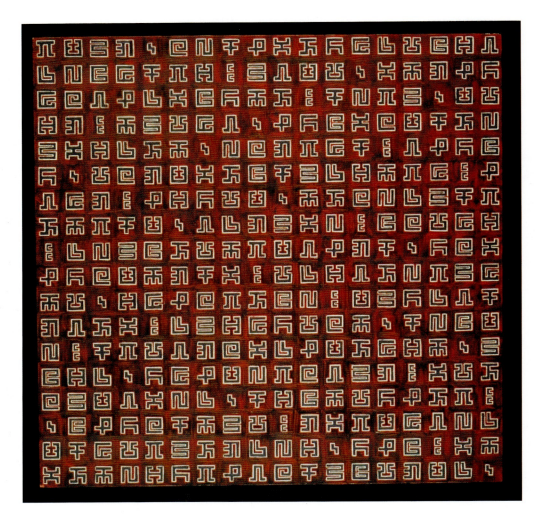

ALLYSON GREY • *Magic Square*, 1990 • oil on wood
http://www.allysongrey.com

CHAPTER 3
LEGAL CONSIDERATIONS

Minty De La Playa

This section covering the legal considerations of psychedelic care services explores a range of legal issues that may impact both event participants and personnel involved in providing psychedelic support. An overview of some of the potential legal risks and consequences is provided with regard to situations including: encounters with law enforcement; consent, confidentiality, and privacy issues; legal protections/fiduciary obligations of support personnel; and other potential legal liabilities in providing psychedelic support.

This chapter should not be viewed as constituting legal advice. It is simply intended to highlight some of the legal concerns that should be considered in relation to the provision of psychedelic care services. As laws vary from country to country and from state to state, qualified independent legal advice should be obtained in order for you to determine applicable laws governing your contemplated efforts.

Legal Issues for Event Participants

INTERACTIONS WITH LAW ENFORCEMENT

Event participants who are experiencing intense psychedelic experiences may find themselves in situations where they are required to interact with law enforcement officials. The presence of law enforcement at festivals and public events is presumably to ensure the safety and security of all participants, but these officials will also be responsible for enforcing the laws of the local jurisdiction, including prohibitions against drug use and public disorder. Although such events may be considered to be private or held on private property, they will nevertheless continue to be subject to the laws of the jurisdiction in which they are held.

There is often an understanding, however, between law enforcement and on-site healthcare personnel, that the immediacy of patient care should override any involuntary remand for a suspected offence. This protection may be codified into applicable law; if so, providers should familiarise themselves with the appropriate statutes.
In any event, providers of psychedelic care services may wish to ensure that such an understanding with law enforcement also applies to their services and is obtained in advance of the event.

Although there may be a greater law enforcement interest in pursuing individuals suspected of assault, trafficking, or other serious offences, notwithstanding that they may need immediate medical attention, it is presumable that lesser infractions involving public intoxication, consumption of illicit substances, or disorderly conduct, should typically give way to patient need in order to reduce immediate harm. Such considerations will necessarily vary by jurisdiction.

There are inherent legal risks to participants who possess and/or consume illegal psychoactive substances and who may come into contact with law enforcement.

CONSENT AND CAPACITY

Individuals who are experiencing intense psychedelic experiences may not have the requisite capacity to make certain decisions concerning their own care, or may not be able to consent to treatment in cases of distress or immediate risk of personal harm. In most cases, psychedelic support may simply involve providing a "safe space" for the individual until the intense experience passes or is otherwise resolved. However, there may be cases where intervention is required, such as when individuals pose a risk of harm to themselves or others, or when medical complications arise.

In severe cases, psychedelic care givers will want to ensure that any services provided do not exceed what might reasonably be consented to by an individual in such circumstances. In other words, the care or treatment provided should only go as far as to ensure that the individual does not pose a risk of harm to themselves or others. The extent to which psychedelic support should be provided in such cases will often be difficult to gauge, particularly since the individual may not have the capacity to indicate the types of preventative services they would consent to.

On the other hand, a failure to refer someone who is in medical distress to appropriate medical personnel may result in other liabilities. It may be difficult if not impossible for people without medical training to identify underlying medical conditions, the effects of regularly used prescription medicines, and/or emergent physical symptoms, any of which might result in harmful or even fatal outcomes when combined with a significant psychoactive experience. Specific efforts should be made to adequately gauge the level of care that is required in each case. Whilst most incidents of intense psychedelic experience will probably benefit from some simple harm-prevention techniques, the care giver should be aware of situations that pose serious health risks to guests and that might require immediate medical attention. If there is any concern whatsoever that an individual needs professional medical evaluation, this evaluation must be obtained without delay. Please see Chapter 11, "Screening", for a more thorough discussion of this subject.

CONFIDENTIALITY AND PRIVACY

As with any patient/practitioner relationship, a duty of confidentiality is required of all care givers with respect to their guest's medical condition and other personal identifying information. The duty will vary by jurisdiction, and will depend on the circumstances of each case. For example, in cases of immediate medical distress, the disclosure of information regarding an individual's consumption of psychoactive drugs may be necessary to ensure proper medical treatment, even though this information may have been conveyed or received in confidence. Typically, a guest's expectations of privacy and confidentiality should be preserved to the greatest extent possible, with the only exception being the "immediate risk of harm" to the individual or others.

"Immediate risk of harm" typically refers to situations where there is a likelihood that the individual may cause harm to themselves or to others. Examples may include ideations of suicide, self-infliction of harm, or violent behaviour towards care givers or other participants. In such cases, it may be justifiable to breach an expectation of privacy or confidentiality to which the individual may otherwise be entitled. The overriding concern should be the health and safety of all participants involved with the care service, and any breaches of privacy or confidentiality should be justifiable, with appropriate notes or documentation cataloguing why such a breach was necessary given the circumstances. Inappropriate breaches may result in liability, so care givers should be sure to document any and all potential breaches.

DEEMED WAIVERS AND PRESUMPTION/DUTY OF CARE

Individuals experiencing situations of psychological or emotional distress brought on by an intense drug experience may seek the help of psychedelic care givers or emergency services personnel. In such cases, there is an onus on all care providers to assist such individuals through their experiences and to provide a reasonable standard of care. As described above, some guests may not have the requisite capacity to provide informed consent for psychedelic care services, but if such services are provided, there is a duty of care on support personnel to ensure that the guest receives the appropriate level of care, or referral to other medical services.

In extreme cases, such as when a psychedelic experience becomes so intense, and care givers have employed their best efforts to provide support or other healing modalities, it may be said that the guest is deemed to have waived any rights to any requisite duty of care. In other words, care providers who use their best efforts to assist someone in distress will often be indemnified from liability during the course of care and support. Such protections are typically provided pursuant to "good Samaritan laws" that exist in most jurisdictions. These laws typically hold care providers harmless for attempting to assist those in distress, assuming that the care provider has acted with reasonable care. The deemed waiver will not apply, however, if the care provider has acted negligently or in bad faith. As such, care givers should ensure that they are providing the best possible care or support in each circumstance, and be ready to refer a guest to other health care providers as appropriate, in order to ensure the health and safety of all participants. Refer to Chapter 14, "Working With Other Organisations", for further discussion on this topic.

Festival and event organisers often include deemed liability waivers as part of their event participation or ticketing processes. The care service leader should seek to ensure that the wording of any such waivers also applies to all participants in their care service.

Legal Issues for Care Givers

Legality of Psychedelic Support Services

In some jurisdictions, the promotion or idealisation of drug use may be considered illegal, and various duties are sometimes imposed on festival promoters to identify and report unlawful activity, such as illicit drug use. This raises the question of whether providers of psychedelic care services, by virtue of their focus on the *after-effects* of drug consumption, *are* actively engaged in the promotion or idealisation of illicit drug use. Yet it is possible that in some cases, law enforcement agencies may consider this to be so.

There are documented cases where a positive duty is placed on festival organisers to actively prevent, eliminate, or report illicit drug activity. It is unclear whether such a duty would extend to psychedelic care providers who interact with users of psychedelic drugs during public events. Although it is presumed by the presence of psychedelic care services that illicit drug use may indeed be occurring at the event, it is more likely that such services will be viewed as being akin to medical care. The duty to report or prevent such activity may, however, be extended to psychedelic care givers depending on the jurisdiction in which the event is being held. Careful consideration should be given to how such care services are likely to be viewed by law enforcement authorities in each particular jurisdiction.

Police officers at the Burning Man Festival in a friendly debate over whether they might have to pull over a "kinetic sculpture" or an "art car". Photo by Jon Hanna, 2007.

Although the presence of psychedelic care implies a "presumption of use", much like the individual possession of drug paraphernalia does in some jurisdictions, there may be an argument to be made that any sanctions on the provision of such care may contravene constitutional protections on the right to freedom of speech or expression. Nevertheless, a careful analysis of relevant laws should be undertaken to ensure that good faith psychedelic care services do not unwittingly fall within the ambit of what is considered to be illegal activity.

Public Policy Initiatives and Harm-Reduction Strategies

In many jurisdictions there is a recognition that harm-reduction strategies are a more appropriate way of dealing with the effects of substance use than traditional punitive sanctions, especially in situations where the likelihood of substance use continuing despite sanctions designed to deter it is high. An example of such a harm-reduction strategy is a needle exchange programme for intravenous drug users; although the use of intravenous drugs may generally be "illegal", there is a public policy argument to be made that providing clean needles to such users may reduce the likelihood of harm in other health-related areas, such as the transmission of diseases including HIV. There is similarly a general understanding that the presence of support personnel at events where psychedelic substances may be consumed could help in pursuing the public policy interest of reducing certain harms among those participants.

Regulatory Frameworks around Public Events

In some jurisdictions, event organisers may legally be required to have an emergency plan in place, and must demonstrate that they have sufficient emergency care providers on hand in an appropriate ratio to participants. It is unclear whether psychedelic support services would serve to fulfil such a requirement, but they are likely to be viewed as auxiliary services that are performed alongside more traditional emergency care strategies. In any case, psychedelic care providers should ensure that the provision of their services does not run contrary to any existing regulations that govern public festivals and events.

Interactions with Law Enforcement: Aiding, Abetting and Entrapment

There is an additional concern that, given the nature of psychedelic care services, care givers may be accused of aiding and abetting in the use and consumption of illegal substances. Although this would generally be contrary to the good faith nature of such services, individual care givers should be cautious about their own interactions with participants to ensure that they are not seen to be participating in the commission of illegal acts. Appropriate training about the laws of the jurisdiction should perhaps be provided to care givers in this regard.

Psychedelic care givers should also be made aware of the possibility of entrapment measures by law enforcement officials posing as festival participants requiring care. Although psychedelic care providers may generally be supportive and sympathetic around users of illegal drugs, they should not place themselves in situations where they are viewed as aiding in the commission of an offence.

The grim tone and content of this last paragraph may rightfully sound disconnected from reality to those who have provided psychedelic care in certain countries (for example, Portugal), and very connected to reality to those who have worked in others (for example, the United States). Each case must be assessed in its own right, taking into account the laws and the norms of its particular jurisdiction.

Potential Liabilities in the Provision of Care: Fiduciary Obligations, Good Samaritan Laws, and so forth

As mentioned above, psychedelic care givers could be held liable for breaches of any duties of care that may be owed to users of their services, even in cases where deemed waiver provisions are provided as a condition of participation at a public event or festival. There may also be fiduciary obligations owed to participants, as well as to festival or event organisers. It is advisable to ensure that such requirements are appropriately researched in advance of providing care. An understanding of local "good Samaritan laws" is also advisable.

Special consideration should be given to the topic of professional medical evaluation. Whilst it may be argued that in the majority of cases, routine medical evaluation—on an ongoing basis once a guest is admitted to the care service—is not necessary, the psychedelic care giver needs to be mindful of the risk of underlying or emergent medical conditions that can have harmful or even fatal outcomes if left without medical intervention. A non-medical care giver who elects to defer or avoid medical evaluation should carefully consider the potential of both legal and personal long-term emotional liability if the participant in distress deteriorates and suffers injury or death. This topic is discussed at much length in various parts of this Manual, and especially in Chapter 11, "Screening".

Human Rights Issues: Discrimination, Sexual Assault, Workplace Violence and Harassment

Individuals who are experiencing intense psychedelic experiences may often be placed in vulnerable situations where their rights to be free from discrimination or harassment may be infringed, either by fellow event participants or by the care givers entrusted to ensure their health and safety. Care givers should be made aware of the rights and protections that are afforded by law to event participants and any additional duties that may be imposed on them with regard to the care owed to vulnerable populations. Care givers are likely to be viewed as holding positions of trust in relation to the care and treatment of vulnerable guests. As such, there may be additional liabilities imposed if care givers misuse or abuse that trust, or if they infringe the rights of those they are expected to protect.

By the same token, psychedelic care givers are also usually protected from discrimination, harassment, and violence inflicted by those to whom they are providing care. Care givers should be adequately trained to ensure that they are knowledgeable about their own rights and about how to handle situations where there may be a risk of harm to themselves or to others.

Ethical and Professional Considerations for Harm-Reduction Practitioners

Although psychedelic care givers may not be subject specifically to the ethical and professional obligations that would otherwise apply to mainstream health care providers, such duties may nevertheless apply to individual care givers who are already a member of a regulated health profession (including, but not limited to, doctors and nurses) and who are also providing psychedelic care services. These professional obligations may extend to the provision of psychedelic care even though regulated health care providers may not be engaged in their own professional practice at that time. The application of these ethical and professional requirements should be explored by individual professionals to ensure they are not breaching any professional codes of conduct.

In some locations, psychedelic care givers may be held liable for providing treatment beyond what is specified within the constraints of their then-current medical training and certification. Similarly, even with an appropriate class of medical training, care givers may require current licensure to provide medical care in the local jurisdiction. Failure on either count may result in civil and/or criminal liabilities.

Since the provision of psychedelic care services at public events and festivals appears to be a growing phenomenon, it may be worth considering whether a uniform code of conduct for those who provide such services should be created. This would help in standardising certain service expectations in the provision of this type of care, and may help in bolstering the legitimacy of such services along with minimising individual liabilities. A starting point for creating such a code of conduct could be the Code of Ethics for Spiritual Guides, developed by the Council on Spiritual Practices (CSP), and included in Chapter 2, "The Principles and Ethics of Psychedelic Support". As that chapter points out, however, the CSP code was developed for a set of circumstances very different than those typical of psychedelic care scenarios at music festivals or other events, and it is mentioned here only as a possible point of inspiration.

Burning The Man in 2003.
Photo by Jon Hanna.

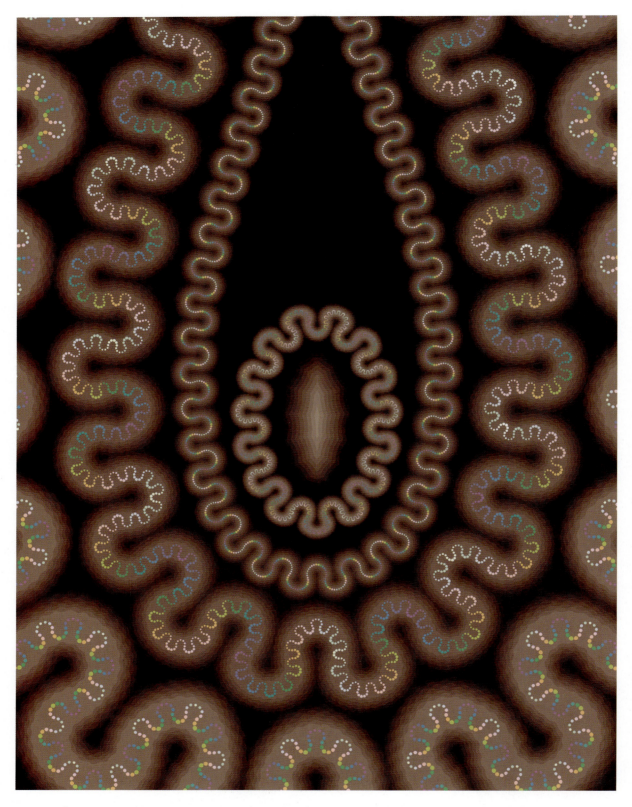

VIBRATA CHROMODORIS • *Inspirazione*, 2012 • digital (Adobe Illustrator)
http://vibrata.com

CHAPTER 4

PLANNING AND FIRST STEPS FOR A NEW PROJECT

Annie Oak

Svea Nielsen

This chapter presents the steps that organisers of a psychedelic care service should take to plan and direct the project. It includes information on how to describe the project to event organisers, collect needed materials, and attract potential volunteers. Some of these topics are also covered in more detail in Chapter 14, "Working With Other Organisations".

Determine if the Community Supports a Care Service

4.1

Before approaching the organisers of a festival or event with an offer to provide a care service, it is important to determine if you have local community support for such a project. Attracting and organising people to volunteer for the service, help finance the needed materials, and undertake the physical labour to create the space is hard work. Your first step should be to determine whether you can gather a community to launch this effort. If there is no comparable service that is provided at events in your area, it is more likely that you can recruit local people interested in participating. You may also want to identify some patrons who can donate money, or community organisers who can help you throw fundraising events.

The creation and execution of an effective care space will often require a single person or a small group of people who have the time and organisational skills to complete a very time-intensive project. Organisers should make an honest assessment of their talents and resources before embarking on the creation of a care space. Each organiser should have a specific set of duties that he or she will be responsible for during the project. Determine, for example, who will be the main contact for the festival organisers, for the medical and security services, and so forth.

Once a core group of organisers have decided to launch a care service, they should commit themselves to working through challenges, difficulties, and the inevitable stress that they will encounter. Organisers should make sure that they have adequate support in their own lives for a demanding project and take special care to stay healthy and positive throughout the process. It is important that all organisers resolve to remain friends and acknowledge each other's contributions no matter how the project plays out.

Create a Budget

4.2

Before asking the community to support a care service, it is essential that you create a budget to acquire the needed materials and supplies. Begin by listing all the anticipated materials that the service will need. Chapters 8, "Logistics" and 9, "The Care Space", provide lists of items that need to be acquired to construct and run a care space. Major budget items may include a structure, beds and bedding, lighting, signs, a heater, cushions, furniture, rugs, water storage, and other supplies. You should also include the costs of transporting materials to the event site, meals and other support for care givers, copying training materials, and an after-party to thank the staff.

Larger events will clearly require more infrastructure. Depending on numerous factors—including how many supplies you can obtain through donations or cull from your own possessions, and where the event is taking place—for a large service at an event with 20,000+ attendees you may need to raise between US $3,000 and $10,000 in order to cover all of your expenses (although this is only a very rough estimate).

Once you have assembled a budget, begin to consider how you will raise the money to create the care space. You can ask festival organisers to help cover expenses, run a crowdsourced fundraising campaign, or ask philanthropists and non-profit organisations for support. It's also possible to throw fundraising parties before or after the event. If your care space is located in a large camp within a festival, you may want to charge each camp participant a fee to help support the project.

Care givers can also help gather clean beddings, snacks, and other items before the event. Encourage those who are helping to create the space to hold small fundraisers among their friends. Start an online mailing list for care space volunteers where you can post project updates and make further appeals for funding and care space supplies. Be reasonable with your budget and make contingency plans in case you don't raise all the money you need.

Contact Organisers of the Event

Once the core care team organisers have determined that they have enough community support and potential funding for a care service, they should then contact the event organisers with a written description of the service. If the service is part of a larger camp, then the description should be sure to note that as well. The care service may also be included in another kind of structure or project such as a tea house, meditation space, temple, café, dance space, or other sort of theme camp.

When describing the care service to event organisers, ask them to put you in contact with members of the medical team, mental health services (if they exist), and security personnel who will be working at the event with you; see Chapter 14, "Working With Other Organisations". Describe the care service in writing to medical and security services. Identify key people within those teams whom you can work with during your planning and whilst on-site. Familiarise yourself with their emergency procedures and make sure that these protocols are reflected in the training materials for your care givers. Make arrangements to meet members of those teams on-site before the event starts.

PLANNING AND FIRST STEPS FOR A NEW PROJECT

Some festivals may provide structures, materials, or funding for a care service. Offer festival organisers a list of items that you wish to acquire and see if they are willing to finance particular materials. If they make specific offers, get this information in writing and make clear agreements as to which materials the care service may take with it at the conclusion of the event, and which materials the event organisers will want to retain. Request a location for the care space that is not directly next to loud music, but make sure that it is near toilet facilities that will be well maintained (see Chapter 9, "The Care Space"). If you can arrange for event managers to make a portable toilet available solely for the use of the care space, make sure that it's okay to keep the toilet locked for use by the care service only. Ensure, however, that event organisers do not place a toilet *directly* next to the care space but at a reasonable distance from it, allowing the facility to be serviced without unnecessary noise, odour, and disturbance.

Once the festival has accepted your care space proposal, make sure that your description of the service is included in a list of festival events and activities. You should contact the event publicist and give them a clear description of the care space and its exact location, which they can pass along to other media. You may also want to create a page on one or more social media sites that describes the care service, tells people how to find it, and attracts people who may want to volunteer or donate to the project. The care service can also be publicised on the flyer for the event, promoted by on-site radio, advertised in the toilets, or announced on stage. Once the event is underway, make sure that the care space has proper signs to indicate its location, and also see to it that you have good lighting at night to allow the space to be found easily.

Determine Team Size

4.4

The number of people necessary for the care service will vary according to the size of the event. If you run a twenty-four-hour care service, the easiest way to determine how many people you will need to staff the space is to calculate how many shifts you will try to fill. Let's say, for instance, that you run four six-hour shifts each day. In some care services, shifts run from midnight to 6:00 am, 6:00 am to noon, noon to 6:00 pm, and 6:00 pm to midnight. Ideally, each shift should include one person with professional mental health training such as a psychiatrist, counsellor, or psychologist. The shift should also ideally include a person with emergency medical training (please see Chapter 6, "Supporting Roles", for a more detailed discussion of the support staff required).

For a very large event of say 60,000 people, try to recruit a care space team of five to ten people per shift. For a medium

Alicia Danforth speaks to potential new recruits at the 2009 Symbiosis Festival in Yosemite. Photo by Erowid.

to large event of perhaps 20,000 people, four to eight people can staff a care space per shift. Smaller events with fewer than 5,000 people can be covered by three care givers per shift. If medical professionals are not available to cover all shifts, the care service should absolutely develop a plan with event medical services to refer guests for medical issues, request an evaluation, or summon an emergency response (although these procedures should really be worked out no matter how many medical professionals are available to fill shifts for the care service itself). Care givers should also be briefed on transport plans in case a guest requires further care at the local hospital. See Chapter 14, "Working With Other Organisations", for more detailed information on how to set up coordinated working relationships with medical staff.

Recruit Care Givers

When organisers (or a single organiser—the care service leader) have determined that a care space is welcome at an event, they should put out a request for individuals who can serve as care givers. This can be done by reaching out to local networks of friends, medical professionals, and organisations that share the goals of the project. For more information about recruiting staff for the care space, see Chapters 5, "Recruiting a Team" and 7, "Building and Training a Team".

When seeking staff, it is useful to provide them with a written description of the service. Add new team members to a mailing list where they can receive updates on how the care service is progressing leading up to the event. Experienced care givers should be identified to run specific shifts and train

PLANNING AND FIRST STEPS FOR A NEW PROJECT

other staff; these experienced care givers are often referred to as the *team leads*. Organisers should determine if they will attempt to staff the care space around the clock or only during certain hours. Simple gifts such as T-shirts, stickers, patches, and pendants can be created as "thank you" tokens for care givers and an inducement for new staff. Creating and promoting a suitable name and graphic logo for your care space project will help get the word out.

Whilst recruiting care givers, it is also important to make sure that they will have access to free tickets and adequate accommodations at the event where you will be serving. Consider constructing a camp where care service members can assemble and cook together during the gathering. If you take this step, make sure the festival organisers set aside the necessary space for your care service camp. If you choose not to camp together, make sure to inform care givers about their options for staying on-site, parking arrangements, and how to get in and out of the event gate. Care space planners sometimes need to submit a list of care givers to the event organisers so that the staff can enter without cost. Make sure care service members have the phone number of a care space organiser (such as the care service leader or team leads) in case they have trouble en route or at the gate. Plan some group activities during the festival outside the care space that can help the care givers to get to know each other and work as a team; again, for more information please refer to Chapter 7, "Building and Training a Team".

Collect Training Materials

Organisers may find that *The Manual of Psychedelic Support* is a useful source on which to base their training materials. Training information should be as concise as possible and delivered to care givers and any other staff (such as support staff, including medics, psychiatrists, nurses, and so forth) online or on paper according to an established Training Plan (see Chapter 7, "Building and Training a Team"). Care givers should be encouraged to receive first aid certification from organisations that offer this instruction. Some care service leaders with larger budgets may be able to provide this training on-site to volunteers via certified instructors.

Organisers should be open to suggestions for additional training materials, especially updated information about specific drugs that participants may be ingesting during the festival. Websites such as the Erowid drug library are a good place for current data about substances that may be a factor in difficult participant experiences encountered by the care givers. The Erowid library includes information on lesser-known substances and new psychoactive materials.

Fire Erowid does her best to send and receive all information with the appropriate level of scepticism at a psychoactive drug information booth at the 2011 International Drug Policy Reform Conference. Photo by Erowid.

4.7 Develop a Work Schedule

Perhaps one of the most important initial steps of planning for a care service is developing a work schedule for completing the tasks required to create and establish the service. These tasks include determining who will gather needed supplies, developing a budget, contacting event producers, negotiating site location, securing gate access, contacting the event medical and security teams, packing and transporting supplies, erecting the care space structure, coordinating camping logistics, conducting training, managing the care service shifts, maintaining the tidiness of the care space, packing up the structure and supplies, cleaning the site, transporting materials, cleaning and organising gear, and returning supplies into storage. Planning for the care service after-party to thank care givers, as well as any fundraising efforts, should also be considered in this schedule.

It is especially useful to recruit care service members who can arrive at the event early to help set up the care space. Another group of staff should be recruited to remain after the event to tear down, pack up, and transport supplies into storage. Core organisers should manage the schedule carefully so as to reduce the potential for burn-out and allow personnel to allocate their energy judiciously. In addition to working in the care space, staff members should also be encouraged to enjoy the events where they provide care; ideally they should eat well, stay hydrated, get adequate rest, and have fun. See Chapter 13, "Team Welfare", for an in-depth discussion about taking care of one's team. It's often useful to point team members to the festival schedule so that they can plan to see specific music or events during the gathering and schedule their service time accordingly. Working in a care service is challenging, but don't forget to enjoy yourself!

FRED TOMASELLI • *Expecting to Fly*, 2002 • photo collage, leaves, acrylic, gouache, resin on wood panel
courtesy James Cohan Gallery, New York/Shanghai
http://www.jamescohan.com/artists/fred-tomaselli

CHAPTER 5
RECRUITING A TEAM

Jonas Di Gregorio

Snu Voogelbreinder

Tom Shutte

Zevic Mishor

Great importance rests on recruiting team members who are mentally, emotionally, and socially equipped to deal effectively with guests who come to the care service for help. Choose care givers with a wide range of skills to cover as many needs as possible that may arise in the care space. These skills can include psychotherapy, counselling, massage, aromatherapy, homeopathy, Reiki, and other forms of bodywork (see Chapter 12, "Complementary Therapies"). Depending on the event, having team members who can speak a range of languages may also be important or even critical to the success of the care service. Due to the nature of the work, the situations care givers encounter, and the general "energy" of the team (both with each other and when working with guests), it is recommended to aim for a more-or-less even mix of male and female care givers. Note that this current chapter does not address specific support staff positions, such as psychiatrist, psychologist, nurse, and so forth; these are covered separately in Chapter 6, "Supporting Roles".

General Points for Recruiting a Care Service Team

5.1

The care service leader must first make a diligent assessment regarding the size of the team and the various roles required (see Chapter 4, "Planning and First Steps for a New Project"). If possible, it is highly recommended that team leads be individuals with whom the care service leader is already familiar, and with whom he/she has worked before.

Ideally, the bulk of the care givers should also be drawn from people already known to the care service leader and to the team leads. This helps ensure that team leads are aware of the individual personality traits and social skills of their team members, as negative or unwanted traits may not be noticed in newcomers until it is too late. Having said this, and of course depending on the ethos of each particular care service and its leader, it is important that care services do not become "insider cliques" that are completely closed to new members; this is an almost certain path to the ultimate demise of the organisation. There are many great people out there with excellent intentions, good skills, and deep experience, who would make valuable additions to any care service team, and such people should be given a chance to join the care service community.

What to Look For in Care Givers

5.2

The following is a partial list of desirable attributes for a care giver to have. Some of these qualities are very difficult to assess prior to actually working with a person, and so would not form a practical part of the recruitment process (see below); however, these character traits should help the care service leaders form a picture in their minds of the kind of individuals they are looking for:

- A friendly, balanced disposition

- Gets along with a wide range of people, not just with those from their own peer group

- Readily shows compassion and a willingness to help others regardless of how attractive or "cool" the other may be (for example, some people may be good at working with "beautiful people", but their compassion and patience drain away with people who are less attractive, overweight, and so forth)

- Other people feel comfortable around them

- Respects personal space

- Is receptive to social cues and body language

- Can communicate clearly and in a way appropriate to those whom they are communicating with

- Does not avoid eye contact

- Can stay calm when faced with difficult situations and does not become angry or frustrated easily

- Is not condescending or patronising

- Does not think they know everything, or that they are always right

- Is open-minded and receptive to unusual ideas without being dismissive

- Is good at listening and really paying attention to what someone is saying

- Avoids gossip and speaking ill of others

- Has had substantial personal experience with psychedelics (including at least one difficult experience or "bad trip"), but is not egotistical about their level of experience

This may sound like a description for some kind of perfect person who does not actually exist in reality! However, people with these attributes are not uncommon; they just have to be found and recognised. Furthermore, following the example of the care service leader and team leads (who must themselves exemplify these attributes), people will hopefully change and improve themselves throughout a single project, and of course, across weeks, months, and years more generally. If potential team members possess some of these attributes but lack others, they may still be recruited to the team, but should be assigned responsibilities that match with their abilities and personalities, and kept away from situations that may bring out undesirable reactions.

Care givers Tania and Greg Manning reward themselves after a long day working in Sanctuary at the 2006 Burning Man Festival. Photo by Jon Hanna.

The last criterion listed above—"Has had substantial personal experience with psychedelics"—is a very important one. Ideally, it is preferable that all members of the team have previously journeyed with psychedelics and other psychoactive substances. This doesn't mean that a person who has never tried them is unable to join a care service. However, it is important to recognise that personal experience is vital in providing an understanding of the states of consciousness that can be produced by the use of psychoactive substances. Personal experience with these sorts of states and their more challenging aspects can help care givers empathise with others who are having difficult trips, and can produce the foundation for a non-judgemental attitude in the care giver.

On the other hand, the fact that somebody has first-hand experience doesn't automatically make him or her a good fit for this work, as they may have unresolved psychological issues of their own that make them entirely unsuitable. Therefore, this point of personal experience should be neither under- nor over-emphasised; it must be considered as one aspect amongst many that will determine whether a candidate is suitable to join a service as a care giver.

Other Points to Consider

Care staff need to be available to participate in training and team-building activities before the event begins. It is useful to have some relatively strong/large individuals in the care service, in case a guest becomes agitated and needs to be restrained so as not to harm themselves or others (this is a not uncommon scenario), although hopefully event security will be available as well. Another important point to consider is having volunteers on the team who, between themselves, can speak as many of the languages as possible that will be represented at the event in order to be able to communicate with attendees from different countries.

One of the main challenges in recruiting a team is to find people who are *reliable*. It is unfortunately common for people to apply and to be accepted as care givers, yet not to show up when the event begins. This can cause a lot of difficulties in the organisation of work shifts, especially when these shifts have already been planned and shared in advance with the care service team. There are a number of strategies that may be useful in preventing such no-shows; the following are a few suggestions. Of course, if the care service leader doesn't feel comfortable with them, other possibilities must be considered. Again, keep in mind that when a project is run on a voluntary basis, the number of candidates who change their mind at the last moment can be high, so it is crucial to pay attention to these aspects:

ANONYMOUS
Untamed, 2014,
watercolour.

- Ask the selected care givers to sign an agreement, prior to the event, that lists their rights and entitlements, and the care service's expectations and requirements. Care givers must understand the responsibilities that they have taken on and commit to performing them.

- Ask the selected care givers to each pay in advance for their own event ticket; then reimburse them after they have completed all of their shifts. This option can be very effective, but at the same time can also be seen as reflecting a lack of trust in the care givers. So, if used, it is very important to explain the reason for this decision.

- Ask the selected care givers to make a symbolic financial contribution (10 or 20 euros/dollars) to help support the costs of the project. This doesn't guarantee that all of the selected candidates will show up at the beginning of the event; however, it should help make the volunteers feel more like they are a part of the project, and it may help filter out the applicants who are not fully motivated to commit. On the other hand, it may seem counter-intuitive and irritating to some that volunteers are being asked to pay, so this approach should be used with discretion!

RECRUITING A TEAM

One cause for concern in selecting team members is that some individuals who have unbalanced or antagonistic personalities, or serious mental disorders, may feel that they are suited to this work, and may initially appear capable and pleasant enough to give the impression that this is the case. In practice, however, such people may hinder rather than help, and get into conflicts with other team members who try to intervene. Such a situation could prove destructive to the whole enterprise, and this reinforces the need for careful screening of potential team members. The motivation for a volunteer wanting to join the care team is particularly important and should be carefully examined; why is it that this person wants to be part of a care service at a festival/party? And, particularly if they have never undertaken this sort of work before, do they have realistic expectations?

Recruiting a Team in Practice

Teams for small care services may be selected by word-of-mouth between friends and acquaintances, but for medium to large care services (around twenty-five care givers or more) it is recommended that a clear and well-defined application process be employed, and that it be applied equally across the board, for newcomers and experienced care givers alike. Using this method, previous experience (especially within that particular care service) would significantly increase one's chances of being selected; however, *all* prospective care givers would still be required to participate in the application process. The overall aims of such an application process would be: to establish a level of fairness and equality; to ensure that unsuitable applicants can be screened out before they reach the training stage; and ultimately, to recruit the best team possible.

The key tool, then, for a "formal" application process is a comprehensive *application form*. A sample of such a form—that may be freely adapted to the needs of an individual care service—is given below. Apart from gathering basic information (including contact and availability details), such a form aims to collect as much information as possible about the applicant, allowing the care service leader (and anybody else involved in the selection process) to decide whether that person would likely make a good addition to the team.

A useful approach with such an application form is to include a list of criteria, requiring that the applicant answer positively to at least some given number of them (for example, half) as a prerequisite for even submitting their form. This helps to narrow the applicant pool in advance, and saves the care service leader time and effort.

The following sample list of criteria can be modified according to the needs of each individual project:

1. Has had prior experience in psychedelic care situations
2. Has had professional experience in a psychiatric ward (as a doctor, nurse, or similar)
3. Has had personal experience with psychedelics
4. Has a professional background in healthcare services
5. Possesses therapeutic and/or massage skills
6. Has undergone first aid and/or CPR training
7. Has an interest (academic, professional, or personal) in psychedelic science
8. Is linked to a harm-reduction organisation
9. Has had previous experience volunteering (in any capacity) at a music festival or similar event
10. Has been recommended by a previous member of this care service
11. Has attended any previous edition of the event

These criteria may be helpful in selecting applicants. Nevertheless, it is recommended that emphasis be placed not only on personal skills and experience, but also on the individual's *motivation*. An inexperienced-yet-motivated, committed, and energetic care giver is likely to contribute more to the team and do more for guests than a veteran care giver who is tired and disinterested.

Generally speaking, in order to clarify these and other points, it is highly recommended to have a conversation (phone call, video chat, or—as a last resort—email) with each candidate before making the final selection. The questionnaire alone is not enough; especially for applicants unknown to the care service leader, it is absolutely necessary to have more direct contact, in order to assess whether they will really be suitable to join the care service team.

5.5 Example Application Form for a Care Giver

The following is an example of an application form for the position of care giver in a "large" care service at a hypothetical music festival. It is based upon a form kindly donated by the Boom Festival's KosmiCare organisation. This form should serve as a good starting point that can be modified for use by any incipient recruitment scenario.

RECRUITING A TEAM

FESTIVAL X — PSYCHEDELIC CARE SERVICE APPLICATION FORM

— PREREQUISITES —

Please note that it is a **prerequisite** for applying to this care service that at least **five** out of the following eleven criteria are true statements regarding your experience. Please circle the number next to any statement that is true for you, and add any relevant comments/clarification at the end.

1. I have had previous experience as a care giver in psychedelic crises situations.
2. I have had professional experience in a psychiatric ward (as a doctor, nurse, or similar).
3. I have had personal experience with psychedelic substances.
4. I have a professional background in healthcare services.
5. I possess therapeutic and/or massage skills.
6. I have undergone first aid and/or CPR training.
7. I have an interest (academic, professional, or personal) in psychedelic science.
8. I am linked to a harm-reduction organisation.
9. I have had prior experience volunteering (in any capacity) at a music festival or similar event.
10. I have been recommended by a previous member of this care service.
    (Please write down the name and contact info for the individual recommending you:)

11. I have attended any previous edition of this music festival/event.

Comments/Clarification:

_____
_____
_____
_____
_____
_____
_____

AREA BELOW IS FOR OFFICE USE

_____
_____
_____
_____
_____
_____
_____

BASIC INFORMATION

FIRST NAME(S):

FAMILY NAME:

PREFERRED NICKNAME:

MAILING ADDRESS:

Street Address

Suburb/Town/City

State   Country   Postcode

MOBILE NUMBER:

Will you have your mobile on during the festival? (Yes / No)

EMAIL ADDRESS:

SKYPE ADDRESS: (If you have one.)

> *The following will only be used to aid in building appropriately diversified shift teams, and in planning logistics.*

SEX: **AGE:**   **COUNTRY OF ORIGIN:**

OCCUPATION: (Or, how do you spend most of your time?)

LANGUAGES SPOKEN: (Please indicate level of fluency for each language listed: *basic / competent / fluent.*)

GENERAL PROFESSIONAL EXPERIENCE: Do you have any relevant work experience that you'd like to tell us about (for example, medical, therapeutic, counselling, harm reduction)?

AVAILABILITY FOR SHIFTS: Do you have any restrictions on which shifts/what days you'll be able to work? If so, please explain.

AVAILABILITY FOR TRAINING: Will you be able to attend the full, mandatory training day being held on-site on _____(date), one day before the official opening of Festival _____(name)?

WORKING FOR OUR PSYCHEDELIC CARE SERVICE

Please explain in up to 500 words why you'd like to work as a volunteer at our care service.

Please explain in up to 300 words what being a "care giver" means to you.
What do you understand to be the basic guiding principles in such work?

Have you ever supported somebody through a difficult drug experience?
If so, please give a brief summary of how you dealt with the situation.

Is there anything else you would like us to know?

VOLUNTEER AGREEMENT

Please review, then print and sign your name (and indicate the date) on the following declaration of intent:

I, _____ , agree to adhere to the following ethical guidelines for the duration of my care work at Festival X:

- I will strive to be a calm, loving, and dedicated presence.

- I will show up on time for each of my shifts, and support the team lead to the best of my abilities.

- I will help keep the care space clean, friendly, and safe.

- I will attend the mandatory training session, and agree to do my best to abide by Festival X's rules, policies, and procedures.

_____

Signature

_____

Date

Please return this application form no later than the ___th of month to:
care_space_volunteers@Festival_X.com

We appreciate your interest in supporting this care service, and we will be in touch with you promptly!

ROBERT VENOSA • *Seconaphim*, 1974 • oil on masonite
http://www.venosa.com

CHAPTER 6
SUPPORTING ROLES

Natacha Ribeiro

Annie Oak

Joan Obiols-Llandrich

The attention of care givers, along with the application of complementary therapies, is not always enough for the optimal care of guests. In critical cases or for specific pathologies, whether they are psychiatric or not, qualified help is mandatory. The purpose of this chapter is to set forth the supporting roles that should be provided, and how they fit into the care service structure. All roles discussed in this chapter relate to the psychedelic care service itself, and *not* to the medical services (which may range in size from someone with a first aid kit to a full medical team) supplied by the event organisers, as part of the overall event itself. These medical services are mentioned in this chapter, and they are discussed in more detail in Chapter 14, "Working With Other Organisations".

Key Supporting Roles for a Care Service

The key supporting roles are the *psychiatrist, emergency medical physician* (that is, *doctor*), *nurse,* and *psychologist.* Fortunately, it is rarely required for them to intervene; however, a medical professional should always be present or at least on-call at the care space. Whilst some care givers may have many academic and/or professional qualifications, these do not necessarily qualify them to diagnose a medical condition nor administer medications. The absence of qualified medical staff may pose risks not only to guests, but also to the care team and to the broader event organisation, depending on the legal environment in which the event is operating. Without access to medical professionals, potentially life-threatening situations are unlikely to be optimally treated. Furthermore, an underlying psychiatric condition, which should influence the nature of care offered to a guest, may go unnoticed. A licensed doctor or nurse would also be qualified to administer medicines, address potential interactions between recreational drugs and other medications, and dispense various treatments.

Clearly, medical teams will vary according to the size of the event and the availability of such volunteers. For a large event (around 20,000 people or more) the ideal team *per shift* for a care service would include:

- 1 or 2 psychiatrists
- 1 emergency medical physician
- 2 nurses
- 1 psychologist

The emergency medical physician and the psychologist could be eliminated if there are not enough volunteers or if there is a small budget; the work of those roles could be done by the psychiatrists, since psychiatrists are qualified medical doctors. However, remember that under this scenario the psychiatrists could get overloaded during heavier shifts.

In a medium-sized event (around 10,000 people) the supporting roles, *per shift*, should be:

- 1 psychiatrist
- 1 nurse

When it is not possible to find medical professionals to fill these positions, or if you are working at a small event (around 5,000 people or less), the care service organisation should develop a plan to work with the event's medical services and/or with the nearest hospital/psychiatric service.

These relationships are especially important when the care service is lacking in doctors and nurses, but of course, *must be established* even if the service has its own full team of medical support staff. Please see Chapter 14, "Working With Other Organisations", for more detailed information on how to set up such coordinated working relationships.

The Psychiatrist's Role

It is highly recommended that a psychiatrist who joins the care team read this section and carefully consider the information contained herein.

At events where psychedelic substances are likely to be consumed by many of the participants, it seems undeniable that a psychiatrist should be a member of the care service team, to help attend to people having difficult drug experiences. Unfortunately, a psychiatrist will not always be present, and this means that severe cases might be referred to event medical services or sent further afield.

When a psychiatrist is available, he or she should be fully integrated with the care service team, participating in the general training and all the activities scheduled, such as ongoing meetings and so forth. The ideal situation would be to have several psychiatrists on board so that each shift has one of them on duty. If only one psychiatrist is available, this individual should be permanently on-call, contactable by mobile phone, two-way radio, or some other system.

The main role for a psychiatrist at a care service is to offer something as apparently simple as *reassurance* for the care team. The whole team feels more confident knowing that if a guest goes downhill and exhibits extreme psychosis, a trained "expert" is there to deal with the situation. Even for members of the team who might be well-versed in psychopathology and accustomed to treating psychiatric patients, if some medication has to be given (a rare situation), a psychiatrist is needed in order to select and administer the correct drug. So hopefully the team will feel reassured that, if a guest shows severe emotional and/or behavioural disturbances, somebody competent is readily available to handle the situation appropriately.

Some guests who are undergoing difficult experiences and not responding well to the efforts of care givers will also feel reassured when a psychiatrist approaches and presents themselves with an introduction like, "Hi, my name is X, I'm a doctor". Notice that there is a difference between saying "a doctor" versus "a psychiatrist"; the first option works better for the simple reason that being a psychiatrist may bear a stigma, and convey negative connotations associated with "madness". So usually it would be better for a guest, when necessary, to be introduced to a *doctor*; after all, psychiatrists *are* medical doctors, so there is no ethical concern about calling them that.

Along with their major function of reassuring the team and the guests, the psychiatrist will have to carry out their professional chores, although in a setting and using an approach quite different from what they might be used to. It has been emphasised in several chapters of this Manual that the care giver should have some personal experience with psychedelics in order to be able to offer the best quality of assistance possible. This principle is also highly recommended for any psychiatrist engaged to work with the care service team.

The kinds of problems seen at an event are usually also attended to in hospital emergency rooms. The procedures there are, obviously, highly medicalised; when the psychiatrist is requested, they conduct an evaluation of the patient's mental state, establish a diagnosis, and often prescribe medication. The general ambiance in emergency rooms is usually a pressured one, with little time allotted "per case".

It is important for a psychiatrist working in a care service to shift from this paradigm. The approach in the care space is much "softer"; the space is nicer and metaphorically warmer compared to an emergency room, human contact and communication are emphasised, and the guiding principle is *not* to administer medical drugs unless absolutely necessary. Of course, it is often the case that care givers have been working with a guest for some time before they decide to call in the psychiatrist. This may mean that by that moment, there is not much more to be done other than dispensing an appropriate drug. However, in some cases an experienced psychiatrist can do a good job controlling acute emotional and behavioural disturbances in a patient without resorting to medication.

Most of the cases will probably be handled by the care givers as described in other chapters of this Manual (see especially Chapters 2, "The Principles and Ethics of Psychedelic Support" and 12, "Complementary Therapies"). Guests presenting with extreme anxiety, highly emotionally disturbed states, and/or paranoid feelings, and hallucinations can improve surprisingly quickly through a vast array of methods, including massage, relaxation techniques, or from the care giver just "being there". The calm and supportive atmosphere of the care space, drinking and eating, and especially, getting some hours of sleep, are all quite helpful. The main issue for many of the guests may be simple exhaustion; they may have been awake for two or three days, dancing or moving for most of that time, and not drinking or eating as required. Independent of the substance(s) taken, getting some rest is very often the best cure. For this reason the importance of silence or at least quiet in the care space must be emphasised, as a main contributor to an optimal therapeutic ambiance.

Not all guests will respond well to a care giver's interventions, and usually the care giver will require a psychiatrist when the situation seems to be beyond their best efforts. A psychiatric evaluation, based on information given by the care giver and on the psychiatrist's own psychopathological exploration, must be carried out. The substance taken and the dosage are not always the most crucial pieces of information, as many (but by no means all) guests will have consumed multiple substances—including alcohol—within a short period of time. The important thing is to form a clear picture of the symptoms exhibited and to proceed to look for the best solution.

Lake Idanha-a-Nova during the 2008 Boom Festival. Photos by Erowid.

As may be expected, guests will usually present with diverse clinical conditions coupled with altered states of consciousness. Such conditions often include emotional or mood disturbances, with deep anxiety being the most common manifestation. Perceptual distortions are frequent. When they reach the level of "hallucinations", what is enjoyable for many can become frightening for others, with subsequent reactions of panic. Speech and thought disturbances are also common, with guests frequently verbalising various paranoid feelings and ideas. The presence of such symptoms leads, of course, to a diagnosis of a psychotic state; usually a brief one, but sometimes longer-lasting.

When all other approaches have failed, pharmaceutical solutions may be called for. As many guests might be reluctant to use them, the decision to recommend them has to be carefully explained to the patient. Any case showing anxiety resistant to soft methods can be alleviated with an anxiolytic medication. Oral benzodiazepines are the first choice. Low doses can work well in most cases; 5 mg of diazepam (Valium) or 1 mg of alprazolam (Xanax), for example, have given excellent results in past care services. In a few cases, the administration had to be repeated.

For psychotic states showing a high degree of behavioural disturbances (auto- or hetero-aggression) or persistent paranoid ideation, neuroleptic treatment may be considered. As the guest might be completely incognisant of the situation, in some cases—even when they are unwilling to accept the treatment—a drug may have to be administered nonetheless. In many jurisdictions it is accepted that some psychotic states require the administration of medication against an individual's will; however, the psychiatrist should carefully take into account the particular legal constraints of the jurisdiction where the event is taking place. See Chapter 3, "Legal Considerations", for a more detailed discussion of this matter. For severe psychotic states, any of the most common neuroleptics can help, with intramuscular injection usually being the preferred route of administration.

Whilst haloperidol (Haldol) has been a common choice, its use is discouraged except in cases of amphetamine overdose. Benzodiazepines are currently preferred for psychedelics. Of the benzodiazepines, with respect to both time-to-sedation and time-to-arousal, midazolam (Versed) has been proven superior to haloperidol, lorazepam (Ativan), and diazepam (Valium), in the sedation of violent and severely agitated patients. Any of these drugs should be administered only by a licensed medical professional.

These kinds of situations require the help of a nurse and a small team of care givers who are ready to adequately restrain the guest. In some cases, where psychotic symptoms are evident but there is a degree of self-insight and self-control, the guest can accept oral neuroleptic medication. Once again, low doses should be enough, such as 1 mg of risperidone (Risperdal), although if necessary this may be increased to 3 mg.

6.3 Special Situations

Depending on the type of event, *alcohol intoxication* may be a frequent scenario, either mixed with other substances or by itself. Although they tend not to come to the care service on their own, severely intoxicated individuals are most likely to be brought in by friends (or by the event's security services). There is not much that can be done other than encouraging the guest to rest and making sure that vital signs are present and correct.

Heroin or other types of opioid addiction are not cases that a care service is ordinarily intended or prepared to deal with. Individuals may come to ask for needles (the organisation should decide in advance if this service will be offered) or with abstinence syndrome, in which case the person should be sent to the nearest hospital.

Psychiatric patients may constitute one of the most challenging types of cases for a care service. Many guests of this type are young people who enjoy music festivals and, of course, have a right to attend them and have a good time. Problems arise, however, when they begin to display psychiatric symptoms, and especially when their condition is exacerbated by the consumption of psychoactive and especially psychedelic drugs. Such individuals frequently end up in the care space. It is often difficult for a care giver to gauge, at least in the early stages of their interaction with such guests, that there is an underlying chronic psychiatric issue, since the guest's behaviour, as well as their verbalised thoughts and emotions, will usually (and understandably) be attributed to the influence of the particular psychoactive(s) consumed. Care givers should be made aware of these matters, and team leads especially should be on the look-out for potential underlying psychiatric conditions in guests. When such conditions become apparent, the psychiatrist should be consulted regarding appropriate courses of action. Please refer also to Chapter 11, "Screening", for further discussion on this subject.

SUPPORTING ROLES

LUKE BROWN • *Alpha Centauri*, 2010 • digital
http://www.spectraleyes.com

CHAPTER 7
BUILDING AND TRAINING A TEAM

Zevic Mishor

This chapter provides guidelines for training a care service team, including care givers, team leads, and any other roles that contribute to a particular care service. The guidelines in this chapter become relevant the moment a team is selected and finalised, as covered in Chapter 5, "Recruiting a Team". Ensuring sufficient and appropriate training for the entire team is a *key responsibility* for the care service leader. Good training is essential for the smooth and successful running of the care service, resulting in team members who understand their roles, follow the correct procedures in different circumstances, and know how to work with guests, whilst simultaneously tending to their own and each other's welfare and well-being. Conversely, poor training may result in confusion, stress, and inferior care being provided for guests, and may lead to some adverse scenarios. Remember that, although rare, it is possible that care givers may have to deal with a life-and-death situation (such as identifying a life-threatening drug overdose, for example). To a large extent, the team's appropriate handling of the situation will depend on the quality of training they've received.

Leadership

It is important to understand that the care service leader's, and likewise the team leads', responsibility extends far beyond providing "just" training. Your task is to *lead* and *mould* your team(s) into a coherent *whole*, facilitating a state of trust, reliance, and loyalty between team members. Such a state is not something that just happens by itself—it must gradually be built-up. Training before an event is the critical stage at which these building processes are set in motion. For a large event, team members may be coming from far-and-wide and many may not yet know one another. Thus, taking into account all of these factors, it is clear that due importance must be accorded to the training phase for the entire care service, whether it begins remotely (long before the event) or not, and whether it consists of several days or just a few hours at the event itself. All necessary steps must be taken to ensure the success of this training phase.

In terms of leadership from the care service leader and the team leads: effective leadership is a topic upon which entire books have been written, and it is beyond the scope of this Manual to give a thorough treatment of the subject. It is important to understand, however, that individuals have their personal leadership style that is most suited to them. Some leaders, for example, are more autocratic, others more democratic, and there is variation along many additional dimensions. No one style is by definition better or worse than any other; all may be equally effective, if practised wholesomely, sincerely and naturally. If three pillars of advice can be given that summarise what it takes to be a successful leader, they are:

(1) *Lead by example*. Whatever you ask of your people, in things small and large—being on time, standards of dress, correct procedures, how to work with guests, being supportive, and on and on—you must absolutely embody and put into action these principles yourself.

(2) *Care for your people*. Actively care for your people, and do your utmost to ensure their welfare. This begins with the smallest of things. For example, simply enquiring with sincerity about a care giver's mood and well-being; or, if somebody asks something of you, making sure you check up on it/do it and then get back to that person. Caring for your people ends with the largest of things, such as doing your best to ensure the provision of facilities, food, and other amenities for your team (see Chapter 13, "Team Welfare", for further discussion on this point). People are usually quite sensitive and intuitive about such matters, and it will quickly become apparent whether the care service leader or a

team lead truly cares for and has the best interests of the team at heart, or is simply paying lip service to these ideals. Note that caring for your people is *not* to be confused with *trying to be liked*, a common and major mistake for many individuals in leadership roles. If you strive to fulfil #1 and #2 above and #3 below, you'll overwhelmingly find that respect, loyalty, and affection follow.

(3) *Know your stuff.* Be knowledgeable about what you discuss, teach, and practise. If there is an area that you are not knowledgeable about and know you should be, do what it takes (*prior to the event*) to learn in order to bridge that gap. This is a core principle of being professional, and of being good at what you do. Of course, nobody expects you to be perfect, nor to never make mistakes, nor to have greater knowledge and experience in all areas compared to your team members. In fact, given the nature of most care services, some team members may have more experience than the care service leader and/or team leads in this work, and many will certainly have more knowledge than them in various relevant fields. This is a positive and beneficial situation, and the sharing of knowledge and experience should be encouraged. However, anybody in a leadership position must have a reasonably good level of knowledge and competency, and should continually strive to improve that level.

Honouring volunteers, whilst holding them to high standards and accountability, is a fine balancing act for the care service leader and team leads, yet one at which they must become adept. We have seen care services either succeed wonderfully, or come close to disintegration and failure, depending on how "management" (so to speak) treats its people. Don't be afraid of making mistakes, but also—depending on your leadership experience—be prepared for a steep learning curve. Do *not* think that as the care service leader or a team lead you always know best, and try to continually be open to constructive criticism and advice.

Create a Training Plan

The training plan is a day-by-day, hour-by-hour schedule that specifies how training will be conducted; what training takes place, where, how, who facilitates it, and who attends it. The training plan is constructed around the training *syllabus*, which is the raw list of the *content* that needs to be covered by the care service team, before the service can open its doors to guests.

Key responsibility for the training plan lies with the care service leader, although it is highly recommended that they formulate it in consultation with team leads (if such exist), and with any other team members who hold or will hold positions of leadership within the care service. At the smaller end of the spectrum, in terms of event size, the care service leader will probably themselves train the small group of care givers who will constitute the service. At the larger end of the spectrum (at major events that support a care service of substantial size) the ideal sequence of training would consist of two phases:

> **Phase 1:** The care service leader spends some time with the team leads (and any others holding leadership roles) for the purpose of training them and for discussing the training of the care givers who will form their teams.

> **Phase 2:** General training for the entire care service, especially the care givers who form its core.

Pre-Event versus On-Site Training

Training may be divided into that which occurs before the event (pre-event), and that which occurs at the site of the event itself (on-site), usually a day or so before the event begins and the care service officially opens. Pre-event training may be conducted through email, face-to-face meetings, or both. The perfect situation would be to train the entire care service team pre-event, thereby allowing them to focus solely on logistics and practical preparations only, once they arrive on-site. If this is not possible (as is often the case), the care service leader should consider face-to-face pre-event training for the team leads only. Any plan to conduct pre-event face-to-face training will probably take much willpower and no small effort to bring to fruition. However, such training is immensely valuable because it will generally be free of the kinds of distractions encountered at event sites just prior to their opening, and it will also allow additional time for the content discussed at the training to be reflected upon and absorbed by team members.

The other option for pre-event training is through email. Depending on the syllabus (see below), email can be used to send (or link to) information for team members to read, and/or audiovisual material for them to view. Email communications may also be used in a more interactive approach; for example, multiple-choice or written questions can be sent out for completion, or team members may be asked to comment on hypothetical scenarios (such as guests with various specific problems visiting the care service). With some imagination, many parts of the training syllabus can be adapted to such an interactive approach. See Chapter 17, "Online Resources and Obtaining Assistance", for sources of relevant online material.

If emails are sent asking team members to go over information or answer questions in their own time, it is important that whoever is coordinating that part of the training *follow-up* and check whether those tasks have been completed. One way of doing this is to ask team members to email back when they've accomplished some or all of the tasks. Another way to follow up is to set a deadline for completion, and then email the entire group on that deadline to ask members to confirm that they've finished their study. Whilst this may seem somewhat formal, "rigid", or "strict", it usually sets a tone of professionalism and fosters achievement within the care service team. If members are volunteers, a facilitator with an attitude of "you're volunteers, so I don't want to be too demanding—just do what you can" will often produce correspondingly mediocre results. Treating volunteers as responsible staff, however, with clear goals and duties, may well produce better results, increasing self-regard and morale.

The above paragraphs have described some possibilities and ideas for pre-event training. On-site training is dealt with separately, starting on page 96.

The team from Check-In, a Portuguese risk reduction group, places bets on how many people on the bridge might not take ANY drugs over the entire course of the 2008 Boom Festival. Photo by Erowid.

BUILDING AND TRAINING A TEAM

Who Facilitates Training?

Whether pre-event or on-site (and for the former, whether face-to-face or via email), team leads—and even general care givers, if they have the knowledge and inclination to do so—should be encouraged to contribute to the facilitation of training. In other words, whilst ultimately *responsible* for proper training, the care service leader under most circumstances should not run the entire training syllabus on their own. At every step of the way, whether sending out emails, teaching a lesson, moderating a discussion, or acting out a mock scenario, *other team members should take part in delivering training to the group*. This approach has numerous advantages: it helps build team cohesion and morale, shares what may be rich and even unique knowledge, gives different individuals a chance to develop their own skills, and reduces the workload on the care service leader. In allocating training tasks to other team members, make a list of what sessions/tasks need to be facilitated/carried out, and ask people to volunteer for these according to their knowledge, ability, and preference. Ensure this allocation is done substantially prior to (ideally weeks before) the session itself, in order to give the facilitators time to prepare for their sessions. Finally, the care service leader (or somebody else who has good experience in this area) should give constructive and useful *feedback* (even if only briefly) to each person who facilitates a training event.

Decide on a Training Syllabus

The structure and the materials contained in chapters from this Manual may be used (and indeed were intended) as the basis for a comprehensive training syllabus. This applies to care services of all sizes. A key decision that those planning the training must make concerns the *content* that will be delivered in training, given the *time available*. This goes back to the initial stage of creating a training plan, as discussed above. This plan should consider the time available (both pre-event, if at all, and on-site), and lay out, by the hour, a detailed training schedule. In deciding what content to place into which slots, take the following into account:

- Pre-event training is likely to be more relaxed and free of distractions compared to its on-site counterpart.

- Pre-event training will probably not be immediately before the event itself. On the one hand this will allow care givers more time to reflect upon and absorb theoretical content. On the other hand, specific, practical information may be forgotten by the time the event itself begins.

- Any training done through email (asking team members to read information, watch a video, answer questions, and so forth) will be the "weakest link" in the training chain.

In light of these points, it is suggested that:

- Pre-event training, if it takes place, should be used for in-depth theoretical discussions, related especially to the type of topics presented in Chapter 2, "The Principles and Ethics of Psychedelic Support".

- Training done by email could cover topics such as the history of psychedelic care services, further material relating to principles and ethics, case studies and impressions of care scenarios that people have experienced and written about, and possibly, drug-specific information (the drug, its effects, common behavioural responses, and so forth).

- Email-based training should not be used to cover critical material. The definition of "critical" must be determined by each care service leader, but generally includes emergency procedures; protocols for coming on and off shift, receiving guests, guest handovers, and other "practical" policies; instructions and discussions relating to care team safety and well-being; and any other safety/well-being/practical/procedural matters.

These suggestions are, as has been previously emphasised, only a general guide. The care service leader must take into account all relevant factors when deciding how best to divide up the training syllabus and construct their training plan.

A Comprehensive Syllabus for Training

The following is a list of topics that could be discussed in training, and also a guide to where the corresponding information for each topic is located in this Manual. The list is not exhaustive, but it aims to be fairly comprehensive; in other words, covering this entire list would be a "best-case scenario", possible when there is a substantial amount of time allocated for training purposes. The list is presented in a loose order of priority (highest priority first), but this order is a suggestion only. As mentioned earlier, the appropriate order of priority for different topics is highly dependent on each unique care service and the event it serves, *and is the responsibility of the care service leader to decide.*

TOPIC (from highest to lowest priority)	LOCATION IN MANUAL
1. Getting to know the care service team: Intros, team structure, roles, and responsibilities	
2. The principles and ethics of psychedelic support: Core teachings on how to care for and work with a guest	Chapter 2 "The Principles and Ethics of Psychedelic Support"
3. Legal considerations: Legal obligations and possible consequences that care givers must be aware of	Chapter 3 "Legal Considerations"
4. Dealing with emergencies: Medical emergencies, violent guests, fire, etc.	Chapter 10 "Running the Service" Chapter 11 "Screening"
5. Team welfare: Ensuring one's own and each other's welfare and well-being	Chapter 13 "Team Welfare"
6. Procedures for running the service: "On the ground" procedures for receiving guests, handing over to other care givers, discharging guests, upkeep of the care space, regular meetings, food arrangements, etc.	Chapter 8 "Logistics" Chapter 10 "Running the Service" Chapter 11 "Screening" Chapter 14 "Working With Other Organisations"
7. Screening: Emphasised here, separate from *"Procedures for running the service"* above, due to its importance. How to screen new arrivals to the care service, correctly make critical first decisions regarding their care, and identify actual or potential emergencies	Chapter 11 "Screening" **Guide to Drug Effects and Interactions**
8. Documentation and other administration: Any forms and other documentation that need to be completed during the operation of the service	Chapter 10 "Running the Service" **Appendix B** "Monitoring, Evaluating and Researching—Recommendations from an Academic Perspective for an Evidence-Based Approach to Psychoactive Crisis Intervention"

TOPIC (from highest to lowest priority)	LOCATION IN MANUAL
9. **After-care of guests:** Discussion about what can be provided for guests once they return to the "ordinary world", particularly those who have had especially difficult experiences. Guests may also return to the care space days after their initial visit, seeking insight and guidance	
10. **Managing risk and improving performance:** Drawing awareness to ongoing activities (such as debriefings) that continually improve the quality of the service delivered and help to reduce risks. Also focus on specific known risks (for example, violence, infectious disease, drug overdose), and how they may be mitigated. An important topic for the team lead and above level, but also for the care service as a whole	**Chapter 15** "Risk Management and Performance Improvement"
11. **Complementary therapies:** Therapies and techniques that may be used with guests by care givers who feel comfortable employing them	**Chapter 12** "Complementary Therapies"
12. **Psychoactive substances:** The specific drugs expected to be consumed at that particular event; their different names, possible symptoms and signs of use and overdose, effects, and so forth	**Guide to Drug Effects and Interactions** **Appendix A** "Street Names for Commonly Encountered Psychoactives"
13. **Discussion of past care experiences:** Drawing on the present care givers' personal experiences from past care services, and also on material contained in this Manual	**Chapter 16** "Case Studies and Impressions"
14. **The care service in its wider educational role:** Discussion of the role of the care service in *educating* the public at large, particularly event-goers who stop by the care service out of simple curiosity	**Final Words**
15. **History of psychedelic care services:** To connect the work at hand to its lineage, broaden the education of your care givers, and reflect on lessons from the past	**Chapter 1** "A History of Psychedelic Care Services"
16. **Other topics:** Whatever else is relevant to that specific care service	

Logistics and General Considerations for On-Site Training

Training scheduled to occur on-site, just prior to the event itself, will undoubtedly be pressed for time. It may also take place under difficult conditions, in terms of mess, noise, half-erected tents, and a partially finished care space. It is important to emphasise that in most cases, prior to the care service actually opening to guests, *training should take priority over the logistical work* of setting up the care space. There will always be pressure to complete the physical set-up, and the care service leader and others in positions of leadership may be under considerable stress to do so. However, it is important to understand that once the service opens, no additional organised, formal training will usually be possible. Furthermore, because most services will be run in shifts (with some of the care givers either sleeping, enjoying their free time, or on-duty at any given time), it is unlikely that the entire care team even *can* be gathered together again in one place after the service opens. Therefore, once on-site, it is very important to give training *top priority* in terms of allocation of the time available before the care service officially opens. This time, when the entire team is present, should also be used to deliver key themes, important messages, and to convey general leadership precepts (whatever they may be), for each care service leader and their team leads.

In scheduling time-allocation, a good approach (depending on how much training is planned and on other logistical tasks that need to be completed) is to begin on-site training three days prior to the service opening. If this is not possible, two days prior should be attempted. Leaving only one day is problematic, because just the arrival and settling-in phase for the care service team can take an entire day. Many distractions have the potential to cut into time allocated for on-site training. *You must fight to ensure that as much time as possible is allocated, and that maximal effort is made to keep the training plan running on track!*

Formats for On-Site Sessions

Whilst the training plan/syllabus that you have created will dictate the *what* of training, there are many different formats in which this content can be presented. At the simplest level, one can imagine a talk delivered by a speaker to listeners sitting on the ground in a tent. From here, one is limited only by the imagination, and by physical and logistical constraints that were known and planned for in advance. General care giver feedback from one particular care service emphasised the importance and value of *role-*

playing scenarios, in teaching care givers to prepare for different situations, and we encourage that care givers be provided with as much opportunity as possible to simulate various scenarios before the opening of a care service.

The following are examples of different formats and ideas that may be used in training:

- A speaker presents a topical lecture to the entire care team

- Facilitators exploit the use of electronic teaching aids, if logistically possible (for example, video and PowerPoint)

- The care team splits up into small groups for discussion and then re-convenes in the general forum

- Similar as above, but care givers split up into pairs

- Groups rotate through "stations", with a team lead (or someone else) facilitating each of the stations

- Groups each prepare a short presentation or a role-playing exercise, and deliver it to the entire team

- The entire team sits in a circle and has an open discussion

- The entire team sits in a circle. Moving around the circle, each person is given a brief period of time to speak; this is useful, for example, when making introductions. Exercise care with this format, however; with a large group it will take a long time to complete the circle, the process can become tedious, and it often results in people at the beginning of the round speaking a lot, and those at the end speaking very little due to running out of time. It is a good idea to have a predetermined maximum number of minutes that each person can speak and to use a loud kitchen timer to mark when that time that has passed.

Ensure that your schedule allows generous time for discussion within sessions (which, considering the calibre and energy of people in most care service teams, will be lively), and for breaks in between sessions. Training is tiring, and there is only so much information that can be absorbed within a given period. Prioritise your sessions, and *don't leave the important ones until last.*

Materials List for Training

Actual requirements will depend on the training sessions that have been planned. The following list is for a hypothetical care service that is large in size (for example, 30–40 people in total on the care team), has access to electricity, and has the means with which to transport larger items in and out of the event (see also Chapter 8, "Logistics"):

- All personal training notes, lesson plans, and other preparatory materials
- Photocopies of the training plan (or a simplified timetable version of it) for all team members
- 2 whiteboards on stands
- 9 whiteboard markers (different colours)
- Image projector
- Portable projection screen on stand
- Laptop
- Electrical cables, power strips, and, where necessary, outlet plug adaptors
- Ample photocopies of any required handouts to give to the team
- A thin blank notebook and a pen for each team member

Team Building Exercises

It is important to include in training some activities that are fun and enjoyable, and that through the very act of doing them help team members to get to know each other and build rapport. The possibilities for such activities are endless; the following list provides a few examples:

- *Warm up Games:* any games that involve walking or running around the area. For example, start with one "chaser", and then anyone that person touches also becomes a chaser.

- *Hugs:* walking around to music, making eye-contact, and being present in the moment. Every time the music stops, hug the person closest to you. There are many variations on this theme.

- *Introductions I:* split into pairs and everyone tells their partners something about themselves. After which, each person introduces their *partner* to the entire team.

- *Introductions II:* the entire team sits in a circle. Going around the circle, each person briefly introduces and makes three statements about themselves: two are true, one is false. The team must then try to guess which statement is the false one.

- *Eye Contact:* split into pairs and simply hold eye contact for five minutes (time is clocked by the person leading the exercise). Then as a group, discuss the emotions and thoughts that this exercise gave rise to.

Burning Man, 2010. Photo by Jon Hanna.

- *Holotropic Breathwork:* if an appropriate facilitator is present and time is available, facilitate a short Breathwork session. This also relates to psychedelic states that care givers will encounter. Beware, though, that such an exercise can be emotionally revealing and intense, and it may not be appropriate for a large group of care givers, especially just before they begin working in a care service.

- *Simulation exercises:* form into groups; then within each group, split into two teams. Have the teams take turns setting up and acting out a care scenario. The first team plays the part of a person undergoing a difficult experience who is accompanied by others: friends, event participants who found the individual in distress, or event security services. The other team responds to the scenario to the best of their abilities. After each exercise, both teams discuss intentions, responses, and considerations for learning.

Sample Training Plan for a "Medium-Sized" Care Service

The following shows one possible training plan for a hypothetical care service consisting of a care service leader, five team leads, and twenty-five other care givers (as well as hypothetical supporting roles such as a nurse and a psychiatrist). The plan is a generic one, of course, but it may serve as a good starting point that can be adapted to particular care services and their requirements.

Note that the on-site schedule below is concerned with training only, and does not make any reference to physical/logistical work for the actual building and setting up of the care space. How to balance training with the construction effort is something that each care service leader must decide for their particular care service.

BUILDING AND TRAINING A TEAM

TIME	SESSION	STAFF	TRAINING ACTIVITIES
PRE-EVENT EMAIL TRAINING (FOR THE ENTIRE CARE SERVICE TEAM)			
Four weeks prior to event	Background for the specific event and care service	Care service leader	Introduce the event and its history, the care service and its history, the care team's structure, and other relevant preliminary points (to be decided upon). Give a brief summary of the individuals who form the team: the team leads' and care givers' names, where they're from, and possibly a little more info. Explain that a proper "meet and greet" will take place on-site. Email a series of clear, easily readable materials.
Three weeks prior to event	The principles and ethics of psychedelic support	Team lead in charge of email training	Introduction to the care approach to be used at this event. Send reading material and a link to at least one relevant video. Ask all care givers to report back, confirming that they've gone over the material. Use material from this Manual.
	Legal considerations	One of the care givers, who happens to be a legal practitioner	Legal issues that may impact both event participants and personnel involved in providing psychedelic support. Discuss potential legal risks and consequences in relation to encounters with law enforcement; consent, confidentiality, and privacy issues; legal protections and fiduciary obligations of support personnel; and other potential legal liabilities in providing psychedelic support. Ask all care givers to answer a twenty-question multiple-choice test and return it via email. Use material from this Manual.
Two weeks prior to event	Drug effects	Team lead in charge of email training	Ask care givers to read about the main drugs that are expected at the event, and have them answer a series of short questions related to specific drugs. Provide care givers with an additional, optional list of substances to read about.
One week prior to event	Case studies	Team lead in charge of email training	Care givers are to read at least *three* case studies, and write a paragraph about their thoughts and feelings regarding at least one of them (for example, how do they think *they* might have reacted in the same situation? What would they have done differently?). Use material from this Manual.

TIME	SESSION	STAFF	TRAINING ACTIVITIES
PRE-EVENT FACE-TO-FACE TRAINING (ONE FULL DAY AT SOMEONE'S HOUSE, ATTENDED BY TEAM LEADS ONLY)			
10:00 – 11:00	Meet and greet	Care service leader	Play an "introductions" game. All team leads should talk about themselves, their backgrounds, and why they volunteered for this care service.
11:00 – 12:00	Role of the team lead	Care service leader	Discussion of what being a team lead entails, presenting specific roles and responsibilities.
12:00 – 13:00	Operations and logistics	One of the experienced team leads	Procedures and responsibilities for the team leads: how shifts are run, what documentation is required, and what specific tasks to complete.
13:00 – 14:00	LUNCH		Determine any special dietary needs in advance.
14:00 – 15:00	Training plan	Care service leader	Plan for the two days of on-site training that will be primarily run by the present forum for the entire care service team. How will these days be structured? Who will facilitate each session? What challenges might arise on-site?
15:00 – 16:00	Principles and ethics of psychedelic support	One of the team leads with previous experience	Discuss the core principles of psychedelic care at this event, especially at the team lead level. What is the overall aim of the service, and what is considered the "best outcome" for a guest? How should team leads allocate new guests to care givers? What can happen in extreme scenarios?
16:00 – 16:20	BREAK		Tea, coffee, biscuits.
16:20 – 17:00	Team welfare	One of the experienced team leads	A key responsibility of the team lead is to ensure the welfare of volunteers. Explain how to do this, and what challenges may be encountered.
17:00 – 17:30	Managing risk	Care service leader	Team leads must be aware of key risks and do their best to mitigate them. Whilst care givers usually focus on a single guest at a time, team leads must always be aware of the big picture during their shifts, in order to proactively prevent adverse situations from deteriorating further.
17:30 – 18:30	Final discussion	Care service leader	Have each person talk about their hopes and fears for the upcoming event. Discuss any other topics that people want to raise. Afterwords, go out for a team dinner at a restaurant.

TIME	SESSION	STAFF	TRAINING ACTIVITIES
ON-SITE TRAINING (ATTENDED BY THE ENTIRE CARE SERVICE TEAM)			
TWO DAYS BEFORE CARE SERVICE OPENS			
14:00 – 15:30	Meet and greet + Team structure	Care service leader	Play *Hugs* (see "Team Building Exercises" above). Everyone plays some sort of an introductions game (in pairs or groups, and then with the entire team). Discuss team structure, and the basic format in which the care service will be run. Finish with the *Eye Contact* exercise (see "Team Building Exercises" above).
15:30 – 17:30	Principles and ethics of psychedelic support	Team leads	Spend approximately thirty minutes discussing the basic principles of providing psychedelic support in the context of this particular care service. Divide into four groups, and rotate through four "stations", each one run by a different team lead. Each station should address one key aspect of psychedelic care. This training can be run in the form of a discussion or by role playing.
ONE DAY BEFORE CARE SERVICE OPENS			
09:00 – 10:00	Roll of the care giver	Care service leader	Expectations, requirements, rights, and entitlements of the care giver.
10:00 – 10:30	Talk by festival organiser	Festival organiser	It's good to have a key staff member from the festival organisers (preferably one of the big "names") briefly speak to the entire team.
10:30 – 11:00	BREAK		Tea, coffee, biscuits.
11:00 – 12:30	Procedures for running the care service	One of the team leads	"On the ground" procedures for receiving guests, handing over to other care givers, discharging guests, upkeep of the care space, regular meetings, food arrangements, and so forth. Includes an explanation and demonstration of the documentation that needs to be filled out.
12:30 – 13:30	Screening	One of the team leads	More specific focus on the initial screening of guests. Include a role-play exercise or two.
13:30 – 15:00	LUNCH		Determine any special dietary needs in advance.

TIME	SESSION	STAFF	TRAINING ACTIVITIES
ON-SITE TRAINING, CONT. (ATTENDED BY THE ENTIRE CARE SERVICE TEAM)			
15:00 – 16:00	Team welfare	Care service leader	Explain the importance of taking care of oneself and each other (within the care service team). Divide into groups and discuss different themes/questions, then reconvene in the general forum to share thoughts.
16:00 – 17:30	Case studies + General discussion	One of the team leads	Split into pairs and go over some case studies of previous care situations that people have written about. Then reconvene in the general forum for an open discussion about whatever anybody wishes to bring up: hopes, fears, general questions, and so forth.
20:00 +	Meditation, chanting, and Opening Party	One of the care givers	Run a meditation/chanting session, and then throw an Opening Party for the entire care service team! Keep it relaxed and low key—big day tomorrow!
DAY OF CARE SERVICE OPENING (ASSUME FIRST SHIFT BEGINS AT 15:00)			
09:00 – 10:00	Dealing with emergencies	Care service leader	Potential emergency situations and how best to deal with them. Discuss with the entire team, and then get a few team leads/care givers to talk about their past experiences.
10:00 – 10:30	After-care of guests	One of the team leads	Round-circle discussion on post-care scenarios; for example, guests who return to the care service to discuss their experiences.
10:30 – 11:00	BREAK		Tea, coffee, biscuits.
11:00 – 12:30	The care service in its wider educational role + General discussion	One of the team leads + Care service leader	Split into groups, discuss, and each group then presents for 5–10 minutes to the entire forum: how do they see the wider educational role of the care service? Care service leader to give some of their own points and emphases, and then in the time remaining, a final discussion on anything at all—whatever topics care givers wish to raise.
12:30 – 13:30	LUNCH		Determine any special dietary needs in advance.
13:30 – 14:30	Any remaining material to cover, and final preparations for opening the care service!		

BUILDING AND TRAINING A TEAM

NAOTO HATTORI • *Untitled* • acrylic on board
http://naotohattori.com

CHAPTER 8
LOGISTICS

Alicia Danforth

Annie Oak

Kaya

Natacha Ribeiro

Svea Nielsen

LOGISTICS is the management of material resources, which include supplies, structures, equipment, and personnel. Aspects of logistics include procurement, maintenance, transportation, inventory, storage (warehousing), distribution, recovery, and disposal. The amount of time and resources needed to prepare for each of these aspects can be large. Starting early by familiarising yourself with the content in this chapter can be a significant step towards ensuring that your project runs smoothly. Regardless of the scope of service your event requires, the sections that follow are likely to contain information that will assist you in planning, budgeting, and implementing a well-run care service.

General Logistical Considerations

8.1

This chapter provides suggestions to cover multiple care service configurations, ranging from small camp-out settings with a few volunteer care givers, to festivals with tens of thousands of attendees and large collaborations between volunteer and professional care givers.

Throughout the chapter you will find recommendations for what is needed to provide a comprehensive and well-prepared care service. Some content is covered in greater detail in other chapters of this Manual. For example, this chapter includes lists related to setting up the care space. After reviewing them, you might want to consult Chapter 9, "The Care Space", for more specific information about that aspect of the project. Cross-referencing with other chapters is recommended, especially if you are implementing a particular component of a care service for the first time. This chapter is intended to provide an overview of *what* you need to consider and acquire to stay organised and well supplied from start to finish. You might want to bookmark and return to it when required, as a quick reference source. Other chapters offer further discussion on *how* to set up, run, and break down the service.

Equipping the Service: Preliminary Fundamentals

8.2

This section provides an introductory, high-level overview of three core components necessary for creating a care service: *Structures*, *Regulating the Care Space Environment*, and *Human Resources*. The lists are by no means comprehensive or complete in this section; they are intended to provide a general sense of what might be required for your project.

The care space should be an aesthetically pleasing environment. Photo of the 2008 KosmiCare space by Jen Zariat.

106   **THE MANUAL OF PSYCHEDELIC SUPPORT**

STRUCTURES

Structures are either permanent or temporary buildings, or open-air spaces in which the care service is provided. Most commonly used are rigid, temporary structures, which provide some privacy and shelter from weather conditions. Some structure types include:

Primary structure: The main structure used for setting up the care space. This can be an existing lodge, house, cabin, etc., or a portable structure brought in and set up for the duration of the event, then torn down and removed at the end. Open-air spaces are non-structure areas set up where the day and night and general weather conditions are reliable and lend themselves to operating without the need for shelter. Please see Chapter 9, "The Care Space", for specific details and considerations regarding the selection and placement of structures necessary for running the service.

Secondary structures: Additional structures, which are generally smaller and used for expanding areas of privacy, storing supplies, as a staff area, for an entrance, as housing to dampen generator noise, and so forth. They may be included within or adjacent to the primary structure, or they may be in another location at the event.

Entrances: A type of secondary structure, often simpler and without sides, located in front of the main access to the primary structure. An entrance provides space for the removal of coats and shoes whilst protecting guests from the elements.

Structures come in all shapes and sizes, so the list below is intended only to present some basic possibilities. In most cases, the care service leader will want to create a customized list that matches the structure(s) needs and budget for their particular care service. We recommend consulting Chapter 9, "The Care Space", for more details on structures, decor, ambiance, and other aspects of an organised and comfortable care space.

Specific types of structures include:

- Dome
- Tent
- Yurt
- RV/Van
- Carport
- Tepee
- Existing building

- Open-air space

- Seating

- Storage

- Portable toilets

- Private space

In addition to thinking ahead about what types of structures you will need, another smart step in early planning is to think about where and how much land-space (in other words, "the footprint") the care service will require. Some points to consider:

- Confirm in advance with the event organisers how large the footprint for the care service can be.

- Have a plan for marking the space you will require with flags, tape, rebar (metal rods used in construction), and so forth.

- Will anything have to happen on the land before structures can be placed there (that is, clearing brush or debris, levelling the ground, digging holes), and do you have the tools to complete such work?

Determine your "must have" priorities well in advance, if possible. Some examples include:

A few of the items popular with guests staying at the KosmiCare space in 2008. Photo by Jen Zariat.

The care space:

- Is close to and has unobstructed access to a road for emergency vehicles, transportation of guests, care givers, and supplies/equipment.

- Is far away from loud noises; peace and quiet is a top priority.

- Is near main event activities; minimising noise may be less important than being near the action.

- Is adjacent to other medical and security services, or is within reasonable proximity of them.

- Is near the event entrance.

- Is near the main camping spaces.

The footprint:

- Is large enough for the primary care space and (optionally) an adjacent camping area for the care service team.

- Includes parking space for care service vehicles.

- Includes room for private portable toilets.

- Includes a designated entrance (with a waiting area for friends/family of guests and care givers).

- Includes some place for a separate headquarters for the care service leader.

- Includes space for secondary structures or outposts that are separate and at a distance from the main care space. For example, the main care space might be removed from the central activities in a quieter area, but your event might benefit from having a presence in a high-traffic area to raise awareness that the care service is available. Space at other sites may be required for secondary structures in addition to the primary space.

Some events take place in locations where structures are provided by the event organisers for the care service team to move right in. The next section covers some basic points to consider when building a care space from the ground up. It's a good idea to make a checklist of items you'll need.

REGULATING THE CARE SPACE ENVIRONMENT

A key element to providing the service, particularly overnight or over many days, is planning for operating during the day and night, and in hot, cold, windy, and/or rainy weather. Preparing for power needs, lighting, temperature control, fuel, pest control (such as rodents and insects), sanitation, and waste removal is important to consider early in planning. A space that is not adequately lit or that is unable to adjust to weather changes by heating or cooling can quickly become dangerous or unusable. It may be necessary to reserve a generator from a rental supply house weeks in advance, or to gather additional essential equipment that is easily taken for granted in other settings. Early in the planning stages, consider the time of year and other aspects of the setting where you will be running the service. The environment and potential weather conditions will not only affect your choice of structure, but may also result in particular requirements for lighting, heating, and air conditioning. Work with the event organisers to identify which resources are available (for example, on-site electricity) or are prohibited (for example, liquid fuels such as kerosene).

Care space structure supplies may include:

- ☐ Generator(s)
- ☐ Cable locks for securing generators
- ☐ Electrical cords
- ☐ Narrow shovel for digging shallow trenches to bury cables (if allowed)
- ☐ Power adapters
- ☐ Power outlets
- ☐ Basic lighting
- ☐ Special lighting (for example, spotlight, decorative lights)
- ☐ Heaters
- ☐ Fans
- ☐ Water tanks
- ☐ Water pumps
- ☐ Water misters
- ☐ Other air conditioning
- ☐ Fuel tanks
- ☐ Fuel
- ☐ Insect netting
- ☐ Waste containers
- ☐ Water drainage
- ☐ Ground covering/tarps

- ☐ Floor coverings
- ☐ Additional shade structures
- ☐ Stakes or rebar for securing structures against wind (plus dedicated plastic caps or tennis balls to cover rebar tops to help protect event attendees from potential foot injuries)
- ☐ Wire, rope, or ratchet straps to secure structures in high wind
- ☐ Grey water disposal system

HUMAN RESOURCES

People are the single most critical resource of a care service. Their participation starts long before the care service opens and continues after it is closed to guests. As an image of the entire operation comes into view, carefully consider how much help you will need. The number of people you can reliably count on to help purchase, load, transport, set up, operate, and tear down will affect nearly every other aspect of your planning.

Whilst most of the planning often seems to revolve around the actual service delivery during the event, effective pre- and post-service organisation and logistics are essential for a successful service. The process of adequately planning all the aspects that go into acquiring and transporting supplies to the site is easily overlooked. Always obtain commitments from reliable people to assist with setting up and breaking down, as well as with provisioning all the supplies necessary to establish the care space and provide for the care service team's needs before and after the event. Generally, the most difficult aspect to staff is breaking down the space and cleaning up after the event has ended. It is never too early to start finding committed volunteers to help you pre- and post-event.

Logistical care service support roles may include:

- Shoppers (pre-event)
- Liaisons with other teams
- Schedule monitors
- Budget/finance assistance
- Promoters/writers
- Loaders (pre-event, for setting up)
- Drivers (pre-event, for setting up)
- Builders (pre-event, for setting up)

- Decorators/artists/sign makers
- Space tenders (cleaning/housekeeping)
- Builders (post-event, for breaking down)
- Loaders (post-event, for breaking down)
- Drivers (post-event, for breaking down)
- Cooks/food preparers

Supplies for the Care Service Leader

The care service leader fills a special role as the chief person responsible for the entire project. That role also requires the foresight (some would say "mind reading") to be able to anticipate the routine as well as the unexpected needs of others. A storage bin dedicated to the care service leader that contains key organisational items and readily available copies of required documents, schedules, and other materials will help reduce stress, ensure smooth operations, and more quickly resolve situations as they arise.

Care service leader supplies may include:

- ☐ Copies of a contact sheet with names and phone numbers for all volunteers, event organisers, and other dept. leads
- ☐ Copies of the event schedule
- ☐ Event layout map
- ☐ Emergency contact information for inter-event and outside agencies
- ☐ Map to nearest emergency medical facility outside the event (particularly if no medical services are present on-site)
- ☐ Tape (clear as well as duct and/or gaffer's)
- ☐ Pens and pencils
- ☐ Wide-tip marking pens (for making signs)
- ☐ Scissors
- ☐ Stapler and extra staples
- ☐ Basic tools
- ☐ Tape measure
- ☐ Tacks
- ☐ Blank paper
- ☐ Lined-paper notepads

☐ Lock boxes for items needing to be secured (and spare keys)

☐ Tissues

☐ Gloves (construction as well as protective latex)

☐ Spare phone chargers

Supplies for Care Givers

This section contains practical tips and lists to help the care service leader and event planners provide for care givers' needs before, during, and after the event. Guests arriving for care may be feeling anxious, vulnerable, and often sensitive to the emotional tone of their surroundings. Taking steps to ensure that the care givers who welcome them are well-fed, rested, and reasonably comfortable goes a long way in making the care space a pleasant place in which to restore and revive during or after a difficult experience.

Some basic questions to ask during the planning phases include:

- Will any care givers or support staff arrive pre-event for set-up? If so, what supplies need to be on hand so that these volunteers can do their work?

- Will care givers or support staff who stay after the event need supplies?

- Will care givers or support staff be provided with food, beverages, and/or snacks as part of the event and/or care service operation?

- Will care givers who unexpectedly work extended shifts have the provisions—food and beverages (coffee/tea)—they need to maintain their stamina and sense of calm?

- What will the care service provide? What will care givers be instructed to bring?

Experienced care givers compiled the checklists below based on a wide variety of event types in different countries. They contain essential supplies for events of any size, as well as "nice to have" items that can help shifts run more smoothly.

SAFETY SUPPLIES
(see also "Safety/First Aid/Emergency/Medical Supplies" below)

☐ Fire extinguishers/fire blanket

☐ Emergency phone numbers/contact information

☐ First aid kit

- ☐ First aid information/book
- ☐ Latex or synthetic rubber gloves (note that some individuals have latex allergies)
- ☐ Map to medical services (event layout or external road map)

Tip: As part of training, instruct care givers on where these items reside in the care space.

IDENTIFICATION AND UNIFORMS
(will vary widely for each event)

- ☐ T-shirts
- ☐ Arm bands
- ☐ Hats
- ☐ Identification badges/pins/laminates (with lanyards or clips to secure them)
- ☐ Stencils and markers or fabric paint for putting logos and the care service name onto clothing and/or banners

Tip: At most events, being readily identified as a member of the care service is desirable, especially if visibility helps those in need to find support. Contact event organisers well in advance of the start of the event in order to coordinate identification items.

SELF-CARE

- ☐ Extra water bottles
- ☐ Personal medication, if required (enough to potentially cover extended shifts, if needed)
- ☐ Snacks
- ☐ Sunscreen/lotion
- ☐ Lip balm
- ☐ Insect repellent

HYGIENE

- ☐ Hand sanitiser
- ☐ Latex or synthetic rubber gloves (especially if the care giver may encounter assistance situations away from the care space)
- ☐ Wet wipes (pre-moistened paper towels)
- ☐ Tissues
- ☐ Mints/breath freshener/chewing gum

PRACTICAL ITEMS

- ☐ Flashlights (and extra batteries)
- ☐ Writing pads, plus lots of pens and pencils (pens can dry out, pencil points can break)
- ☐ Maps
- ☐ Whistle (to call for assistance outdoors)
- ☐ Change of clothes (anticipate that your clothes may become soiled or get wet from inclement weather)
- ☐ Watch
- ☐ Snacks

HOUSEKEEPING

- ☐ Tea kettle (electric or gas)
- ☐ Space heaters, fans
- ☐ Broom, dustpan, and other cleaning supplies
- ☐ Rugs, soft floor, or ground covering
- ☐ Disinfectant spray or air freshener
- ☐ Refrigerator or secure food storage
- ☐ Rubbish bins or bags

8.5 Supplies for Guests

This section includes checklists of provisions and resources that the care service may offer to its guests. The goal is to identify what is necessary for a supportive guest experience in a safe setting. When guests arrive, they often need little more than gentle reassurance and a few comforts to help them feel better. Offering a moist towelette to an exhausted, dirty, or distraught guest can be an excellent first step towards establishing rapport. Supplies for attending to basic bodily needs should be a priority.

ACCOMMODATIONS
(refer also to **Chapter 9, "The Care Space", for more info on items—such as shelter and bedding—required for housing care service guests**)

- ☐ Bedding (cots, mats)
- ☐ Pillows
- ☐ Seating

- ☐ Sheets
- ☐ Blankets
- ☐ Fabric for privacy screening
- ☐ Portable toilets
- ☐ Small tent (for guests whose care requires more privacy)
- ☐ Extra sleeping bags

FOOD AND BEVERAGES
(see also "Food and Water" below)

- ☐ Water (*providing an ample supply of fresh, clean water is essential to any event*)
- ☐ Tea
- ☐ Electrolyte drink mix
- ☐ Fruit
- ☐ Chocolate
- ☐ Jerky (dried meats) for grounding
- ☐ Veggie, vegan, gluten-free for restricted diets

Tip: Ask about your guests' food allergies before offering food. Some events restrict food service for legal reasons. Check with the event organisers in advance if there is any question about what is permissible or if permits are required to serve food.

HYGIENE

- ☐ Tissues, wet wipes
- ☐ Vomit buckets
- ☐ Urine bed pads or other absorbable, disposable material
- ☐ Waterproof plastic sheets for incontinence issues
- ☐ Sunscreen
- ☐ Feminine hygiene (pads/tampons)
- ☐ Air freshener
- ☐ Lip balm

Tip: Lip balm should not be reused. Keep a small supply of sealed lip balm sticks to offer as gifts to guests in need. Dispose of any used lip balm that guests leave behind.

COMFORT

☐ Spare, clean, warm clothes/hats/gloves to be given away to those in need

☐ Earplugs

☐ Soft toys/teddy bears/comfort objects

☐ Small isolation dome or privacy area

☐ A "designated private" (that is, for the care service only) portable toilet, kept locked when not in use by guests

☐ Art materials (for drawing, painting, and so forth)

☐ Books and magazines

☐ Drug education materials (when appropriate). Can include classics from the psychedelic genre, such as books or articles by Huxley, Watts, McKenna, and Leary

☐ Spare sleeping bags for friends of guests and overflow, or for replacement in case others become soiled

Transportation

Transportation is a vital aspect of planning for a care service, even if it means just getting yourself to and from the location. Walking, driving, biking, and other modes of moving supplies and people to the site should be planned in advance. Every event is different and your transportation needs will vary each time. Items to consider include: vehicle size (and parking needs), availability, rental costs, parking fees, and fuel costs.

In addition to getting yourself and your personal gear to and from the site, you will need to arrange in advance to have adequate, reliable transportation for structures, staff, and supplies. Basically, the care service will need to have a plan for at least three categories of transport:

TEAM TRANSPORT

- Will all care givers arrive at one entrance?
- Will they have a designated parking area?
- If so, will they need parking passes?
- Will a shuttle service from the entrance to the care space be provided for care givers?
- Will any team members require post-event transport to local bus, train, or air transportation?
- Will a designated vehicle be available for the duration of the event for care service use?

EQUIPMENT AND SUPPLY TRANSPORT

- Will there be a designated entrance for deliveries?
- Will special space be required for parking large vehicles?
- Will a staging area be set up for vehicles to load and unload?
- Have you considered the costs for rentals, fuel, and other related expenses in your budget?

TRANSPORT FOR GUESTS

- Sometimes care givers are called upon to find a guest in another location at the event in order to bring that individual to the care service or to the person's campsite.
- Does the care service have qualified drivers and vehicles equipped for special transport of guests? If not, consider a back-up plan for transport to and from other areas of larger events.
- Do other teams (for example, medical or security) have vehicles/drivers available to help transport care service guests?

Possible transport types and associated items include:

- Vans
- Large trucks
- Pickup trucks
- Motorised carts
- Cars
- Emergency transport
- Scooters
- Bicycles
- Fuel and/or electrical recharge station
- Rental fees
- Parking costs
- Parking passes

At minimum, a designated vehicle reserved solely for the care service will be most helpful. Consider having bicycles or other small vehicles available as well.

Tip: As part of basic training, all care givers should receive instructions on when it is *not* appropriate to provide transportation for guests. There may be medical, personal safety, and/or insurance reasons why guest transport by members of the care service is not recommended in some situations.

8.7 Safety/First Aid/Emergency/Medical Supplies

Every country has its own unique laws addressing medical services and the qualifications necessary to provide care; this Manual is unable to provide a comprehensive guide to medical services by country. We encourage you to check with your local medical community regarding questions of care. Please see Chapter 3, "Legal Considerations", for a more detailed discussion of these issues. For the purpose of this Manual, we offer basic recommendations that are broadly applicable regardless of where the care service is located.

At minimum, it is highly recommended that all care spaces have a first aid kit on hand in order to treat cuts and abrasions, sunburn, headache, and other forms of mild pain.

The supply lists provided below are intended to serve as a guide only, and may not include items relevant to your geographic area. We encourage care service leaders and (ideally) team leads to be trained in first aid. Whenever possible, you should seek to have duly licensed medical personnel on-site (see Chapters 6, "Supporting Roles" and 14, "Working With Other Organisations"). If previously trained volunteers are not available, we encourage you to provide at least cursory first aid training, sufficient so that care givers will be able to manage minor wound care and understand how vital it is that they protect themselves from infectious disease. It is critical that all care givers be taught that if there is any question whatsoever regarding the possibility of medical need, a medical evaluation by a licensed practitioner must be obtained without delay.

IMPORTANT ITEMS TO CONSIDER FOR YOUR SAFETY PLAN (please see Chapters 6, "Supporting Roles" and 14, "Working With Other Organisations", for more detailed information)

1. Determine whether the event will have on-site medical services.

2. Consider what is necessary when operating a service without on-site medical support from both a legal and ethical perspective.

3. Plan ahead and contact medical services at the event to establish a relationship.

4. Have a basic medical kit available.

5. Confirm the location of the nearest off-site medical service or hospital.

6. Display the telephone number for the nearest emergency medical service in an *obvious, easily accessible* place.

7. Keep a printed (and on-hand at event) map of the route to the nearest medical service(s). In some cases, these might be local services that are not on the event grounds.

8. If possible, have a vehicle ready on-site in case an emergency transport becomes necessary.

9. Establish a procedure and train care givers on how to manage a situation that progresses from basic, first-encounter triage into something serious or life-threatening.

10. Discuss the topic of "patient abandonment"; this is a common legal issue in the industrialised world.

If your care service is small with minimal resources, will you have access to a nearby medical service with the supplies listed below? If not, what is your back-up plan in case guests present with or subsequently develop urgent medical needs?

MINOR WOUNDS

- ☐ Bandages (adhesive, elastic, gauze roller, and so forth)
- ☐ Sterile gauze
- ☐ Saline sterile water (for cleaning wounds or washing out foreign bodies from eyes)
- ☐ Antibacterial soap (with water for superficial wounds)
- ☐ Antiseptic (wipes/sprays/solutions to apply to wounds)
- ☐ Adhesive tape (hypoallergenic)

PERSONAL PROTECTIVE EQUIPMENT

- ☐ Disposable sterile gloves (latex, nitrile, neoprene, vinyl)
- ☐ Eye goggles (for protection if a guest is spitting)
- ☐ Pocket mask/face shield (for respiratory resuscitation)
- ☐ Hand sanitiser
- ☐ Compressed air horn (for making a very loud sound for signalling purposes)

INSTRUMENTS AND EQUIPMENT
(to be used only by appropriately trained and/or licensed personnel)

- ☐ Trauma shears or scissors
- ☐ Tweezers
- ☐ Surgical razor or scalpel
- ☐ Suture kit or sterile disposable surgical stapler
- ☐ Alcohol 70% (for sanitising equipment or unbroken skin)
- ☐ Irrigation syringes (for medication)
- ☐ Flashlight/penlight
- ☐ Chemical cold packs
- ☐ Thermometer
- ☐ Cotton swabs
- ☐ Sphygmomanometer (for measuring blood pressure)
- ☐ Stethoscope
- ☐ Glycaemia (blood glucose) measuring kit

BASIC MEDICATIONS

In most cases these may be self-administered by a guest and/or offered by a care giver without medical training and licensure. In some jurisdictions, these should only be available to guests who voluntarily elect to use them.

- ☐ Sugar
- ☐ Aspirin
- ☐ Paracetamol/acetaminophen, ibuprofen, or other non-steroidal anti-inflammatory drugs for pain relief
- ☐ Anti-diarrhoea medication, such as loperamide (Imodium)
- ☐ Oral rehydration salts, electrolyte solutions
- ☐ Non-prescription antacids and other medications to treat upset digestive systems (for example, Tums, Pepto-Bismol)
- ☐ Non-prescription nasal decongestants
- ☐ Non-prescription antiseptic/antibiotic ointments, sprays, creams, moist wipes, or liquids; for example, povidone-iodine, benzalkonium chloride, Neosporin, or similar "triple antibiotic ointment" (containing bacitracin, neomycin, and polymyxin B)

LOGISTICS

- ☐ Burn ointment/aloe vera gel
- ☐ Non-prescription anti-itch medication
- ☐ Non-prescription cleansers (for example, Tecnu or Zanfel) and treatments (calamine lotion or hydrocortisone cream) for poison oak/poison ivy/sumac
- ☐ Non-prescription anti-fungal cream
- ☐ Vaseline

ADVANCED MEDICATIONS

Note that in many countries or jurisdictions, the following items may only be prescribed and dispensed by a licensed medical practitioner. In practice, this section is provided only for those care services that have such people on staff. This is not a comprehensive list. Any definitive list must be compiled and reviewed by a licensed medical professional.

- ☐ Epinephrine auto-injector (brand name EpiPen) for anaphylactic shock (note that in some jurisdictions, guests can self-administer)
- ☐ Codeine, tramadol (Ultram) for severe pain (note that in some jurisdictions these may only be administered by a licensed medical professional)
- ☐ Antihypertensives (for example, captopril)
- ☐ Antiemetics (for example, ondansetron or metoclo-pramide)
- ☐ Local anaesthetic for suturing
- ☐ Antihistamine, such as diphenhydramine (Benadryl)
- ☐ Benzodiazepines, such as diazepam (Valium), alprazolam (Xanax), lorazepam (Ativan)
- ☐ Salbutamol/albuterol for acute asthma attacks
- ☐ Insulin for severe hyperglycaemia in diabetics

Internal and External Communication Plans

8.8

Having well-considered communication plans is very important. Even at the smallest events, being able to reliably reach others is essential. At large event sites, it is mandatory to establish commonly understood names for specific areas so that care team members directed to a particular location can reliably find it. As the scale of the event grows or is complicated by difficult terrain, the need for wireless communication becomes increasingly vital. In areas with cellular service you may not need to consider any additional items, although you should be careful of relying entirely on a cellular network; different cellular service providers may or may not supply coverage at the event location. In some locations, established cellular service providers may become overwhelmed by the volume of participants' use, and cell services may suddenly become unavailable. It is essential to determine cell service availability on location well before the event begins, otherwise the network may fail you at a critical time of need.

In the absence of (or as a backup for) cellular service, consider renting or purchasing radios capable of reaching across the entire event area. There are many technical aspects to radios, such as whether they need to be licensed, what frequency they operate on, and their transmitting power, portability, and battery charge duration. Consult a radio sales or rental professional to discuss which solution is right for you. Make sure that the care team gets trained in radio protocols and learns to check their battery levels and replace batteries as needed.

Wireless communication equipment may include:

☐ Cell phones (confirm there is service on-site in advance)

☐ Two-way radios

☐ Radio earphones

☐ Radio headsets

☐ Radio holders

☐ Other radio accessories

☐ Batteries/battery chargers

Tip: Sometimes *what* gets communicated is as important to plan for as the technology of *how* communication takes place. For example, care service leads may need to train care givers and others on how to appropriately discuss the use of psychoactive substances over the radio or in person with guests and others outside of the care service. Local laws should guide communications policies. In all cases, the care service lead must be responsible for informing the care service personnel about what standards are expected for protecting guest confidentiality and for relaying sensitive information. *Assume at all times that electronic communications—particularly radio—will be monitored.* In some jurisdictions, therefore, any over-the-airwaves mention of anything to do with illegal substance use is strongly discouraged. In other jurisdictions, however, there may be official law-enforcement and government-level support for the care service (as a harm-reduction organisation), and communications may take place more freely.

INTERNAL COMMUNICATION WITHIN THE TEAM

Effective communication within the team should be taken very seriously by the care service leader—from the beginning of the project, during the training phases, and throughout the operation of the service. Encourage people to debrief together and be sure there is enough time between shifts so that care givers can transfer knowledge of shift issues and guest status to the oncoming team. Supplies that might assist effective internal team communication include:

☐ Whiteboard (inside the care space) + whiteboard markers

☐ Shift schedules

☐ Sign-up sheets

☐ Bulletin board at entrance (for posting messages)

☐ Pens

☐ Pencils (for hot areas where pens will dry out)

☐ Seating for a designated debriefing area

☐ Extra maps

☐ Extra training materials, such as manuals

☐ Logs/paper/binders/clips/organisers (for data collection)

EXTERNAL COMMUNICATION WITH OTHER EVENT TEAMS

Establishing good communication with teams outside of the care service can be essential to running the care space effectively. For some events it is necessary to use technology, such as radios, to communicate between several crucial teams. For example, for safety and other logistical reasons, a communication plan linking the care service, medical services, security services, official law enforcement, and event organisers may be desirable or even required.

If possible, try to schedule a brief presentation about the care service to the whole staff of the event during one of their meetings, or at least with the event medical and security teams. In the planning phase, check with the event organisers to find out if they might include a mention of the care service on their flyers, website, or other event information sources.

EXTERNAL COMMUNICATION WITH THE PUBLIC

Consider how you want to communicate about the care service to event attendees and the general public, if relevant. Be sure to have an appealing, colourful sign that identifies the entrance of the care space. If possible, it is great to post fliers with information about the service in locations such as bars, eating areas, bathrooms, dance floors, and other areas where event attendees are likely to see them.

In countries with fewer legal restrictions, consider including announcements about the care service in all media (radio, TV, website, etc.) that the event is using to advertise and promote itself. If local laws are prohibitive, collaborate with the event organisers to figure out how to notify their customers about the care service in advance of the event. Please see Chapter 14, "Working With Other Organisations", for more detailed information about publicising the care service to event participants.

Food and Water

Water is the most important item to have on hand. If tap water is not available on-site, you must carefully consider the care service's anticipated usage. Not having enough is an obvious problem; yet significantly over estimating puts excess demand on volunteer time, in loading, transporting, and warehousing the stock.

Food has additional concerns such as refrigeration, heating, preparation, and/or cooking. In some countries or municipalities there may be a requirement to obtain a health permit before providing food to staff and/or participants. Meal-specific shopping lists exceed the scope of this book. However, some general items are listed below to assist you with high-level planning:

- ☐ Potable water
- ☐ Perishable groceries (for short-term events and/or where refrigeration is available)
- ☐ Non-perishable groceries
- ☐ Refrigeration
- ☐ Freezers
- ☐ Coolers/ice chests
- ☐ Ice and/or an electric ice maker
- ☐ Dry ice
- ☐ Storage containers

LOGISTICS

- ☐ Food preparation supplies
- ☐ Plates (washable/recyclable or disposable)
- ☐ Eating utensils (washable/recyclable or disposable)
- ☐ Cups (washable/recyclable or disposable)
- ☐ Dishwashing items (bins/biodegradable soap/drying rack/towels)
- ☐ Waste storage and removal
- ☐ Covers (to keep out pests)
- ☐ Picnic cloth/table for serving

Tip: Consider in advance the best ways to serve food and beverages. Can you minimise the need for disposable materials? Are individual water bottles preferable to using paper or plastic cups? Can non-plastic disposable items be burned? Is it possible to reduce the amount of waste associated with food service? Is heating or refrigeration necessary?

SNACKS

Most care services do not provide full meals for guests for a variety of legal and logistical reasons. However, in the case of long visits, it may be appropriate to arrange for an occasional meal to assist in stabilising the guest. Snacks are another matter; they should be available for both care givers and guests alike. Fruit, bread/crackers, and chocolate are usually appreciated. Often, just a little comforting food can calm down an agitated guest.

MEALS

A hungry stomach makes for an unhappy care giver, so be sure your people are eating properly, and having meal breaks during their shifts (if applicable). If your care service assumes responsibility for providing meals to care givers, pay special attention when planning the menus. If you have care givers with specific dietary requirements, consider the extent to which you are able to provide for them, including vegetarian, vegan, gluten- and casein-free, low-carb, or culturally appropriate (such as kosher) food.

BEVERAGES

Providing an ample supply of fresh, clean water is essential to any event—we can't repeat this point often enough. In addition, tea and coffee are very much appreciated by the care service team and guests alike. Just remember that excessive consumption of tea, coffee, or other caffeine-containing beverages can be dehydrating.

Accommodating Rain/Heat/Severe Weather

IN CASE OF RAIN AND COLD

See that the shelter is waterproof and that any electrical connections and devices are kept dry at all times. Ensure that there won't be a river of mud flowing inside if the ground is not flat. If puddles are a possibility, keep some straw to cover the muddy places of your shelter. The care service should also keep a supply of clean used (donated) clothes to give away to guests—for warmth, if needed, and because folks in crisis sometimes take off and lose all of their clothes.

IN CASE OF HEAT AND SEVERE SUN

Some guests may arrive with severe sunburn. If possible, have some soothing lotion for minor sunburns, or consult medical staff for assistance in more severe cases. If heat-related conditions, such as heatstroke, are a possibility, confirm in advance that all care givers are briefed on the signs that indicate that medical attention may be needed.

Make water available to everyone (care givers and guests) all the time. Water has a great relaxing effect.

IN CASE OF WIND

Be sure that everything is properly tied down. If wind is even a remote possibility, include items such as wires, cords, rebar, stakes, or other equipment for securing structures and equipment in your packing lists.

Tip: If your event is located in an area with any potential for serious wind, secure your structures with rebar and ratchet straps on every corner. Uncovered rebar is sharp and presents a serious injury hazard to participants, especially at night, so cover any rebar ends with dedicated plastic caps, old tennis balls, or even plastic bottles, and mark the rebar with LED lights for visibility at night. If the ground does not support rebar (for example, you're on a rocky patch or an asphalt surface), obtain large plastic storage drums and fill them with water, then tie the ends of the structures securely to the plastic drums. A 200-litre (55-gallon) drum full of water weighs over 200 kilos!

Set-Up and Break-Down

Lists for this section will vary widely depending on the scope of your event. Content for this section is also covered in "Equipping the Service: Preliminary Fundamentals" (on page 106), as well as in Chapter 9, "The Care Space". You can use the suggestions below to start your planning for set-up and break-down, and then add or omit items to customize your lists to meet your unique care space needs.

LOGISTICS

Tip: Will composting be part of your plan? If so, remember to add the items you'll need before, during, and after the event.

Items required for set-up and break-down may include:

- ☐ Tools for clearing brush (pruners, shovels, hoes, rakes)
- ☐ Debris removal supplies and transport
- ☐ Tarps (tarpaulins)
- ☐ Flags (for marking the care space footprint)
- ☐ Measuring tapes (including at least one that is fairly long)
- ☐ Construction equipment (cranes, skip loaders)
- ☐ Tools for digging (post hole diggers, trenchers, shovels)
- ☐ Tools for assembly/disassembly (spanners/wrenches, screwdrivers, hammers, saws, etc.)
- ☐ Work gloves (various sizes)
- ☐ Fasteners (rope, twine, zip ties, string, fishing line)
- ☐ Tape (gaffers, duct, electrical, reflective)
- ☐ Clips/carabiners
- ☐ Bungee cords
- ☐ Rebar
- ☐ Ratchet straps
- ☐ Stakes
- ☐ Broom/cleaning supplies
- ☐ Dustbin/heavy-duty garbage bags
- ☐ Ladders
- ☐ Scaffolding
- ☐ Work lights
- ☐ Long heavy-gauge electrical cords
- ☐ Electrical cord splitters/power strips/short electrical cords
- ☐ Power distribution boxes (distros/spider boxes)
- ☐ Temporary shelter (tents)
- ☐ Poles (for supports, signs, decor)
- ☐ Storage bins/sacks/cabinets

- ☐ Shipping materials
- ☐ Hay bales
- ☐ Shower stalls/curtains/camp showers
- ☐ Evaporation tubs/pool liners/fans/pumps (for management of grey water)
- ☐ Inventory lists/binders

Privacy and Noise Control

Choosing the care space and camp location usually comes with trade-offs. A common question event organisers ask themselves is, "Should we set up the care service near the main event activities (such as dance floors) for visibility and easy access, or is it more important to be away from the core of the action, where the environment is quieter?" Either option has its benefits and drawbacks.

In some cases, making extra provisions for privacy and noise control becomes necessary. Below are checklists and tips to help improve the care space by tending to the privacy and noise control needs of guests.

PRIVACY

Consider what a visit to the care space would be like from a guest's perspective. Would they feel sufficiently out of the public eye to rest and restore themselves? Is the entrance to the care space shielded from curious onlookers? Can accommodations be made in a shared space to partition off some more private areas? Supplies that might assist with the logistics of creating private or "private feeling" spaces include:

- ☐ Fabric, tapestries, blankets, or sheets for creating partitions
- ☐ Cords, posts, poles, or piping to support partitions
- ☐ Eyeshades/sunglasses
- ☐ Seating outside of the entrance to the care space for friends or camp-mates waiting for guests
- ☐ Small tents or a separate space for guests who feel a strong desire for temporary isolation

NOISE CONTROL

Despite best efforts to locate care services away from major sources of noise, sometimes there is just no way to keep the booming bass, generator noise, revellers, or other audio distractions from interfering with optimal care. Some of the following suggestions, however, may help:

LOGISTICS

- Request access to maps of key event installations (for example, sound stages and communal eating areas) as early as possible in planning, to maximise the opportunity to choose the quietest spot.

- Keep a large supply of "single use" foam earplugs to give away.

- Play soft ambient music within the care space.

- Post signs requesting quiet in the immediate surroundings.

- Keep a list of other chill spaces, bonfires, and peaceful areas in nature near the care space for guests who would like a transitional space before resuming full activities or returning to their campsite.

- Try positioning the care service camp as a noise buffer zone around the care space (so long as care givers can still get a good night's sleep!).

- Be aware of variable responses to ambient noise sources; for example, the whirring of an electric fan can be either soothing or intolerable, depending on a guest's state of mind.

Tip: Place generators as far from the care space as possible, which might mean using long and heavy-gauge power cables. Consider erecting a noise-containment structure (hay bales can help) around generators, as well as digging shallow trenches for burying power cables (if possible, without overly disturbing the land).

Conclusion

The above sections constitute a comprehensive, although by no means exhaustive, presentation of logistical items and considerations for establishing, running, and packing-up a care service. To the first-time care service leader, our lists may appear daunting in their scope, diversity, and sheer number of items. Remember, though, that they are largely generic, and not all care services will require all items (and some items, such as physical structures and meals, may be supplied by the event itself). Adapt our suggestions to create customized checklists that suit the needs of your project.

Adequate forward planning will help one to comprehend the various categories of logistical requirements. The care service leader must assemble a capable leadership team who will assist in these matters. With practice, logistical planning and tasks become less daunting; indeed, for some experienced care givers who have worked in various roles—including as care service leaders—they have become almost second nature.

Sandra Karpetas relaxes after her CosmiKiva care giver shift at the 2004 Boom Festival. Photo by Jon Hanna.

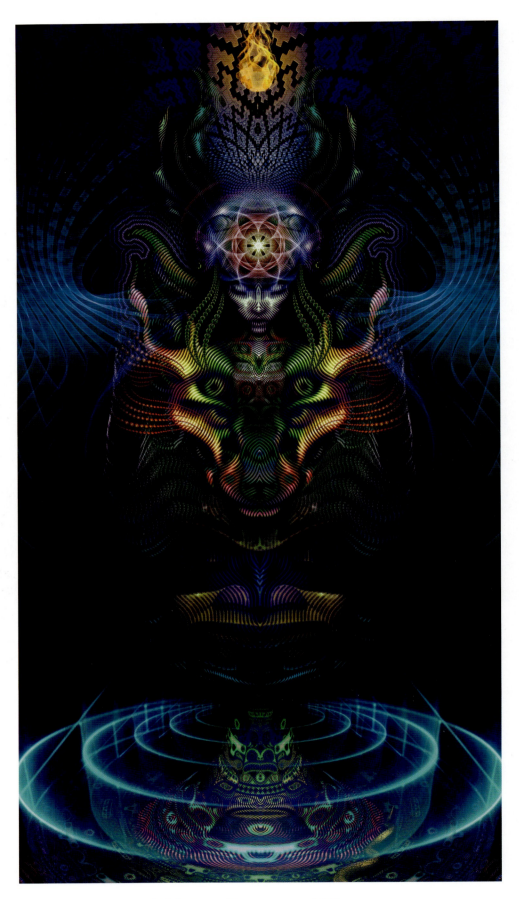

LUKE BROWN • *Foxy Methoxy*, 2011 • digital
http://www.spectraleyes.com

CHAPTER 9
THE CARE SPACE

Kaya

Snu Voogelbreinder

The care space is a dedicated area or structure set aside and equipped for the purpose of providing comfort and aid to those in need. It is ideally made available for the duration of the event. A space may be "self-serve", temporarily staffed, or staffed full time (this Manual is generally based on the latter model). Additionally, a space may be a temporary location, sometimes created spontaneously, in response to a particular and often unanticipated need.

The terms "set" and "setting", when applied to psychedelic experiences, refer to the "mindset" and "physical environment" influencing the experience of the guest requiring help. A thoughtfully designed space seeks to address the mental and physical needs of the individual in order to move them towards a positive state of mind and body. The design of the space is intended to provide a healing and supportive atmosphere that will facilitate an improvement in guests' experiences.

A space may range from simple to elaborate in design, and may be operated by one person (which is not ideal, since assistance is often needed) or a large team of staff. The pursuit of the "perfect space" is not necessary; the primary goal should be to provide an area to the best of your abilities where the majority of people may feel safe, comfortable, and supported. Sensory overload is a common problem at festivals, and the space should be designed to minimise unnecessary stimuli.

There are many aspects to consider when planning a suitable space and selecting the items necessary to provide care. There are fundamentals to take into account, yet you must also remain open-minded and prepared to adjust your approach to suit the changing needs of the individual or situation. The environment you create works in conjunction with care givers to provide care. When planning and setting up the space, take the time to consider the many aspects that may influence your guests' state of mind, which can range from elation to extreme distress.

The material found in this chapter, focusing on the care space environment itself, is complemented by (and in some cases overlaps) that found in Chapter 8, "Logistics". When planning a care space we encourage you to revisit the information contained in both chapters.

Location

9.1

In general, the care space should be located a reasonable distance from performance areas, busy and noisy zones, and camping sites, but not be so remote or obscure that it is difficult to find. If the event has a medical service, then the space should be situated close by in case medical attention is required. There should be convenient access to clean toilet facilities, water, food, and if needed, electricity. The approach to, and the area around, the space should be open and clear of dangerous objects such as broken glass, protruding branches, unmarked stumps, rocks, or ditches.
If feasible, illuminate the path to the care space at night.

When possible, it is important to keep a cell phone on hand in the space with a list of phone numbers for emergency services, including ambulance and medical staff, event security services, and the event organisers, as well as numbers for the members of your care team. Some events are held in remote areas where cell phone coverage may be limited or non-existent. When choosing the location for your space check cell phone coverage; if no cell service is available, discuss emergency communication options with the event organisers. See Chapter 8, "Logistics", for more details related to communications.

OPEN-AIR VERSUS INDOOR SPACES

Care spaces will be located inside a building or structure in most cases, but this is certainly not a requirement. Some environments lend themselves to choosing open-air spaces because of consistent mild weather, day and night, and may contain natural features (such as trees or cliffs) that offer ample shade and wind protection. Open-air spaces should be considered only when there is great confidence in the weather, and when the open-air space offers benefits and environmental protections similar to a good indoor area.

TEMPORARY SPACES

There may be times when an immediate need arises unexpectedly; you might come across a person in a crowd or near a performance area in distress, or there may be no designated space for providing care. The material in this chapter, and indeed the entire Manual, may also be used to guide the care you provide in the absence of a dedicated space.

If you find yourself in this situation you should immediately seek the help of at least one other person. Never leave an individual in distress alone; rather, rely on other people to retrieve whatever you need. If the individual is able to move, safely escort them to a quiet area and set up a temporary care space. What follows in this section applies as much to handling the individual case as to serving large festivals.

Structure Selection: Size and Suitability

When planning for the space or structure, first consider the size of the event and the environment. A 50,000-person festival will necessitate a larger space, more supplies, and a larger crew of care givers than a 200-person gathering.

It is vital to anticipate the environment and weather for the duration of the event. A poorly designed or inadequate structure could collapse from wind, become soaked with rain, or become either too cold or too hot, making it unusable. A structure that becomes unusable in poor weather conditions can make bad situations worse for people in distress, not to mention for yourself and your care givers. Ensure that your structure will be adequate for day and night temperatures, and withstand rain and wind if expected. If you are unfamiliar with the geographic location of the event you should be able to locate historical weather data; or, ask local residents what the weather is typically like. *When in doubt, prepare for all possible weather conditions.*

THE CARE SPACE

When planning the structure of your care space, ask yourself: Do you have adequate human resources to match the requirements of the space? Structures such as geodesic domes meet many of the recommendations, but require significant time and human resources to assemble and break down. The number of dedicated people available before and after an event, to help set up and take apart the space, are an important factor in structure selection. Once more, please refer to Chapters 8, "Logistics", and 4, "Planning and First Steps for a New Project", for further information.

Design and Aesthetics

The shape, form, and aesthetic of a space are important criteria to consider. Rounded, organically shaped or flowing spaces tend to be aesthetically pleasing and supportive of a positive atmosphere. As a general guide, if there are other options available, do not use spaces that are hard, angular, cold or dreary. Often, however, one must use whatever structure is available rather than an ideal one. In such situations you can augment a structure's interior to create an organic and flowing environment by shaping the space through the use of art, lighting, and hanging fabrics.

DIVIDING THE CARE SPACE: PROVIDING FOR PRIVACY

It is generally recommended to create separate sections within the space to provide for small groups, private areas, food and beverage service, reception, and supply storage. Throughout the space, ideally in each section, keep small bins, plastic garbage cans, or buckets, and paper towels readily available in case of nausea and vomiting.

At some points guests may wish to congregate, whilst at other points they will prefer to have some time alone. Dividing the space to set aside some areas to offer greater privacy (and perhaps lower light levels) will add functionality and diversity. Areas of greater privacy are necessary as some people may wish to talk but feel uncomfortable opening up in the presence of others, or may simply need somewhere to lie down and work through things by themselves, whilst knowing that a care giver is present near by if needed.

Hanging fabric can create partitions that add privacy, whilst also producing a soft, aesthetically pleasing environment.

It is important to monitor your space, particularly the areas that offer some privacy and are occupied by more than one person, as there is the potential for the space to be used for sexual activity. This is unacceptable in the care space, since it may disturb other guests and also presents problems with potentially biohazardous fluids and clean-up.

Soft, artistic illumination is key; this archway would make a great care space entrance. Carey Thompson's Starport 2.012 was a portal between the Man and Center Camp at the 2012 Burning Man Festival in Nevada. Photo by David Arnson.

LIGHTING

Illumination of the space should be sufficient to allow guests and care givers to move about in a safe and relaxed manner. Overly bright light, however, can cause discomfort or even pain to those under the influence of psychedelics due to enlarged pupils that cannot easily adapt to high or dramatically changing light levels.

Whenever possible select diffuse lighting (Chinese lanterns or reflected light) instead of hard light (bare light bulbs or work lights). In setting up the lighting for the space you may wish to have some areas brighter and others darker in order to accommodate the different needs of guests. However, diffuse white light should constitute the majority of the lighting in the space. White light is the most visible, and adequately lighting the space will require fewer white light bulbs than it would take to achieve a similar level of brightness using coloured bulbs (although coloured light may be attractively employed as an accent).

Candles are discouraged due to their potential risk for accidental fires or burns. If candles are used, they should be placed in safely enclosed containers that will shield the flame and prevent spillage of hot wax. Place candles and any open flame far away from anything flammable, and where

THE CARE SPACE

they will not be accidentally knocked over. If candles or open flames are used, it is essential that fire extinguishers be kept in the space and that all staff members know their exact location and how to safely operate them.

DECORATION AND ART

The choice of colour and decoration dramatically alters a space and influences its atmosphere. The goal should be to create an area that encourages feelings of relaxation. Art, like colour, can be used to instil a particular emotion or mood in guests. Artwork inspires creativity and adds a richness to the space, encouraging the imagination. As with colour, individuals' response to art is highly variable and subjective; therefore, particular care must be taken when selecting imagery. Don't include so much visual stimuli that it could become disorienting. Non-threatening transformative art, as well as nature photography, are great for providing a calming focus for contemplation whilst working through a difficult experience. Interesting sculptures and other appropriate objects in the space may serve a similar purpose, with an added tactile component in some cases. Potted plants make an excellent addition to the space; preferably they should be non-toxic (and non-psychoactive!) in case a guest ingests part of a plant when no one is watching.

COMFORT

The floor may be covered with carpets and rugs, or left partially open, exposing the ground for people who wish to feel the grass or earth beneath their feet without wandering away from the care space.

A central area in the space where people may take off their shoes and put their bare feet in clean sand could be provided; this has been found to be a very grounding experience. A central spot is also a good location for a heat source, if necessary, as it provides a natural area to congregate for guests who want to be near other people.

Throw-cushions, pillows, bean-bag chairs, and couches are preferable to plastic or fold-up seats (although they are more bulky to transport). Large pillows, futon mattresses, or foam pads are perfect additions to the space. Inflatable PVC beds—whilst light, compact, and convenient—are easily punctured and can quickly become useless trash. (If these are brought, remember to also bring patch kits, and to put protective tarps under, and blankets on top, of any inflatable mattresses.) It is recommended that you should cover resting areas with sheets, which can be easily replaced if they become soiled.

Depending on the climate, there may be a need to heat or cool the space to maintain comfort. An open fire is not practical, due to ventilation requirements and other safety concerns (such as accidental burns or the spread of fire). Therefore, alternatives need to be provided, including electric or gas heaters (preferably without exposed elements that could be touched when red hot) and electric fans.

Clean blankets should be kept available if needed for extra warmth, or for psychological comfort. *Do not underestimate the positive effect that a single blanket can provide to a cold guest undergoing a difficult psychoactive experience.* From experience, we have found that blankets are one of the first items that a care service runs short of, so make sure you stock up adequately.

The Sonic Environment

The space should encourage connection and communication, but maintain regard for the needs of others. Care givers should speak softly or at a low conversational volume when possible. This may in turn encourage guests who are making excessive noise to quiet down and relax. Shouting or angry tones should of course be avoided, but there is nothing wrong with loud laughter—it can be contagious, after all! If it goes on for too long, however, anyone suffering paranoid thoughts might feel that people in the space are laughing at them. Some people experiencing difficulties may require a safe space where they are permitted to express themselves through sound without being judged, so occasionally some noise that could unsettle others might not be avoidable.

Many people find the gentle sound of flowing water to be calming and pleasant. If the space is fortunate enough to be situated near a stream or brook, this is great, as long as there is not undue risk of someone stumbling out and accidentally falling down the bank and injuring themselves or drowning in the dark. If you have access to an artificial waterfall or similar device that circulates water over some rocks, this makes an adequate substitute for a natural waterway with regard to the sound, and it may be visually attractive as well.

Music is an option for use in the space, although it may be difficult to agree on what sort of music is acceptable to everyone in this context, and its presence can even be distracting or can intensify someone's difficult experience. Care givers may decide that no music is the best option, although in a festival or party situation it is likely that music from outside the space will still be audible. Guests may need some temporary separation from the goings-on of the rest of the festival, including music, and for this reason it may be best to have the space music-free.

If the care team does choose to incorporate music into the space at times, instrumental, non-intrusive music with a harmonising feel and without strong beats is recommended. The music should not be too weird, excessively sentimental, highly religious, or bland. If there are any signs that the music is disturbing somebody's state of mind, it should be faded out and switched off.

Air Quality

It is not uncommon at festivals for people to offer incense or "smudge sticks" of burning sage, and to smudge a space with these materials. For some guests the use of these substances can be beneficial and calming; for others, however, especially considering that some psychoactive drugs increase mucogenesis (phlegm) and congestion, the presence of pungent fragrances can add unnecessary distress, or worse, trigger an asthma attack. Care givers should be made aware of these issues, and act accordingly.

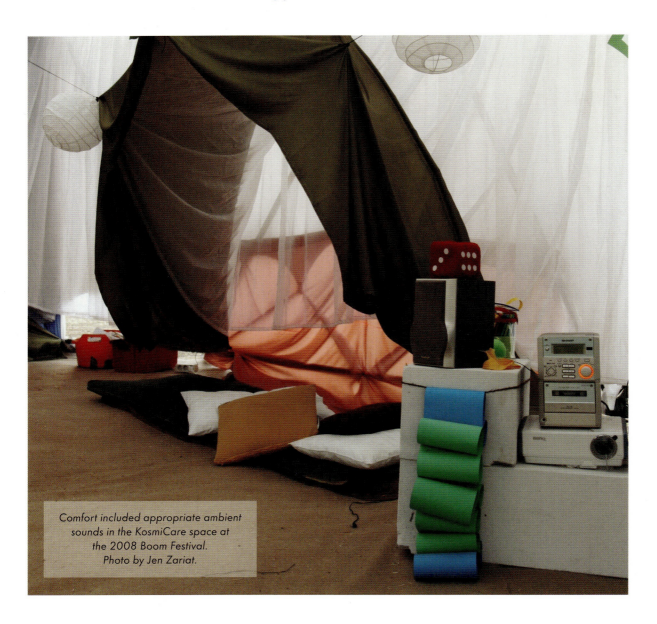

Comfort included appropriate ambient sounds in the KosmiCare space at the 2008 Boom Festival. Photo by Jen Zariat.

Reception Area

Care should be taken in the reception area of the space. People who enter should be able to approach care givers and ask questions about the function of the service. In fact, this should be encouraged, as it helps spread the message about the kind of work the care service does, and generally educates festival-goers. The reception area and entrance, however, must not become blocked, noisy, or crowded.

Individuals often find it difficult enough to approach someone for help whilst in their altered state; having an entrance filled with people talking busily only serves to repel the cautious, timid, or paranoid potential guest. It can be useful to have some kind of privacy screen at the entrance, as many curious passers-by want to see what goes on inside, their imaginations perhaps fired-up by images of a "house of horrors" within! Such a privacy screen helps reduce unnecessary traffic at the entrance to the space. In order to offer a sense of privacy and separation from the outside, there should also be some division of the inside from the reception area.

Having a "shoes off" policy can help to keep the space clean and set a nice atmosphere; entering the space then becomes a bit of a special exercise. This should not be harshly enforced though, just presented as a guideline. Provide a chair at the entrance where folks can sit to remove their shoes, and have a designated, well-lit space available for storing them (since it should be made as easy as possible for guests to locate their shoes and put them back on with minimal frustration).

A sign near the front door identified and described the KosmiCare space at the 2008 Boom Festival. Photo by Jen Zariat.

THE CARE SPACE

Food and Drink

The care space provides resources to support the mind, body, and spirit. We have covered many aspects so far, but it is imperative not to neglect the important roles of nourishment and hydration. Some of the most common causes of distress are the result of dehydration, hyponatremia (low sodium), hypoglycaemia (low sugar), and lack of sleep. The care space should be equipped to address each of these issues. Food can also be a pleasant sensory distraction, whilst offering nutrition that may help the body and mind cope with difficult experiences. The vitamins, amino acids, proteins, minerals, sugars, fatty acids, and antioxidants that food contains have beneficial effects on the nervous system, mental outlook, and coherence in general, and on the body as a whole. Cell function is nourished, neurotransmitters replenished, blood sugar stabilised, and free radicals neutralised. Never offer food to people who are not completely awake or who show signs of nausea; giving food to people in these states can be dangerous.

FOOD AND BEVERAGE RECOMMENDATIONS
(see also **"Food and Water" in Chapter 8, "Logistics"**)

Food

A key element in restoring well-being is providing quality food. Food offerings need not be expensive nor complex, although it is good to have at least a couple of different choices available for guests. Drugs affect appetite as well, in terms of desire and tolerance for food. Food options should be nutritious, easily served, and preferably require no special preparation. Foods such as chips or cookies, whilst easy to offer, do not provide the steady release of energy necessary to restore well-being. Strong-smelling or meaty foods should be avoided, as guests may have an amplified sense of smell in an altered state, and such odours can quickly pervade an indoor area.

By far the easiest choice to offer is fruit, either dried or fresh (though fresh is best). Fresh fruit could include grapes, apples, oranges, pears, and bananas. Dried varieties may consist of apple, raisins, mango, papaya, and dates. Fruit has the advantage of coming in its own package and requires no special refrigeration or storage. When selecting fruit to offer, consider the accompanying clean-up; some fruits in their fresh form, such as mango, pineapple, melons, and papaya, can be very messy, leading to soiled bedding, floor, clothes, and hands. Grapefruit (and grapefruit juice) should be avoided because it can potentiate some psychoactive drugs. Unroasted pumpkin and sunflower seeds are rich in essential fatty acids (EFAs), which are beneficial to the nervous system; a lack of EFAs in the diet may have a negative effect on mood and brain function (it might help to tell the guest this, as even just the idea of eating something with known beneficial content may help make them feel better, as a sort of placebo effect). For fruit it can be convenient to have a small serving dish or bowl with which you move around the space, being mindful of hygiene if guests touch food that they are not going to eat themselves.

Bread or crackers are another option, preferably with some choices of spread to liven them up. They can be a good way to quickly get something simple and carbohydrate-rich into the stomach if the guest hasn't eaten anything substantial in a while. Although bread can quickly go stale, crackers tend to stay fresh for far longer. Chocolate can have a mild anti-depressant effect, at least partly because it tastes and feels so good in the mouth. Chocolate is a popular snack that goes fast; everyone will want some! Note, however, that chocolate quickly melts in heat, and usually needs to be refrigerated.

Nuts should be avoided due to potentially serious and even fatal allergies; a susceptible guest in an altered state may partake before realising what they are eating, which will create a very problematic scenario in the care space.

Beverages

Sometimes all a guest needs is a cup of hot tea to get into a more positive mindset, and this should be available at all times. If a guest shows no signs of nausea you should offer them food and beverage. Remember that drinking a cup of tea is something that many have done on numerous occasions whilst sober, so the ritual and the memories associated with it can help a person to ground and feel quiet and restful.

When offering a hot beverage to a guest, be sure that it is in an appropriate container so that it will not spill or scald anyone. Sugar added to the tea, apart from being a tasty sweetener, increases blood sugar levels, which can help to clear the head and take away confusion. There are hundreds of different herbal teas available, many of them believed to have various calming, revitalising, cleansing or healing properties. See Chapter 12, "Complementary Therapies", for some suggested herbal teas and their properties.

Water

Bulk water dispensed from jugs is the most common and easiest beverage to provide. Ensure that there is an adequate quantity on hand or that there is easy access to a water source to refill as needed. A pinch of table salt can be added to regular water without altering the taste. A steady supply of water is also necessary for making other beverages, such as tea.

Hot Cocoa

For many people hot cocoa (hot chocolate) is a tasty and comforting drink that brings delightful memories of childhood and good times; it is also mildly nutritious. It is most convenient when pre-made and stored in a large thermos or dispenser, as the preparation of individual servings can lead to sticky messes.

Indian Chai

Found throughout the world, chai is a spiced tea blend that contains black tea and an array of other herbs, depending on the individual blend (common ingredients are cardamom, ginger, cinnamon, and cloves). Chai usually has a small-to-moderate amount of caffeine from the black tea (about one-third as much as coffee), and its mild stimulant and mood-improving effects are believed to be due to a synergy of all the herbs it contains. Indian-style chai can be brewed in bulk ahead of time and is a delicious drink to promote the flow of positive vibes. Chai can range from mild to highly spiced. In some countries (such as Australia and the United States), chai is often boiled with milk or a milk substitute such as soy milk, and served with honey; others brew it without any kind of milk. Milk-brewed chai is not appropriate for vegan or lactose-intolerant guests; hence, you should either use a milk substitute (other than nut milks) or brew the chai using only water, and then allow guests to add the milk or milk substitute of their choice.

Coffee

In general, coffee should not be offered, as it is a strong stimulant and diuretic; coffee can aggravate an altered state rather than ground it. For guests who express the need or desire for sleep, serving coffee, chai, or any other caffeine-containing beverage is not recommended. However, coffee should be on hand for care givers to help them get through their shift. And if a guest really wants a coffee and is sure it will help them deal with things, then they probably know themselves best and should not be denied the request.

Sports (Electrolyte) Drinks

Sports drinks contain a relatively high proportion of electrolytes, and often plenty of sugar. A natural electrolyte alternative is pure coconut water.

SET-UP AND SERVING

Plan for ample rubbish, recycling, and (if possible) compost bins, and keep a supply of heavy-duty garbage bags on hand. Include sufficient space for food and drink storage (including plates, cups, and relatively safe forms of cutlery) and an area for basic food preparation and dish washing (if provided). Position the serving area where it can easily be accessed from both inside and outside the space, and where spills will not disrupt operations or unnecessarily soil bedding and linens.

Maintenance

The cleanliness of the care service space throughout the event plays an important role in the perception and utility of the area. Unnecessary dirt and clutter can undermine the best efforts of the care givers.

Care givers should be suitably equipped and expected to share in the responsibility of keeping the space relatively clean and neat throughout its use. Cleaning the space is not a big chore and care givers should understand that a clean space complements the assistance they are providing. Little actions to maintain the space throughout the event improve the atmosphere and make tear-down easier.

Care givers should keep an eye out for instances where they can aid each other, which ultimately helps everyone in the space. If staff members notice something that needs doing, and they don't have immediate responsibilities, they should attend to it themselves rather than wait for somebody else to do it. This is an attitude that the care service leader and team leads can foster in their people by leading through personal example.

BIOHAZARD CLEAN-UP

There may be times when a guest can't help but leave behind biohazards such as blood, vomit, urine, or faeces. It is vital that the care service be equipped to clean up such messes.

The recommended procedure is: wear gloves and eye protection, remove any soiled bedding and place it in a bag clearly marked "biohazard" and set aside for washing later. For spills on other surfaces use an absorbent material (kitty litter, corn starch, or similar products) to completely soak up the spill. Using something disposable like note cards, cardboard, or plastic, scoop up the absorbent material and place in a plastic bag. Spray the remaining area with disinfectant, wipe clean with paper towels, and contain everything in a plastic "biohazard" bag for later disposal.

THE CARE SPACE

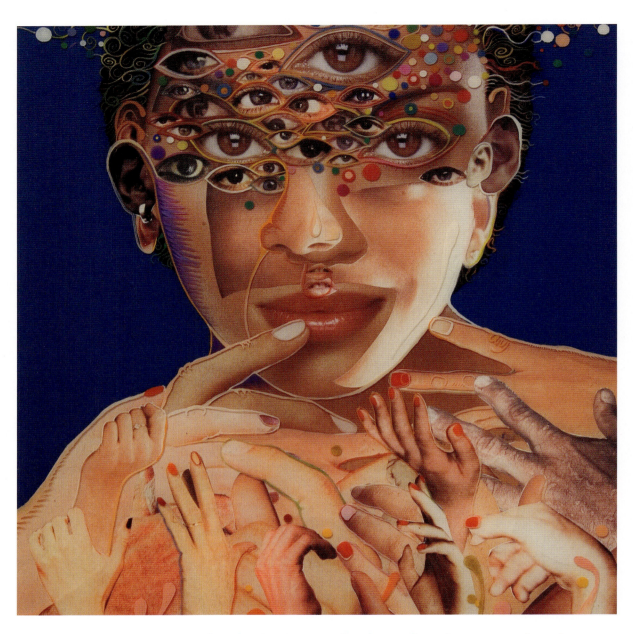

FRED TOMASELLI • *Perfect Skin*, 2006 • mixed media, acrylic and resin on wood panel
courtesy James Cohan Gallery, New York/Shanghai
http://www.jamescohan.com/artists/fred-tomaselli

CHAPTER 10
RUNNING THE SERVICE

Annie Oak

This chapter addresses the practical tasks that need to be carried out to ensure that the care space serves guests effectively. It includes a list of tasks that care givers should consider when they arrive on-site, during the event, and at the conclusion of the project. Some of the themes dealt with in this chapter are covered in more detail in Chapters 7, "Building and Training a Team"; 8, "Logistics"; 9, "The Care Space"; 11, "Screening"; 13, "Team Welfare"; and 14, "Working With Other Organisations".

Gathering the Team On-Site

It is likely that your care givers will arrive on-site for the care service at different times, either before or sometimes during the event. It is helpful to have a strategy in place to make sure that each care giver knows where they need to be, when they need to be there, and for what purpose. Members of the care service team who arrive early to help construct the care space should know exactly where to find the site, and have their arrival passes or tickets taken care of ahead of time. Space should be arranged for those arriving early to park (if required) and camp. A meal plan or a kitchen space should be set up for care givers if they are not preparing meals at their own camps.

Once the care team begins to assemble on-site, one or two people should be designated to welcome other care givers as they arrive and help facilitate construction of the care space. Supplies and equipment should be unpacked and organised for easy access during the event. An inventory of such supplies and equipment should be created and a list of needed materials drawn up for last minute purchase if required. Requests for additional supplies can be posted before the event to the care service mailing list, if one exists and if time permits. See Chapter 8, "Logistics", for a detailed discussion and equipment list related to establishing the care space.

Prior to the opening of the care service, a schedule should be circulated among the care service team indicating shift rosters. Depending on the particular care service, different considerations will need to be taken into account when assembling care givers into shifts. These can include gender (in order to have both genders represented in each shift), age (including a balance of older and younger people), and languages spoken. The shifts may need to be adjusted throughout the event, and an updated schedule should be posted in a central place. Those who are leading shifts (usually referred to as the "team leads") should confirm their schedules both prior to the event and also upon arrival at the care space. Organisers should create a master contact list for the entire care service team, including phone numbers and camp locations (if disparate) during the event.

The care service leader—and any others on the "leadership team"—should set a time when they hold a daily meeting with team leads in order to review concerns about the care service and address any issues that arise.

10.2

Receiving Guests

Prior to officially opening the care service, organisers should review with care givers all procedures related to interacting with guests, including receiving, handover to another care giver, and discharge. This review should constitute a core part of the care service Training Plan (see Chapter 7, "Building and Training a Team", for more detailed information). Different care services may approach these procedures in various ways; no matter which method is used, however, guests who arrive at the care space should be greeted warmly by the team lead or by a care giver who asks for their name. You may want a single person to serve as the greeter, who then assigns each guest to a compatible care giver in that shift. Whatever the set-up, the team leads must keep themselves well-informed and up-to-date *at all times* regarding which guests are present in the care space, their basic situations, and who is taking care of them.

A care giver should lead guests to a place where they can sit down and make themselves comfortable. A special area of the care space should be designated for incoming guests to sit and talk with care givers. If the guest arrives with friends, they should also be made comfortable inside the care space.

If appropriate, guests and their friends should be offered a cup of water, herbal tea, or other beverage upon arrival. Those who are having difficulty sitting can be led to a bed/sleeping pallet where they can lie down and be covered with a blanket if they are cold. Once the guest is comfortably seated and introduced to the care giver, they should be asked why they chose to come to the care space. The guest should be given time to explain why they are there and what services they are seeking. If they are present, care givers should also give the guest's friends time to explain what circumstances prompted them to bring their friend to the care space. Of course, all this is assuming that the guest can speak and/or is with friends. In some cases, individuals (often brought to a care space by medical or security services) are in a state of "meltdown", simply requiring a space to lie down and receive basic physical care. In other, more rare cases, guests may be highly agitated due to the psychoactive substance(s) they consumed and/or underlying mental health issues. They may not understand that they have arrived at a psychedelic care service and may associate event security services with official law enforcement and feel that they are being detained. The team leader must respond swiftly to agitated guests and if necessary, enlist care givers or event security to restrain physically aggressive guests. A doctor should be consulted to intervene pharmacologically in extreme cases (see Chapter 6, "Supporting Roles").

RUNNING THE SERVICE

Once inside the care space, some guests may wish to talk about an experience they are having, others may simply want to rest and rehydrate. If a guest requests medical care, or if it is apparent that they need medical assistance, they should be brought promptly to the nearest medical service area, or a medical provider should swiftly be summoned to provide an evaluation. Guests receiving medical care should be given some privacy, if possible, within the care space. This might be accomplished with curtains and/or other barriers that separate the care space into different areas (see Chapter 9, "The Care Space").

Documenting Guests

Care services may elect to collect assorted types of information about each guest who enters the care space. Here we give a brief outline regarding guest documentation; please see Appendix B, "Monitoring, Evaluating and Researching—Recommendations from an Academic Perspective for an Evidence-Based Approach to Psychoactive Crisis Intervention", for an in-depth presentation of this subject. There are some sound reasons for data collection, but it should be done without making the guest feel uncomfortable. The most important reason to collect information about guests is to provide medical personnel with information about an individual should he or she require medical care. Knowledge of what substances a guest may have taken or any illness that the guest has experienced could be critical for providing effective and timely medical assistance.

The other pressing reason to collect information about guests is to provide continuity of care between different shifts of care givers. Whilst a face-to-face hand off between care givers is ideal (preferably in a way that involves the guest),

10.3

Even when their shifts were over, members of the 2010 KosmiCare team were still debriefing much of the time. Photo by Erowid.

when a new shift starts every six hours, it is useful to be able to refer to written records for each guest. This is especially true if the guest is sleeping when a new shift arrives.

A third reason for collecting information may be for research and strategic/future development purposes; a care service that can demonstrate its effectiveness based on empirical data is more likely to attract support and funding from various organisations—especially from the event organisers themselves—for its next instalment. Chapter 15, "Risk Management and Performance Improvement", provides an in-depth discussion on metrics and key performance indicators, whilst Appendix B, "Monitoring, Evaluating and Researching—Recommendations from an Academic Perspective for an Evidence-Based Approach to Psychoactive Crisis Intervention", gives a comprehensive treatment of this subject.

Some items that care space intake forms should cover include:

- Name/Nickname

- Date and time of arrival

- Native language (at international events)

- Who (if anybody) was with the guest upon arrival, and a contact phone number for that individual as well as the names and numbers for any known friends

- Where (and, if possible, with whom) the guest is camping/sleeping/staying

- Substance(s) and amounts ingested, if known

- A brief description of the guest's experience before arriving at the care service

- The name of the care giver the guest was initially assigned to, and a list of other care givers who worked with the guest

Other information that should be noted on the intake form includes whether the guest had been to the care space on a previous visit, and any requests for medical care or professional mental health services. Care givers should also note changes in the activities of guests, such as agitated behaviour, upset stomach, periods of sleep, requests for food, and messages for friends. When a guest leaves the care space, a note should be made on the intake form indicating the departure and describing the guest's state of mind at the time.

Each care service will have different procedures for where and how these forms are stored, but they must be kept in a safe and secure location. It may be useful for the care service leader/team leads to review all of the collected information on a regular basis, in order to attempt to determine whether there are any trends in: the requests for assistance, the drugs guests have taken, how many guests are served at different times of day, etc. Any useful hypotheses or conclusions should be shared with the entire care service team.

The care service leader will need to decide if and when to share the guest intake information with other groups who might request this data. Such groups may include medical personnel, professional mental health counsellors, official law enforcement, or festival organisers. Laws related to the privacy of this information may vary in different countries. As a general rule, care givers should be expected to keep a guest's information confidential unless there is a compelling reason to share it, such as providing details to medical personnel who are treating the guest. See Chapter 3, "Legal Considerations", for more details regarding confidentiality and privacy issues.

Handoff Procedures

10.4

Different care services will elect to run different types of schedules. Some services may operate only during certain hours; others run twenty-four hours a day in four six-hour shifts (for example: from midnight to 6:00 am, 6:00 am to noon, noon to 6:00 pm, and 6:00 pm to midnight). As each new shift commences, it is imperative to have a procedure where the outgoing care givers brief their incoming colleagues. Ask each care team member to wear a watch and to be on time (that is, at least a few minutes early) for their shift; this is a basic responsibility, and lateness should not be tolerated. Most volunteers readily understand and accept punctuality as a fundamental condition for professionalism.

Once they have arrived, the incoming shift should sit down with the outgoing care givers and review the circumstances of the guests who are present in the space. During this review, information on the intake form for each guest should be examined and passed along to the incoming care givers who can continue to annotate and update the information. Important information to convey includes the ongoing presence of the guest's friends or family and their needs, if any.

The briefing during the transition from one shift to another should be conducted by the team leader, who calls on each member of the shift to present first-hand observations about the guests for whom they have cared. Whenever possible, incoming care givers should be introduced to the guests by the person who has worked most directly with that particular guest. Some consideration should be taken to match guests with the incoming care givers who may best assist them; this is a key responsibility of the team lead. If a guest expresses any discomfort with a new care giver, that person should be replaced with another care giver. Although this situation is rare, it may happen for a variety of reasons; care givers must accept that it is not anything "personal" about them, but simply a mismatch amplified by the crisis state that the guest is experiencing. Team leads should keep an eye out to determine how well their team members are working with guests and adjust accordingly.

At the end of each shift, the care givers should be given an opportunity to debrief with the colleagues they have just served with. The team leads should check in with their people to see if they need to talk about an experience with a guest or make suggestions for improving the service. Some care service leaders (or for their own shifts, team leads) may institute a "buddy system", in which care givers are paired together for the duration of the event. They are then encouraged to share experiences and receive support from their buddy at the conclusion of each shift. Since volunteers in psychedelic care services tend to be communicative people, however, this system may not be necessary. The care service leader may also ask team leads to form an advisory group that is accessible to members of the care service for follow-up questions and conversations, both during and after the event. Providing psychedelic crisis services can be challenging work, and every effort should be made to support the care givers. Please see Chapter 13, "Team Welfare", for more on this topic.

Smaller organisations helping at the 2008 Boom Festival had to close during the event's slow hours, so that their staff could get some sleep.
Photo by Jen Zariat.

RUNNING THE SERVICE

Contacting Other Services

Prior to opening the care space, the care service team should have a plan for interacting with external organisations, including on-site medical and security services, as well as the festival organisers. Detailed information about working with other groups is provided in Chapter 14, "Working With Other Organisations".

All care givers should have a basic idea of the other support services at the event, but it is most important for them to understand the emergency medical and security procedures. Care givers must know exactly where the nearest medical service is located and how to contact it. If event medical personnel want specific information about a guest, be prepared to gather basic data on that person and write it down for medical staff to review. It is similarly important to know how the security services at the event operate and how to contact them if required. For a discussion on internal and external communication, see Chapter 8, "Logistics".

If law enforcement organisations arrive at the care space, make it clear to them that it is a safe space where people in vulnerable states are seeking rest. Suggest that any law enforcement activities take place in some other location, outside of the care space. If they continue to demand entry, do your best to stand firm, and ask them to speak to festival organisers first.

If a guest requests a referral to other event services, including medical, mental health, or law enforcement personnel, locate the appropriate service provider and introduce them to the guest. A private space should be found for such conversations, outside of the care space if possible. If guests say that they would like to obtain follow-up care after the event, suggest that they contact professional counsellors on-site for a referral.

Shutting Down the Care Service

If it is not possible for the care service to assemble enough people for a given shift, it may be important to place a sign on the door of the care space, stating that the service is temporarily closed, and indicating when it will reopen. This may be considered "normal" for some care services, yet entirely unacceptable for others (for example, those who have a prior agreement with event organisers to provide around-the-clock service). If the service runs as planned throughout the event, send out an announcement (if possible) in the last few days, telling event attendees when you will be closing. It is useful to give people advance warning that the service will not be available after a certain time.

If the event is subject to extreme weather conditions, consider keeping the service open to provide shelter to people who are caught in the storm. Designate care givers to help clean the care space daily, and encourage those serving on each shift to tidy the space as they work. Maintaining a clean and neat care space should be emphasised as a basic responsibility for all care givers on shift. Well in advance of the event, try to recruit a group of people who will help break down and pack up the care space when the event is over. Don't forget to organise an after-party for care givers and other volunteers on-site before everyone leaves. Check in with the care service team after the event to see if they have any suggestions, concerns, or feedback that can help improve the care service; *we recommended preparing a written care giver feedback form for this purpose.* For a detailed description of the logistical aspects of break-down, once more please see Chapter 8, "Logistics".

Burning Man, 2003. Photo by Jon Hanna.

RUNNING THE SERVICE

ALLYSON GREY • *Jewel Net of Indra*, 1988 • oil on wood
http://www.allysongrey.com

CHAPTER 11
SCREENING

Twilight

Whether at the care space or somewhere on the event grounds, when an event participant who may require assistance presents to the care service, an initial assessment is the first step in determining appropriate support. This chapter covers the necessary factors that must be considered during that assessment: participant and care giver safety, basic medical evaluation, mental and emotional stability, and determining when external assistance is required.

Care services specialise in assisting participants under three broad circumstances:

- Non-life-threatening psychoactive drug issues
- Non-life-threatening emotional or interpersonal issues
- Depression or disturbed mental states

When presented with a possible situation in which care service assistance may be appropriate, the care service team should develop, publish, and train a specific protocol that all care service staff should follow to qualify, route, and treat the affected participant(s) appropriately.

As a prerequisite to the contents and actions covered in this chapter, care givers are expected to have already determined what support exists at the event in terms of emergency services, licensed medical care, security services, any other organised assistive functions, and law enforcement (see Chapter 14, "Working With Other Organisations").

Situation Safety 11.1

Before starting any initial evaluation of a participant who may need assistance, the first requirement of care givers is to assess the safety of the location. Is it safe to approach the participant without endangering the care giver and/or further endangering the participant? Is there any risk from structural failure, fire, traffic, exposed electrical wires, flowing water, or other potential dangers? *If so, seek immediate assistance from the event organisers or designated responsible parties.* Only proceed when it is safe to do so.

The second consideration applies to care givers, as well as to the participant in distress and other event participants; if there is any threat of violence, particularly if any form of weapon is involved, care givers are—first and foremost—responsible for their own safety. If they attempt care of a violent individual and are injured in the process, there are now two problems: the violent individual *and* the injured care giver. *Regardless of your best intentions, do not compound the problem.*

Once their own safety is assured, care givers should work to help remove the threat from other participants, who may be endangered by an apparently violent individual. This typically means making an immediate request for assistance from other event staff such as security services, medical support, and/or law enforcement. Carefully consider enlisting other event participants to help, particularly if security or medical assistance is not forthcoming.

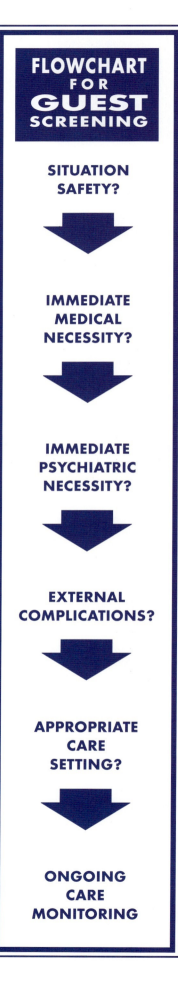

FLOWCHART FOR GUEST SCREENING

SITUATION SAFETY?

⬇

IMMEDIATE MEDICAL NECESSITY?

⬇

IMMEDIATE PSYCHIATRIC NECESSITY?

⬇

EXTERNAL COMPLICATIONS?

⬇

APPROPRIATE CARE SETTING?

⬇

ONGOING CARE MONITORING

Why is it so important to get help with a violent participant? Many clinical studies have examined correlations between mental health issues and the increased likelihood of homicidal behaviour, particularly when accompanied by the ingestion of alcohol. As individuals using psychedelics may have far more intensely emotional experiences than those using alcohol, the risk of encountering a mentally unstable individual who may engage in violent behaviour must be considered as part of any preparation for the operation of a psychedelic care service.

Immediate Medical Necessity

Evaluate the following:

- Is the individual responsive?
- Does the individual have a pulse?
- Is the individual's airway clear?
- Is the individual breathing?

If the answer to any of these questions is "no", this is a crisis: **seek immediate medical assistance**. If the care giver is qualified, remember the ABCs (or, preferably, the CABs) of first aid and take appropriate actions, including CPR if indicated.

- Does the individual show any signs of injury, including bleeding, broken bones, or burns?

If so, **seek immediate medical assistance**.

Next we reach a part of the assessment where the responses will depend upon what services are available at the event. Consider each item carefully and formulate a response based on what services are present.

Immediate Psychiatric Necessity

- Does the participant appear to be suicidal?
- Does the participant appear to be in danger of harming themselves (either on purpose, or by accident)?
- Is this potentially a psychiatric emergency or a significant mental health issue?

These situations indicate a need for psychiatric care. If there are qualified, licensed staff available to help, request their immediate assistance.

If no such people or support organisations exist at the event, carefully weigh your ability to deal with the situation as well as what resources are available to you. For example, consider two scenarios:

CPR: ABC NOW CAB?

In 2010, the American Heart Association changed the order of the steps that one follows whilst performing cardiopulmonary resuscitation (CPR). They now recommend "CAB" over the previous "ABC" approach. This means that one *first* gives the chest compressions ("C"), then performs an airway ("A") check, and then begins the breathing ("B") via mouth-to-mouth.

SCREENING

1. *The participant is engaging in behaviours that can result in harm—striking self with hard objects, cutting self, or otherwise attempting self-mutilation.*

In a situation of this nature, safely restraining the individual from carrying out any self-destructive behaviour is the desired course of action. However, accomplishing this may be challenging for several reasons:

- Care givers could get hurt in the attempt.

- Use of restraining devices may be illegal in the event jurisdiction if not applied by a licensed professional.

- Physical restraint of the individual may be deemed "assault and battery" by local law enforcement.

- If applied improperly, restraining devices can result in a reduction of circulation and/or respiration that can cause serious harm or death to the restrained individual.

Care teams should determine to the best of their ability how to handle such a situation. In particular, means for arranging transportation of the individual to the nearest qualified healthcare provider is essential.

2. *The participant has chosen to suddenly discontinue prescribed antipsychotic medication and has become severely unstable and combative.*

In many or most cases care givers will be unaware of the discontinuation of medication that has resulted in severely unstable behaviour. This situation—which is not uncommon at longer festivals—may be further compounded by the recreational use of psychoactive substances. These factors can precipitate a psychiatric crisis, the manifestations of which may result in harm to the individual and/or to other people.

Again, this situation should be carefully planned for by care teams, including the possible need for restraint and transportation to the nearest qualified healthcare provider.

External Complications Requiring Assistance

11.4

In the process of assisting a participant, there may be additional circumstances discovered surrounding the initial situation:

- Is there a possibility of associated physical assault?

- Is there a possibility of domestic violence associated with the participant's condition?

- Is there a possibility of associated sexual assault?

Situations such as these may result in a need for a crisis team, event medical services, security services, law enforcement, and/or other event-designated parties. **Request immediate assistance if such circumstances are suspected**.

It is particularly important to consider whether an individual —such as a friend or significant other—who brought in the affected participant for care may have been involved in an untoward manner. If the affected participant shows fear or anger towards another individual who may have been recently present, care givers should attempt to determine the nature of the fear or anger from the affected participant or accompanying party.

Optimal Location for Assistance

Once the individual has been screened and appears to be suitable for care service assistance, the next determination is the best location where assistance can be provided. The care space set up for the event will always have limitations in terms of beds, space, and care givers. Before bringing someone into the care space, care givers should consider whether the participant in need may be assisted in another supportive location, where additional care givers can come to help, if required.

If safe and appropriate, first consider assisting participants in a supportive environment that provides a familiar atmosphere and, with any luck, friends and festival-mates. This should be a comfortable space where the participant's friends are willing, ready and able to assist. As trained care givers are usually few in number, ideally the care giver would be able to transition care of the affected participant back to the individual's own companions.

Assisting a participant in need may not be possible in such a location if the individual's friends or camp-mates are themselves unable to provide reliable assistance. Furthermore, a history of conflict between the participant in need and one or more of his/her friends or camp-mates signals a negative and inappropriate care setting. In such cases, seek another location for assistance.

If it is not appropriate to assist the participant in camp/with friends, and the problem is not sufficiently debilitating that it would preclude standing or walking, a seated conversation in a nearby space that is quiet and relatively open may be the most appropriate location for assistance.

If the participant's camp is not an option, or if the individual is unable to be appropriately looked after in an open space, the participant should be supported in the care space itself. However, there are two remaining considerations:

1. *The participant may refuse to go to the care space for assistance.*

Some event attendees who appear to be in need of help may resist or refuse going to a care space. If the care space seems to be the best option, but the individual refuses, there is typically no justification for compelling a participant to go there. Whilst frustrating, this is a frequent circumstance and should be anticipated by the care team.

2. *The care space may be full.*

Bringing a person in distress to the care space only to find it full can present a serious challenge. Even if unable to communicate verbally, the individual may perceive the situation and become more distressed as a result. Whenever possible, care givers should call ahead to determine if the care space has room available for one more person.

Once a guest is accepted into the care space, care givers should assess the suitability of the care giver(s) who will be assigned to care for the individual. If there is only one care giver, there isn't much choice. If there are several possible care givers available, the team should consider the participant's specific needs. Are there any trigger issues that would render a particular care giver inappropriate for the interaction? Is the nature of the situation—for example, relational/interpersonal issues—something for which one care giver may be better qualified than another? Is the apparent nature of the substance more appropriately cared for by one care giver over another? Does the individual in question have any gender concerns? (The latter question is especially important if there is any possibility of domestic violence or assault of any nature that contributed to the individual's need for care service.)

Each case needs to be carefully evaluated so that the most appropriate care giver can provide the best assistance possible to meet the guest's specific needs. In practice, however, care space staff may be scarce at times, so the care service team is encouraged to develop competency in many areas.

Ongoing Assessments

At times, particularly involving lengthier situations, circumstances change over the course of providing assistance to an individual. It is therefore worthwhile to periodically review the issues surrounding the development of the guest's care. Carefully consider what has changed in the time since the last assessment. At minimum, care team staff should usually re-assess each situation on an hourly basis for the duration of assistance, and document any findings.

11.6 Situations Requiring Assistance

MEDICAL EMERGENCIES

If at any time during care a guest is believed to be experiencing a medical emergency, notify event medical services immediately. Remain calm and focused, keep the individual safe, pay attention to breathing and other vital signs until the staff from medical services takes charge. Provide the medics with any relevant guest information that you are aware of, referring to the care space documentation on the guest to refresh your memory and for any further details.

When an individual is having a challenging experience with psychedelics, sometimes it is best for everyone to simply monitor that person from a distance. Photo by Erowid, 2008.

When requesting medical assistance, communicating the following pieces of information will help the medical staff to determine the nature and urgency of the situation:

- Location of the individual(s)

- Approximate age

- Gender

- Primary issue (for example, lacerations, a broken leg, chest pain, seizures, severe bleeding)

- Incident type (for example, a fall, illness)

- Consciousness: Yes/No (if yes, are they alert?)

- Breathing: Yes/No (if yes, are they having difficulty?)

Note that the guest's name is not on this list. If possible, find out this information, but **do not transmit individuals' names over the radio in medical situations**.

One care giver should stay with the guest whilst waiting for the medical team to arrive.

SHANNON THERON • *Sea of Dreams*, 2014 • acrylic on acrylblock
http://plus.google.com/+ShannonTheron/posts

MENTAL ILLNESS

Despite the care space's quiet and safe environment, it cannot effectively treat those whose psychedelic or spiritual difficulties are masking more serious psychiatric emergencies. Whilst they may not have shown symptoms on arrival, if you believe a guest could be experiencing serious mental and/or emotional distress beyond the bounds of the care that you could provide, or if the guest appears to be undergoing a psychotic episode, review the screening protocol above and arrange for the appropriate assistance, including possible evacuation to a hospital for further evaluation and/or medical attention. Such a situation may become apparent rapidly, or it may happen after several hours (or more) of symptoms that don't appear to be improving. Remember that the duration of some psychoactive drug experiences can extend to thirty-six hours or more.

When participants requiring assistance arrive at the care space, there should be a protocol in place to interview them and obtain information about their situations and any medications prescribed and normally used by the participant, in addition to any psychedelics or other drugs they may have ingested at the event. Please see also Chapter 6, "Supporting Roles", for further discussion.

VIOLENT BEHAVIOUR

If a guest displays any violent behaviour towards themselves or others, move yourself, participants in the care space, and staff to a safe distance. Do not intervene. Immediately contact event security and/or law enforcement, as well as the medical team if required, for assistance. If the violent person has a friend or family present in the care space, enlist that person to help calm the violent individual. Your steadiness, calmness, and equanimity in a violent (or potentially violent) situation are the best means to de-escalate the mood. Care space staff should under no circumstances be asked, nor expected, to put themselves in harm's way.

The medical team will determine whether the participant requires a mental health evaluation. Further recommendations and actions should be provided and taken by a licensed medical professional. At some events, medical staff may have an approved sedation protocol for use at their discretion. Whilst many approaches to psychedelic therapy discourage the use of sedation in the event of an adverse drug experience, the decision to use a sedation protocol lies entirely with medical staff.

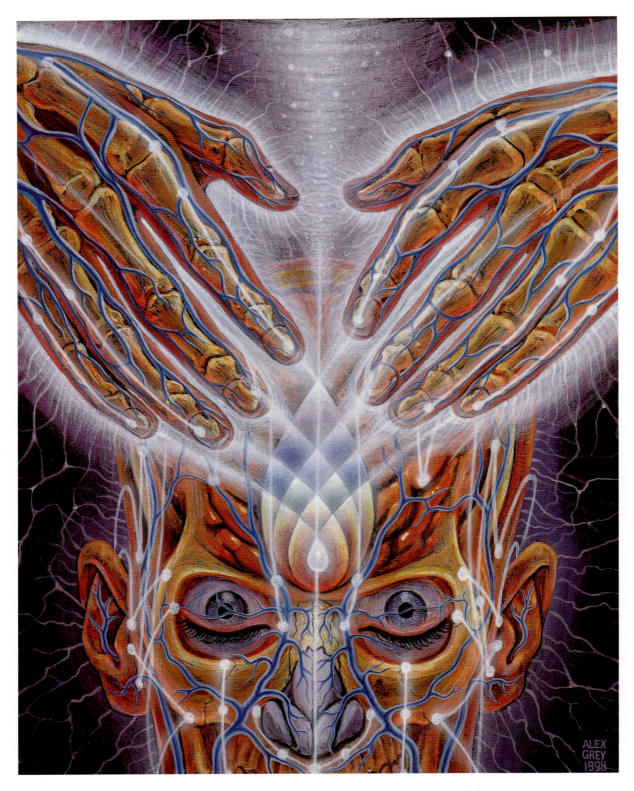

ALEX GREY • *Lightweaver*, 1998 • acrylic on linen
http://alexgrey.com

CHAPTER 12
COMPLEMENTARY THERAPIES

Snu Voogelbreinder

Alexandre Quaranta

Ben Atkinson

Kaya

Natacha Ribeiro

In addition to human support and talking through an experience, and when medical intervention is not necessary, some supplemental therapies that complement "standard procedure" may be beneficial. The intent of many of these therapies is simply to assist in relaxing and grounding a guest. Some therapies may be used as relatively safe tools to help guests explore their problematic states and find a way out of them. Certain therapies require care givers with some level of specific expertise, whereas others can be facilitated by any care service team member. No complementary therapies should be pushed upon a guest; guests should simply be made aware that these options are available if they wish to use them.

This chapter should *not* be seen as an instruction manual in the use of such therapies—we simply mention some of the relevant and safe options that exist, and describe how they may be useful.

Laughter

If care givers are able to encourage humour and laughter in guests, this can be very beneficial. In many cases it is indeed true that laughter is the best medicine. Preferably this should not be forced, although even laughing for no particular reason can lead to an improvement in mood and outlook.

Deliberate voluntary laughter is a tenet of laughter yoga. Put simply, the body doesn't recognise the difference between actual laughter and fake laughter—it produces the same physiological responses. So, to gently encourage a guest to laugh deliberately for no purpose can be very effective. Laughter can also be contagious. If a care giver consciously initiates a deliberate laugh it can lead a guest into laughter. Make sure, however, that the guest knows you are not laughing at them.

Breathwork

Often the first step in assisting someone who is mentally distressed (which is likely to also manifest in increased heart rate and chaotic, shallow breathing) is to encourage them to breathe slowly and deeply, preferably breathing in through the nose, and breathing out through mouth or nose (whichever is most comfortable for the guest). A team member can assist in this regard by breathing with the person to set an example and give a feeling of solidarity. This should be continued until the person has noticeably calmed down and pulse has returned to normal. More specific meditative focused breathwork may be used later if called for, led by a team member experienced with such techniques.

Adjusting your breathing can powerfully change what you are experiencing, as these novice Holotropic Breathwork students are learning at the 2006 Mind States conference in Costa Rica.
Photo by Jon Hanna.

12.3

Meditation

Meditation, contemplation, and intelligent mobilisation of attention have much to offer as a way to not only recover peace in an extreme situation, but also to trigger a deep understanding that will have a positive (and hopefully, lasting) impact on the guest. Meditation can awaken a pure self-awareness, peaceful consciousness, and blissful acceptance. However, it is important to note that there have been rare cases of people suffering unwelcome mental disturbances when engaging in dedicated meditation; especially when in a strong altered state of consciousness to begin with, some people might find that meditation increases their unpleasant symptoms. In a Buddhist monastery, this would be understood as a normal (and temporary) phase of spiritual growth. Yet in "normal" modern Western society, this cultural perspective is lacking; such instances are usually treated as mental illness and suppressed. Ideally, the care giver would be personally familiar with meditation, and have the experiential certainty that a very dark and negative state can be transformed or dissipated if properly approached.

There are many kinds of meditation, hence the term "meditation" means different things to different people. Guests who are quietly sitting in the care space, appearing to be doing nothing, may in fact be actively meditating by themselves, perhaps due to the sheer force of their experiences. Hopefully, such people will be able to resolve their own difficulties without further assistance, and they simply require a safe space in which to do so.

A guest who is in need of direct assistance may benefit from being led through a guided meditation; this consists of an experienced care giver encouraging the guest to relax whilst sitting or lying in a comfortable way (preferably with a straight back) and then asking the guest to bring contemplative attention to one (or a series of) thing(s), such as imagining a flower of a particular colour, or paying attention to their own breathing. However, a guest may often be too physically and mentally stimulated to sit or lie relatively still in order to attempt meditation, and other more active therapies should be considered.

The following books discuss some practical methods of directing attention towards the transformation of suffering:

Kabat-Zinn, J. (2013). *Full Catastrophe Living: Using the Wisdom of Your Body and Mind to Face Stress, Pain, and Illness.* New York: Bantam Books.

Wolinsky, S. (2006). *Hearts on Fire: The Tao of Meditation.* California: Quantum Institute, Inc.

COMPLEMENTARY THERAPIES

Yoga

Care givers may offer guests the opportunity to engage in some bodywork, enhanced body awareness, and light stretching; all this can be done through (gentle) hatha yoga, among other possibilities. Yoga can be of help to ease a guest into a grounded state, and to aid in harmonising body and mind through the clear flow of energy.

In some cases, a yoga (or other bodywork) session in the peak of a psychedelic trip can be a great experience, which at the same time relieves anxiety. However, in other cases it can (at least in the beginning of the session) enhance anxiety because of the increased energy flow and awareness. Guests should be informed that they are, of course, free to stop at any time.

The care giver offering a yoga session should be aware of the state of the guest, and not push the idea of yoga too much if the guest has experienced a strong energy awakening, since yoga could bolster this powerful energy and make the experience much more dramatic and intense. If a guest consents to bringing this on, in order to attempt to resolve an internal crisis, then it may be acceptable to engage in deeper yogic exercises.

Nude yoga should never be suggested by or involve the care giver. Photo by Anonymous.

12.5 Tai chi and qigong exercises are slow, graceful forms of martial arts, using harmonious, balanced movements around a grounded core; this slow-motion flow is great for calming, focusing, and centring a person. People who do not already know a routine of moves will require someone experienced to lead by demonstration.

Massage

12.6 **It is generally good** to have at least one care giver who is a trained masseur or masseuse, to treat people who are tense (and who consent) to a massage—including tired care team members! It is important to remember to *ask permission* from an individual before treating them in this way. Massage performed by untrained hands can still have a calming influence, but such untrained staff should avoid any strong manipulations that may have adverse effects; these care givers may wish to stick to simple neck-and-shoulder, feet, or head massages. People with some training in reflexology may also choose to work on particular areas of the hands and feet that relate to mental processes. In our context, this is not strictly a matter of physical therapy, nor of sensual pleasure; the aim is to assist in dissolving emotional/mental and physical tension. The care giver offering a massage should be of clear and pure intent, and preferably be skilful and experienced in detecting those places where the guest is manifesting tension. Massage should be discontinued if the guest being worked on shows any signs of sexual arousal, in line with the ethics of psychedelic support. Likewise, any touching in massage should avoid potentially erogenous spots on the areas such as front torso, upper thighs, buttocks, genitals, and the surrounding areas.

Reiki

12.7 **Reiki requires** a practitioner, and a guest willing to lie or sit and relax with eyes closed whilst the Reiki session takes place. The intention of Reiki is to direct the clear flow of the guest's portion of vital/universal energy by "laying on of the hands" without actually touching the guest. Reiki practitioners believe that the energy flows through the therapist and becomes captured by the recipient (the guest), according to the recipient's need, without any negative interaction of each other's energy. It is a safe and gentle complementary practice that can bring peace, balance, reduce anxiety, and dissolve emotional blockages. As it doesn't require actual touching, it is a good alternative to massage with guests who are uncomfortable being touched, or in order to avoid the possibility of sexual arousal.

COMPLEMENTARY THERAPIES

General Physical Activities

Taking part in some simple activity, particularly in nature, can be very beneficial in shifting the mindset of the guest. This may work by providing a distraction, or a new area of focus, or even just by becoming active in a recreational way, with any attendant positive changes in the nervous system that such activity may bring. Activities beyond the actual care space should be supervised by a care giver, and the guest may feel more comfortable and able to find benefits if the care giver takes part in the activities as well. Some suggested activities with positive potential include going for a walk, going for a swim or a dip in water, and non-contact recreational games such as throwing and catching a ball or a Frisbee.

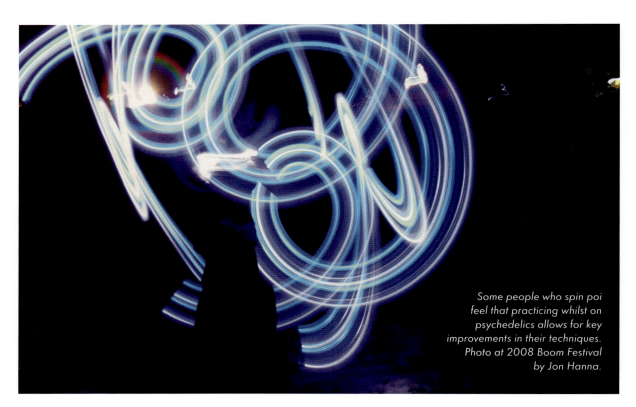

Some people who spin poi feel that practicing whilst on psychedelics allows for key improvements in their techniques. Photo at 2008 Boom Festival by Jon Hanna.

Shamanic Therapies

Shamanism and altered states of consciousness naturally go together, whether the guest has intended this or not. Situations that may best be understood from a shamanic or healing perspective often arise when people undergo difficult psychedelic experiences. However, as this Manual is largely confined to operating within a system of "sitting but not guiding", the intervention of a "shaman", or attempts to engage the guest in a guided shamanic voyage, are ethically precluded without explicit consent from the guest. Nevertheless, there remain some techniques that guests could try themselves that may help and cannot hurt.

For example, some experienced users of ayahuasca find that troubling visions can be dispelled by "blowing them away" with the vital force and intent of focused breath. An attitude of humble fearlessness can be encouraged, and guests may call on a protector (such as the spirit of an animal with which the guest feels an affinity; guardian angels, if the guest's religious beliefs support such beings; the spirits of a guest's ancestors; or God, if the guest feels this is appropriate) to assist them in bravely facing what is troubling them.

Philosophical Enquiry

Guests may be able to find a way out of their "problem states" if they are cleverly questioned about what they are experiencing. A guest doesn't need to be fully functional for the freeing effect of well-adjusted enquiry to take place. Such questioning can give birth not only to great and deep existential and philosophical insights that dissolve the "bad trip", but also to a certain level of lasting understanding. In a way, this approach is a variety of the Socratic method, triggering insights in the mind and in the heart of the guest. If the care giver is calm, genuinely warm-hearted, kind, and patient—absolutely confident in creating the perception that the guest can consciously disassemble and overcome a "problem state"—then a good configuration is in place for the play of questions to unfold.

There is no real recipe for learning the skill of asking the right question or the right set of questions at the right time, in the right way. However the study of neuro-linguistic programming, for example (or other approaches that have developed tools to precisely model and deconstruct a state or a skill), can be employed to "reverse engineer" the creation of the state and the fixation of attention that the guest is engaged in. Care givers might ask themselves, "Regarding this unique person in this unique situation, which questions could help this individual become aware that he or she is bigger than the state being experienced, that this state can be deconstructed, and that inspiration can come through the channel of intuition?"

The kinds of questions that are helpful should bring the guest to consciously direct their attention towards a precise aspect of their experiences, investigate it, and give up certainties and presuppositions that will ultimately be recognised as being only thoughts that are harmless bubbles in their awareness. With such questioning, attention follows a process of naturally de-fixating—ungluing itself from what has trapped it—and recovering its freedom for creating and experiencing what is here and now.

Such questioning will not work with everybody all of the

COMPLEMENTARY THERAPIES

time, but when it does work it is a great exploration both for the care giver and the guest. It works very well for anxiety or guilt; for example, "Could you teach me to be as anxious as you are now?" worked very well with one person under the influence of LSD. He was exaggerating all the thoughts and worries he was having, thus not allowing his attention to move on. At some point (and this was a clear sign of the shift), he was introducing humour into his explanation of how to create anxiety (what to think about, where to focus, and how to fix one's attention).

"How do you know you are correct to create guilt right now? How do you prove that you need to experience this guilt?" worked well with another person under the influence of cannabis. Playing with doubt and certainty, he realised that the guilt he was experiencing had no real grounds and no creator other than himself. This realisation led him from a "bad trip" to deep existential and philosophical insights.

Sometimes a nonsensical question before or after "intelligent" questions can precipitate the deep shift and freeing of attention (and we really do mean a nonsensical question, rather than a Zen koan).

In some cases the guest will start to resist the questioning after a while. At such a point, it is often appropriate to stop. Nevertheless, something happens even when resisting the rise of awareness expansion. We remember a young man coming out of the influence of a strong dose of LSD, who was not yet back into an ordinary state. After a while he said, "Too much questions!" But he said this in a way that meant, "I got it, there is no real problem. Okay? Let me enjoy what is left of my 'problem' state!" Freedom was there, and awareness was back in the driving seat.

Recommended readings:

Books on neuro-linguistic programming by Robert Dilts; see http://www.nlpu.com/NewDesign/NLPU.html

Books by Stephen H. Wolinsky; see http://stephenhwolinskyphdlibrary.com/downloads.html

Fenner, P. (2007). *Radiant Mind: Awakening Unconditioned Awareness*. Canada: Sounds True, Inc.

Exposure to Beauty

By exposure to beauty, we mean offering guests the option of putting their attention towards something powerfully beautiful or awe-inspiring, whatever that might be: a quote, an object, something in nature, a sensation, an expression of art, and so forth (for art therapy, see below). When in an

12.11

altered state of consciousness the effect of this activity on the guest can be profound, and potentially turn around a difficult experience. There is intuitive skill involved in choosing how to suggest this redirection of attention, to contemplate an expression of beauty with a certain freshness and spontaneity. The care giver should have an understanding of the workings of attention in general and what we could call a playfulness and lightheartedness with all the possibilities that are at hand. When a redirection of attention is offered or suggested—ideally without even being noticed—it should be presented as an option, not a duty.

Beauty is in the eye of the beholder. What is viewed as beautiful or inspiring is different for different people. Also, something a person may normally find beautiful could be experienced as horrifying or simply uninteresting when in an altered state of consciousness, and vice versa.
Directing the attention towards the ugly or horrible, or allowing one's self to contemplate such things, is of equal value in developing a balanced and realistic experience of life—indeed, a person may realise that there is beauty even in these things, and learn not to judge by appearances and/or conditioned responses to them. However, it may simply make the situation worse to fill the imagination with (what a guest finds to be) horrible images; so for the sake of assisting an individual to move out of a difficult space, such an approach should not be promoted by care givers (although guests may choose to look at whatever they wish).

Experience has shown that exposure to well-chosen imagery can be effective with cases of anxiety and paranoia. Let's illustrate this with a story. A man in his mid-forties was starting to regress deeply into memories of his birth, and was experiencing anxiety and strong physical pain. He was instructed by the sitter that it was okay to fully experience whatever arose, and to trust the unfolding and blossoming of this memory without resisting. At this point, he started to become a little bit paranoid, whilst at the same time describing lucidly his projection on the sitter, who was hallucinated as the devil with vivid imagery. The situation was becoming very problematic: rising anxiety, rising paranoia, strong hallucinations, and physical pain possibly due to resistance. In other words, it was becoming a hellish state. The sitter spontaneously presented a high-quality and beautiful picture of an Indian mystic (Sri Anandamayi Ma). Since the man was in a strong psychedelic phase, he started to see the face in 3-D and the body within the picture gave the impression of coming out of the page. At the same time he was amazed and awed by the beauty of what he was seeing and the archetypal dimension of what he was connecting with. At that point anxiety was dissolved in wonder, and paranoia was no more. The only

Painting at the 2013 Lightning in a Bottle Festival near Lake Skinner. Photo by David Arnson.

thing left was an intense energy state which wasn't all pleasant, but which was stabilised by contact with a tree (see "Tree Grounding" below).

Another example again featured a case of strong anxiety, which was poetically dissolved whilst the guest, who was lying down, was offered the opportunity to contemplate the dance of the falling petals of the flowers of a cherry tree that the care giver was shaking, offering a kind of petal shower. Here, wonder beholding beauty acted to dissolve the anxiety. The surrounding nature was in this case the ally, and whenever nature is available as an ally in its demonstration of beauty, it should be offered as a source of contemplation for a guest in difficulty.

Viewing beautiful films can engage and inspire a guest, and also divert and distract attention from negative thought streams. Powerful non-verbal films are especially appropriate, as they are less likely to confuse a guest in an altered state. Headphones and a laptop or tablet computer should be used to prevent the film disturbing others in the care space.

Art Therapy

Both looking at art (see also "Exposure to Beauty" above), and creating their own art, can be beneficial to guests. Each gives the guests a focus for their attention that may lead to healing thought processes, helping the guests work through whatever personal issues may be giving rise to psychologi-

12.12

Creating art whilst under the effect of a psychedelic can be very rewarding. Byron Bay Acid by Zevic Mishor, 2010.

12.13

cal difficulties. Any art used to decorate the space may be repurposed for viewing and meditation, and it may also be desirable to have appropriate art books for guests to look through. Some basic art supplies—such as paper, pencils, water-based paints, brushes, and modelling clay—may be kept on hand in case they are requested or a care giver wishes to offer them.

Music Therapy

In general, there is not likely to be any music playing openly in the care space, due to the difficulties of pleasing everybody, especially with numerous guests present in strongly altered states. However, music can play a powerful role in changing the direction and content of a psychedelic experience; when chosen wisely, it can be exquisitely fascinating and even enlightening. Conversely, some music may make a guest's experience even more difficult and intense. How a person reacts to any given choice of music in such a state of mind may vary at different times and in different circumstances, and of course, depending on their personal tastes. A good compromise to enable access to music (should the guest request it) is to have available some kind of device to play recorded music through headphones or earphones, so that a guest may listen without affecting others. It would be helpful for at least one care team member, enthusiastic about music, to assemble selections of tracks from a wide range of styles into playlists that may be acceptable and enjoyable to people in powerful states of consciousness. Compilations

COMPLEMENTARY THERAPIES

of such playlists could be shared online between different teams, to help encourage the collection of tried-and-tested music, so that a wide variety of potentially appropriate music is readily available if needed.

Instrumental music is preferable, because lyrical content may be inappropriate for guests in fragile and suggestible states. Generally, fast, dark, or disturbing music should be avoided. However, if the guest is a fan of heavy metal, for example, it may be that the music the guest loves gives him or her the strength and grounding to transition out of whatever hell the person is trapped in; for another individual, however, the same music may *take* that person *to* hell! Guests may discover that they find solace in a style of music they normally wouldn't listen to, such as classical music or improvised jazz. In these states, music can serve as a meditational focus, giving listeners something to become absorbed in and think about other than their previous distressing thoughts and feelings; or, music can become a vivid accompaniment to the movement of those thoughts and feelings, carrying the guests through their experiences on painted chariots of sound rather than leaving them to struggle on foot, so to speak. When a person really identifies with the music, it can move the mind in ecstatic ways and may even help steer the guest's experience towards a melodic resolution.

Biofeedback Devices

Biofeedback devices measure and monitor some physiological data (such as heart rate, body temperature, skin conductivity, brainwave frequencies) and offer a real-time representation of this data (usually visual and auditory feedback, such as a flashing LED and a beeping sound), enabling users of these devices to train their minds and bodies to be consciously adjusted into more relaxed states. There are several biofeedback devices on the market today—at reasonable prices—that may be useful to help a person experiencing difficult states to obtain some relief.

For people who are not familiar with meditation, or who find meditation to be difficult, biofeedback devices may allow quicker entry into a meditative state, if the appropriate frequency is selected. Caution should be exercised when using devices such as "strobe goggles", as a guest may be susceptible to epileptic fits under the intense stimulation.

Tree Grounding

Healing with trees is an option that has to be considered seriously due to its high efficacy, its riskless aspect in the huge majority of cases, and its easy availability in many situations (although perhaps not in the middle of Burning

Man or other treeless spaces). Tree grounding can bring harmonisation and pacification of a difficult and powerful psychedelic state, thanks to the presence and "structure" of the tree (both physical and metaphysical, as explored deeply in shamanism). The effect is very positive and can provide excellent results in cases of anxiety, sensory overload, loss of vitality and coordination in the body, and for people who are flying high but off-centre, or concerned by their loss of cognitive or physical functionality. In some cases, when an individual is strongly resisting an experience (because it is not the right moment to go deep into an issue, for example), tree grounding allows the person to dissipate some of the powerful energy, which can be "safely absorbed" by the tree. For people experiencing paranoia or mistrust of others, a tree can be a neutral friend they can turn to. There is no need for any particular beliefs, skills, or world view for this to work. All that is required is a willingness to try it and open up to whatever may happen. Of course, the care giver having personal experience with this and also taking part—as with anything else—will definitely help to give the guest faith in the therapeutic possibilities, rather than worrying about looking or feeling silly by hugging a tree.

The idea here is to offer and structure an opportunity for a guest in which their heightened and amplified sensitivity, imagination (possibly hallucinations), and empathy are focused in sensing a chosen tree, identifying with this tree, and naturally (that is, without any conscious intent in this direction, and simply as a by-product of the special attention paid to the tree in this intense state) experiencing a sense of being grounded and at peace. In other words, the expansion of sensitivity and perception that may have led to anxiety and a problem state is put into the service of restoring well-being and peace through an intense empathic connection with a tree, either by touch or by sitting near it. With the kind encouragement and presence of the care giver, the guest can either simply contemplate the tree or get very physical with it, hugging it, or leaning against it and merging with it, with a sense of the spine becoming the trunk, experiencing the deep roots as being nourishing and stable.

In some rare cases, a guest can be overwhelmed by the amazing perceptions experienced when connecting with a tree, and the guest may feel anxious and want to disconnect. Unless the care giver has subtle perceptions of what is happening and can imagine and suggest options to dissolve this anxiety, so that the guest will fully enter the positive grounding aspect, then the guest's desire for disconnection must be respected.

COMPLEMENTARY THERAPIES

In other, less-rare cases, becoming "one" with the tree and being pacified by it transforms into making love to the tree, with highly aroused sexual energy exhibited. Women, especially, may sometimes fuse with a gigantic phallus and experience strong orgasmic waves. This may be a very positive thing for the guest, but the care giver will have to check that allowing this energy to unfold is okay within the context of the situation, and that the dignity of the guest can be protected from onlookers.

Practical concerns in choosing a tree include checking that there are no sharp spines, sticky sap, poison ivy, wasps, ants, stinging caterpillars, or similar deterrents present.

Aromatherapy

Essential oils and aromatic natural substances can be useful in facilitating calmer states of mind in distressed people. Essential oils are usually dispersed into an indoor area with the aid of vapourisers or tea-light "burners", which heat a mixture of water and essential oils from below. More simply, a bottle of essential oil can be uncapped and held under the nose to inhale the scent. "Aromatic oils" are cheap imitations of essential oils, or blends containing mostly alcohol, and should be avoided.

Burning blended incenses in the care space should generally be avoided as some people may find the smoke irritating, and the aroma crude and heady. The team might wish to have oil vapourisers constantly in use throughout the space, though care should be taken to select scents that most people are likely to find pleasant and therapeutic. For example, many people find patchouli to be too cloying, and some people find scents such as rose geranium and balm of Gilead to be unpleasant. On the other hand, scents including sandalwood, rose, clary sage, tangerine, lavender, lemon balm, lemongrass, and sweet basil are pleasant and acceptable to a large range of people, and can have relaxing and uplifting effects. Peppermint is believed to improve concentration, relieve shock and nausea, and it can also be a mild stimulant (see "Herbal Teas" below). One consideration against the use of essential oils in the care space is that a small minority of people have allergic reactions to a variety of otherwise innocuous scents.

Herbal Teas

In the context of psychedelic care, strongly stimulating herbal teas should be avoided. Relaxing teas and those with noteworthy antioxidant properties are most appropriate. Some common herbs have properties that are usually harmless, but which may strengthen or alter the effects of some medications or psychoactive drugs that the guest may have consumed. For example, passionflower (*Passiflora incarnata*) is often used as a sedative and anxiolytic (relieves anxiety), but its mild inhibition of monoamine oxidase (MAO) enzymes in the body may strengthen the effects of some psychoactives, and/or have unforeseen interactions with some antidepressants. St. John's wort (*Hypericum perforatum*) should also be avoided; it is a weak MAOI that increases serotonin levels, which may be contraindicated with some recreational psychoactives. To avoid breaching the duty of care, large doses of any herbs should not be administered in this context if normal doses appear to be having no effect. Herbs that are generally accepted as safe may not be so for all people if very large amounts are taken at one time or over an extended period.

Some examples of useful herbs are listed below. Note that "infusion" here refers to soaking the herb(s) in water that has just come to the boil; usually with caffeinated tea the infusion takes place for only a few minutes before the herb or tea bag is removed; however, with many herbal teas, where astringent tannins are not as much of an issue, the herb or bag may be left in the cup whilst the tea is being drunk.

CAMOMILE

Camomile (*Anthemis*, *Chamaemelum* and *Matricaria* species) generally has sedative, anxiolytic, antispasmodic and mild analgesic effects. The flowers, and sometimes the leaves and stems, are prepared by infusion. Note that because camomile may cause uterine contractions that can lead to miscarriage, the United States National Institutes of Health recommend that pregnant and nursing mothers avoid consuming it; keep in mind that women may sometimes be pregnant without yet knowing of their condition.

HOPS

Hops (*Humulus lupulus*, female flowers) are generally used in beer brewing for their bitterness, although they also have calming sedative properties and are used for this reason in herbal medicine. Hops may be prepared by infusion. The main drawback is that the herb is very bitter and the taste may not be tolerated, although honey can help somewhat with this.

LAVENDER

Lavender (*Lavandula* species) has anti-inflammatory and antiseptic effects, and it has been purported to help with depression and anxiety, possibly due in part to the aroma of the herb, which most people find very pleasant and comforting. It may be prepared by infusion (usually blended with other herbs), or the herb or its essential oil may be used in aromatherapy (see "Aromatherapy" above). Fresh flowering cuttings can simply be handled lightly and held to the nose for smelling, and they're also beautiful to look at in a psychedelic state.

LEMON BALM

Lemon balm (*Melissa officinalis*) has relaxing tonic properties, can improve mood and enhance mental performance, and may also relieve nausea and headaches. It can be prepared by infusion, or the herb or its essential oil may be used in aromatherapy (see "Aromatherapy" above).

LIMEFLOWER

Limeflower (or lime tree), also known as linden and basswood (*Tilia* spp.), is not related to the citrus lime. It is used as a sedative nerve tonic, and relieves muscle tension and high blood pressure. It should be used in moderation in this context, as some limeflower constituents (such as kaempferol) have, or may have (such as quercetin) MAO-inhibiting activity, which may strengthen the effects of some psychoactives. It can be prepared by infusion.

PEPPERMINT

Peppermint (*Mentha x piperita*) is a mild stimulant, and may be helpful if a guest is in a state of shock or feeling nauseated. It can be prepared by infusion, or the herb or its essential oil can be used in aromatherapy (see "Aromatherapy" above).

ROOIBOS

Rooibos or red bush tea (*Aspalathus linearis*) has become popular outside of its native South Africa as a tea substitute, although it contains no caffeine (or similar alkaloids), nor does it act as a stimulant. It is of interest here due mainly to its antioxidant properties, which may be helpful to anyone who is under stress (due to drug use, staying awake for long periods, working too hard, and so forth). The herb is rich in ascorbic acid (vitamin C, which also might help take the edge off a powerful psychedelic experience), as well as minerals and protein. Additionally, it is a mild antispasmodic. However, rooibos also contains quercetin, which may have a MAO-inhibiting effect that could strengthen the effects of some psychoactives. It is prepared by infusion, often with milk and honey stirred in.

ROSEHIP

Rosehips are the dried fruits of the "dog rose" (*Rosa canina*); they are made by infusion into a pleasant-tasting tea that is rich in vitamin C.

SKULLCAP

Skullcap or scullcap (*Scutellaria lateriflora*) is a sedative and antispasmodic nerve tonic. The main drawback of the herb is its unpleasant bitterness. It is prepared by infusion, though it may be best in blends that improve the flavour, as well as with honey.

VALERIAN

Valerian (*Valeriana officinalis*) generally acts as a sedative, anxiolytic, and nerve tonic, although in people who are already fatigued, or with old herb, it may instead have stimulating effects. Roots more than one year old should not be used. Due to concerns of potential cytotoxicity in the fetus and hepatotoxicity in the mother, it is recommended that women avoid consumption of valerian root during pregnancy. The roots are prepared by infusion; often an alcohol tincture may be used, diluted in water.

Burning Man, 2003. Photo by Jon Hanna.

COMPLEMENTARY THERAPIES

LUKE GRAY • *PMS, 2013* • Staedtler Triplus Fineliner and watercolour
http://www.lukegray.net

CHAPTER 13
TEAM WELFARE

Svea Nielsen

João Gonçalves

This chapter intends to be a microcosm of the macrocosm, as the team's welfare is like a mirror of the welfare they'll be able—or *unable*—to provide to guests who come to the psychedelic care service. Here we wish to offer some basic suggestions regarding what is important in order to run a care service from the perspective of the team working in this environment. As many of these points have been raised in other chapters of the Manual, here we intend to briefly summarise them and make them easily accessible.

The Importance of Team Welfare for the Entire Project

In many care service projects that we've seen, the main focus is placed on the guests who will be provided with care, and the team *behind* that care becomes too easily forgotten. Hence, in this chapter we provide some tips and advice that will help the whole project: both the guests and the project's main drivers, the care givers! The care givers have key positions in many additional areas that these kinds of projects seek to fulfil, not solely related to the direct care of the guests. Care givers, for example, are the people who promote these types of projects and create them at events. They are also the people who educate members of the public about the therapeutic, philosophical, and spiritual uses of psychedelics, as opposed to the drugs' negative and often frightening "recreational" image, which is common in most modern societies.

The Basic Needs

The starting point concerns the basic needs of the team. Events may take place in very harsh conditions in terms of weather, camp arrangements, and noise, not to mention the toll taken by working day after day (depending on the event duration) with guests in crisis. The care service leader must ensure that the team has the following four basic needs fulfilled:

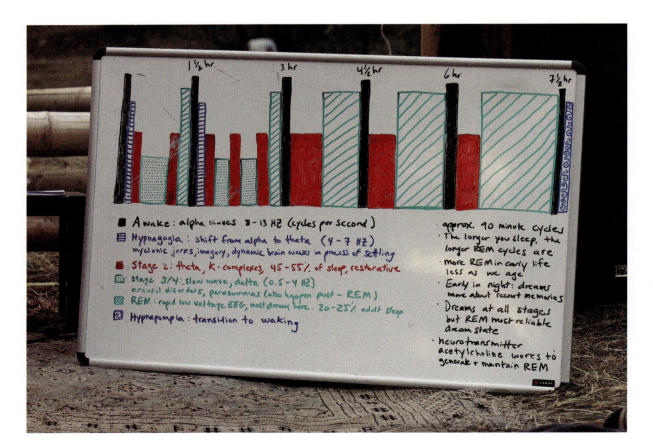

Clearly, it was very important for everyone at the 2009 Symbiosis Festival to be getting enough sleep. Photo by Erowid.

- **Water:** Direct access to water is imperative.

- **Food:** Is it provided by the event organiser or not? Will the care service prepare its own food? Whatever the arrangements, hungry care givers make for stressed and unhappy care givers.

- **Sleep:** Does everybody have a proper place to rest?

- **Hygiene:** Convenient access to toilets and showers is a must.

The General Working Environment

The quality of the general working environment, and especially relations within the team, is as important as the above basic needs in ensuring a harmonious, effective, and fun care service. Several topics, especially regarding leadership, have already been raised in Chapter 7, "Building and Training a Team". Here we return to some of those points and consider a few additional aspects.

It is recommended that name tags be worn by all care givers. If some care givers prefer to remain anonymous, they might be encouraged to choose a nickname, pseudonym, or even a number for their name tag. Name tags are very useful in helping the team to get to know one other, and in allowing guests to know the team. Flags from various countries can be added to the name tags in order to indicate the language(s) spoken by each care giver.

Shifts should be clearly defined in advance so that care givers can plan when to rest, when to party, and when they are working. Time must be allowed between shifts to enable the outgoing and incoming teams to exchange information regarding guests, general running of the service, and so forth. Therefore, teams coming on shift should arrive 15–30 minutes early, to enable a proper handover to occur. The roles and responsibilities of care givers should be made clear so that, without too much hierarchy, they still know where they can find help or advice when in need. The team lead has a key role in arranging shift rosters and allocating tasks to individual care givers. Team leads also have a key role to play in the motivation of the entire team; this begins with *leadership by personal example*. Leads must also remember to provide care givers with feedback about their work, and to generally, regularly, and sincerely enquire about their well-being. We recommend creating a system allowing volunteers to make suggestions, verbally or in writing, to express their own challenges and to present new ideas or solutions they may have discovered.

Help the Team to Help Itself

Ideally, the care service team should run smoothly and be an exemplar of harmonious collaborative work. Team-building sessions, in the course of training, will assist in achieving this goal. At the beginning of the project it can be helpful to make a list of relevant skills possessed by individual care givers; for example, those who can offer massage, homeopathy, or have a good knowledge of drug–drug interactions. This list should be available at a central notice board in the care service, so that everyone has access to it.

It is important to encourage care givers to debrief with one another. The changeover time between shifts is usually allocated for a more practical and formal exchange of information, so care givers should use quiet times (on- or off-shift), meal times, or chance meetings and other moments spent together, to share thoughts and feelings on a deeper level.

Since team leads may be overwhelmed by moment-to-moment circumstances and be generally quite busy, it is recommended that the team look after itself; a well-formed and cohesive team can do this. Care givers should check periodically with one another to see how everyone is doing. Shifts are long, and care givers may be having their own fair share of spiritual and/or party experiences when off shift, affecting their ability to cope with other

people's crises. Care givers should therefore be encouraged to share their experiences and emotional states with one another, or just to check every now and then to make sure that the other team members are doing okay. Even the most experienced and committed care giver can get into difficult places at unexpected moments, and the team has to be ready to support them.

Let the Team Run in a Chaordic Way

In the end, we hope that your team will be able to feel comfortable enough within the project, and with their physical and emotional needs met, to be able to work in a *chaordic* way. "Chaordic" refers to what some people believe is a fundamental organising principle of evolution and nature. It is the behaviour of any self-governing organism, organisation, or system that harmoniously blends characteristics of chaos and order, with neither element dominating the other (Hock 1999). Accordingly, we believe that if the care service team feels well taken care of, it will rise to meet any issues—small or large—that occur during the course of its work with all of its creative ability and resources. Team members themselves, as well as the guests, can only benefit and grow from such an approach.

References

Hock, D. (1999). *Birth of the Chaordic Age*. Berkeley, California: Berrett-Koehler Publishers.

Training the KosmiCare team at the 2012 Boom Festival. Photo by Susana Santos.

MARTINA HOFFMANN • *Alien Ascension, 2007* • oil on canvas
http://www.martinahoffmann.com

CHAPTER 14

WORKING WITH OTHER ORGANISATIONS

Annie Oak

Natacha Ribeiro

Whilst providing a psychedelic care service, the care service leader should strive to work effectively with other organisations on-site. This section offers practical suggestions for how to approach and build relationships with the event organisers, medical services, and security personnel. It also offers helpful tips on how to fit into the existing services, publicise the care service, and adjust to the culture of the event. For those producing care services at events in countries that support the on-site testing of drugs, this chapter will consider the benefits of such testing and other harm-reduction strategies. Some of the topics covered in this chapter are also discussed in Chapter 4, "Planning and First Steps for a New Project", and we recommend that you consult the material there, too.

Contacting Event Organisers

14.1

A well-developed care service can offer great benefits to event organisers, allowing them to provide targeted assistance and complement existing resources. When approaching a festival where a care service may be welcome, the potential care service leader (or leadership team) should first examine the existing services that will be available at the event. They should also determine which event organisers are the primary contacts for proposing a psychedelic care service. If the top organisers have delegated the event's medical and/or mental health services to a subgroup of outside contractors, the care service leader should first contact the central group of organisers and then ask for introductions to outside staff or subcontractors as required.

Once the care team have determined whom to speak with, they should prepare a brief presentation of the services that they would like to offer and begin a dialogue with event organisers to discuss how they could contribute. Appropriate written materials describing the care service should be offered, along with the names of contacts and their qualifications. Parts of this Manual provide examples of written material that may be presented as evidence of the well-considered, rigorous, and professional approach that the care service will adopt and exemplify.

Throughout these discussions, the care team can determine what services are planned for the event and how they can appropriately tailor their own offerings to compliment the culture and expectations of event organisers. If event organisers indicate that they might indeed welcome a psychedelic care service, the care team should share information about their staff selection process and their training strategy. They should indicate who would be the main care service contact people (the care service leaders) during the event, and whether they are seeking help in staffing the care service.

Determining Possible Sponsorship

14.2

The care service leader should also determine whether the event organisers can afford to fund some or all of the care service. Can the event provide free tickets, lodging, and/or meals for care givers? Is there an existing physical structure that can be used for the care space, or can the event help defray the cost of establishing a shelter? If the care service is planning on setting up their own structure, they may need to work with those in charge of placement at the event to determine where the care team can camp or lodge during the event.

The care service leader might also explore the possibility of selling some sort of product or food item at the event to help defray the cost of the care service. At events where sales are made, the care service can inform customers that proceeds from the sales will help cover the cost of aiding festival participants in psychedelic crisis. The care team could also—with approval from event organisers—explore possible outside sponsorship, or hold fundraising parties to assist in covering the expenses to provide the service.

Working with Event Medical Services

If appropriate, the care service should work with core organisers to develop complimentary procedures for working with existing medical services. Any such procedures must, of course, be intimately coordinated with the care team's internal medical procedures (see also Chapter 6, "Supporting Roles"), and indeed, the care team's psychiatrist(s), medic(s), and nurse(s)—if they exist—should be instrumental in the formulation of these complimentary procedures. The care service team could work with existing emergency medical services at an event to develop, for example, protocols that would be included in the training of their respective staffs. Each team could be shown the exact location of each other's facilities, become familiar with their counterpart's intake and documentation procedures, and agree on what kinds of situations would best be served by each group. Care givers might be trained, for instance, to refer all medical questions and emergency medical needs to event medical staff, and set up a system to walk participants in need of medical care over, send a runner to get assistance, or contact medical staff via phone or radio. If members of the care team are expected to present information about participants they bring to medical services, a checklist of vital information should be provided that can be included in care giver training. Emergency medical providers should also be briefed on the role of the care service team and should train their staff to refer people in need of these services. Protocols for transferring guests and follow-up care could also be developed as needed by both groups.

Especially in cases when qualified medical professionals are not an organic part of the care service team, close communication between the care team and event medical services and/or the nearest hospital must be set up. This should be planned months prior to the event, with participation of the hospital management and the event organisation. All service details, such as medical transport from inside the event to a main road, and then to and from the hospital itself, must be determined in advance.

Direct communication between the care service team and event medical services should begin before the event. Ideally, there should be a gathering one or two days prior to the event's opening, in which medical professionals and care givers get to know one another and their respective specialties. This is especially important at small events, which are less likely to have medical professionals working directly within the care service. Event medical staff can share information with the care service team about what to look for in a possible emergency situation with a guest, and what steps to follow in such cases. Care givers should make sure that the event medical staff understand how they approach difficult psychedelic experiences. Members of the care team with first aid or emergency medical training should also identify themselves.

Making medical staff aware of how the care givers assist guests can be challenging because medical professionals may have little to no personal experience with altered states of consciousness—or have some level of discomfort with those who are under the influence of psychedelic substances. For this reason, training should ideally be delivered by health professionals from the care service who have some experience with psychoactives (and especially psychedelics). When possible, this training should include teaching medical staff the difference between treating a medical condition (such as cleaning a wound, for example) versus assisting a person having a difficult psychedelic experience. Medical staff should also be instructed how to act in a first contact with this kind of guest, and how to identify when someone is having a difficult experience. It would be beneficial to help them understand how vulnerable a person feels in this state, perhaps using analogies to treating those with psychiatric conditions or children, for example. All medical professionals, especially doctors, should be reminded to be on the lookout for any medical conditions that may alter consciousness, including dehydration, kidney or liver problems, infections, psychiatric and neurologic pathologies, and so forth.

Working with Event Security and Law Enforcement

14.4

Security services and law enforcement (that is, police) can work with the care service to direct participants to the care space. With the assistance of event organisers, the care service leader should make early contact with representatives of event security and law enforcement who will be on location during the event. The care team could present information to these groups about the services they offer and the physical location of the care space. Contact information can be exchanged between the care team leader and representatives from event security or law enforcement in order to allow for efficient communications, the seeking of assistance, and/or resolution of any questions during the event. Security and law enforcement are often relieved to have a place to bring highly altered participants where they can be cared for before rejoining the gathering. The care service should enquire about protocols used by these groups and develop a strategy for discussions with these personnel, if needed, in a private area outside of the main care space. If there is any possibility that law enforcement may be hostile to the activities of the care service, the care service leader should work with organisers to understand the rights of care givers and their guests, and to develop a system to request mediation or legal assistance if necessary. See Chapter 3, "Legal Considerations", for further information on this topic.

Working with Drug-Testing Services

In some jurisdictions events can provide services that allow their attendees to test drugs on-site. The results of these tests can potentially indicate if dangerous substances that may harm participants are being distributed. If testing services are available, a protocol should be developed to allow drug

Energy Control, a Spanish risk-reduction organisation, conducted thin-layer chromatographic drug testing for attendees at the 2008 Boom Festival. Photo by Jen Zariat.

testers to alert the care service to the presence of specific dangerous substances and how they are being distributed; this would help care givers to better assist event attendees who might be impacted. In such situations, it might also be possible to have substances tested that were ingested by those seeking support from the care service.

When drug-testing services are offered at an event, a protocol to alert event medical services may also be useful. If the drug testing is done off-site, arrangements should be made to rapidly test substances and quickly return the results during the event. Ensuring the privacy of participants during testing is an important consideration. The care service and event organisers should also discuss how information about possible dangerous substances might be publicised generally to participants at the event.

Publicising the Care Service

There are different ways to publicise that a care service will be available at an event. A description of the service and its location can be included in advertising for the event, or in programmes/schedules presented online, or in printed form at the event's entrance. Posters, stickers, and flyers can also provide information on-site about the care service (hang some in the bathrooms), as can radio programmes received by participants. Information services at the event could be told about the care service, and outreach to the press might include mention of it. Informing DJs and other performers who can make announcements from stage may also be a good strategy, as is simple word of mouth, encouraging participants to tell others that the service is available.

Some events may be hesitant to publicise a care service because they are concerned that it may somehow be interpreted as official sanctioning of drug use, or paint the gathering in an unflattering light. If this is the case, information about the care service could still be distributed to specific services on-site who can then provide referrals for participants in need. If there *is* no official psychedelic care service provided at an event, operators of chill spaces could use some of the concepts in this Manual to help train their staff in common sense approaches to assisting people in psychedelic crises without the benefit of organised services.

Learning from Other Organisations

Care services should be open to adapting approaches and best practices developed by groups that provide similar services. Those organising a care service should try to forge relationships with others working in this field, and include on board individuals with previous experience who can bring their knowledge to share with the group. See Chapter 17, "Online Resources and Obtaining Assistance", for a fairly detailed list of existing psychedelic care groups, as well as harm-reduction organisations providing related services, from around the world.

During the debriefing of care givers at the end of an event, information should be noted that could improve the next version of that care service, or indeed, assist other care services more generally. This data could be shared directly with other groups or used to update and expand this present Manual. Care givers can also use their own best judgement to test out new procedures or techniques in the field and then report back about their utility. As standards of care evolve, care givers should try to implement the most useful and effective techniques for providing assistance to guests. Updated information about how to work with other groups in an effective and collegial way can help make better use of existing expertise, with everyone benefiting.

PowerPoint projections provided daily drug-testing details at the 2008 Boom Festival. Photo by Erowid.

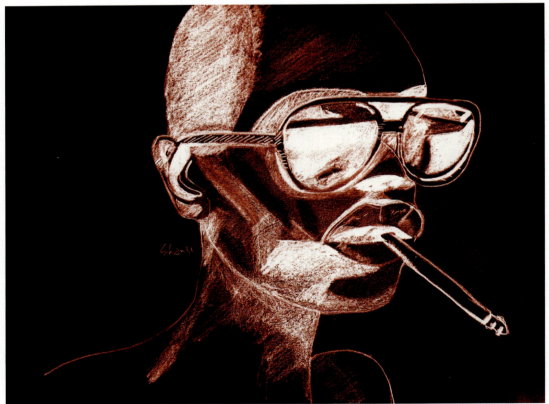

SHANTIQ • *ich bin sehr cool*, 2009 (top) • oil painting
aj24ebene, 2008 (bottom) • graphite pencil drawing
http://www.saatchiart.com/shantiq

CHAPTER 15
RISK MANAGEMENT AND PERFORMANCE IMPROVEMENT

Twilight

Risk management is a common-sense approach to minimising the likelihood of bad things happening to guests and care givers. This is fundamental harm reduction. Risk management is an essential discipline for anyone responsible for the organisation of harm-reduction efforts. Its applicability extends from very small gatherings to large festivals.

Risk management is important because it allows care givers to do the following:

- Gain increased awareness of the overall concept of risk minimisation

- Consider and anticipate what could go wrong in a situation

- Provide advanced mental preparedness for what might occur, and what steps could be taken to minimise adverse outcomes

- Do the right thing when the need arises

- Eliminate or minimise negative outcomes to guests and staff

- Minimise the likelihood of getting sued

The Fundamentals of Risk Management

Risk management can broadly be categorised into two fundamental components:

- Loss prevention: What actions can we take to minimise the possibility of adverse events?

- Loss control: When an adverse event has taken place, what actions can we take to minimise the present or future damage?

Loss prevention is about considering what potential risks exist in any given situation. Five questions need to be asked:

- What are the risks?

- How likely are they to occur?

- What are the consequences if they occur?

- How can we avoid them or minimise the possibility of their occurrence?

- What should we put in place to minimise the possibility of their occurrence?

Loss control is about what happens when something has already gone wrong. Three questions need to be asked:

- What can we do right now to make the situation better in the immediate future?

- What can we do to make the situation better in the longer term?

- What can we do to minimise our chances of being sued?

As an example, consider the scenario of an intoxicated participant falling from a tall art structure made of scaffolding and vibrantly coloured lights. Looking at the structure before participants arrive, we can apply loss prevention as a framework for understanding:

- What is the risk?

A participant, intoxicated or otherwise, is attracted to the colours, chooses to climb the art structure, falls, and sustains a serious injury.

- How likely is that to occur?

If it's an intriguing art structure and it appears to be climbable, we acknowledge that people may wish to climb it and therefore list it as a potential risk.

- What are the consequences if a participant falls from the structure?

There could be significant injury and/or mortality.

- How can we avoid this happening?

We could post cautionary signs advising participants not to climb.

We could have people stand guard at the base of the structure.

We could make it difficult to approach.

We could make it difficult to climb.

- What **should** we put in place to minimise the possibility of injury?

We could build fences and/or anti-climbers around the art structure, rendering it unattractive for people to attempt to climb.

Next let's consider a scenario where a group of intoxicated participants climbs the art structure, and the art structure partially collapses. One of the participants falls and breaks a leg. Immediately, we apply loss control measures:

Climbing onto art structures whilst inebriated is probably a bad idea. Uchronia, aka "The Belgian Waffle", was constructed on the playa at Burning Man in 2006 under the direction of artist Arne Quinze and entrepreneur Jan Kriekels. Photo by David Arnson.

- Assess the situation.
    1. Are the other climbing participants in danger?
    2. Is it safe to approach the injured participant?
    3. Might the structure collapse further?
    4. Could another climber fall from above?
    5. Are there exposed wires that could cause electrical shock?
    6. Who is available to help?
    7. How severe is the injury?
- Create a perimeter to keep curious onlookers away from the collapsed structure and the injured person.
- Get qualified medical assistance to the injured participant quickly.
- Safely assist the other climbers down from the structure.
- Stabilise the injured person and arrange for transport to an appropriate healthcare facility.
- Keep an open and honest communication with participants (and if necessary, the media).
- Document carefully every step taken to respond to the situation, care for the injured person, and do the right things (this could ultimately prove very useful in the event that legal action ensues).

Whether it involves sympathetic counselling for a distraught participant or the handling of a major catastrophe, the more situations that can be carefully thought through in advance, the more likely we will be better prepared to handle what comes our way. Flexibility and careful consideration for the needs of all participants are expected of all individuals associated with harm-reduction efforts.

Every individual associated with harm reduction should be encouraged to constantly assess and suggest ways in which participant assistance can be better delivered, as well as ways to minimise the liability of an adverse outcome.

Organising a Pre-Event Risk Assessment

To better prepare care givers, a group risk assessment exercise is encouraged. Ask staff to list as many items as they can that could conceivably go wrong. Prioritise those events into the likelihood of their occurrence, then categorise each item in terms of its severity if it were to happen (this typically

15.2

results in a lively discussion). This exercise focuses thought on what could happen that care service staff may reasonably be expected to deal with.

For the events that your group believe are reasonable to expect, decide how you will generally manage each of them. A simple framework:

- *Avoid:* Is there any way that the given risk could be avoided or eliminated in the first place?

- *Reduce:* What could be done to mitigate against the potential risk?

- *Share:* Is the responsibility of risk shareable with another party (for example, event medical services)?

- *Accept:* If none of the above are possible, your team should have a plan to completely handle this item.

If the risk falls squarely into your area of responsibility, discuss and create a loss control plan listing actions to be taken in the event that the risk materialises. Care givers should be trained in the processes and procedures set forth for each applicable risk.

Training staff in risk management techniques may be made easier through the use of illustrative published scenarios. In such a document, real-world examples are set forth for review. What was the originally perceived problem? What was done? What was ultimately discovered to be the underlying or actual problem? How was the problem resolved? How could the problem have been handled better?

Common Event Risks

Every event has its own specific risks, and these should be evaluated carefully. There are also risks that are common to most events. The following basic list presents risks that should be considered and addressed before the event. Common risks include:

Harm-reduction efforts that:

- Are inadequately funded

- Are insufficiently organised

- Are insufficiently staffed for the shifts and/or volume of affected participants

- Have insufficient support from event leadership

- Have insufficient availability of and/or access to trained medical emergency responders

RISK MANAGEMENT AND PERFORMANCE IMPROVEMENT

- Have insufficient means of safe, timely transportation for:
    1. *Staff needing to go to participants who require care*
    2. *Participants needing to go to the care space, and/or*
    3. *Guests needing to be taken to a licensed medical facility*
- Have a potentially adverse relationship with law enforcement
- Have insufficient processes and documentation (forms) for recording relevant events surrounding care that could be provided to medical responders and/or could be relied upon in a subsequent legal action

Care givers who:

- Are insufficiently organised
- Are insufficiently trained
- Are insufficiently prepared
- Are insufficiently insured, or uninsured
- Are overworked
- Are overstressed
- Are undernourished
- Are inadequately rested
- Do not have an effective means of rapid communication in adverse situations
- Show up for shifts in an altered state
- Attempt to provide care beyond their licensure and/or accreditation

A care site that:

- Is situated inappropriately because it is:
    1. *Too noisy*
    2. *Too far from medical services*
    3. *Too far from vehicle transportation*
- Has insufficient supplies
- Has insufficient privacy
- Has insufficient warmth and/or cooling
- Has insufficient support to safely handle a participant who becomes violent or combative

No amount of risk management efforts will encompass everything adverse that could happen. For the organisers, understanding and addressing the risks before the event is of substantial benefit as you plan your activities. With the information, understanding, and insights gained from the exercise, better plans and processes can be developed regarding how best to respond to unexpected/unforeseen events. When presented in training, the risk management exercises can help staff understand how to assess an evolving situation, consider the options available, and prepare for the best resolution possible.

15.4 Performance Improvement—Learning to Do Better from Our Experiences

In pursuing harm-reduction efforts, event organisers are acknowledging that some attendees will likely choose to participate in activities that are of risk to themselves, and these risks may be of such a nature as to require intervention by volunteers and/or event staff. Further, it would be wishful thinking to hope that over time, attendees will reduce or eliminate their choices of risky activities, when in all likelihood, the probability of increased risky activities will rise as an event grows in size.

Harm-reduction efforts are typically initiated when a perception of need meets one or more people with the responsibility and the determination to make them happen. Whilst this can occur through foresight and planning, harm-reduction activities often arise after a serious adverse event has occurred, or a series of lesser events has elevated such concern that the organisers realise that something should be done to prevent a serious event in the future.

Once harm-reduction activities are in place, however, the problems are not solved. Despite the best efforts of those responsible, adverse events may continue to take place or increase in number and severity. It is at this point that people begin to ask the question, "How can we do better?" This brings us to the topic of *performance improvement*. Please note that Appendix B, "Monitoring, Evaluating and Researching—Recommendations from an Academic Perspective for an Evidence-Based Approach to Psychoactive Crisis Intervention", also gives a comprehensive presentation on this subject.

15.5 How Do We Know How We're Doing?

There are different perspectives of performance. As harm-reduction leadership, at the end of an event we may ask the question, "How do we think we did?" Our answers may well be different than answers from the perspectives of the event organisers, the guests we looked after, or even the care givers themselves. Such is the nature of subjective perception.

To address this question and move it into the objective realm, we need to look at numbers that relate directly to some measurement of how well we did. These are our metrics, otherwise known as key performance indicators or performance measures. Whilst metrics may initially appear more appropriate in a business setting, they're how we can objectively quantify, account for, project, and sometimes defend our performance.

The following is a brief introduction to the use of metrics for performance improvement. There are many useful online references to performance improvement, and interested readers are encouraged to study them. The metrics used here are a starting point for illustrative purposes only; they may or may not be applicable for any given event.

Basic Metrics for Staffing and Volume of Service

Let's start with a count of how many staff hours were spent during the event looking after guests in our care space:

- How many people were trained to work as care givers?
- How many individuals worked as care givers?
- How many hours was our care space open?
- How many hours were worked by care givers?
- How many shifts were worked by care givers?
- How many shifts had fewer care givers working than we expected?

If we're staffing a care space, we'll have specific hours during which we wish to offer our services. We'll also have people signed up to work specific shifts during the event. We'll keep track of that in something like a duty roster, which will probably be maintained in a spreadsheet. This sets a baseline for performance and provides us with insights into our staffing and scheduling:

- How many people attended the event?
- How many people did we care for in our space?
    1. *Usually itemised by day*
    2. *Sometimes itemised for each hour of each day and/ or each shift*
- How long did each guest stay in the care space?

From these metrics, we start to get an idea of which of our shifts are popular and need more staff than others. When assessed with respect to the number of people attending the event, we can extrapolate for the next event what our staffing needs might be if the event had, say, 20% more participants.

Expenditures

- How much did we spend for harm reduction?

    1. Staff
    2. Infrastructure
    3. Training
    4. Durable equipment
    5. Supplies
    6. Transportation
    7. Food and beverages

- How many meals were served to care space guests?
- Number of vehicular transports to/from the care space?

We will often be asked to submit budgets and justify each line item in them. Every year, we should have a detailed record of what we spent, and how much more we could expect to spend if we increased our service levels, and/or the number of participants at the event increased.

Adverse Metrics: Things That Shouldn't Happen

Unlike volume and productivity statistics, adverse metrics are used to record events that should not happen. We can use these as items to study carefully and set targets for improvement in successive events.

INABILITY TO PROVIDE SERVICE

- How many participants did we turn away from our care space due to lack of care givers?
- How many participants waited for more than thirty minutes to be taken care of due to lack of care givers?
- On which days and between what hours did we turn away people in need or make them wait more than thirty minutes to be seen?

One of the first things we want to know is whether we had enough people to provide our intended service. Were we completely overrun with participants in need? Did we ever have to turn away participants in need because we didn't have the staff, or make them wait long periods of time before we could help them? If we answer "yes" to these questions, it's probably safe to say that we could have used more care givers. In preparing for the next event, we will look at what happened, then plan for and recruit more care givers so that we won't have delays in helping our guests.

If we can't take care of an individual in need due to staffing, that is a risk. If that person suffers a seriously adverse event due to our inability to care for him/her, we will have failed to provide the level of care we expected, and that was expected of us.

SERIOUS EVENTS

- Number of violent guest episodes in the care space
- Number of guests requiring urgent transfer to medical services
- Number of guests vomiting
- Number of guests apprehended from our care by law enforcement

SATISFACTION

- Number of guest complaints, typically grouped by category
- Number of care giver complaints, typically grouped by category
- Satisfaction survey scores

Complaints are unfortunate, yet they also represent an excellent opportunity to understand more about how performance could be improved. Each time a complaint is voiced, it should be recorded in writing and followed up on. Complaints should be evaluated and discussed during the event as close to the time that the cause of the complaint occurred as is possible. This allows for some situations to be resolved before the involved parties depart the event. Such resolutions can leave a lasting impression and can be very valuable in creating a positive perception of care space and harm-reduction activities.

Satisfaction surveys may be created and provided to participants to gain further insight into specific areas of harm-reduction operations. Generally, a satisfaction survey would include ten or fewer key items, and each item would be scored by the respondent on a descriptive basis of best to worst.

MY EXPERIENCE WITH CARE SPACE STAFF (CARE GIVERS) WAS:

Please check the box that most accurately reflects your opinion.

Thank You!

☐ Excellent
☐ Good
☐ Fair
☐ Poor
☐ Unacceptable
☐ Not Applicable

It is strongly recommended that any survey conclude with a question asking for an overall rating; something along the lines of: "All things considered, my experience with the care service was...". Despite whatever may have happened that brought them to the care space (which clearly may not have been pleasant), the overall score should focus on their perception of how well the care space served them.

Additional explanations or comments by survey respondents may provide details that can be quite useful in understanding the respondents' perceptions, as well as planning for how to do better in the future.

15.9 Ratios: Count Metrics Related to Volume Metrics

If metrics are to be used for purposes of evaluation over time, it is often useful to standardise them based on the volume of service as a denominator. Let's look at a simple metric:

- Percentage of total event participants using the care space

If over three successive years your care space served 60, then 100, than 150 participants, it would be a very different story if the total number of participants at the event was the same over those three years versus if it doubled each year. If the total event participants was the same, say 1,000, you clearly would have a growing trend in the need of your services:

$$\frac{60}{1000} = 6\% \quad | \quad \frac{100}{1000} = 10\% \quad | \quad \frac{150}{1000} = 15\%$$

Expressed graphically:

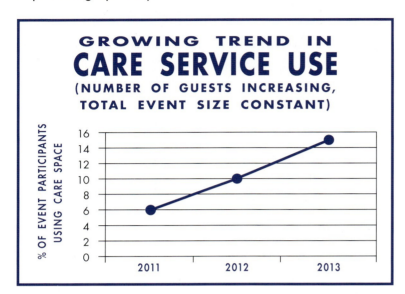

Alternatively, if your event were doubling in participants each year, from 1,000 in 2011 to 2,000 in 2012, and 4,000 in 2013 the graph would look very different:

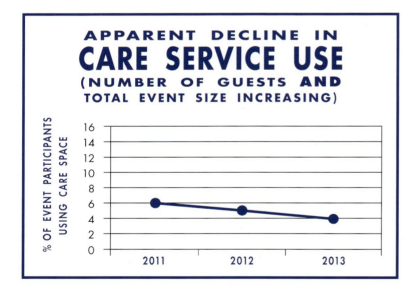

Ratios are particularly useful for metrics such as:

- Average time spent with a guest in the care space:

    Total number of hours guests spent in the care space divided by the total number of guests served

- Percentage of guests requiring medical assistance:

    Total number of guests requiring medical assistance divided by the total number of guests served

- Percentage of guests filing care service complaints:

    Number of complaints divided by the number of guests

If you are using metrics to show progress over time, graphs are essential. Few people can withstand the onslaught of pages of numbers and make sense out of them, and fewer are motivated to do so. Graphs help readers to quickly understand what's happening with any given measure of performance.

Practically, performance improvement for harm reduction is best accomplished by finding one or more people passionate about doing better and interested in working with numbers and spreadsheets. Harm-reduction leadership works best with those individuals who understand trends as well as unexpected events, and then use this information to develop means to improve the overall performance of the group. Finally, the harm-reduction metrics can be used to showcase the group's activities in quantifiable terms to event organisers and other interested parties, and to demonstrate group performance, emerging challenges, and improvement and expansion of service over time. Once more, please see Appendix B, "Monitoring, Evaluating and Researching—Recommendations from an Academic Perspective for an Evidence-Based Approach to Psychoactive Crisis Intervention", for further information on this subject.

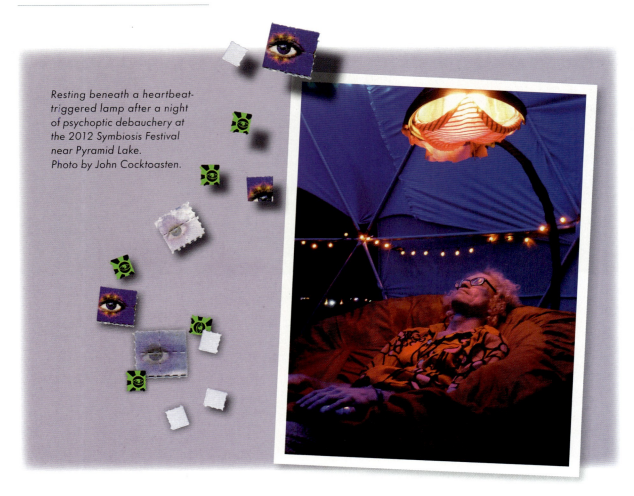

Resting beneath a heartbeat-triggered lamp after a night of psychoptic debauchery at the 2012 Symbiosis Festival near Pyramid Lake. Photo by John Cocktoasten.

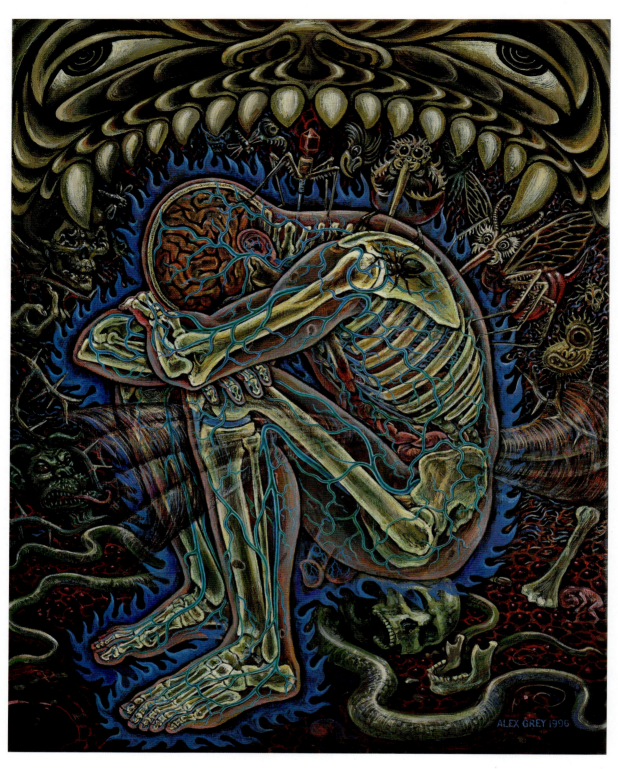

ALEX GREY • *Despair*, 1996 • acrylic on linen
http://alexgrey.com

CHAPTER 16
CASE STUDIES AND IMPRESSIONS

Constance Rodrigues

Berry

Constantinos Efstratiou

Grace Liew

Jack Lieberman

Joan Obiols-Llandrich

João Gonçalves

Jonas Di Gregorio

Karin Silenzi de Stagni

Kim Penders

Mimi Peleg

Rick Doblin

Tracy Dunne

Zevic Mishor

The following case studies and impressions were written by different authors, based on their personal experiences as care givers at events. They are presented here to provide readers a "taste" of different situations that may be encountered in a care service setting. These accounts are also well-suited for use in the training phase of a project, as material for thought or discussion, and as suggestions for role-playing scenarios.

Each account is presented in two parts. Accounts begin with a concise "case study" that summarises the service provided. The case studies are broken down into the following seven subheadings:

1. Initial Observation
2. Key Issue
3. Psychoactives Involved
4. Medical Care
5. Time in Care
6. Final Outcome
7. Notable Points/Lessons Learned

This summary is followed by a more detailed and lengthy "impression", in which the author shares personal observations and feelings, and generally describes the unfolding of events in more detail. For many of these authors, English is not their native tongue; we have done some basic editing on the accounts, but have endeavoured to preserve the original tone and flavour of these recollections. All names have been altered and events (such as the particular music festival or gathering) have not been identified, in order to protect the identities of guests and any other persons involved.

It is highly recommended that care givers—especially those who have not fulfilled such a role previously—read at least some of these case studies and impressions, and consider how they would respond in a similar situation, prior to their beginning work at an event.

Potentially Suicidal Guest Gone Missing

INITIAL OBSERVATION: *What was the first condition that the guest presented with upon coming or being brought to the care service?*

The guest, an amicable man in his twenties, was having a challenging time with the after-effects of an LSD experience. He was, however, suffering not just from these after-effects (the drug had been taken several days earlier), but also dealing with some mental health issues that had been affecting him (possibly for years).

KEY ISSUE: *In the course of providing care, what turned out to be the core condition or challenge that had to be handled?*

Obsessively recurring thoughts that the guest found very negative and very difficult to deal with, his brooding on suicide, and his extremely low self-esteem.

PSYCHOACTIVES INVOLVED: *What substances (if any) relevant to the incident had the guest consumed?*

The guest had taken some LSD.

MEDICAL CARE: *Was there a need for medical intervention (that is, any treatment beyond interaction with a care service volunteer)?*

There was no need for medical intervention.

TIME IN CARE: *How much time did the guest spend in the care service?*

The guest stayed in the care space for the night and partially through the next day, leaving in the afternoon.

FINAL OUTCOME: *What was the condition of the guest upon discharge from the care service?*

During his stay in the care space, "Tom" went through self-therapeutic activities, including some writing, and this seemed to be rather positive and strengthening. He left the space lucid, in the company of a care giver who took him to his tent, and he had the intention of meeting one of his friends with whom he would leave the event that day.

NOTABLE POINTS/LESSONS LEARNED: *What was done well, and what could have been improved upon or done differently? Are there any other notable points from this case?*

Firstly, the importance of being a good listener became obvious. Even when there are deep psychological issues at hand—far beyond the acute effects of a single drug session—and these issues clearly will not be resolved in the context of the care service, the importance of being an empathic fellow human being, listening, and providing comfort is still paramount. Secondly, if thoughts regarding suicide are expressed, one should inform the team lead and the care service leader, and take advice with them as to how to act. In fact, in any difficult situation, the value of involving fellow care givers and getting their advice cannot be overstated.

An attendee reintegrates near the water at the 2012 Eclipse Festival in Australia. Photo by Maddie Radnan.

IMPRESSIONS

The event for which we were providing a care service, a large music festival, was coming to an end after several tumultuous days. It had been an amazing and inspiring festival, yet also emotionally draining and tiring. On the last shift for the entire care service, beginning in the morning, I took over the care of one particular guest, let's call him "Tom", who had come in the previous evening. Tom was an amicable man in his twenties, who was having a challenging time with the after-effects of an LSD experience. Apparently he had taken the drug several days earlier, and it had put him in a difficult frame of mind. I had obtained some details about Tom from the care giver who had been with him during the night, but in the next few hours, after he woke, I would find out much more about him.

It became clear that Tom was suffering not just from the after-effects of the drug, but was also dealing with some mental health issues that had affected him, possibly for years. The LSD experience seemed to have brought these issues to the fore for him to contend with. That morning he told me about a personal matter that was deeply shameful to him, but that he found difficult to change or control. He also said that a few days ago he had swum out into the nearby lake, with the thought of killing himself. At some point, however, he had decided to swim back to shore. We spent several hours talking. He was a very intelligent and communicative man, and I think that the simple act of discussing and confiding these things (which he had probably kept very private) was doing him good. Tom spoke of constantly recurring thoughts—thoughts he could neither control nor stop—that were affecting his mood and self-esteem almost the entire time. He also told me that he was an avid poet and writer, and so I gave him paper and pens to write with. During periods when I left him, he wrote with great energy, filling up many sheets of paper, and this seemed to be a positive activity for him.

Tom had a group of concerned friends who came to visit him, and generally he seemed to have a good level of emotional support at the festival. He was to meet one of these friends in the afternoon, and together they would drive home. By late morning the event site was already being taken down, along with tents, facilities, and so forth, and our care space was also being packed up. Tom's tent was a good distance (over a kilometre) away from the care space, so I offered to accompany him there. By this time we had built a good and warm rapport, and despite his protesting that there was no need, I insisted on walking with him anyway. We arrived at his small, one-person tent, by now standing alone (other tents had been taken down) in a clearing. Here I felt a decision point—I could help him take down the tent and pack, and then personally make sure that he connected with his friend, or I could say goodbye and leave him to it. I was physically and emotionally exhausted at this stage; it had been a very long festival. I made a half-hearted offer to help him pack, but he shrugged it off, saying that all was good, that I had done enough, and that he would be fine on his own. We embraced, and I returned to the care space.

As I was packing up my own gear, I felt a growing sense of unease. I had left this person, who had spoken about suicide, alone. Although fellow care givers reassured me that even accompanying Tom to his tent was beyond any obligation I needed to perform, I decided to follow-up on it; I felt it was the most correct thing to do. I went to where I remembered his tent to be, and it was gone. I then went to the installation where he told me he'd be meeting his friend, and spoke to the people there. They knew Tom, but he had not made contact with them. What followed was a horrible few hours, where I walked kilometres in the burning sun, across a massive festival ground, looking for Tom. A feeling of dread grew upon me, and I became almost distraught, fearing the worst. Tom's friends searched for him as well, but to no avail. At one stage they even found clothes by the lakeside, with nobody there, and called my phone to ask me what Tom had been wearing...

After several hours I received a call. Tom had been found! I felt giddy with relief. I spoke to him briefly on the phone, and wished him all the very best.

Working with Tom in the care space was a challenge in itself, but not unpleasant. He was talkative, we formed a good connection, and he disclosed much to me as we built trust. The main point here was to be an attentive listener, and especially, to be absolutely non-judgemental. Even as he told me about some fairly sensitive topics, I accepted him first and foremost as a human being, with all the rest being just the details. The crunch came when I decided to accompany him to his tent; I feel I should have seen it through all the way; that is, made sure that he had physically connected with his friend. Different care services will have different protocols and guidelines on such things, but if somebody talks about suicide, a care giver should exercise an extreme degree of caution —including getting advice from a team lead and/or the care service leader—before deciding on how to "discharge" the guest.

Being Aware of Our Limits

INITIAL OBSERVATION: *What was the first condition that the guest presented with upon coming or being brought to the care service?*

The care giver found himself with a man who was in a very weak condition. He had a fever, and had been experiencing vomiting and diarrhoea for a couple of days.

KEY ISSUE: *In the course of providing care, what turned out to be the core condition or challenge that had to be handled?*

Leaving the care service in order to accompany the guest to the hospital was a real challenge, firstly because his physical condition was very worrying, and secondly because he was under the effects of psychoactive substances.

PSYCHOACTIVES INVOLVED: *What substances (if any) relevant to the incident had the guest consumed?*

The guest had taken some psychoactive substances in the previous days, but it was clear that these were not the main reason for his condition.

MEDICAL CARE: *Was there a need for medical intervention (that is, any treatment beyond interaction with a care service volunteer)?*

After a long consultation with a doctor and another care giver, the team concluded that the best course of action was to call for an ambulance and take the guest to the nearest hospital, where he was given some intravenous vitamins and minerals.

TIME IN CARE: *How much time did the guest spend in the care service?*

The guest arrived in the morning, went to the closest hospital and returned to the event in the afternoon.

FINAL OUTCOME: *What was the condition of the guest upon discharge from the care service?*

Soon after treatment at the hospital the guest felt a lot better and was able to swiftly recover. Within a few hours he expressed a desire to return to the event. On the way he told the care giver that he was very grateful for the support he had received and that he was now ready to go out and look for his friends by himself.

NOTABLE POINTS/LESSONS LEARNED: *What was done well, and what could have been improved upon or done differently? Are there any other notable points from this case?*

In any care service it is important to assess the contextual limits of the intervention, especially during risky situations involving a physical condition that the service cannot treat.

IMPRESSIONS

I was asked by the team lead to take care of a man who was in a very weak condition. He had a fever and had been experiencing vomiting and diarrhoea for a couple of days. He had also taken some psychoactive substances in the previous days, but it was clear that these were not the main reason for his condition. After a long consultation with a doctor and another care giver, we concluded that the best course of action was to call for an ambulance and take the guest to the nearest hospital. When the ambulance arrived I was asked to go with him, to keep an eye on his condition. My care service shift was nearing its end, but I decided to accept the request and rode with the guest in the ambulance. When we arrived at the hospital he was given some intravenous vitamins and minerals; these seemed to make him feel a lot better, and additionally, the air conditioning and the silence of the place helped him to rest and recover.

After some hours the guest felt so much better that he wanted to return to the festival. I suggested that he stay in the hospital a little longer, but he said that he was feeling better and wanted to go back. We therefore made our way back to the event by taxi, and once there, he told me that he was very grateful for the support he had received and that he was now ready to go out and look for his friends by himself.

Initially I wasn't comfortable with the idea of taking the guest into the hospital, but upon arriving there, I realised that the safer and most correct choice had been made. Considering that he was very weak and had not been able to feed himself for a couple of days, and that we didn't have the equipment to carry out an intravenous injection of vitamins and minerals, I think that it was appropriate to accept our limits and call the ambulance.

16.3 A Rollercoaster of Emotions—From Hell and Back

INITIAL OBSERVATION: *What was the first condition that the guest presented with upon coming or being brought to the care service?*

The guest was a woman who stood at the entrance of the care space chatting freely with one of the care givers, and seemed mainly interested in the philosophy of a psychedelic care service. It didn't take long until she expressed what she was actually doing there, and pretty soon the normal chatting turned into gibberish and then into random screaming, crying, and a rollercoaster of emotions. She seemed like she was slipping in and out of strange patterns of thought, and these were loops of desperation from which she couldn't escape.

KEY ISSUE: *In the course of providing care, what turned out to be the core condition or challenge that had to be handled?*

The core condition that had to be handled was the psychological condition of the guest. This woman showed no capability to distinguish between her thoughts and reality. Her thoughts could best be described as being those of a person experiencing a really tough dream. She experienced parts of her childhood, would forget her identity, would identify other people wrongly, and near the end would express herself using religious ideas. The main challenge for the care giver was to stay focused and calm. Focused, because of the fatigue that had built up in the previous days; calm, because the situation was pretty demanding, both psychologically and physically.

PSYCHOACTIVES INVOLVED: *What substances (if any) relevant to the incident had the guest consumed?*

The guest had taken one 100-microgram LSD blotter.

MEDICAL CARE: *Was there a need for medical intervention (that is, any treatment beyond interaction with a care service volunteer)?*

Even though there wasn't a need for medical intervention, this guest had to be carried to a restricted chamber set up especially for cases that might otherwise disturb any of the other guests present in the main care space area.

TIME IN CARE: *How much time did the guest spend in the care service?*

The guest came in the evening and left the next day.

FINAL OUTCOME: *What was the condition of the guest upon discharge from the care service?*

After spending a whole night in the care space, when the guest woke up she was totally fine, apart from being shaken up by the psychological ride she had faced for hours in a row. This was an experience that had changed her and she felt grateful towards everybody who had helped her over the course of the previous night.

NOTABLE POINTS/LESSONS LEARNED: *What was done well, and what could have been improved upon or done differently? Are there any other notable points from this case?*

One of the biggest achievements of the project was that a group of people who previously didn't know each other were able to work as a solid team within such a short time of coming together. The care giver felt that he had a supportive network on hand all throughout the intervention of this episode. Perhaps in certain circumstances it would be a good idea for care givers to dress in distinguishable outfits; in that way, our roles would be much more visible to people.

IMPRESSIONS

When I heard of a project that was going to set up a psychedelic care service, I immediately wanted to participate in it; and, as it turns out, it offered me a unique chance to be part of something magical. In this report I recount the most impressive story that I assisted with during my time as a volunteer. From my perspective this story contains a lot of the elements that are important to the job at hand: it was extremely intense, it took a long time, and it didn't really stick to the official "work schedule". It showed clearly how we should expect nothing less than the unexpected when working at a psychedelic care service.

On this particular night I didn't have a shift at the care service. I was simply enjoying my holiday, hanging around watching the setting sun. Eventually I ended up helping out a fellow human being until four o'clock in the morning! I was pretty tired from the previous days. My plans were to see the sun set and then head off to bed, but something else was thrown at me, and before I knew it a story unfolded that seemed surreal at certain points. As the sun set, a young lady (I will call her "Eve"), came to sit next to me and my friend. At first it seemed like nothing out of the ordinary, just a person interested in finding out what exactly we were doing. This happened a lot at the entrance of the service, and we always made sure someone was standing guard in order to explain to these people what we were doing and why they could not enter our installations.

The conversation was mostly about the event, and how we were experiencing it, what we liked and didn't like. After fifteen minutes of chatting it became clear that Eve had taken one hit of acid, about an hour before. It is strange to see how under certain conditions people seem to talk freely about their use of drugs. It is even more interesting to note how the shared experience of using certain drugs seems to transcend any cultural differences that might otherwise be a possible hurdle for making a connection. I guess one might say that the effect of drugs is not bound by cultures.

The print of the blotter was the one with Albert Hofmann on his bike. I immediately thought, "Well, that should be maximum 100 mics, so it should be a light dose". I could not have been more incorrect. Even if it was a light dose, it triggered a far-reaching experience.

At a certain point Eve picked up my name, which turned out to sound a bit like her ex-boyfriend's name. Our conversation took place in English, even though this wasn't any of our native languages. She told me she was working at the event too. She already had some experience with psychedelic substances, although this kind of setting—being among thousands of strangers in an unfamiliar place—was new to her. She started by saying that she felt like she had to come to the care service, that something was calling her there and how she felt like it was some "kind of a portal". I reacted by smiling, not saying anything, sometimes nodding to make sure she knew I was still listening. I was just leaving her with the thoughts she was playing with, and could definitely notice how the LSD was starting to take effect.

Pretty soon her normal chatting turned into gibberish, and not much later random screaming, crying, and a rollercoaster of emotions. Eve went from hysterically happy to almost manically sad; laughter and crying followed one another like sides of a coin being flipped. I quickly realised that she needed help. She started calling out to somebody whose name did sound like mine, and started blabbering a bit about calling her mum. Pretty soon she started to mix up English and her native language. It seemed like she was slipping in and out of strange patterns of thought, and that these were loops of desperation from which there was no apparent escape.

Eve was in a totally disorientated state of mind, and one of the ways that you could notice this was the manner in which she used her voice. She would go from whispering to screaming without any discernible trigger, or at least nothing visible to us. I could clearly see in her eyes that she was viewing something completely different than most of the people there. You could tell that she was focusing on places where there was nothing to be seen. Even when talking to me sometimes, I could see how she seemed to focus a little bit above my eyes instead of looking at them. This to me was a clear sign that "Eve had left the building…". It was as if someone had a finger on a button, and when this button was pressed Eve would disappear, to be replaced by what appeared to be only automated thought patterns.

A few people who were also hanging around at the entrance then did something I will never forget, and this should be prevented at all times. Because we had other guests

LSD blotter making the rounds at the 2010 Boom Festival. Photo by Erowid.

inside the service also attempting to get a grip on their experiences, I tried to get Eve to keep her voice down. She would only partially react and sometimes still go off into bursts of screaming. As a result, some people who were sitting close to us started to make remarks about this directly towards Eve. It goes without saying that she did not understand, and as a result got even more confused. Apparently these people, who were not from our team, weren't aware of what was happening, even after I and several others told them that this girl was having a hard time. This should have been avoided by all means. The truth is that those remarks made at Eve contributed to her growing state of confusion, and she picked up on all remarks hinted at her.

In her state it was impractical to let Eve go inside the care space where some of the other guests were sleeping, as she would have greatly disturbed the peace inside. At the same time, walking away alone with her didn't seem like a solution, as I would be by myself if the situation developed into an even harder experience. It was only afterwards that I realised how this decision turned out to be a really wise one. It became increasingly difficult reasoning with Eve. She was wondering what she did wrong, why people were reacting as they were to her. For me, it was clear that she was heading towards a total psychological collapse, so I asked some other care givers to come help me and sit near by just in case. By now, an hour had passed. After all this time, she still was going in and out of sanity, being a happy little creature one second and the saddest person alive the next.

I will try to give a description of one example of how this translated into behaviours in Eve, recounting her words, describing the expressions on her face and the intonations that went hand-in-hand with them. Eve was talking in two different languages, jumping from one to another, speaking in English and in her mother tongue, a language of which I couldn't understand a word. I can only say I was happy at the time to have someone in the vicinity who could translate part of what she was saying. It would go slightly like this, "I have to call my mum. I have to tell her that everything is okay. Can I call my mum, Jay?" (Question directed at me, although she was confusing me with her boyfriend the whole time.) "Jay, where are you? You are so far away. Jay, please call me. I really have to call my mum right? I really have to. Jay, don't leave me, Jay... But it is late, maybe my mum is asleep. What if she is asleep? Should I call my mum, Jay?"

The intonation of her voice made it all seem even weirder. She would whisper, then scream, then whisper, and so on. She would talk with a high-pitched voice followed by a low one, sometimes switching in the same sentence. She would

CASE STUDIES AND IMPRESSIONS

take her mobile phone out of her pocket, and then put it back, only to get it out again a second later. She kept on repeating the same things, but in different order and with different intonations. This was all accompanied by an array of facial expressions that seemed to be out of this world. Her face would literally change with every episode that exploded into existence.

I decided the best thing to do, as always, was to remain contained in my own energy and calmness, and try to be a pillar of steadiness for Eve by just being present, breathing calmly, and not being alarmed by anything.

In the meantime Eve wanted to go to the toilet, so I asked some female co-workers to escort her there. I explained to them the situation, what Eve had taken and when she took it, and her current condition. I also told them how long I had been sitting with her. This felt really important to me, because you do start to feel responsible for someone as soon as they take shelter under your wings.

Once they left, I felt temporary relief. I finally had some time to reflect on what had just happened. From the start until this point, over two hours had passed. It was supposed to be a quiet night for me—enjoying the sunset and the stars and then off to bed—but it turned out to be something completely different.

In those two hours I witnessed and partly felt the emotions and the energy that was raging inside Eve's body. Although the aim is not to get involved emotionally or energetically, it is not possible to completely detach from these things, as a little will always trespass through any defences you might have. The thing that helped me the most during this time was knowing that I had people backing me up, as I realised at that point that Eve's journey would take her long into the night... But I told myself, "She is safe now, she is being taken care of", and I felt as though I had just walked out of a huge amusement park ride, totally shaken and trying to rearrange myself. During this moment of reflection I noticed something really interesting: my tiredness had disappeared during this whole period. It is fascinating to see how easily our consciousness influences our physical condition. As soon as I slowed down again, the tiredness hit me very hard and I planned on going to sleep.

I was grounding myself a bit again when I heard someone scream from the direction of the toilets, and I quickly realised it was Eve; the female care givers were now in need of some aid. Eve had become completely deranged, and was getting pretty aggressive towards the people who were trying to help her. I quickly got up from my place, cleared my head, and ran over to the other volunteers. Again I was amazed at how rapidly I adjusted to the situation, revived once more from my tiredness, putting on my so-called psychological battle helmet again.

By the time I arrived there, Eve was foaming from her mouth, and was frantically trying to get out of the grip of the volunteers. I stepped in and tried to subdue Eve physically, by holding one of her arms, and we managed to get a little bit of control over her largely uncontrollable physical movements. It was amazing to see how strong a person really can be physically in these sorts of situations.

To be clear, restraining Eve was only done because, at this point, she had started to physically harm herself and the people around her. Two more male volunteers came to help, and together with three female volunteers we carried Eve towards the care space. We decided as a team that it would be best to put her in the restricted space that was set up especially for cases that might disturb the others present in the main care space. This turned out to be a very good choice, and we finally got Eve to lie down in this place.

It took four people to hold her down, one on each leg and each arm. The power that came from her was unimaginable, it seemed as if the energy of a complete galaxy was rushing through her and driving her body to do physical things that were simply not possible. Eve lingered in this strange outbreak—screaming, kicking, laughing, and crying—as if all these emotions could combine into one at the same time.

It is also hard to describe how much a person changes during these experiences, concerning the appearance of their face and their body language, as I had the chance to witness with Eve. The young girl who is sitting quietly next to you in one moment, is kicking and spitting at you an hour later, eyes popping out and facial expressions totally blown out of proportion. Remaining calm was the only thing we could do, especially for Eve's sake.

After following her for another hour, I asked someone to take over because I was getting too tired. Soon I was relieved from my duty and I could finally go to sleep. I had a very good rest because I was really exhausted. After I woke up, the first thing I did was walk out to the care space, because I was wondering about Eve's follow-up. It turned out she came to her senses, only four hours after I left. I got to hear a wonderful story from my fellow volunteers about how, in the end, she started to say she was Shiva and all was love, falling asleep afterwards. In the morning she was totally fine, apart from being shaken up from the psychological ride, which is to be expected after an experience of this magnitude.

I will never forget this night. And although I didn't talk to Eve any more afterwards, I felt I had done a good job. I was totally surprised when more than half-a-year later I opened my mailbox and found a message from Eve in it. In this mail, she told of how she experienced the night, and how I was a big help in keeping her in some touch with reality by sitting and talking with her. Eve explained how the experience had changed her, and she expressed how grateful she was towards everybody who helped her that night.

She admitted she had never been so disorientated before, not knowing her name or even what she was, convinced that she "had to find out; that it was some sort of game and that the care service was the place to get directions, like a starter kit", and thus she asked all those questions. She also shared the fact that she had "reverted back to childhood experiences" and somehow convinced herself that she was "still four years old", believing her former life until then had only been a nightmare and the real life was at this event all day, every day! Her experience didn't sound mad from the outside, for Eve was facing a serious mind-boggling puzzle, as she herself describes:

> "Eventually I collapsed while my mind travelled at light speed and at a certain point I started counting from the second to the millisecond to the microsecond to the pico-second until TIME ZERO! I believed I was like the alarm clock of creation, the ONG NAMO, the one who awakens first and wakes up all the others and starts organising things for the coming age."

The experience had been a lesson for her, as it made her realise how "profoundly narcissistic" she was and how she "got stuck at some early developmental stage of grandiose ideas about the self and delusions of being of vital importance to the world".

What is interesting about the message is that it gives me feedback on what Eve experienced; because, as I stated before, she was definitely experiencing a different reality. It also shows the great degree of paranoia involved.

For me, as a care giver, the hardest thing to do might have been keeping faith in the positive outcome of this experience. And in a way, I had to do this for both of us. I hope this story shows clearly that one has to expect the unexpected when doing this kind of work, and one has to stay grounded and in control of oneself.

16.4 Struggling for Control Under Marijuana

INITIAL OBSERVATION: *What was the first condition that the guest presented with upon coming or being brought to the care service?*

When the guest, a middle-aged European woman, was brought to the care service she was agitated and paranoid, very scared. She had come to the event for the first time with a certain theme group, but she didn't know anybody, neither in this group nor at the event. She'd developed symptoms that were worrying her, and she felt like she was losing her control, on top of thinking that people around her were hostile.

KEY ISSUE: *In the course of providing care, what turned out to be the core condition or challenge that had to be handled?*

The key issue was how to handle a condition characterised by a fear of losing control. This condition can present itself in many situations involving various substances.

PSYCHOACTIVES INVOLVED: *What substances (if any) relevant to the incident had the guest consumed?*

The guest had smoked marijuana.

MEDICAL CARE: *Was there a need for medical intervention (that is, any treatment beyond interaction with a care service volunteer)?*

There was no need for medical intervention.

TIME IN CARE: *How much time did the guest spend in the care service?*

The guest spent about one-and-a-half hours at the care space.

FINAL OUTCOME: *What was the condition of the guest upon discharge from the care service?*

The care giver and guest had a somewhat philosophical discussion about the issues the guest was facing, and that helped her calm down. As the guest felt more self-confident, the care giver walked her down to her own bus. She left the care service with her own concept of "self-control" changed, finding her new outlook to be very insightful.

NOTABLE POINTS/LESSONS LEARNED: *What was done well, and what could have been improved upon or done differently? Are there any other notable points from this case?*

The primary challenge for the care giver in this situation was to maintain a calm demeanour at all times. Establishing trust is also important, so that the guest can allow the process to unfold without trying to maintain control.

IMPRESSIONS

I was working in the care service of a large event when a middle-aged European woman was brought in. She was agitated and paranoid, very scared. I sat down with her in a quiet corner of the space and asked her what was going on. She said that she had come to the event with a certain theme group and that she knew no one at the event or in the group, and it was her first time here.

She also decided to try smoking marijuana for the first time when it was offered to her! After smoking, she developed symptoms that worried her, as she proceeded to get very scared and paranoid, thinking that people around her were hostile. She felt like she was losing control, and she was the kind of person who prided herself on her "self-control".

I decided that being a calm presence and listening to her was the best strategy to use, at least at first. Afterwards I decided to engage in a somewhat philosophical discussion about the issue of control, and I explained to her that the more she struggles to maintain control, the more scared and paranoid she may become. I tried to persuade her that the best thing for her to do was to surrender to whatever was happening to her, and that this strategy could very well serve her in normal life, too. She really found the whole concept quite insightful; this was new information for her.

After about one hour she was feeling well enough to return to her bus and I walked her back there.

It is important not to underestimate the psychoactive effects of marijuana, which can be quite challenging; even if it's not normally considered a problematic drug, in fact, it can be. Someone experiencing it for the first time can have quite a profound, and sometimes disturbing experience with it. It is important to remember to try to facilitate a positive learning experience by working with the difficulties presented.

When the Care Giver Feels Healed

16.5

INITIAL OBSERVATION: *What was the first condition that the guest presented with upon coming or being brought to the care service?*

The guest, a male, arrived at the care service and stood in the immediacy of the facilities with some friends. He was sort of sitting, sort of reclining on his side, and he seemed very concerned with what people were saying and doing behind him. When the care giver stared at him, he seemed uncomfortable. He had large pupils, was profusely sweating from his forehead, and generally seemed like he was "coming on" to something.

KEY ISSUE: *In the course of providing care, what turned out to be the core condition or challenge that had to be handled?*

The guest wanted to talk about the paranoia he felt, a delicate matter for him because he was experiencing it intensely, and without knowing it, he was bringing into the discussion a topic that had also been familiar to me, the care giver, at one point in my life. Thus, whilst simultaneously helping someone to address a state of mental confusion as a care giver, I remembered my own throes and was confronted with an experience that was totally unexpected and that turned out to be significant for the both of us.

PSYCHOACTIVES INVOLVED: *What substances (if any) relevant to the incident had the guest consumed?*

The guest had taken a "large dose" of MDMA and was feeling the full effects coming up when arriving at the care service.

MEDICAL CARE: *Was there a need for medical intervention (that is, any treatment beyond interaction with a care service volunteer)?*

There was no need for medical intervention.

TIME IN CARE: *How much time did the guest spend in the care service?*

The guest spent around seven hours at the care space.

FINAL OUTCOME: *What was the condition of the guest upon discharge from the care service?*

As the sitting proceeded, and the guest managed to untie some of the knots of his challenges, "his eyes were wide and glaring, like an explosion of happiness and bliss on his face". After spending some hours with his care giver during the day, outside by the lake, he rested inside. That same evening he went back to his friends.

NOTABLE POINTS/LESSONS LEARNED: *What was done well, and what could have been improved upon or done differently? Are there any other notable points from this case?*

A difficult experience can not only be averted or tuned down, but can actually turn into a positive healing one, not only for the guest but also for the care giver.

IMPRESSIONS

In my second daytime shift at the care service, I had gone out with someone earlier in that day to see if anyone needed help at the dance floor. It was a quiet day and even though it was hot and the festival had already been going for a long time, the number of guests in the care space was low, so I was sitting in front of our installations with other care givers.

At some point a group of people arrived and among them was one young man with a beard whom I remembered seeing in days prior. As they approached our facilities, this man and his friends sat down outside, and I saw that with them was one man whom I did not remember meeting the other time (in this story I have called this person "Uri"). He was sort of sitting, sort of reclining on his side, and I noticed he was very concerned with what people were saying and doing behind him. He seemed uncomfortable and as I increased my attentions towards him I noticed he had large pupils, was sweating on his forehead a lot, and generally seemed like he was "coming on" to on something

I offered him some water and returned my focus to the conversation. After a minute or so, the man I met the other day said that he had met Uri and they talked for a while; apparently Uri was somewhat disorientated and in a far-out place. Now the man wanted to move on, and he asked if it was okay if they could leave Uri in our care. In that moment, I understood the intent of the meeting and replied, "Of course". Uri was welcome and would be taken care of as much as we could provide.

They said goodbye and I made contact with Uri for the first time for real. I asked how he was and he said he didn't really feel all good. I asked why, and he shared with me that he had taken a large dose of pure MDMA and was feeling the full effects coming up. It was his first time taking this drug and even though he seemed very open and was opening up more, he felt he wasn't fully right. I said that this was exactly what the care service was for and if he wanted I could sit with him, offering him a hug and a listening ear.

As he talked for a while and drank some of the water, he would occasionally stop his speech in the middle of a sentence, probably whilst he experienced that feeling of "goosebump waves" rising up from the stomach area to the top of the head. He didn't seem to give in, and was still looking over his shoulder every now and then. I do not remember who brought it up, but after a while Uri and I came to the conclusion he would feel better at the waterside, as there he could watch the water and be more secluded. I said if he could wait a minute I would fill up my bottle of water and come back. By that time I had noticed somewhat paranoid behaviour, and in our conversation he had mentioned that he had heard a talk the evening before about how MDMA was used to heal in a psychological setting and he had intended to do something like that with his trip. I anticipated something might come up, and told the other volunteers I would return later.

Uri and I walked off to the waterside, sitting down. After a short conversation he asked me how long the come on should take and if there was any way he could make it come on easier; whilst he asked this, he seemed rather tense. I replied that it would probably pass more easily if he let go a bit and allow the experience to enter at its own pace. I used an analogy of a hot bath, as one doesn't jump into a hot bath all at once. You first enter a little bit with your foot and as your body adjusts itself you enter more and more until you are submerged.

After that we both sat upright for a while, our feet tucked under us, and we stared at the lake and the small waves that were slowly sloshing onto the shore. For a while, we exchanged glances and drank water often.

At some point he expressed his gratitude for this opportunity and we started to talk again. His talk basically revolved around paranoia, and in the conversation that ensued, it came up that I'd had paranoia as well at one point in my life. We talked about this and he asked how I had overcome it. I explained that I had allowed all of my paranoid energy to symbolically flow into a rock, and then I cast that rock into a lake. After that moment, I could always refer any paranoid idea to that rock at the bottom of the lake and overwrite it with a positive and healing thought instead. On one hand, you recognise it as something real; but on the other hand you, have chosen not to stay with that paranoia and you choose healing instead.

He decided to do the same, and even picked up a marker to write "paranoia" on a stone. I feel I must state at this point that I never suggested he would or could do anything during this conversation. I continuously allowed him to speak his mind and only elaborated on my own thoughts when he asked for conversation. He sat with the stone in his hands for a while and talked. By this time I noticed that I was pretty much out of the conversation mode, as if I had taken a backseat in his mind and we were not really having a dialogue. His words seemed more a manifestation of thought than an attempt to relay thoughts from one human to another. Perhaps he was addressing his paranoia directly? I have no idea and no way of knowing.

A long while after this I replied to something and before I finished my sentence, he suddenly stood up and I thought to myself, "Uh-oh… this time I said too much! He's going to run off!" But then I saw something else. He had walked about fifteen metres away from the water and then he ran at it at full speed. He gave a really angry and primaeval shout, all the way as he ran. I could feel it crawling up from my toes and reaching into my own spine, it was intense! As his feet hit the water he threw the stone with all his force into the lake!

He watched it plop into the water and almost fell over as he sat down again. His eyes were wide and glaring, like an explosion of happiness and bliss on his face. He laid his head down in the sand and lay there giving off deep sighs and saying little.

The hours after this were filled with more talking and eventually he moved into the care space to rest for a while. He said he would like to smoke some weed and I advised against this as it might bring up the paranoia again. He understood and eventually was able to fall asleep.

I met Uri a couple of days after his experience and he was still radiant and happy. In the evening of the day we had discussed his experience, he'd found his friends and they had a good conversation. One could see he was really busy integrating the whole experience into his life. We both felt happy for him and we hugged. I wish that we'd have exchanged emails, so I might have heard from him again.

From this experience I learned that even the most difficult moments in my own life can apparently be of help to others. A lot of the humans on this planet tend to pretend that we are all smiles and giggles but I know from my personal experience that this is not the case, as we must always find a balance between "dark" and "light".

The acknowledgement that came from externalising my paranoia into that stone as a symbol has really helped my life experience move forward and I hope that it has helped Uri as well. I also felt that the notion "giving is receiving" has been more true than ever after that conversation with him, because it was the first time I had told anyone outside of my close circle of friends about my paranoid past.

Since then, I have received the courage to talk about it with others as well, discovering a path to puncture an apparent bubble that revolves around a sensitive subject like paranoia. I have noticed that numerous people have had these experiences and no one seems to talk about them because they are so ugly. Now that this subject has spilled out for me, I've been able to actively discuss it in many conversations.

16.6 Lost and Found—The Love Bond

INITIAL OBSERVATION: *What was the first condition that the guest presented with upon coming or being brought to the care service?*

Scouting for potentially risky situations, a couple of care givers walked around the event and found someone sitting on the ground by himself. He was a middle-aged Asian guy, and he was in distress, looking quite anxious, alone and lost. He held his hands as if he was praying and it was hard to understand what he said. He was also crying and expressing a lot of sadness, but seemed to be physically all right.

KEY ISSUE: *In the course of providing care, what turned out to be the core condition or challenge that had to be handled?*

It was challenging following someone who—under the effects of LSD—considered himself responsible (and suffered with that thought) for being lost from his wife and friends, and had virtually no possible way to contact them whilst he was at the event.

PSYCHOACTIVES INVOLVED: *What substances (if any) relevant to the incident had the guest consumed?*

The guest had taken LSD.

MEDICAL CARE: *Was there a need for medical intervention (that is, any treatment beyond interaction with a care service volunteer)?*

There was no need for medical intervention.

TIME IN CARE: *How much time did the guest spend in the care service?*

The guest came during the night and left on the next day; overall the time at the care space was more or less ten hours.

FINAL OUTCOME: *What was the condition of the guest upon discharge from the care service?*

After spending the whole night at the service, the guest was still heavily shaken, crying and expressing feelings of sadness, dishonour, and shame for hours in a row. He wasn't the least bit aggressive or paranoid; his fight seemed to be entirely within himself, with his own values and beliefs. It was only in the morning when his wife showed up that the missing element he needed in order to build himself back up came into play. The couple remained in the care service and, after spending some time with his wife, the guest started to recover from his crisis and he left the place smiling.

NOTABLE POINTS/LESSONS LEARNED: *What was done well, and what could have been improved upon or done differently? Are there any other notable points from this case?*

Close friends or relatives can play a major role in a guest's recovery. Language can sometimes be a problem and non-verbal approaches can be quite useful in providing care.

IMPRESSIONS

At the beginning of the shift, the other volunteers and I were ready for another night of psychedelic emergency services. Nothing much was happening, so a volunteer and I were chosen to walk around the festival and look for potentially risky situations. We walked around for an hour or two, and most people seemed to be all right, enjoying the festival. Here and there we found a few people lying on the ground, but when we approached them everyone expressed that they were okay. It seemed a quiet night, so we decided to go back to the care space.

As we were returning, we spotted someone sitting on the ground by himself. He was a middle-aged guy of Asian nationality. We approached him and he seemed to be in distress. We tried to communicate with him; the guy looked quite anxious, alone and lost. He was holding his hands as if he was praying and it was hard to understand what he said. He was also crying and expressing a lot of sadness, but seemed to be physically all right. Patiently, we tried to communicate with him; he could understand English, but spoke a mixture of English and his mother tongue, and none of us understood him.

Slowly we managed to talk with him and we persuaded him to come to the care service. As we walked, we got to know a bit more about him and his situation: he was with his wife and friends at the festival, all of them took LSD, and they became separated. He felt responsible for losing his wife and was in a spiritual crisis, overridden with guilt and shame. It seemed as if his own culture, one in which honour and duty play a crucial role, enhanced the impact of his emotional crisis.

We spent some time with him at the care service space, but as our shift ended, someone else was assigned to follow him and we went for some rest. In the morning I returned and asked about our friend; he had been there all night and was still heavily shaken, crying and expressing feelings of sadness, dishonour, and shame for hours in a row. Volunteers had been around him and were trying to comfort him. It must be said that he wasn't the least bit aggressive or paranoid; his fight seemed to be within himself, with his own values and beliefs.

As the morning went on, an Asian woman came to our entrance; she had been looking for her husband all night and finally somebody told her he might be in our space. We took her to our friend, and immediately she recognised her husband and embraced him. We left them both alone—we could see she was the missing element to rebuild this guy's emotional balance. She comforted him, embraced him, and even gave him a massage.

After some time with his wife in there, the guy started to recover from his experience, and the couple smiled and left the space about two hours later. He was still shaken by the emotional and spiritual crisis, but now he was able to understand the world was not ending that day because of his "faults". They were both very thankful and we felt glad with the happy ending for this situation.

Frequently at a large event, the person who most needs help won't be at the centre of attention; instead this person going through a difficult psychedelic experience might be lost and hidden in some dark corner, or alone inside his or her own tent! Often a person won't be able to look for help or won't feel comfortable seeking it. These are challenges to a good psychedelic emergency service; and the bigger the event, the higher the likelihood that some individuals won't get the attention they could use. We're aware that it isn't remotely possible or even reasonable to go inside each tent at the event to monitor the well-being of participants, but the situation I have described shows the importance of trying to inform the public and staff that help for these kinds of situations is in a specific place and can be found whenever necessary.

This case also brings two important aspects to light: close friends and relatives can play a major part in the support process, if they are available and willing to help. But if they are unwilling, or if they are rejected by the guest, then it might *not* be a good idea to involve them. Also, even when there is a language barrier (either because the language is different or because the speech of the person has turned incomprehensible), one is still able to help an individual in a lot of ways. Remember that the spoken word is just *one* of the channels of communication available, and with a person going through a psychedelic crisis, often a verbal conversation won't be the most effective means to communicate.

16.7 The Symbiotic Bond

INITIAL OBSERVATION: *What was the first condition that the guest presented with upon coming or being brought to the care service?*

CASE STUDIES AND IMPRESSIONS

The two guests arrived at the care service whilst having delusional thoughts; they were frightened and very suspicious of what was going on, not really feeling at ease with the fact that they had been brought to the care space.

KEY ISSUE: *In the course of providing care, what turned out to be the core condition or challenge that had to be handled?*

Upon the arrival of the guests, immediately one condition presented itself as a challenge: the guests (a couple of friends going through a similar experience, after having ingested LSD for the first time) couldn't be separated, and the care giver had to work not with just one person going through crisis, but with two! As the girls' experiences shifted between a sensation of hopelessness and a sensation of pleasure, these were variables taken into account whilst caring for them, balancing opposing extremes as they surfaced.

PSYCHOACTIVES INVOLVED: *What substances (if any) relevant to the incident had the guest consumed?*

Each of the two guests had taken 150 micrograms of LSD.

MEDICAL CARE: *Was there a need for medical intervention (that is, any treatment beyond interaction with a care service volunteer)?*

There was no need for medical intervention.

TIME IN CARE: *How much time did the guest spend in the care service?*

The girls stayed for the whole night, spending about ten hours at the care space.

FINAL OUTCOME: *What was the condition of the guest upon discharge from the care service?*

After spending a whole night in "treatment", the guests left the next morning, fully vitalised and ready to enjoy the party in a safer way.

NOTABLE POINTS/LESSONS LEARNED: *What was done well, and what could have been improved upon or done differently? Are there any other notable points from this case?*

Reading through the whole report, one can think of the need for a follow-up. With persons who are not frequent users, or with those who try a substance for the first time and go through an intense experience, it makes sense to have a counselling session post-stay at the care service. Some people leave the event feeling that they still need to talk about their experience in order to process unfinished issues.

IMPRESSIONS

Early in the night, a nineteen-year-old girl ("Gabrielle") and her eighteen-year-old friend ("Kate")—high on LSD (150 micrograms each)—were brought in by the paramedics. The two girls, who had taken LSD for the first time, weren't really aware that the paramedics (all male in this situation) were friendly professionals, so they kept thinking that the paramedics would harm them in some way. Possibly experiencing fears of rape (something that can occur within an psychoactive crisis experience), they were very scared in the beginning, asking many questions; we reassured them they were in a safe space where nothing bad was going to happen. The team on that shift decided that only female care givers should take care of the girls, in order to hopefully decrease their delusional thoughts and paranoia.

Gabrielle's physical condition was stable but she was feeling somewhat lost and hypothermic, switching between passively lying down and suddenly going outside to smoke or to see the stars. She was having intense visions and her eyes looked spaced-out whilst she was shifting between total focus (especially when we asked questions) and detaching all of a sudden, not really listening to anything any more. She was so awe-struck with the experience that she couldn't put it all into words; at the same time, she wanted to pay attention to her friend who was slightly younger. One could see they had a strong bond, so the best option for this sitting experience was to have a female care giver work with the two of them.

Another care giver and I did the girls' intake. They ate some apples and lay down together in sleeping bags; and when the girls had proper shelter and seemed more grounded, they were left with just one care giver who sat with both of them. One could notice how Kate was caressing her friend's face with the tip of her fingers in a very delicate manner and both girls seemed to derive great pleasure from this. Later on, their symbiotic bond allowed them to sleep together coiled with each other in foetal positions, an image that was like a soothing portrait. The care service is not only a container for people ridden with despair, anxiety, fear, and feelings of hopelessness, but also a warm, peaceful "womb" where guests can really feel safe and nurtured.

Once their basic needs were met (warmth, food, water, and toilet), we opted to give the girls enough space to explore their sensations, whilst simultaneously keeping an eye on them. During a sitting experience it's important to pay attention to issues of personal boundaries, as the guest often feels rather sensitive with every move and might need very little interaction with the care giver, without any dialogue.

The issue of trust between the care giver and the guest is an important topic to address as well. Gabrielle, who seemed overall more dynamic than Kate, would often go outside the care service on her own whenever she wanted, and those moments were also a suitable grounding strategy for her. However she remained in the area near by and would always return to us.

Kate felt insecure and complained about hallucinations; she didn't seem to be coping with the experience as well as Gabrielle. My colleague gave her some information about LSD and explained how long it would take to come down, how all of it was just temporary. Kate kept checking for Gabrielle whenever she went outside; but after a while, realising that her friend just needed some fresh air and would always return, she felt more at ease. The girls left the next day, back on their feet and ready to enjoy the party in a safer way.

The care giver is the one who makes the assessment of whether the "bird can fly outside the nest" or not, and most likely this can happen successfully, except if the guests might hurt themselves or others. In either situation, I feel that it's good to remain assertive whilst working simultaneously with flexibility, so that we don't look like we're policing the person.

If we endeavour to build bonds with empathy, resonating with a sense of mutual self-respect, everything can flow better. Even when guests have ended their stay at the care service and are off to the party renewed and reborn, they may come back again later to say "hello" or to have a chat with their care givers. Often when guests return for a conversation, they are sober rather than being under the influence of any substance.

Addressing the personal development issues and inner conflicts that initially surfaced during a psychedelic crisis experience can be therapeutic for a guest, but doing so usually takes time and effort. Post-crisis conversations between a care giver and his or her guest may help to further the guest's process of personal transformation whilst the guest is able to maintain a more typical level of self-awareness and cognition.

Psychiatric Patients Also Enjoy Festivals

16.8

INITIAL OBSERVATION: *What was the first condition that the guest presented with upon coming or being brought to the care service?*

The individual was brought by a friend who informed the care service that the guest suffered a psychiatric condition and was on medication, which it was believed that he had abandoned the use of over the past few days. He was not willing to cooperate and presented serious behavioural disturbances. He didn't speak at all and he was grimacing in a spectacular way, moving all his facial muscles at an incredible pace. He was in a very weak condition, had a fever, and had been experiencing vomiting and diarrhoea for a couple of days.

KEY ISSUE: *In the course of providing care, what turned out to be the core condition or challenge that had to be handled?*

The guest probably had a bipolar condition and was in the middle of a manic phase. On top of this, there was a suspicion that he had taken some psychoactive substance and that he had dropped his prescription treatment.

PSYCHOACTIVES INVOLVED: *What substances (if any) relevant to the incident had the guest consumed?*

Nobody really knew for sure, but there was a suspicion that the guest had taken some psychoactive substance, whilst having dropped his treatment with a prescription psychiatric drug.

MEDICAL CARE: *Was there a need for medical intervention (that is, any treatment beyond interaction with a care service volunteer)?*

This guest had to be treated by the psychiatrist in the care service.

TIME IN CARE: *How much time did the guest spend in the care service?*

The guest came in the evening and left the next day, but later on he was brought back again to the care service.

FINAL OUTCOME: *What was the condition of the guest upon discharge from the care service?*

After sleeping a few hours the guest left, but he had taken one of the care givers' bags and disappeared. On the following day he caused some serious trouble around the event and security services brought him back to the care space. The event was over and the installations were being dismantled, so there was no choice but to evacuate the guest to the closest hospital in the area with a psychiatric ward.

NOTABLE POINTS/LESSONS LEARNED: *What was done well, and what could have been improved upon or done differently? Are there any other notable points from this case?*

With the guest being evacuated to a psychiatric hospital ward, in certain ways it was a sad ending, but the case also showed that although psychiatric patients have a right to go to festivals and have fun, they must also be prudent, maintain their treatment, keep their resting hours, and avoid the recreational use of psychoactive substances.

IMPRESSIONS

As the only psychiatrist at this care service, I took care of many interesting cases. One of the most complicated was a European guest, I'll call him "Mathias". I was requested by the team lead at night, on the last day of the festival, to attend to a guest who was not willing to cooperate and presented serious behavioural disturbances. He had been brought by a friend who informed us that Mathias suffered a psychiatric condition and was on medication that he had abandoned a few days previous.

Mathias was not speaking at all, but he was grimacing in a spectacular way, moving all his facial muscles at an incredible pace. As he was reluctant to respond to my questions, I decided to imitate his grimacing. It seemed to work and, little by little, a minimal communication began to be established.

He was incoherent, nonsensical, hyperactive, moving around the whole space, and probably having hallucinations, although this cannot be assured. His friend had the medication usually taken by Mathias: quetiapine, a neuroleptic tranquilliser, and lamotrigine, a mood stabiliser. This medication and the symptoms shown by Mathias confirmed my suspicion about his diagnosis.

Mathias probably had a bipolar condition and was in the middle of a manic phase. There was a suspicion that he had taken some psychoactive substance, but nobody really knew, and also that he had dropped his psychiatric treatment. The result was in front of me. After about an hour of surreal conversation I convinced him—don't ask me how—to take his medication. So he swallowed three 300-mg tablets of quetiapine—a total of 900 mg, which is quite a high dose; but he was accustomed to it, as he recognised that this was his regular daily dose. We skipped the lamotrigine, which is not so fast acting. He seemed to be more peaceful and I left him with his friend who was very helpful during the whole process.

He slept for a few hours and apparently moved away. But he had taken one the care givers' bags and disappeared. On the following day, I was called again; Mathias had caused some serious trouble around the festival, had been restrained by the security services and brought again to the care space. The festival was over and the space was being dismantled, so we made the choice to evacuate Mathias to the closest hospital in the area with a psychiatric ward.

16.9 "Is This Really Me?"—Regaining Identity

INITIAL OBSERVATION: *What was the first condition that the guest presented with upon coming or being brought to the care service?*

This guest, a young girl, was found on the dance floor doing an amazing choreography of strange postures, completely freezing in between the postures for some 20–30 seconds. It was a cold and very windy night and she was dressed in her bikini top and a miniskirt, her knees were wounded, and her hair tangled with dry plants. Four firemen had surrounded her and they literally seemed afraid of her. She appeared to be totally out of reach, not even registering the care giver's hand movements in front of her face.

KEY ISSUE: *In the course of providing care, what turned out to be the core condition or challenge that had to be handled?*

The core condition of the girl was confusion and various degrees of dissociation. When she came to the service, she couldn't see or talk. Then, when she regained more connection and feeling in her body, the challenge was to stop her from being worried or agitated, and even from experiencing shame. Sometimes the care givers had to chase her and gently bring her back to the sitting spot. Taking care of her wasn't difficult, but it was a challenge to turn such a dissociative experience into a warm and happy one.

PSYCHOACTIVES INVOLVED: *What substances (if any) relevant to the incident had the guest consumed?*

The guest had taken a red micro-star containing about 130–150 micrograms of LSD.

MEDICAL CARE: *Was there a need for medical intervention (that is, any treatment beyond interaction with a care service volunteer)?*

This guest was initially assisted by the firemen, who contacted the paramedics. She was then brought to the care service, and no further medical intervention was required.

TIME IN CARE: *How much time did the guest spend in the care service?*

The guest came in the night and left the next day.

FINAL OUTCOME: *What was the condition of the guest upon discharge from the care service?*

This guest had a full build-up experience followed by a plateau where she was losing it, and in the course of the night spent at the care space, her coming down to a saner state of mind was as evident as it was amazing. The report below is very descriptive and dwells on many of the details of her full return and recovery.

NOTABLE POINTS/LESSONS LEARNED: *What was done well, and what could have been improved upon or done differently? Are there any other notable points from this case?*

Friends usually have an important role to play in bringing a guest to the care space when the person needs to be helped. However, sometimes an individual becomes lost from their group of friends and is experiencing psychoactive effects that induce a strong disconnection from reality. Some of the people attended to by the care service reach states of mind bordering on the psychotic, and they have virtually no possibility to ask for help. Thus, finding them at large events is sometimes a stroke of luck. With this guest in particular, the successful intervention of the care service was preceded by cooperation with other partners: the firemen and the paramedics.

IMPRESSIONS

I didn't have any shifts that day but I hung around the care space for most of the day and evening, and late in the night my working mates told me to go and sleep; I guess I looked tired, but I was feeling like the night was still young! So I headed to the main dance area and then saw a young woman in her bikini top and a miniskirt on a very cold and windy night, now crawling on the mat, with her knees wounded and hair tangled with dry plants, doing an amazing choreography of strange postures! She would struggle with passion and a lot of strong freaky emotion and then freeze in the next pose for some 20–30 seconds. She was dancing a slow painful trip, looking lost and out of contact with this reality. She couldn't stand up, didn't feel like lying down, and she was tensing her muscles so much that she would lock her movements into a pose, propped up on her knees.

I looked around and realised that four firemen had already circled her, all of them keeping well clear of the "cosmic beast"! They were literally frightened of her...; they would all take a step back every time she moved towards them! I knew they were attempting to secure her, and at the same time they were waiting for assistance, as one of them was communicating with the paramedics through the radio. I tried to talk to the girl, but she was totally out of reach, not even registering my hand movements in front of her face. I asked the firemen to bring her to the care space in a car, and I walked there on my own, waiting for her arrival.

She was going through an intense trip, confused and lost. She would sit down for a minute, then jump up trying to walk towards somewhere, then forget her intention and collapse back on the floor! She appreciated the grounding effect of my touch and started following simple instructions like, "Stay with us!" I was assisting her with another of our care givers.

Within five minutes she started speaking in a very British accent, her words emphatic and dramatic with long spaces in between, sometimes striving to place more than three words together in a sentence. She would say things like, "Embarrassment, cold, confusion, so strong, is it really me? Acceptance, safety, trust, why everything?" Her emotions were changing quickly; she was struggling to make sense of her surroundings and attempting to regain her identity.

A "Starlight Kush" cannabis clone displayed by Oaksterdam University's booth at the 2009 Harmony Festival in Santa Rosa, California.
Photo by Erowid.

CASE STUDIES AND IMPRESSIONS

She was verbal, attempting to answer questions like, "What is your name?", "Where you are from?" and trying to explain her situation without any success for a good whole hour. Then, she managed to put some clothes from our stock on by herself but needed assistance with her socks. During her moments of restlessness and agitation, shame or insecurity, she really appreciated my hand supporting her back and shoulders, a friendly pat on the shoulders and a quick back rub to shake off that chilly feeling.

Her Kundalini was travelling wildly up and down her spine, to a point she felt so relaxed and excited she started touching me in intimate spots in a very sensual way. I had to gently remove her hand, reflecting that the "brotherly or fatherly" approach would be more ethical for all of us. Flashes of heat would make her take some clothes off again but the bitter cold around her was forcing her to get dressed and wrapped in one of our sleeping bags. After a while she felt more secure—calm and appreciative of our company—and started saying longer phrases, still struggling to put events in order.

Within half an hour more she could say her name with certainty, and she would ask ours and remember where we all came from. She started getting concerned about her looks, feeling the mess on her hair and trying to pull out the thorns and plants, but she would try to pull her hair out many times and we had to gently persuade her to stop. By now, three hours had passed and we had gathered interesting facts together, as she had confirmed them enough times to be confident that she was telling the truth. She was a sixteen-year-old girl on her birthday night, and this was her first psychedelic experience; she was on a red micro-star LSD trip of 130–150 micrograms, a large dose especially for such a young person.[1]

The few of us who were with her sang her happy birthday, and for the first time we saw sincere happiness shining in her eyes! I was glad to see how she was checking and evaluating her looks. We also offered her a cup of tea. "I

---

[1] Compare with 16.3, "A Rollercoaster of Emotions—From Hell and Back", above. In that Impression the author describes 100 micrograms of LSD as a *light* dose, whilst here, 130–150 micrograms is labelled *large*. These discrepancies illustrate how different individuals are affected by psychoactives in varying ways, yet also how different people—including experienced psychonauts—conceive of similar doses differently. Be wary of jumping to the conclusion that a certain dose will be light, medium or strong for a particular person, especially someone you've never met before. As always, remember that *set* and *setting*, as well as *dose*, each play a fundamental role in determining the strength and quality of a psychedelic experience.

would love a cup of Earl Grey", she said. But we only had camomile, and she gratefully accepted that. Just the fact that she could remember that she loves Earl Grey made me feel confident that she was returning at a steady pace.

By this point she was accurately reflecting upon the events of the night in perfect chronological order, feeling a bit guilty that she had caused such a mobilisation. Now that she was so present—aware and enjoying, letting long breaths flow from her lungs and lowering her stressed-out shoulders—we gave her a short massage. Her body had been so tense since those poses on the dance floor and now she was coming all the way from a hazy, abstract, and "melted space", back into touch with reality and connecting to the sensations of her body, regaining her sense of identity. She seemed really focused on planning her next moves whilst she was empathising with the worries of her friends who must be missing her; yet she also blamed them for letting her down.

It was 4:30 am, dark and cold. She felt like going outside the care space to enjoy the rest of her night but she could also feel the need to rest. The acid was still giving her uncomfortable boosts of energy whilst she was struggling to stay in

A soft reassuring voice and gentle touch can help mellow out an anxious tripper, encouraging a longer stay at the care space if needed.

her sleeping bag. The team was aware that it was important for her to remain a bit longer and that a soft reassuring voice and presence would help her to mellow down and wait for a couple more hours more until she was feeling stronger. This girl, who earlier that night had resembled a creature lost in a bizarre compulsive choreography, struggling with nature and the elements, fully ego-shattered and absent from her body, was slowly returning to her emotions, ego, persona, and self.

Around 5:30 am, her concerns would not allow her to rest or enjoy our company any longer; she really wanted to find her friends and she was very confident about finding her way to her tent, but we offered our escort. As we walked towards the dance floor, the other volunteer and I were high from sheer exhaustion by now, and the girl was feeling optimistic. The sun was greeting everybody with its morning warmth. Although the music and the crowd called to her, she was sober enough to remember her goal and destination, and she easily found her tent. Surprisingly, she was my neighbour!

This girl went through a full circle over twelve strong hours under the effect of LSD, having a complete return and recovery, and I felt our mission had been accomplished.

Some days later I passed by to check up on my neighbour, to see if she was well and rested, and to make sure she had no hangovers or unprocessed emotions. When I came to her camp, her friends called her out; she just put her head through the tent door and quickly assured me that she was fine. I didn't want to interrupt her longer. I felt happy and proud, with a smile on my face! I rank this case as my best because I got it literally thrown at my feet. It was an early intervention at a critical time, and she was definitely in need of psychedelic care.

I also felt that the other care givers on this shift were very complementary to each other the whole time, advising, backing themselves up, and supervising, with the goal of relieving that girl by taking the psychedelic load off her shoulders.

The "Violent Hooligan" in a Spiritual Seeker

16.10

INITIAL OBSERVATION: *What was the first condition that the guest presented with upon coming or being brought to the care service?*

Violence, both physical and verbal.

KEY ISSUE: *In the course of providing care, what turned out to be the core condition or challenge that had to be handled?*

The guest had apparently taken a cocktail of psycho-actives that rendered a generally peaceful being a danger to himself and others. The core concerns were: getting hit, being bitten, contamination with microbes from his bodily fluids, physical abuse whilst holding the guest down, and verbal abuse.

PSYCHOACTIVES INVOLVED: *What substances (if any) relevant to the incident had the guest consumed?*

The guest had taken ketamine, as well as something between "a few drops" and "an entire bottle" of liquid LSD.

MEDICAL CARE: *Was there a need for medical intervention (that is, any treatment beyond interaction with a care service volunteer)?*

Medical care was involved, delivered by event paramedics. Security services also intervened.

TIME IN CARE: *How much time did the guest spend in the care service?*

The guest spent eight to ten hours at the care space.

FINAL OUTCOME: *What was the condition of the guest upon discharge from the care service?*

The guest's friends picked him up once he had returned to a stable condition.

NOTABLE POINTS/LESSONS LEARNED: *What was done well, and what could have been improved upon or done differently? Are there any other notable points from this case?*

A care giver losing his temper in self-defence and tired desperation helped shift the energy of the guest enough so that he was able to begin responding in a positive way. Sometimes, when the conditions are extreme and the approach taken to assist a guest becomes overwhelming, shifting gears can help.

IMPRESSIONS

Somebody shouted a colour code of alert and the ambulance was already there, with the doors opened whilst the security was fighting a strong young man down. He was quick, aggressive, and just losing the last of his clothes! He was very agile, desperately trying to escape, crawling into the hard earth and scratching in many places. After he managed to free his hands from the grip of a security guard, he took a fist-full of dust and ate it! He was in despair and crying, whilst at the same time he was very disruptive and threatening.

I tried to restrain his head to stop him from hitting it on the ground, but the guy was too strong to hold, and he would start spitting (targeting our faces), putting his finger up his rectum, then trying to touch us, and attempting to bite anything close to his mouth!

By now we were eight people working to detain him—four security personnel and four care givers—and still the man was putting up a fight. I ran to bring the stretcher, adding four pillows and two mattresses to make it softer. By the time the stretcher was next to him, ten people were holding him down and a well-built security guard was kneeling on his chest!

As we were keeping him still, a paramedic ran to the car, fixed an injection, and shot him in the thigh. We placed him on the stretcher and it was a struggle to bind him down! He resisted the whole time, still spiting and biting, even with his mouth full of earth and his eyes rolling around. He was trying to pull his penis off many times, and we had to keep a firm grip on his wrists against the stretcher until we immobilised his hands with the help of two cushions and the straps! We had to place two mattresses against the edges of the stretcher so that he couldn't hit his head against the metal frame and we tightened up the belts as much as possible.

He was screaming and he kept saying, "I will beat you up! I know you now! I will find you and kill you!", as well as things like, "Who am I?", "Is this really happening?", "Am I really?", but quickly changing back to violent threats.

We offered him water to wash his face and mouth; by now he had eaten earth three times and thrown dust all over his face. He would bite the plastic water bottle and crush it; we had to pull it away with much force!

When we managed to get him into a special safety zone within the care service, he was still immobilised on the stretcher. After disinfecting our hands, we put on latex gloves and tried to keep our eyes away from his spitting.

By now some of his friends had arrived and we asked them to keep talking to him in their own language. They were not really getting through to him, but they could occasionally distract him from spitting on our faces by shouting, "You better stop that behaviour now!" I asked them if he was usually this violent and aggressive, and they said that he is a very calm and sweet person, interested in yoga and meditation, a spiritual seeker rather than a violent hooligan!

He had a crew cut and a big tattoo, tense muscles and a strong body-build… he didn't look like a spiritual seeker right now; he was in a demonic state, eyes rolling, blowing his nose with force, covering his face with snot, and spitting all the time. He kept sliding his hands away from the grip of the belts tied up around him, and he tried to pull off his penis three or four times more. We kept on tying him back and placing the pillows tightly against his thighs and stomach so he couldn't reach his centre line, and we kept on readjusting the belts to have the maximum hold possible without suffocating him.

Suddenly, he bit the water bottle again! Every time he would cover his face with snot and spit, I had to take a big thick diaper, reach his face, and wipe him clean without giving him a chance to bite me (although he tried many times). After a good hour had passed, it came a point when I started losing my patience with him, as all our approaches were useless: talking calmly and brotherly wasn't helping, joking around didn't come through, begging him for his cooperation was not giving results, and now was the time for a harsher approach. I screamed something like, **"Stop treating me as if I was security! I am here to help you!"** I felt as though I shocked everybody who was there; my voice was loud and angry, and my phrase clearly expressed *my own* experiences and projections. It was out of context and unfair to the security personnel. However, it did help to calm the guy; and by now the injection was setting in; as his muscles relaxed, his powers gave way to a struggle to find rest. He finally drank some water and started dozing off.

He had been keeping four of our people on full alert for more than two hours, during which time three or four of his friends came and went. They told us that he had been taking a lot of ketamine over the last four days, and then he took ten drops of liquid LSD, but soon after that he bit the whole bottle and apparently drank it all! His friends, who were each starting to trip on two drops of LSD just as the security had earlier intervened, wanted to stay there, but their friend was going to be sleeping for some hours, so they had better things to do. They promised to drop by many times and to be there when he woke up. I must have slept like a rock after that, yet I woke up still full of adrenalin. Back at the care space, I was told that the guy we treated had left with friends, and that he was calm, sweet, and very thankful—an amazing difference.

I saw him at a crossroads at the festival and he truly was thankful. He even fell on his knees when I told him we had a plastic bag with his mobile phone and dirty clothes. It was wonderful to see him so different and happy! I wish I could see him again and chat more.

It was a tough job with a pleasant ending, and it made me really appreciate the backup of the paramedics and security, the need for training to deal with difficult and violent cases, and the alertness of our group. It also made me think of the dangers of the work: getting hit, contaminated with microbes from receiving bodily fluids, and potentially being bitten!

I felt so warm to receive thanks and to know that I protected him from the darker self we all hide inside. It is always amazing to see a human being like a wild dangerous beast one day, and the next day like a saint, the hope of humanity!

Water Grounds a Guest in Discomfort

INITIAL OBSERVATION: *What was the first condition that the guest presented with upon coming or being brought to the care service?*

Agitation, incoherence, and discomfort that manifested in hyper-energy.

KEY ISSUE: *In the course of providing care, what turned out to be the core condition or challenge that had to be handled?*

The key issue was that the guest needed grounding.

PSYCHOACTIVES INVOLVED: *What substances (if any) relevant to the incident had the guest consumed?*

It was unclear whether or not the guest had taken anything, and if so, whether the effects were getting stronger or weaker.

MEDICAL CARE: *Was there a need for medical intervention (that is, any treatment beyond interaction with a care service volunteer)?*

There was no need for medical intervention.

TIME IN CARE: *How much time did the guest spend in the care service?*

The guest spent about two hours at the care space.

FINAL OUTCOME: *What was the condition of the guest upon discharge from the care service?*

After sleeping, the guest woke up able to converse.

NOTABLE POINTS/LESSONS LEARNED: *What was done well, and what could have been improved upon or done differently? Are there any other notable points from this case?*

From this experience I came away with an appreciation for the grounding power of water. Although there were potential hazards involved in swimming, the benefits greatly outweighed the risks.

IMPRESSIONS

One evening I was at the care space when a woman came in who was extremely agitated. She was talking, standing up, and moving around but she was not very coherent. I entered the scene and decided to hang out for a while and see if I could speak with her. I tried to figure out what she was talking about and what was concerning her. It was too difficult for her to be clear about her issues and she continued to grow agitated. I stayed in the tent with her for around an hour. It wasn't clear whether or not she had taken anything and, if she had, whether the effects were getting stronger or weaker. It seemed like she was in a plateau of hyper-energy, not very verbal and certainly not comfortable. The general temperature was also quite hot. I had just come in from swimming in the lake that was only 20–30 metres away when I started talking to her. I thought to myself how unusual it was that we had this care space right near a lake. I started thinking about how grounding water can be in times of stress and considered seeing if she was interested.

I thought it might be too dangerous and reviewed all of the inherent risks involved for a long time. I figured that if I stood on the other side of her, towards the deeper water, I could keep her safe. There were also a lot of people already in the water. I asked if she wanted to go to the lake and the idea

If appropriate care is taken, water can be grounding in times of stress. Photo from the 2006 Mind States conference in Costa Rica by Jon Hanna.

immediately appealed to her. We walked to the water and went in. She dove in and I dove in ahead of her. I had a short moment of hesitation, considering whether she was self-destructive. The water was a great relief to her; she was able to get out some physical energy and demonstrated that she wasn't self-destructive.

After five or ten minutes in the water I suggested we head back to the dome. When we got back, she finally relaxed and was able to lie down. I tried to project a sense of tranquillity and meditated a few feet away from her. She grew increasingly quiet, falling asleep after fifteen minutes; it was very peaceful. She was able to converse when she awoke.

From this experience, I came away with an appreciation for the grounding power of water. Though there were risks involved, I carefully considered each of them and decided that the potential benefits greatly outweighed the risks.

Over-Anxious, Overwrought, and Overwhelmed—Kosmicare UK, a Care Service Leader's Point of View

There are so many things to consider when managing a psychedelic support service. Over the years we have encountered many problems, with event organisers and workers not understanding what the service is about, and even with care givers thinking that volunteering at the service is just an easy way to attend an event "for free". The following is a case study that emphasises some of the problems faced by the care service leader, and how they were resolved in this particular instance.

INITIAL OBSERVATION: *What was the first condition that the guest presented with upon coming or being brought to the care service?*

The guest was a young woman about twenty-four years old; she was alone and verging on tears. She looked lost and scared.

KEY ISSUE: *In the course of providing care, what turned out to be the core condition or challenge that had to be handled?*

The woman was extremely anxious and overwhelmed by the emotions she was mentally and physically feeling. She was looping from the darkest, deepest despair to euphoria.

PSYCHOACTIVES INVOLVED: *What substances (if any) relevant to the incident had the guest consumed?*

The guest had taken hash cakes.

MEDICAL CARE: *Was there a need for medical intervention (that is, any treatment beyond interaction with a care service volunteer)?*

There was no need for medical intervention; the guest had already been to the medical tent and was medically fine.

TIME IN CARE: *How much time did the guest spend in the care service?*

The guest spent approximately thirteen hours at the care space.

FINAL OUTCOME: *What was the condition of the guest upon discharge from the care service?*

The guest was extremely tired when she left the service and was escorted back to her tent. She was given a flyer and told to return at any time throughout the festival if she felt the need to do so.

NOTABLE POINTS/LESSONS LEARNED: *What was done well, and what could have been improved upon or done differently? Are there any other notable points from this case?*

It was obvious that even though the medical service knew about us they didn't really understand how we help people. It would have been a good training exercise for the medical team if they had been available just to observe this case. It also showed the importance of having both male and female care givers available at any given time.

Eighteen months after the event, the guest emailed the service, thanking us for our good work. (This shows the value of distributing flyers providing an email address for the service.)

IMPRESSIONS

We arrived at the festival site—an event at which we had never worked before—with only a skeleton crew. This is a regular situation that we encounter, not being able to ensure that all the volunteers are on-site for training. Some of our volunteers work, and so cannot attend a day or two before the start of the event. And in this case I am describing, the guest needed our help even before the event had officially started.

We had just finished setting up and decorating our structure and we were preparing to go to bed. It had been a long, busy day (we had travelled from another festival), when we heard a knock on the door and there was "Silvia". She looked lost, confused, and on the verge of tears. We invited her into the space and a male colleague sat and talked with her whilst I made her a cup of tea. It was obvious when I returned that even though my colleague was an experienced care giver, she felt uncomfortable with him. He called me over, introduced me, and when he saw her relax he quietly slipped away.

Silvia explained that she'd got to the festival early and her friends had not yet arrived. She had set up her tent and decided to have some hash cakes before going to sleep. She was badly affected by them and became scared, and she eventually sought help from the medical tent. She explained that the staff at the med tent had good intentions but did not know what to do; they suggested that she telephone her parents (!), which frightened her even more. She explained that she had seen us setting up throughout the day and had actually spoken to another care giver in passing, so she came to seek our help.

It became obvious that Silvia was looping: from a dark despair (during which she thought she was going to die), through to normality (when she realised that this was going to be a long trip but knew it would end eventually), to euphoria (when she actually didn't want the trip to be over).

The only thing I could do was to keep her warm, listen to her, and reassure her that I wouldn't leave her and she would be all right again, and that whatever she wanted to do—whether it was crying, drinking tea, screaming, or going for a walk around the site (all of which she did)—it would be okay and I would be there for her.

Silvia was in our care for approximately thirteen hours. We were exhausted at the end of the journey, but we had both learned so much.

As a care service leader I realised many things, such as the acute lack of understanding from the medical team. Even though I had been to see the medics earlier in the day, it was only after talking to Silvia, and her telling me what had happened at the medical tent, that I realised I had to go back and meet with them again and make the situation very clear about the needs of our potential guests. After meeting with them the following day and discussing Silvia (she was someone they could relate to; a real live person) they had a much better understanding of what our service offers. They continued to work with us very well after that and we have worked with the same team at other festivals quite successfully.

Going the extra mile really hit home for me; I was extremely tired when Silvia arrived needing help, and even though I had not slept, I knew it was important for me to stay awake and give her my full attention to help her through her journey in a positive manner.

The following day, when the rest of the team looked to me for guidance, and all I wanted to do was sleep, I realised that the skills of leadership include the capacity to organise one's own work and that of others. This requires attending to several activities simultaneously, prioritising, and switching gears as necessary. It includes dealing with unexpected crises, obstacles, or interruptions, and effectively getting back on track, to prevent further crises.

I learned that a clear head, calm demeanour, and the ability to delegate are essential when running a successful service. *It is also essential to have a co-leader of some sort to share the workload* (one person cannot be on-call twenty-four hours a day); it also means you have assistance rather than isolation in dealing with any problems that arise. Making sure that the correct team is chosen is crucial; it is important for morale and the smooth, successful running of the care service. Members should be aware of their abilities and should be encouraged to ask for help if they need it. There are always challenges in the care service and a strong team can act as a support mechanism for all care givers, working together to improve the service. The team certainly supported me that day; the workload was organised between them, allowing me a few hours rest and recuperation.

I would like to share a quote from Silvia, which she wrote after the experience and granted permission for us to use in the Manual:

> "I was severely anxious and very overwrought and very overwhelmed by the physical sensations in my body as a result of the ingestion of too much of a good thing. The anxiety was in my mind, as well as in my body. Tracey was an angel to me when I badly needed one. My mind was a very difficult place to inhabit that night and she possessed great patience and empathy, which she generously shared with me to guide me through the experience.
>
> I was shattered for most of the festival thereafter. But one thing is certain in my mind. I truly honestly deeply do not know how I would have come safely through the experience, were it not for her guiding light."

Being part of a psychedelic support service is hard work and can be emotionally, physically, and financially draining at times, but the benefits far outweigh the down times. It enhances your life tremendously; and the satisfaction of doing something successfully that you wholeheartedly believe in is the most incredible feeling ever; it restores your faith in humanity. Just reading Silvia's email reaffirms that services such as ours, if done well, are the most valuable resource that a party, event or festival can offer their clientele.

Experiences as a Care Service Leader

There is so much to consider when managing a psychedelic support team! I could tell many stories of cases, but none would be more important than the impressions from the point of view of a care service leader. I would like to share some of the challenges we faced through the years working at festivals, hoping that our lessons can be of help to those people who want to start a psychedelic care service.

ABOUT VOLUNTEERS

Many people are very keen to come to a festival, and they may see volunteering as an easy way in. But as a service leader we have to choose our volunteers as best as we can, because they are the backbone of the work. Never trust other people to bring friends along to help; always go through the steps of having potential crew fill out a form, and make sure that the applicant understands the seriousness of the task. When volunteers live in different parts of the country or abroad, it can be very difficult to organise training. We have tried many times to ask people to arrive two days before the event, but in our experience most people don't come "early", because they are unable to get extra holiday time off from their jobs. This is a tricky thing, because we can't work without volunteers... yet it's difficult to work if the volunteers have no training. We have learned to compromise; we ask people to arrive as soon as they can and accept it if they can arrive only the same day the festival starts. We always make teams by mixing new volunteers with more experienced ones, and we encourage the newbies to seek help whenever they need. We coach them as they work, and try to make time for revision, evaluation, and personal support.

Another common problem we used to have was when volunteers arrived at the festival, but did not come to work, or missed their shifts. We resolved that problem by requiring applicants to make out a cheque to our organisation for a value even higher than the price of the festival ticket. If they come to all their shifts, the cheque is returned to the volunteer or destroyed; otherwise we cash it as compensation for the inconvenience.

Some people may sound very good on paper, but they turn out to be not-so-good in reality. A few people we've worked with had lots of impressive qualifications, but it ended up that they weren't team players; they set themselves apart from the group, creating friction and conflicts. It is always good to check the references given and to be ready to put the volunteer in a different roll/task if they are not fit for a particular job. For example, once I encountered a very judgemental and condescending new volunteer; she was not empathic with the people in need and, on the contrary, was talking down to them as if they were stupid. I decided to remove her from sitting, and gave her work at the kitchen, where she was in charge of making cups of tea; in this way, she was still involved with the team but not directly involved with the people in crisis.

Most times volunteers go through emotional problems themselves. This can be because they are dealing with lots of deep existential situations that the care service guests are going through, and these can act as a mirror to their own life situations; sooner or later something triggers their own fears and challenges, and they find themselves in a conflict. It is important that the care service leader be ready for this. In our experience, it happens to nearly every volunteer at least once! That's why the team must be very reliable and support each other. Nevertheless, it's the responsibility of the service leader (and also team leads) to try to resolve such issues as soon as they arise. We have had many cases like this, but I'll present an especially serious one as an example, because it also relates to the predicament of not having enough volunteers.

We had a friend of the team, a vibrant and charming person who was there to help organise the group. However, I didn't want him to sit because he was suffering from bipolar disorder and often felt depressed and helpless. Unfortunately, we didn't have enough volunteers, and one night around the fire circle he started to talk to a woman who was suffering from depression. She was self-harming and not taking care of her personal appearance. After talking to her for a short while, he realised he couldn't help her and called another colleague to step in. Whilst he was with me, reporting the case, he said, "Look at the state she is in! I think it would be better if she killed herself!" But at the same time that he made this statement, he realised that he was actually talking about himself. Immediately after he realised this, he fell into a deep depression and had suicidal thoughts that lasted for days after the event. I had to follow him very closely, talking to him every day, and a week later assisted him in entering a suicide help clinic, where he was admitted for five days until the crisis ceased. Thankfully he is still alive today.

Another problem we encounter is that many of the people inclined to do sitting work have been or currently are involved at some level with sharing or selling substances. In some ways I see this as a natural consequence of the subject, because in the best case scenario, any well-intentioned, conscious dealer of psychedelics would be there for a friend or customer if/when things go wrong, giving direct counselling or providing information about other similar reactions that they may know of. These are the people who often have great hands-on experience assisting intoxicated individuals who are struggling with an experience brought on by mixing compounds or consuming high doses. An academic psychologist or serious researcher will have fewer chances to do a practical intervention, due to legal obstacles; they may have access only to personal or conceptual information. However, a person who has been sharing/dealing drugs will have had a larger number of encounters with the dark side of psychoactive drug use. I believe that a good mix of knowledge and skills is the best formula for a care service team, provided that everyone has great tolerance, openness, and willingness to learn from each other. The only problem is that sometimes the old clients of such individuals come to the care space looking for drugs! For obvious reasons this is a big NO when we are trying to run a respectable, legal care service. It's a difficult subject to talk about... a hot potato. Whilst I must validate the invaluable knowledge of non-professional peer volunteers, it's imperative that a care service leader never ignore the possibility of prospective care givers or their friends sharing or selling substances, or the situation may backfire on you. Be clear with your team at the first meeting: the care service can't be filled with dealers, so they must please make all their friends and/or clients aware of this whilst they are volunteering. Let them know that anyone who breaks this rule will be removed from the team, no exceptions.

ABOUT FESTIVALS

Many times festivals don't want to advertise the existence of a psychedelic care service; they feel that doing so will be admitting that there will be drugs on the premises. We praise the people who include a care space at their event as being responsible and conscientious. We thank them for caring about the well-being of their guests and assure them that our presence will reduce dramatic situations and the escalation of cases to a point where outside services are required.

When dealing with organisers it is important that the event's leaders understand specific points from the beginning. Some things are negotiable, and some aren't. For example, you can compromise with regard to food for the volunteers, or having water near by, but you should never compromise about safety. You should demand a radio to communicate with the medical and security teams, if the need arises. We have suffered the negligence of event organisers who failed to give us a radio and we had to rely on stewards to contact the medical team. Because of this we decided to buy our own radio set. This is an important point: I highly recommend that every project consider having their own means to communicate with the medical and security services.

Sitting is demanding work and ideally a care service should be open twenty-four hours throughout the duration of the festival. Many small festivals don't want to provide enough tickets for the care service team; they think that because it's a small festival, "ten sitters will be plenty". We came to realise that it is practically unsafe to work with less than twelve people for a three-day event, regardless if the festival is a very small one. So again, do not compromise on the size of your team or you will find yourself flat-out tired, attempting to do more than you possibly can.

In terms of the location of the care space, it is important to have a good spot at the festival, somewhere quiet but not too far from the action. Look for hazards like pits, holes, or rivers near by. Think of how the place will affect the people who need the space but are totally disorientated. Have a big illuminated sign and easy access for an ambulance to arrive if necessary.

ABOUT THE SPACE

Make sure that the space is respected as a sanctuary at all times. We have had many situations where it has been necessary to intervene. Sometimes friends want to come to check how a guest is doing; this is okay, but many times these people are under the influence themselves and they may become loud and disturbing to other guests. It is important to ensure that non-guests do not "take over" the space as if it were their own.

Resting reveler reduces regurgitation risks at the 2009 Symbiosis Festival in Yosemite. Photo by David Arnson.

CASE STUDIES AND IMPRESSIONS

I always say that a good festival is one where we have the care space free most of the time. As a contrast to most business models, a care service with fewer guests is a measure of effective work; it means that attendees are being provided with good information and they are making responsible decisions. However, accidents can and will happen, so never lose your alertness, even when it looks like all is peaceful. Do not allow the use of the space as a chill-out; it is better to be empty and ready than full of sleeping people whom you will have to awaken and move out if somebody in crisis appears.

BE READY

Things can happen before the event starts. We were very relaxed a day before the festival started; the tent was up, but no decorations or beddings were in place. Some of the volunteers decided to open a bottle of rum and were partying away when we got a call from security services; a young guy had fallen into the river, and doctors were examining him but they needed dry clothes and a place for him to stay under supervision—he was very drunk and hypothermic. Luckily, I was sober and could deal with the situation, even in the messy environment and with my entire team inebriated! At least one sober person must be on guard at all times, and preferably more than one.

Things can happen after the event finishes. In our experience, the crew may themselves need support when the festival ends, as the crew party can be more over-the-top than the whole festival put together! So be ready for casualties. We had one very serious case in which a crew member overdosed on GBL by accident when everyone was packed up; even the medical team was gone. We had to stay one extra day, caring for him until he returned to baseline.

Some people might think that because a care service is available, this means that they can take higher doses, since we will care for them. Discourage this attitude if and when you come across it. We have had friends bringing their friends to do "heroic doses" of DMT in front of our tent, in order to feel safe whilst they took something they'd never tried before, even at a low dose. Unfortunately, I only realised this was occurring as it was happening! Understanding the nature of the substance, I couldn't display anger or abruptly ask them to go away... I had to be cautious and talk sweetly to the friend who was lighting the pipe. I explained that this was trespassing on our ethical ground rules, and that he was confused about our role at the event. We provide a safe space, but this is not an encouragement for the use of drugs. I could only talk to the friend, and I had to wait for the person who was tripping to go through his peak and come back before I could have a word with him... And even then, it wasn't possible until the next day to sit down and seriously explain how misguided their decision to smoke near the care service was. As a leader, one has to be vigilant about these issues; on occasions, I had volunteers smoking inside the tent (because it was empty), or using the privacy of our space's curtains to weigh substances (because they didn't have good lights in their own tents!). Any such inappropriate activities must be shut down as quickly and discreetly as possible.

What we have learned is that staffing a psychedelic care service is both a very demanding and a very rewarding job. It is not to be taken lightly. As a coordinator, one has to be on top of things without dominating the group. Leave space for growing. Have others to rely on. Be humane and speak up if you are tired and need support. The team becomes a family. Treat them with respect and love, and you will receive the same in return.

Good luck!

Refreshingly cool and dark during the heat of the day, this kiva/tepee structure was a more private space for psychedelic journeys at KosmiCare during the 2008 Boom Festival. Photo by Erowid.

VIBRATA CHROMODORIS • *Below Zero*, 2012 • digital (Adobe Illustrator)
http://vibrata.com

CHAPTER 17
ONLINE RESOURCES AND OBTAINING ASSISTANCE

Xavier Urquiaga A.

Svea Nielsen

Annie Oak

This chapter provides Internet links to various online resources and harm-reduction organisations. Whilst fairly comprehensive, it is by no means exhaustive. The website of the Multidisciplinary Association for Psychedelic Studies (MAPS) also provides a list of relevant resources.

General Resources

Code of Ethics for Spiritual Guides
by the Council on Spiritual Practices (2001)
http://csp.org/code.html

The *Code of Ethics* is also reproduced in Chapter 2, "The Principles and Ethics of Psychedelic Support".

"Psychedelic Crisis FAQ" by Erowid (2005)
http://www.erowid.org/psychoactives/faqs/psychedelic_crisis_faq.shtml

Erowid is *the* website for information on psychoactive drugs. This publication gives a good summary and provides a useful list of things that can be done to help in a psychedelic crisis.

Erowid Experience Vaults
http://www.erowid.org/experiences/

Over 24,000 first-person trip reports, reviewed and searchable by several criteria. The most comprehensive resource of its type in the world.

Green Dot Advanced Ranger Training Manual
by Burning Man (2012)
http://rangers.burningman.com/wp-content/uploads/GD-manual-2012.pdf

The training manual for the Green Dot Rangers, who provide peer-based counselling at the Burning Man Arts Festival.

DÁT2 Psy Help Manual (2013)
http://daath.hu/dat2/psy-help/dat2-psy-help-manual-EN.pdf

This "psy help" (that is, psychedelic/psychological/psychiatric help) manual is a practical guide to harm reduction at parties and festivals, focusing on psychedelic emergencies and spiritual crises. It draws together practical knowledge on drug-related harm reduction, discusses the requirements for the helpers as both individuals and team members, and provides practical details about the psychedelic support process, including various ethical considerations.

"Crisis Intervention in Situations Related to Unsupervised Use of Psychedelics"
by Stanislav Grof (1980)
http://www.psychedelic-library.org/grof2.htm

An excellent piece of writing by one of the leaders in the scientific research of psychedelics, from his classic book, *LSD Psychotherapy*. In a psychedelic crisis, we often think that the drug has created the problem. But actually, we are usually dealing with the dynamics of the unconscious.

Erowid information booth at the 2009 Symbiosis Festival in Yosemite. Photo by Erowid.

Grof stresses that LSD sessions in which the emerging gestalt is not complete are conducive to negative emotional and physical after-effects and "flashbacks".

"Using Psychedelics Wisely"
by Myron J. Stolaroff (1993)
http://www.erowid.org/entheo_issues/writings/stolaroff_using.shtml

A valuable point of view from the author: "Interestingly, this concept of the trained user does not appear in the literature. But it is precisely the trained user who can best take advantage of the unfathomed range of wisdom and understanding contained in the far reaches of the mind. There seems to be no limit to the dimensions of understanding that can be experienced by the explorer who has the courage, integrity, and skill to navigate them. With integrity, and with the support of appropriate disciplines and friends, one can bring back a great deal for the betterment of oneself and mankind."

Session Games People Play: A Manual for the Use of LSD
by Lisa Bieberman (1967)
http://www.luminist.org/archives/session.htm

An excellent guide, aimed at first-time experimenters with LSD, but containing insightful and well-written material that should be of great interest to any psychonaut and psychedelic crisis care giver. First published as a pamphlet in 1967, shortly after LSD was made illegal in the United States.

"A Note on Adverse Effects"
by Lester Grinspoon and James B. Bakalar (1983)
http://www.druglibrary.org/schaffer/lsd/adverse.htm

From Grinspoon and Bakalar's book *Psychedelic Reflections*, this chapter reviews the literature on adverse effects of psychedelic drugs. In summary, bad trips and mild flashbacks are common and even expected, but are usually considered a mere nuisance—and occasionally even an opportunity—rather than a danger. There is no good evidence of organic brain damage or genetic alterations as a result of psychedelic drug use. Bad trips usually become deterrents before they become dangerous.

"'Bad Trips' May Be the Best Trips"
by Walter Houston Clark (1976)
http://www.druglibrary.org/schaffer/lsd/clark2.htm

Clark's article, which appeared in the April 1976 issue of *FATE* magazine, contains a first-person account from someone who underwent treatment in a controversial Mexican clinic that was inducing "bad" trips in their patients. Dr. Salvador Roquet deliberately disturbed his subjects to bring their worst fears and issues to the surface. He had a successful (apparently positive) outcome for nearly 3,000 patients.

How to Treat Difficult Psychedelic Experiences: A Manual
http://www.maps.org/images/pdf/Psychedelic-Harm-Reduction-2014.pdf

Written by a psychedelic therapist and originally posted as part of MAPS' Rites of Passage Project, this concise article has recently been adapted as "Appendix A" within *The Zendo Project Harm Reduction Manual*. It covers the "Role of the Sitter, Facilitator", "Varieties of Psychedelic-Induced Crises", "Working and Being with Psychedelic Emergencies", "Aftercare", and "Related Readings".

"Ethical Caring in Psychedelic Work"
by Kylea Taylor, M.S. (1997)
http://www.maps.org/news-letters/v07n3/07326tay.html

An article from the *MAPS Bulletin* that presents some ethical considerations for psychedelic sitters.

"Working with Difficult Psychedelic Experiences"
by Brandy Doyle (2001)
http://www.maps.org/news-letters/v11n2/v11n2_14-17.pdf

An article from the *MAPS Bulletin* that reports on a care service at a festival in Columbus, Ohio. An interesting quote: "In a sense, the young people who find themselves in a tent like a psychedelic Civil War hospital really are war victims,

Brad Burge staffs the Multidisciplinary Association for Psychedelic Studies (MAPS) information booth at the 2009 Symbiosis Festival in Yosemite. Photo by Erowid.

casualties of the Drug War that prevents open communication and responsibility regarding psychedelics".

**"Ground Central Station at the Boom Festival: Creating a Safe Space for Working with Psychedelic Crises"
by Sandra Karpetas (2003)**
http://www.maps.org/news-letters/v13n1/v13n1_37-40.pdf

An article from the *MAPS Bulletin* that reports on the care service provided at the 2002 Boom Festival. This was the first time that the service was set up as an official project by the Boom organisers in collaboration with MAPS.

Bad Trip Guide
http://www.badtripguide.com

A good site to help someone prepare for a trip, including the why, what, how, where, and so forth.

Preparación para una Sesión con Enteógenos
http://www.imaginaria.org/sesion.htm

This site provides a good Spanish language introduction to the psychonautic use of enteogens, covering all aspects of a basic session.

***Meeting the Divine Within: A Manual for Voyagers and Guides and Supplemental Information*
by The Guild of Guides (2010)**
http://enlightenment.com/entheo_manual.pdf

This manual brings together the insights of a number of guides who have been working quietly behind the scenes over the last forty years to facilitate maximally safe and sacred entheogenic experiences.

ONLINE RESOURCES AND OBTAINING ASSISTANCE

"Ground Control: A Sitter's Primer"
by The Teafærie (July 22, 2007)
https://www.erowid.org/psychoactives/guides/guides_article2.shtml

An excellent general overview of basic protocols and best practices for those who would act as sitters or "ground control" for psychedelic psychonauts. Also check out the author's short supplementary piece, "Spiritual Emergence Kit".

"Interview with Kosmicare UK founder Karin Silenzi de Stagni" by Robert Dickins (November 19, 2013)
http://psypressuk.com/2013/11/19/interview-with-KosmiCare-uk-founder-karin-silenzi-de-stagni

One of our Manual authors, Karin Silenzi de Stagni, speaks to the *Psychedelic Press UK* about her British psychedelic care service.

Videos

Working With Difficult Psychedelic Experiences: A Practical Introduction to the Principles of Psychedelic Therapy by Donna Dryer (2011)
https://www.youtube.com/playlist?list=PLF78A33465DDA48D2

A twenty-minute video produced by MAPS that presents information about how to take care of someone who is undergoing a difficult psychedelic experience. Good material to use for training purposes.

Psychedelics in the Psychiatric Emergency Room by Julie Holland, MD, video and transcript (2010)
http://vimeo.com/16702478
http://www.erowid.org/culture/characters/holland_julie/holland_julie_ps21c_presentation1.shtml

An interesting thirty-minute video (and transcript thereof). Dr. Holland shares lessons she learned in a psychiatric emergency room at Bellevue Hospital Center in New York City. She also describes the potential therapeutic use of MDMA in the treatment of schizophrenia. Holland is the editor of *Ecstasy: The Complete Guide*.

Safer Festival Intervention at O.Z.O.R.A. 2012: The Haven by Jonas Di Gregorio (August 23, 2012)
http://www.youtube.com/watch?v=fdoPjsMct1k

A short video by one of our Manual authors, Jonas Di Gregorio, about The Haven care space at O.Z.O.R.A. Festival in Hungary, 2012.

17.3 Discussion Forums

Bluelight's Harm Reduction Forum
http://www.bluelight.ru/vb/forumdisplay.php?forumid=144

Drugs-Forum
http://www.drugs-forum.com/index.php

The Lycaeum
http://www.lycaeum.org/forums/

The Shroomery
http://www.shroomery.org/forums

17.4 Some Organisations Working in Psychedelic Care and Harm Reduction

EUROPE

Agência Piaget para o Desenvolvimento (APDES)
http://www.apdes.pt/v1/

Alice Project
http://www.alice-project.de

Checkit!
http://www.checkyourdrugs.at

Chill out
http://chillout-pdm.de/verein

Correlation Network
http://www.correlation-net.org

Crew
http://www.crew2000.org.uk

DÁT2 Psy Help
http://daath.hu/dat2/psy-help

Democracy, Cities and Drugs Projects
http://www.democitydrug.org

DrogArt
http://www.drogart.org

Drug Scouts
http://www.drugscouts.de

Drugcom.de
http://www.drugcom.de

Drugs Just Say Know
http://www.know-drugs.ch/home.htm

Energy Control
http://www.energycontrol.org

European Cities On Drug Policy
http://www.ecdp.net

European Foundation of Drug Helplines (FESAT)
http://www.fesat.org/en

European Monitoring Centre for Drugs
and Drugs Addiction (EMCDDA)
http://www.emcdda.europa.eu

Eve & Rave
http://www.eve-rave.net

Fêtez Clairs (Celebrate Clear)
http://www.fetez-clairs.org

Jellinek
http://www.jellinek.nl/

KosmiCare Boom
http://www.boomfestival.org/boom2014/boomguide/kosmicare

Kosmicare UK
http://www.kosmicareuk.org

Lab57 Alchemica: Laboratorio Antiproibizionista Bologna (Alchemical Lab57: Anti-prohibitionist Laboratory of Bologna)
http://lab57.indivia.net

Modus Vivendi
http://www.modusvivendi-be.org

Movida Project
http://www.comune.venezia.it/flex/cm/pages/ServeBLOB.php/L/IT/IDPagina/58737

Progetto Neutravel (Neutravel Project)
https://www.facebook.com/Neutravel

Nightlife Empowerment & Well-being Network (NEW Net) / Safer Nightlife
http://www.safernightlife.org

PartyProjekt-Odyssee (Party Project Odyssey)
http://partyprojekt-odyssee.de

PartySmart
http://partysmart.org/index.php?file=public/home.php

Peer Involvement
http://www.peerinvolvement.eu

Progetto Nautilus (Nautilus Project)
http://www.progettonautilus.it

Psicologi Senza Frontiere (Psychologists Without Borders)
http://www.psicologisenzafrontiere.org

Q de festa (Q Festival)
http://www.qdefesta.cat

Quality Nights
http://www.qualitynights.be

Safer Clubbing
http://www.saferclubbing.ch

Safer Party
http://www.saferparty.ch

DanceSafe information booth at the 2011 International Drug Policy Reform Conference. Photo by Erowid.

Spora
http://www.spora.ws/en

Techno+
http://www.technoplus.org

THE UNITED STATES
(see also Chapter 1, "A History of Psychedelic Care Services")

Burning Man Emergency Services Department (ESD) & the Green Dot Rangers
http://www.brcesd.org
http://rangers.burningman.com/ranger-teams

The Burning Man Emergency Services Department (ESD) and the Green Dot Rangers both provide services to participants at the annual Burning Man Festival in Nevada. The Burning Man ESD runs a Mental Health Branch that provides psychiatric services for distressed participants at the event's Sanctuary space, and the Green Dot Rangers provide peer counselling at this location.

DanceSafe
http://www.dancesafe.org

DanceSafe provides harm reduction and peer-based educational programmes to reduce negative drug experiences and empower young people to make healthy, informed choices. DanceSafe is known for bringing pill-testing services to the rave and nightlife communities in the United States, where their volunteers staff harm-reduction booths at raves, nightclubs, and other dance events.

The Rainbow Family of Living Light

The Rainbow Gathering has assembled each year since 1972 on National Forest land in the United States and is coordinated by a loose affiliation of people called the Rainbow Family of Living Light. The Gathering offers health services run by a group of volunteers called the Center for Alternative Living Medicine (CALM). Psychedelic care services are provided by Brew HaHa, a CALM subcamp.

Rock Med
http://www.rockmed.org

Rock Med was created in 1973 to serve participants at large concerts in the San Francisco Bay Area. Since then, it has branched out to provide care at sporting events, marches, fairs, circuses, and other large gatherings. The group now has about 1,200 volunteer doctors, nurses, and CPR-certified care givers, and serves at more than 700 events a year in Northern California.

Spiritual Emergence Network (SEN)
http://spiritualemergence.info

A site for spiritual counselling, with a database of therapists aware of the profound impact that psychedelics can have.

White Bird
http://whitebirdclinic.org

White Bird is a non-profit human service agency based in Eugene, Oregon, that runs health clinics and has provided medical care at festivals for over forty years. A collective of largely volunteers, White Bird offers free primary care to the homeless and runs CAHOOTS, or Crisis Assistance Helping Out On The Streets, a mobile crisis intervention team.

INTERNATIONAL

EcstasyData.org
http://www.ecstasydata.org/index.php

"EcstasyData.org is an independent laboratory pill testing program run by Erowid Center, and co-sponsored by DanceSafe and Isomer Design. Launched in July 2001, its purpose is to collect, review, manage, and publish laboratory pill testing results from a variety of organizations."

Harm Reduction International
http://www.ihra.net

Volunteers for Erowid and the Portuguese risk reduction group Check-In conduct thin-layer chromatographic drug testing at the 2010 Boom Festival. Photo by Erowid.

LUKE GRAY • *Fountain of Youth*, 2013 • Staedtler Triplus Fineliner and watercolour
http://www.lukegray.net

FINAL WORDS

Psychedelic care services—in their modern form—have been around since the 1960s, yet it appears that a new era is underway, characterised by more care spaces than ever before, and increasingly organised, professional, and well-trained care service teams (that we hope will only continue and expand). There are many reasons for this growing trend; they include the gradual revival and re-legitimisation of psychoactive drug research around the globe; the fact that large music festivals are now being regularly held and run in a competent and responsible manner; the shifting of focus and attitudes of some national policy makers (in Europe especially) from prohibition to harm reduction; and the emerging availability of a great number of novel psychoactive substances for which there is little research or experiential knowledge. Importantly, the most significant efforts at setting up and running new care services are coming largely from within the "psychedelic community" itself; brave initiatives by men and women who are personally familiar with the psychedelic space, generally love music festivals, and have identified a pressing need for care work. They are well-aware that such care spaces can and do bring light to guests in their darkest hours of need, and may make the difference between a horrific, scarring experience, and a difficult yet ultimately radiant and liberating one.

This Manual contains practical information intended to be scalable to care services of different sizes. Many of the care givers, team leads, and care service leaders who have volunteered at large events and helped write this material began their care work in far smaller settings, sometimes without any budget and in an impromptu capacity. Indeed, the principles presented in this Manual can be put to use during informal care situations, in which no structured care service is present.

We aimed to be as thorough as possible with the material, yet we also wish to emphasise: **do not be daunted** by the myriad details covered herein! Whether you're a care service leader, a care giver, a seasoned psychonaut, an enthusiastic novice, or anything else, you will rarely be alone; there will usually be capable and experienced people around you, whom you can turn to for help and advice. Indeed, as repeatedly highlighted, the *people* who make up a care service team are its absolute core; how they're trained, treated, and motivated to work with one another will be the decisive factors in making or breaking a care project. We cannot emphasise enough the importance of care givers taking care of and looking out for one another.

One of the Impressions related in this Manual contains the fitting remark: *"we should expect nothing less than the unexpected when working at a care service"*. Indeed, at some points a care space may be calm and peaceful, yet at others it may well resemble a war zone. In the latter cases, the care givers are truly on the front lines, doing what they can based on the sum total of their experience and training in order to provide care and comfort to guests in need. When one keeps in mind the overall purpose—to help people and to bring in whatever love and healing can be brought to a

Hooping (left) and dancing (right) were popular activities at the 2009 Harmony Festival. Photos by Erowid.

given situation—one can rarely go wrong. Having said that, it must be emphasised again that psychedelic care services may involve life-threatening situations; corners cannot be cut in following procedures to assess whether trained medical support is required, nor in seeking it out if it is.

It is the dream of countless people involved in this "space", including many working at care services (and many of those who wrote this Manual), that the modern Western world will come to adopt a more balanced, realistic, and hopeful outlook regarding the positive potential of well-established psychoactive plants and molecules, compared to the largely negative and ill-informed attitudes prevalent in mainstream contemporary societies. In this vein, care givers at psychedelic care spaces should see themselves also as educators and ambassadors, both to the attendee populations whilst they are at events, and to the public at large in their daily lives.

To all these worthy ends just mentioned, we encourage you the reader to go out, share, and apply the knowledge contained in this Manual wherever it is needed.

May you keep doing good things!

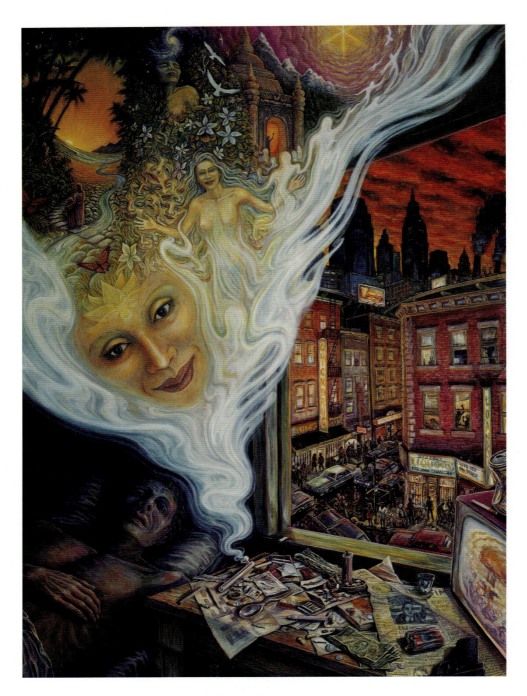

MARK HENSON • *Illusion of Reality, 1993* • oil on canvas

http://markhensonart.com/all-art-gallery-shop/illusion-of-reality

*Most of us who were raised in the '60s and '70s have "been there"/"done that",
or knew someone who had "been there"/"done that"
We may have visited someone like this poor soul...*

In a shabby room, in any big city, a broken man lies dead or near death. From his pipe, a vision of what all of humanity seeks wafts towards the ceiling. Paradise, the face of a woman, brotherhood, harmony with nature and spirit, the heart of human existence is but a vision. His table is filled with a cornucopia of escape mechanisms, anything to quash the pain of existence. A nuclear bomb goes off on the TV set, as the newspaper proclaims the next war. The toxic environment was not the drug of his choice. The room overlooks a desolate urban nightmare. Pollution hangs over a garish street scene. Ladies of the night stand on the corner; cops roust folks on the opposite street as Krishna devotees sing their mantras hoping to bring a bit of divinity to the situation. In the hotel across the way, an artist peers through his window. In rooms nearby, various people escape in their own ways from their collective self-created miseries.

It's our war on us.

— Commentary by Monti Moore

Appendix A

STREET NAMES FOR COMMONLY ENCOUNTERED PSYCHOACTIVES

Zevic Mishor

Christopher J. Ward

Daniel Leuenberger

Emma Metcalf

Igor Domsac

Isla Camille Duporge

Jacob Potkonyak

João Gonçalves

Kai Schulze

Karin Silenzi de Stagni

Kim Penders

Marc B. Aixalà

Maria Carmo Carvalho

Natacha Ribeiro

Snu Voogelbreinder

The following lists are intended as a quick reference: an alphabetically ordered guide for "translating" street names of commonly encountered psychoactives into their more standard versions (for example, cannabis, cocaine, LSD, and so forth). In this first edition of the Manual, we present names in six languages: Dutch, English, French, German, Portuguese, and Spanish. Where possible, we have tried to preserve region-specific information (for example, usage of a term in Australian- versus American-English, or European- versus Mexican-Spanish). Botanical names are given, as per standard practice, in *italics* (for example, *Salvia divinorum*); however, more commonly used terms are written normally (for example, cannabis, psilocybin-containing mushrooms, and so forth).

These lists must be considered a work in progress; indeed, the very knowledge they are attempting to capture is constantly changing due to the nature of day-to-day spoken language. We welcome any additions or feedback, which can be provided to us at http://www.psychsitter.com.

DUTCH

STREET NAME	PSYCHOACTIVE
Acid	LSD
Ballon	Nitrous oxide
Blow	Cocaine
Bruine	Heroin
Chrystallen	MDMA
Coke	Cocaine
Een Blowtje	Cannabis
Gras	Cannabis
Hasj	Hashish
Ket	Ketamine
Liquid	GHB
M	MDMA
Magic Truffels	Psilocybin-containing mushroom sclerotia
MD	MDMA
Molly	MDMA
Paddos	Psilocybin-containing mushrooms
Pep	Amphetamine
Philosopher's Stones	Psilocybin-containing mushroom sclerotia
Shit	Hashish
Skunk	Cannabis
Smack	Heroin
Snelle	Amphetamine
Special K	Ketamine
Speed	Amphetamine
Stoeltjes	Psilocybin-containing mushrooms
Stuff	Hashish
Tripcactus	Mescaline-containing cacti
Trips	LSD
Truffel	Psilocybin-containing mushroom sclerotia
Vloeibare	GHB
Vloeibare XTC	GHB
Weed	Cannabis
Wiet	Cannabis
Witte	Cocaine
Zegels	LSD

MDMA may be sold pressed into pills (as shown here from the 2010 Boom Festival), or it may be available as crystalline chunks or powder. Photo by Erowid.

Commonly described by dealers at the 2008 Boom Festival as being "mescaline", these very tiny stars were actually LSD microdots. Photo by Erowid.

The "Fly Agaric" (Amanita muscaria) contains the psychoactive chemicals ibotenic acid and muscimol. Due to their sometimes-less-than-pleasant effects, other mushrooms—those that contain the psychedelics psilocybin and psilocin—are much more popular among festival attendees. Photo by Jon Hanna, 2009.

STREET NAMES for **COMMONLY ENCOUNTERED SUBSTANCES**

ENGLISH

STREET NAME	PSYCHOACTIVE
5-MEO	5-methoxy-dimethyltryptamine
Acid	LSD
Adderall	Salts of racemic amphetamine and dextroamphetamine (prescription drug)
Angel Dust	Phencyclidine (PCP)
Angel's Trumpet	*Brugmansia* and *Datura* species (contain tropane alkaloids)
Base	Cocaine freebase (USA and UK) — OR — Methamphetamine (in impure form; Australia)
Biccie	MDMA (pill, often containing adulterants; Australia)
Biscuit	MDMA (pill, often containing adulterants; Australia)
Blue Meanies	Psilocybin-containing mushrooms (*Panaeolus cyanescens*, although sometimes applied to any bluing psilocybin mushroom)
Brown	Heroin, usually freebase (UK)
Brug	*Brugmansia* species (contain tropane alkaloids)
Bud	Cannabis (female flower cluster)
Bulbs	Nitrous oxide (when in metal bulbs / cartridges sold for making whipped cream)
C	Cocaine
Changa	DMT (Dimethyltryptamine) mixed with a herbal smoking mixture that includes a mono-amine oxidase inhibitor (MAOI)
Charas	Cannabis (concentrated resin preparation)
Charlie	Cocaine
China White	Heroin
Choof	Cannabis (Australia)
Chronic	Cannabis (not to be confused with smoking blends marketed as "Kronic" that may contain synthetic cannabimimetic agents)
Coke	Cocaine
Crack	Cocaine freebase — OR — Methamphetamine crystals (Australia)
Crank	Amphetamines (general term)
Crystal	Methamphetamine
Cubes / Cubies	Psilocybin-containing mushrooms (*Psilocybe cubensis*)

A variety of packages used to market 5 mg tablets of 2C-B (4-bromo-2,5-dimethoxyphenethylamine). Scan by Jon Hanna, 2014.

The Banisteriopsis caapi vine contains monoamine oxidase inhibiting harmala alkaloids, allowing the DMT from Psychotria viridis to become orally active in an ayahuasca brew.
Photo from the 2006 Mind States conference in Costa Rica by Jon Hanna.

Moulded with a Mesoamerica glyph, this disc containing delicious Belgian chocolate plus 16 grams of Psilocybe atlantis sclerotia was the perfect vehicle for a psychedelic experience at the 2010 Boom Festival. Photo by Erowid.

STREET NAMES FOR COMMONLY ENCOUNTERED SUBSTANCES

ENGLISH CONTINUED...

STREET NAME	PSYCHOACTIVE
Datura	*Brugmansia* or *Datura* species (contain tropane alkaloids)
Desoxyn	Methamphetamine (prescription drug)
Dex	Amphetamines (prescription drug)
Dexedrine	Amphetamines (prescription drug)
Dexxies	Amphetamines (prescription drug)
Dimitri	DMT (Dimethyltryptamine)
Dinger	MDMA (pill, often containing adulterants; Australia)
Dope	Heroin (also used for Cannabis)
Draw	Cannabis (UK)
Eccies	MDMA
Ecstasy	MDMA
Elf Spice / Spice	DMT (Dimethyltryptamine)
Fanta	GHB (Australia)
Fantasy	GHB
Fly Agaric	*Amanita muscaria* mushrooms
Foxy / Foxy Methoxy	5-Methoxy-DIPT (5-methoxy-di-isopropyltryptamine)
G	GHB
Ganja	Cannabis
Gas	Nitrous oxide — OR — Methamphetamine in impure form (Australia)
GBH	GHB
Gear	Heroin (Australia and UK)
Glass	Methamphetamine
Gold Tops	Psilocybin-containing mushrooms
Grass	Cannabis
Green	Cannabis
H	Heroin
Hammer	Heroin
Heads	Cannabis (female flower clusters; Australia)
Herb	Cannabis (although could also refer to any herb)
Hippy Crack	Nitrous oxide
Ice	Methamphetamine
Jazz Cigarette	Cannabis cigarette (although this one sounds like an archaic and obsolete term, it is still used with humour today)

STREET NAME	PSYCHOACTIVE
Jimsonweed	*Datura* species (contain tropane alkaloids)
Junk	Heroin
K	Ketamine
K Bombs	Ketamine (instead of MDMA in street tablets)
Kim	Ketamine (intramuscular) [K IM]
Kitty / Kit Kat	Ketamine
Laughing Gas	Nitrous oxide
Liberty Caps	Psilocybin-containing mushrooms (*Psilocybe semilanceata*)
Liquid	LSD in a (usually) clear liquid carrier substance
Liquid Ecstasy	GHB
Lucy	LSD
Magic Mushrooms	Psilocybin-containing mushrooms (although might also be applied to *Amanita muscaria* or *A. pantherina*)
MD	MDMA
Meow Meow	Mephedrone
Mep	Mephedrone
Methedrine	Methamphetamine
Molly	MDMA
Moonflower	*Datura* species (contain tropane alkaloids)
Mushies	Psilocybin-containing mushrooms
Nang	Nitrous oxide
Nitrous	Nitrous oxide
Nos	Nitrous oxide
Panther Cap	*Amanita pantherina* mushroom
Paper	LSD (blotter paper)
Pep	Amphetamines (general term)
Peruvian Torch Cactus	*Trichocereus peruvianus* (contains mescaline)
Peyote Cactus	*Lophophora williamsii* (contains mescaline)
Pharmahuasca	DMT (Dimethyltryptamine) + Pharmaceutical monoamine oxidase inhibitor (MAOI, often moclobemide), taken orally
Pill	MDMA (pill, often containing adulterants, although can also be used for any tablet)
Pinger	MDMA (pill, often containing adulterants: Australia)
Pot	Cannabis
Psilos	Psilocybin-containing mushrooms
Rock	Cocaine freebase

STREET NAMES FOR COMMONLY ENCOUNTERED SUBSTANCES

ENGLISH CONTINUED...

STREET NAME	PSYCHOACTIVE
Rush	Mephedrone
Sally / Sally D	*Salvia divinorum*
San Pedro Cactus	*Trichocereus pachanoi*, and sometimes other *Trichocereus* species (contains mescaline)
Shabs	Methamphetamine (Australia)
Shabu	Methamphetamine (Filipino)
Shards	Methamphetamine
Shrooms	Psilocybin-containing mushrooms
Sid	LSD
Smack	Heroin
Smoke	Cannabis
Special K	Ketamine
Speed	Amphetamines (general term)
Speed Bombs	Methamphetamine / amphetamine (instead of MDMA in street tablets)
Spliff	Cannabis or Cannabis + Tobacco (either as a rolled cigarette or as a generalised term)
Subs	Psilocybin-containing mushrooms (*Psilocybe subaeruginosa*)
Tabs	LSD (either as tablets or on blotter paper)
Tar / Black Tar	Heroin (America)
Tree Datura	*Brugmansia* species (contain tropane alkaloids)
Trip	LSD
Tripstacy	2C-x or 2C-T-# (instead of MDMA in street tablets; Australia)
Wacky Baccy / Wacky Tobaccy	Cannabis
Weed	Cannabis
Whippits / Whip-its	Nitrous oxide (when in metal bulbs / cartridges sold for making whipped cream; derived from the brand-name "Whip-it!")
Whizz	Methamphetamine (in impure form; Australia)
X	MDMA
Yarni	Cannabis (Australian indigenous term)

"Angel's Trumpet", "Brug", "Datura", "Jimsonweed", and "Moonflower", are all names given to plants from the Brugmansia and Datura genera, which contain somewhat dangerous deliriant/hallucinogenic tropane alkaloids that often produce bad trips when taken recreationally. Photo from the 2006 Mind States Costa Rica conference by Jon Hanna.

One of the "Rainbow Roll" Cannabis sativa/C. indica hybrid strains from a 2011 Northern California medical marijuana garden. Photo by Erowid.

"San Pedro" (or Echinopsis pachanoi [= Trichocereus pachanoi]) cacti is a visionary sacrament used by some indigenous and mestizo shamans within South America; it contains mescaline, similar to peyote (Lophophora williamsii) used by the Native American Church in the United States and the Huichol Indians in Mexico. Due to the nausea and vomiting associated with mescaline, San Pedro is not as popular on the festival circuit as other psychedelics or empathogens, such as LSD, mushrooms, or MDMA. Photo by Jon Hanna, 2014.

STREET NAMES FOR COMMONLY ENCOUNTERED SUBSTANCES

FRENCH

STREET NAME	PSYCHOACTIVE
Acide	LSD
Amphé Thai	Methamphetamine
Bat	Cannabis (cigarette; Quebec)
Beuh	Cannabis
Beuher	Cannabis
Beurre de Marrakech	Cannabis (dissolved in butter)
Brun	Hashish
Buvard	LSD (blotter paper)
C	Cocaine
Cartons	LSD (blotter paper)
Champ	Psilocybin-containing mushrooms
Champignons Magique	Psilocybin-containing mushrooms
Champis	Psilocybin-containing mushrooms
Chichon	Hashish
Coco	Cocaine
Coke	Cocaine
Com	Hashish
Cône	Cannabis (cigarette)
Cristaux	MDMA
De But	Cannabis
Ecstasy	MDMA
Exta	MDMA
Goutte	LSD (drop)
Hash	Hashish
Herbe	Cannabis
Herbe des Dieux	*Salvia divinorum*
Joint	Cannabis (cigarette)
K	Ketamine
Keta	Ketamine
Ligne	Cocaine
Magie-juana	Cannabis
Marron	Hashish
MD	MDMA
Micropointe	LSD (microdot)
Mush	Psilocybin-containing mushrooms (Quebec)

"Changa" smoking mixtures containing DMT and harmala alkaloids—such as this sample photographed at the 2010 Boom Festival—have become increasingly popular in recent years. Photo by Erowid.

Known as "Laughing Gas", "Hippie Crack", "Whip-its" (a brana), "Nang", "Nos", "Bulbs" (for the small metal cartridges that it comes in when sold as a propellant for making whipped cream), or "Ballon" (in Dutch, for the balloons from which it is commonly inhaled), nitrous oxide is often a popular psychoactive at festivals. Photo of various brands of spent nitrous cartridges by Jon Hanna, 2014.

This crystalline MDMA was being sold at the 2010 Boom Festival under the street name "Sass", a slang term that has also been used for MDA and other chemically similar empathogens. Some dealers/users claim that "Sass" is a "more natural" (or less refined) version of MDMA or MDA, due to their belief that a precursor chemical that can be used in the production of these drugs, safrole, was created out of sassafras oil obtained from the root of a tree in the Sassafras genus. Photo by Erowid.

STREET NAMES FOR COMMONLY ENCOUNTERED SUBSTANCES

FRENCH CONTINUED...

STREET NAME	PSYCHOACTIVE
Ouinj	Cannabis (cigarette)
Pano	LSD (blotter paper)
Parachute	MDMA (powder wrapped in paper)
Pétard	Cannabis (cigarette)
Petri	LSD
Pills	MDMA
Pilon	Cannabis (cigarette)
Pilon	MDMA (Switzerland)
Plomb	MDMA
Poudre	Cocaine
Psilo	Psilocybin-containing mushrooms
Rabla	Heroin (cheap variety)
Rashasha	Opium
Salade	Cannabis
Salvia	*Salvia divinorum*
Sav	Hashish (large block)
Savonette	Hashish (large block)
Seum	Hashish
Shit	Hashish
Shroom	Psilocybin-containing mushrooms
Space Cake	Cannabis (cake)
Special K	Ketamine
Speed	Amphetamine
Speedball	Heroin + Cocaine
Splif	Cannabis or Cannabis + Tobacco (cigarette)
Stick	Cannabis (cigarette)
Tarpé	Cannabis (cigarette)
Taz	MDMA
Teuchi	Hashish
THC	Cannabis
Tige	Cannabis (cigarette)
Toncar	LSD (blotter paper)
Tonj'	Cannabis
Trace	Cocaine
Trait	Cocaine

STREET NAME	PSYCHOACTIVE
Trip	LSD
Truffes	Psilocybin-containing mushrooms
Un Dard	Cannabis (cigarette)
Weed	Cannabis (cigarette)
Xe	MDMA

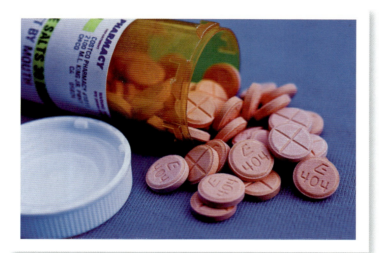

Depicted to the left are 30 mg scored generic Adderall pills, a prescription stimulant made from a mixture of four racemic salts: amphetamine aspartate, amphetamine sulphate, dextroamphetamine saccharate, and dextroamphetamine sulphate.

On the street, various amphetamines may be known as "Crank", "Dex"/"Dexies"/"Dexxies", "Feijão Mágico", "González", "Pep", "Pepp", "Pille", "Snelle", and, most commonly, "Speed". Photo by Jon Hanna, 2014.

Available as a prescription called Desoxyn (and formerly sold using the brand name Methedrine), methamphetamine hydrochloride is a popular stimulant on the illicit market; users may consume it orally, snorted, smoked, or injected. On the street it is known as "Crank", "Crystal", "Glass", "Ice", "Meta", "Meth", "Shabs", "Shabu", "Shards", "Speed", "Tweak"/"Tweek", "Whizz", "Yaba", "Yama", and various other names. Photo by Erowid, 2014.

STREET NAMES FOR COMMONLY ENCOUNTERED SUBSTANCES

GERMAN

STREET NAME	PSYCHOACTIVE
Acid	LSD
Adam	MDMA
Angel Dust	PCP
Bombe	Amphetamines (packed into a cigarette paper and swallowed)
Braunes	Heroin (not clean) — or — Hashish
Buff	Cannabis — or — Hashish
C	Cocaine
Candyflip	MDMA + LSD
Cokie	Cocaine
Cookie	Cannabis cookies — or — Hash cookies
Crystal	Methamphetamine
Deep Purple	LSD
Diaz	Diazepam
Dope	Hashish
E	Ecstasy — or — Amphetamine
Engelsstaub	PCP
Ethnoflip	MDMA + Psilocybin-containing mushrooms
Ganja	Cannabis
Gras	Cannabis
Grünes	Cannabis
H	Heroin
Hero	Heroin
Hohes	Cocaine
K	Ketamine
Koks	Cocaine
Lady	LSD
Liquid Ecstasy	GHB
Mandy	MDMA
Nexus	2C-B
Pappe	LSD (blotter paper)
Peace	Hashish — or — PCP

STREET NAME	PSYCHOACTIVE
Pepp	Amphetamine
Pille	Amphetamine — or — MDMA — or — Other drugs in tablet form
Pilze	Psilocybin-containing mushrooms
Pollen	Cannabis
Pott	Hashish
Psilos	Psilocybin-containing mushrooms
Puder	Cocaine
Rakete(n)	LSD + PCP
Rotze	Cocaine
Schnee	Cocaine
Schore	Heroin
Sherman Hemsley	PCP
Shit	Hashish
Shore	Heroin
Ticket	LSD
Tiefes	Heroin
Weed	Cannabis
Weißes	Cocaine
Yaba	Methamphetamine
Yama	Methamphetamine
Zettel	LSD (blotter paper)
Zeug	Heroin

Four hits of the "Shiva" blotter acid that was making the rounds at the 2010 Boom Festival; each hit was reportedly quite strong. Photo by Erowid.

STREET NAMES FOR COMMONLY ENCOUNTERED SUBSTANCES

PORTUGUESE

STREET NAME	PSYCHOACTIVE
Ácido	LSD
Alberto	LSD
Alface	Cannabis
Base	Cocaine freebase
Bazucada	Cocaine
Bitola	Ecstasy
Branca	Cocaine
Brita	Cocaine
Canhão	Cannabis (cigarette)
Cartolina	LSD (blotter paper)
Castanha	Heroin
Cavalo	Heroin
Chamon	Cannabis (concentrated preparation)
Charro	Cannabis (cigarette)
Charutos	Cannabis (cigarette)
Chinesa	Heroin (smoked)
Chinesinha	Cocaine (smoked) — OR — Heroin (smoked)
Chuto	Heroin (injected) — OR — Cocaine (injected)
Coca	Cocaine
Cogumelos	Psilocybin-containing mushrooms (also used for psychoactive mushrooms in general)
Crack	Cocaine freebase
Cristal	MDMA (in crystalline form)
Cuguis	Psilocybin-containing mushrooms (also used for psychoactive mushrooms in general)
Daime	Ayahuasca
Drop	LSD (liquid)
Erva	Cannabis
Falopa	Cocaine
Farinha	Cocaine
Farlopa	Cocaine
Farlupa	Cocaine
Feijão Mágico	Amphetamine
Fumos	Cannabis

STREET NAME	PSYCHOACTIVE
Ganza	Cannabis
Gelatina	LSD
González	Amphetamine
Gota	LSD (liquid)
Haxe	Cannabis (concentrated preparation)
Haxixe	Cannabis (concentrated preparation)
Hofmann	LSD
Keta	Ketamine
Kiza	Cocaine
Kruguers	Psilocybin-containing mushrooms (also used for psychoactive mushrooms in general)
Manuel Damásio	MDMA
Mário	MDMA
Mário Dias	MDMA
MD	MDMA
Mel	Cannabis
Miau-miau	Mephedrone
Micro	LSD (microdot)
Mushys	Psilocybin-containing mushrooms (also used for psychoactive mushrooms in general)
Paiva	Cannabis
Papel	LSD
Parpalho	Cannabis
Pastilha	MDMA (pill, often containing adulterants)
Pó	Cocaine (commonly, but can also mean heroin)
Polen	Cannabis (concentrated preparation)
Pombo	Cannabis
Porro	Cannabis (cigarette)
Roda	MDMA (pill, often containing adulterants)
Selo	LSD
Speed	Amphetamine
Speedball	Cocaine + Heroin (injected)
Tilha	MDMA (pill)
Trip	LSD
Túlia	Cocaine
Wella	Cannabis
Xito	Cannabis

STREET NAMES FOR COMMONLY ENCOUNTERED SUBSTANCES

SPANISH

STREET NAME	PSYCHOACTIVE
Abuela	Ayahuasca
Abuelita	Ayahuasca
Aceite	Hashish (oil)
Ácido	LSD
Ajo	LSD
Alfalfa	Cannabis
Angoleña	Cannabis
Apaleao	Hashish
Arimba	Cannabis
Avispa	Heroin
Azúcar marrón	Heroin
Bacalao	Heroin
Bazuco	Cocaine freebase
Bellota	Hashish
Bernice	Cocaine
Biberón	GHB
Bicho	LSD (South of Spain) — OR — MDMA (pill; Argentina)
Bombeta	MDMA
Breva	Cannabis (cigarette)
Brown	Heroin
Buco	Heroin (injected)
Burro	Heroin
Caballo	Heroin
Californiano	LSD
Caliqueño	Cannabis (cigarette)
Camerusa	Cocaine
Camisa	Cocaine — OR — Heroin
Candelo	Cannabis (cigarette)
Canuto	Cannabis (cigarette)
Champis	Psilocybin-containing mushrooms
Chicle	Hashish
China	Hashish
Chino	Heroin (smoked)

*The humble poppy seed pod (Papaver somniferum), source of painkilling opiates such as morphine and codeine, and inspiration for semi-synthetic opioids such as heroin and oxycontin.
Photo by Jon Hanna, 2009.*

*The Erythroxylum coca plant is celebrated in Bolivia, where it is commonly chewed, brewed as tea (shown here), and incorporated into various foods, including candies and an energy drink launched in 2010 called Coca Colla. Such uses do not seem to be as problematic as the pure alkaloid cocaine can sometimes be.
Photo by Jon Hanna, 2014.*

*Alcohol remains one of the most popular psychoactives at many festivals, as this wall of beer available at the 2008 Boom Festival attests to.
Photo by Erowid.*

STREET NAMES FOR COMMONLY ENCOUNTERED SUBSTANCES

SPANISH CONTINUED...

STREET NAME	PSYCHOACTIVE
Chipiturca	Cannabis
Chiri	Cannabis (cigarette)
Chiva	Heroin
Chivo	Heroin (Mexico)
Chocolate	Hashish
Chufla	MDMA pill
Churro	Cannabis (cigarette)
Chute	Heroin
Coca	Cocaine
Coca Cola	Cocaine
Cois	Cocaine (Mexico)
Cono	LSD
Copos	Cocaine
Costo	Hashish
Cristal	MDMA — or — Cocaine freebase (Mexico)
Dimitri	DMT (Dimethyltryptamine)
Dulce	Cocaine
Eme	MDMA
Estrella	LSD
Éxtasis	MDMA
Éxtasis líquido	GHB
Farla	Cocaine
Farlopa	Cocaine
Faso	Cannabis (cigarette)
Filete de merluza	Cocaine
Fina	Cocaine
Flai	Cannabis (cigarette)
Flan	Cocaine
Fly	Cannabis (cigarette)
Fuel	Hashish
Ful	Hashish
Gallo	Cannabis (cigarette)
Gamba	Cocaine
Gena	Hashish
Goma	Hashish

STREET NAME	PSYCHOACTIVE
Gota	LSD
Grifa	Cannabis
H	Heroin
Henna	Hashish
Hongos	Psilocybin-containing mushrooms (although this is also the common word for mushrooms in general; Mexico & Spain)
Huevo	Hashish
Jaco	Heroin
Jaimito	LSD
Jali	Hashish
Jamila	Cannabis
K	Ketamine
Keta	Ketamine
Kit Kat	Ketamine
Lenteja	LSD
M	MDMA
Macoña	Cannabis
Mai	Cannabis (cigarette)
Mamuco	Cannabis (cigarette)
Mandanga	Cannabis — OR — Cocaine
Manteca	Heroin
Manzanero	Amphetamine
Marchosa	Cocaine
Mariachi	Cannabis + Hashish
Mefe	Mephedrone
Merca	Cocaine
Meta	Methamphetamine — OR — Methadone
Miau	Mephedrone
Micropunto	LSD (microdot)
Mois	Cannabis (Mexico)
Monguis	Psilocybin-containing mushrooms
Mota	Cannabis
Nena	MDMA (pill)
Nevadito	Tobacco or Cannabis cigarette, mixed with Cocaine
Nevado	Tobacco or Cannabis cigarette, mixed with Cocaine

STREET NAMES FOR COMMONLY ENCOUNTERED SUBSTANCES

SPANISH CONTINUED...

STREET NAME	PSYCHOACTIVE
Nexus	2C-B
Nieve	Cocaine
Orange	LSD
Paja	Cannabis (cigarette)
Pala	Cocaine
Pasti	MDMA (pill)
Pastilla	MDMA (pill)
Pepas	MDMA (pill)
Perico	Cocaine
Peta	Cannabis (cigarette)
Petardo	Cannabis (cigarette)
Pichu	Amphetamine
Pico	Heroin
Piedra	Hashish
Pirulas	MDMA (pills)
Pito	Cannabis (cigarette)
Pitxu	Amphetamine
Plata	Heroin (smoked)
Polen	Hashish
Porro	Cannabis (cigarette)
Postre	Cocaine
Postura	Hashish
Pote	GHB
Potro	Heroin
Priva	Alcohol
Reina	Heroin
Rosamaría	Cannabis
Rula	MDMA (pill)
Saltaperico	LSD
Secante	LSD
Sello	LSD
Special K	Ketamine
Speed	Amphetamine
Speed Ball	Heroin + Cocaine
Tacha	MDMA (pill)

STREET NAME	PSYCHOACTIVE
Tailandesa	Heroin
Tatano	Heroin
Tate	Hashish
Tobogán	Heroin (smoked)
Toque	Cannabis (cigarette)
Tostis	MDMA (pills)
Trinqui	Alcohol
Tripa	LSD
Tripi	LSD
Trócolo	Cannabis (cigarette)
Trompeta	Cannabis (cigarette)
Troncho	Cannabis (cigarette)
Turrón	Heroin
Vitamina K	Ketamine
Volcán	LSD
Yerba	Cannabis
Yoe	Cannabis (cigarette)
Zarpa	Cocaine

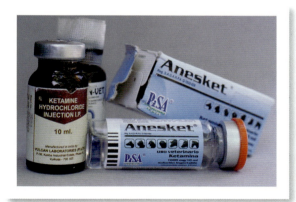

A few different brands of injectable ketamine. On the festival market, ketamine is more frequently sold as a powder, which is taken intra-nasally. Photo by Jon Hanna, 1999.

In recent years, several powerful psychedelics, such as bromo-dragonfly (shown left), DOI (shown right), and some NBOMe compounds (not depicted), have begun to appear on blotter. These drugs have a different risk profile associated with each of them, as compared to LSD, and unfortunately they are sometimes misrepresented or mistaken for LSD. BDF and DOI blotters shown are from the 2008 Boom Festival. Photo by Erowid.

GWYLLM LLWYDD • *Event Horizon*, 2014 • India ink, digital corrections
http://www.gwyllm-art.com

Appendix B
MONITORING, EVALUATING AND RESEARCHING— RECOMMENDATIONS FROM AN ACADEMIC PERSPECTIVE FOR AN EVIDENCE-BASED APPROACH TO PSYCHOACTIVE CRISIS INTERVENTION

Maria Carmo Carvalho

Mariana Pinto de Sousa

Implementing a successful care service doesn't solely depend on your capacity to guarantee a skilled and trained team, appropriate intervention strategies, or adequate resources. Furthermore, an appraisal of these factors frequently isn't really formed until well after work in the field has commenced. This seems to be the case with all interventions occurring where guidelines and experiences haven't been systematically reported and documented, as often occurs in the case of psychedelic support. It is every intervention agent's responsibility to contribute in order to change this scenario.

The only way of doing so is to *monitor* your activity, making sure you have accomplished your intervention goals, and to share the product of your work with your colleagues. This is the kind of approach that will allow you to grow from spontaneous and informal action into an evidence-based care service. Please note that some topics in this Appendix are also covered in Chapters 10, "Running the Service" and 15, "Risk Management and Performance Improvement".

Specific motives that justify keeping a detailed account of the work done by a care service are diverse and may vary from one context to another. In this chapter we briefly present central arguments for recording the results of your project, and we offer short instructions and practical examples on how to implement this process. We will go over three important reasons for researching, monitoring, collecting feedback, and documenting your psychedelic care service.

After carefully examining the legal landscape within the jurisdiction of the event, you should consider recording the results of your interventions for clinical purposes. The diversity of guests and situations you will encounter, and the need to pass on information to a team colleague during interventions, are only a couple of the reasons why you should think about this kind of data collection. In "Feedback and Monitoring" below, we will provide examples of basic information you could collect to allow an effective transmission of relevant clinical details during a guest's stay at the care space. We will also emphasise how this effort can contribute to growing knowledge in the field of psychedelic support.

Another valuable benefit to documentation is that it provides a means for evaluation. The only way to assess a project's efficacy is to plan goals and measure your outcome. Did you achieve what you initially set out to attain? Advanced intervention team leaders are those who have studied their own processes and efficacy, who continuously improve their strategies, and who aspire to standardised (yet evolving) intervention guidelines that help in future implementations. This means that even though socialising and passing on knowledge to the larger community of colleagues who share your interests is always relevant, the product of evaluation efforts is primarily directed at yourself as a care service leader, and at your promoting entities (such as the event organisation) and other partners.

Evaluation may be conducted in various ways. You may choose to study intervention processes, intervention outcomes, or both; you may choose to use quantitative indicators, qualitative approaches, or both. The important thing to keep in mind is that you will guarantee appropriate evaluation as long as you make sure you are addressing your project's specific goals whilst designing your evaluation process. This means there is no optimal single way of evaluating—it is always good as long as you make sure it is appropriate for you project's characteristics. Since it is impossible for us, without knowing your project's specific goals, to present targeted suggestions on how to perform evaluation, we will share some basic principles and present examples based on our experiences in "Evaluation" below.

Finally, where legal considerations do not preclude the ability to do so, you may wish to consider using your care service for scientific research purposes. Care services for psychedelic support at recreational settings present unique opportunities to get in touch with research subjects who can be difficult to sample elsewhere. Data regarding their personal backgrounds and experiences is a potentially precious contribution to scientific knowledge in many diverse domains (including pharmacology, health studies, psychology, anthropology, sociology, criminology, and more) and research themes (risk behaviour, drug use patterns, life trajectories, transpersonal experiences, psychopathology, and so forth). Implementing research is a demanding task, and it is clearly not an essential requirement for the effective facilitation of a psychedelic care service. So our purpose here is simply to present examples of what *could* be achieved, should you have the required resources and skills, and decide to go ahead with conducting some manner of scientific study. We develop this approach under "Research" below.

1. Feedback and Monitoring

Gathering basic information about your guests and their experiences at the care service ensures you get feedback about what is happening, allowing you to monitor your interventions in the field. That information is useful for clinical purposes, since it provides you with an opportunity to get to know your guests and decide how to best respond to their needs. In the field you will encounter a diversity of individuals presenting varying requests, symptoms, and predicaments. It is often the case that you will expect some of these situations, whilst others may catch you off-guard. During care work you will also find the need to pass along information from a guest to a colleague or team lead who replaces you in the next shift, or to medical personnel who become involved with a guest's care. There is much variation between care services in terms of event type, number of care team members, and complexity of team management. As an event and its corresponding care service increase in size, the challenges posed to gathering data about guests are also expected to increase.

Below we outline some of critical aspects you should consider regarding data collection. When building your data collection forms, you should endeavour to use easily manageable formats that facilitate consultation of the information whilst in the field (when you need it), and provide a structure for future data analysis (if applicable). We will present suggestions on how to do this, along with practical examples.

There are a couple of distinct options for keeping track of the work being done. You may choose to monitor individuals and open a single care record for each uniquely named (identified) *person*. Or, you may choose to record each individual *visit* attended to by the service, regardless of the identity of the guest. These two options present different implications if the same individual comes to the service on more than one occasion. In the first option, you identify your guest, open the record only once, and always use the same record if the guest visits again at a future time. In the second option, you assume you are only accounting for the situations that received help regardless of the guest's identity, so you open a new record for each situation attended, even if some of these records may refer to the same person. The recommendations we present below refer to the first option. In our opinion, it is useful to know what happened in the previous visit(s) when dealing with a repeat customer; how did the guest respond to the earlier intervention(s)? However, keeping track of all your guests might be a difficult challenge, especially at larger events.

IDENTIFYING GUESTS

You must find some basic method for identifying your guests, even though the collection of personal data is potentially concerning within the operation of a care service related to the use of illegal substances (see Chapter 3, "Legal Considerations"). As shown in Figure 1, "Data Collection Regarding Guests' Identification", we suggest you collect data concerning the guest's *name* or *nickname*, *age*, and *nationality*. Approaching guests using their *names* is an important strategy for building rapport. Frequently, *age* can be estimated; if you don't have a way of knowing a guest's age precisely, use this alternative. *Nationality* helps you decide on which language the care giver should use whilst interacting with the guest; when possible, care service staff should make efforts to communicate in a guest's native tongue. When you are assembling a team, knowledge of guests' expected nationalities (based on the known pattern of attendance for that festival) is useful for planning the languages required by the care service.

You should also include a checkbox that informs you if it is the first time a guest has been at the service during the event, whether they have visited the service previously, or if you simply can't determine that information accurately. From our experience, *distinguishing between first admissions and re-admissions poses a major challenge*. The only way of solving this is to gather data concerning guests' identification as well as information about the number of previous occasions they visited the service.

The Arc of Reflection by Amy Stabler was a twenty-foot tall arc of mirrors built on the playa at the 2003 Burning Man Festival.
Photo by Jon Hanna.

Finally, we also suggest you ask about the guests' previous attendances at that particular event. From our experience of evaluating a large-scale care service (KosmiCare at Boom 2010), we noticed that 68% of the guests were visiting the event for their first time (Carvalho, Pinto de Sousa, Frango, Carvalho, Dias, & Veríssimo 2011). This poses the possibility that guests less familiar with a particular event's dynamics might be the ones more likely to find themselves in need of assistance.

INFORMATION ABOUT ARRIVAL

You should try to gather as much information as possible about how your guest arrived at the care service (see Figure 2, "Data Collection on Arrival"). If the individual didn't walk in alone, identify *who brought the guest* (this person may also be able to provide relevant information about the situation and how the guest was found); the *date* and *time* the guest arrived; and *which care giver* was assigned to the case. Also keep a running list of the other care givers who followed. As the number of guests increases, these are the crucial pieces of information that help you situate a new arrival and sometimes determine whether the guest has been at the service before.

VISITOR DEMOGRAPHICS		
1. Name:		
2. Age: ☐ Actual ☐ Estimated		3. Gender: ☐ Male ☐ Female
4. Nationality and language(s) spoken:		
5. Number of times at the service: ☐ One ☐ Two or more		6. Number of times at the event: ☐ One ☐ Two or more

People who first encounter a guest in trouble are the ones who are often most able to offer details that will help in understanding the guest's needs, particularly in situations where the individual isn't communicating verbally. At large-scale events, a guest might be brought in by other event services in the field (including medical and security services), by other staff at the event, by care service staff, by friends, or by a well-meaning passer-by. If the guest has lost consciousness at any point or if they have trouble recalling what happened prior to the admission, they will probably ask you about the circumstances that brought them to the service once they become more coherent. To be able to offer this feedback is frequently reassuring for the individual. In cases where the guest was brought in by friends, it is very important to keep track of and stay in touch with these people—they are the ones most likely to provide relevant information such as which substances were consumed, their quantities, the time(s) of ingestion, combinations, and any details on medical and/or psychiatric history. Most of all, friends may be able to offer reassurance and grounding for the guest who is likely to be suffering from all the insecurities that an unexpected and painful experience usually brings up.

The date and time of a guest's arrival have implications for team organisation that surpass the mere identification of the situation attended. From our experience evaluating a care service, these data have helped us realise that the care service was receiving more guests on specific days of the event, which was a large scale festival that lasted for a total of eight days. In our example of Boom 2010, these were the days immediately following the beginning and immediately preceding the end of the event. Data on times that guests were received furthermore allowed us to understand that the number of guests at the care space peaked during the afternoon (15:00 to 23:00) (Carvalho et al. 2011). Future editions of the same intervention at the same event might take advantage of this information to improve human resource management.

Information regarding *substance use* is central at this point and you should allocate specific attention to a number of details including not only the substance names, but also quantities, timing of ingestions, the setting/context of

FIGURE 1:
Data Collection Regarding Guests' Identification

> People who first encountered a guest in trouble are the ones who are often most able to offer details that will help in understanding the guest's needs, particularly in situations where the individual isn't communicating verbally.

ARRIVAL

7. Date:	8. Time:	9. Care Giver #1:	10. Care giver #2:

11. Guest was brought in by:	☐ Him-/herself ☐ Friend ☐ Paramedics ☐ Care giver ☐ Other
12. If brought in by friends, did they stay with the guest?	
13. Describe the guest's physical condition	
14. Describe the guest's psychological condition	
15. Describe presented symptoms and their severity	
16. Describe relevant physical or mental health history	

17. Regarding guest's psychoactive substance uses, describe each product, quantity of ingestions, ingestion day(s), ingestion time(s), ingestion context (where, with whom), and ingestion method (oral, smoked, injected, other)

	Product	Quantity	Day	Time	Context	Ingestion method
17-a.						
17-b.						
17-c.						
17-d.						
17-e.						

18. This guest was brought in because he/she was:	18-a. Any additional notes related to question #18:
☐ having an intentional but difficult experience related to PAS ☐ having an accidental experience related to PAS ☐ having a personal crisis not related to PAS ☐ having a mental crisis concurrent with PAS use ☐ having a mental crisis without any PAS use ☐ not having any sort of crisis (explain reason in 18-a)	

FIGURE 2:
Data Collection on Arrival Related to the Use of any PsychoActive Substances (PAS)

...some substances are being used in such high prevalence that their consumption is frequently under-reported.

ingestions (where, with whom), method of ingestions (how), and if interaction with alcohol existed. From our experience, some substances are being used in such high prevalence that their consumption is frequently under-reported. This happens because guests tend to consider their common use as normalised behaviour that, in their perception, seems less relevant. This is the case primarily with alcohol and cannabis. Knowledge of these, however, is important for intervention; for example, a guest may have been ingesting stimulants (such as amphetamine or cocaine) alongside alcohol (a depressant), which can affect treatment choice. Our documentation has found substance use to be the most common source of symptoms presented by guests, even though other factors, including contextual emotional effects and health or psychiatric history, may also be of prime importance.

A final aspect to consider at the initial stage is a summary description of *symptoms* presented and an evaluation of the *type of crisis situation*. Symptoms and their evolution during intervention will also be part of a distinct section of the record that is solely dedicated to intervention. However, a summary of the most visible signs of distress presented by the guest upon arrival will allow for a quick overview of the situation and aid initial decision-making. From our experience, you can expect a wide variety of crisis situations that present for assistance. At Boom Festival 2010, from an approximate total of 120 guests who visited the care service, we noted that 76% presented situations related to difficult intentional experiences with a psychoactive substance (PAS); 8.3% were mental crises that also involved the use of a PAS; 7.4% of situations didn't correspond to any sort of psychological crisis (for example, information and first aid requests); 5% related to mental (psychiatric) crisis without PAS use; 2.5% related to accidental experiences with a PAS; and 0.8% had to do with personal crisis (due to emotional and contextual factors) not related to a PAS (Carvalho et al. 2011). Knowledge of this breakdown helps you better prepare the team in terms of training emphasis.

In our experience, psychiatric situations, whether involving PAS use or not, tend to be the most demanding on a care service's resources, and are the ones you will probably feel least prepared to deal with. They are also the ones with higher probability for unsuccessful intervention, occasionally even resulting in the transfer of the guest to a medical/psychiatric facility. These guests are more likely to arrive earlier in the event, and they tend to stay for longer periods of time. They are also more likely to require prescription drugs. Despite these challenges, and provided that there is appropriate medical/psychiatric assessment and supervision, in our opinion the care service remains the most suitable place to attend to these individuals' needs at an event. To better respond to these situations, the help of qualified staff is essential. The skills required have to do not only with adequate medical and psychiatric training, but also with a good understanding of the dynamics of recreational drug settings and substance-using communities.

INTERVENTION PROCESS DESCRIPTION

This is perhaps the richest section of your data collection, since it provides feedback on clinical decisions, contains detailed qualitative content to evaluate the success of the intervention, and gathers knowledge about your guests and their PAS experiences for research purposes.

We suggest you gather information on a number of general topics that summarise your guest's episode, and then simply record in the most systematic way possible what happens, following a timeline of the guest's stay at the care space (see Figure 3, "Description of Intervention Process").

> *We suggest you gather information on a number of general topics that summarise your guest's episode, and then simply record in the most systematic way possible what happens, following a timeline of the guest's stay at the care space...*

INTERVENTION			
19. Summarise the psychological issues that the guest was dealing with during the intervention:			
20. Describe the guest's primary emotional states during the intervention in chronological order (for example: hyper alert, anxious, calm, etc.):			
21. Summarise therapeutic strategies used with guest that seemed to help most (for example: listening; sitting with quietly; talking; music therapy; walking around; holding; wanted to be left alone, etc.). Also describe strategies used that were less helpful:			
Date:	Time:		Care giver:
Date:	Time:		Care giver:

FIGURE 3:
Description of Intervention Process

Whilst previous sections should be completed at the moment of arrival, the intervention section should be filled out during the course of care, and completed just after the guest's situation has resolved and the guest has left the care space. In this process you should register information that tells a "story", with a clear time sequence of major events, guest reactions, and care givers' decisions and their impact on the guest.

As for general topics, we suggest you try to start with a short summary of the psychological issues the guest was dealing with when intervention began, the guest's primary emotional states, and how these developed. Also include a short summary of any therapeutic strategies to which the guest responded positively. After this, simply register all major reactions, events, therapeutic decisions and strategies, and their impact on the guest, along a timeline.

INFORMATION ABOUT DEPARTURE

Your basic records for Feedback and Monitoring of intervention should conclude at the time your guest leaves the care service. Take notice of two aspects: the *date and time* the guest left, and *how* the guest left. Date and time allow you to know how many hours were spent in the care space, and thus the average length of intervention per guest or type of situation—for the care service as a whole—may eventually be calculated. For example, at KosmiCare's intervention at the 2010 Boom Festival we concluded that 52% of all guests attending the care service stayed for between one and five hours. This means that all remaining guests (48%) stayed at the care service for a minimum of six hours, which represents a considerably more lengthy intervention (Carvalho et al. 2011).

> **Take notice of two aspects: the date and time the guest left, and how the guest left.**

DEPARTURE

22. Date and estimated number of hours that the guest stayed at the care service:

Date:	Time of arrival:	Time of departure:	Approximate number of: ☐ hours _____ ☐ days _____

23. Indicate how guest was released from the care service:

☐ On his/her own   ☐ Other (describe) _____
☐ Escorted by friends/relatives/partners   _____
☐ Escorted by care giver   _____
☐ To off-site medical or mental facility   _____

24. Describe guest's current psychological condition:

25. Describe guest's current physical condition:

Knowing how your guest left the care service is an important indicator to evaluate your intervention efficacy. Following the above example, we established that 67% of the guests left the care service on their own, which largely indicates intervention success. Guests may also leave with friends, partners, or relatives; be escorted by a care giver back to camp; or, less frequently, be transferred to another health service outside the event.

It might also be useful to consult your intervention process notes and have a small summary describing the guest's psychological and physical condition on departure (Figure 4, "Data Collection on Departure").

INFORMED CONSENT

When personally identifiable data is being collected, we recommend you ask guests to sign an informed consent document (Figure 5, "Example of an Informed Consent Form"). You may present a small text with a general overview of your feedback and monitoring goals, or your evaluation goals, or even your overall research purpose. Consider including a request for a contact email that allows you to check up on the person at a future date, if that is relevant to your intervention or research. This request should ideally be presented by someone other than the care giver assigned to the guest.

You should expect a range of different reactions when an informed consent request is presented. It may be that the person feels grateful and is willing to contribute to your work in any way possible; it may be that the guest finds it okay to give the information but wants to leave the care service as quickly as possible, and isn't interested in taking the time to

FIGURE 4:
Data Collection on Departure

> **Consider including a request for a contact email that allows you to check up on the person at a future date, if that is relevant to your intervention or research.**

INFORMED CONSENT

All of the guest data collected at this care service is kept 100% confidential.

Within that framework of confidentiality, we are conducting scientific research that will help us increase and share knowledge regarding the use of psychoactive substances within a variety of social environments, and the unique—and sometimes challenging—mental spaces that can be inspired by the consumption of psychedelics. Information concerning your experience whilst at the care service is of great importance for us. We would very much appreciate if you agreed to allow us to use—within an entirely anonymous context—the data collected during your stay for research purposes. Please indicate your preference and sign below:

☐ **YES** I have been informed about the objectives of this research project, and
I agree to the anonymous use of information collected during my stay at the care service.

☐ **NO** I have been informed about the objectives of this research project, and
I DO NOT agree to the anonymous use of information collected during my stay at the care service.

*If you agree to participate, we would be interested in checking back in with you in a few months.
If that would be okay, please neatly print your email address below.*

EMAIL: _____

SIGNATURE: _____ DATE: _____

FIGURE 5:
Example of an Informed Consent Form

> You should expect a range of different reactions when an informed consent request is presented.

read and sign a document; or it may be that the guest totally rejects (and sometimes regards with intense suspicion) the idea of his/her information being used in the future. From our experience, verbal consent can be considered valuable for our purposes—if this is the case, register what occurred so you will know later why the document wasn't properly signed. If you find yourself in the scenario where a guest totally refuses to cooperate, we recommend that you destroy all personal information (for example name, age, nationality, and any notes that contain information referencing personal data, such as the names and phone numbers of friends), but retain a global record of the situation so that you can still use it as a simple indicator of the project's activity.

See Chapter 3, "Legal Considerations", for a further discussion regarding consent and record keeping. *Please note that informed consent documentation may not be deemed valid and/or legally binding when signed by an individual in any altered/intoxicated state.*

2. Evaluation

Data collection suggestions presented above for Feedback and Monitoring purposes already constitute a valuable contribution to your intervention evaluation. In the following, however, we will give a broader overview on what may be accomplished through evaluation, the questions you can expect to answer, and further indicators you may want to consider. We'll start with a short introduction to the origins of evaluation practice and what its general goals are.

Systematic empirical methodologies for intervention evaluation began to appear in the 1950s, mostly in the fields of education and human resources (Illback, Zins, Maher & Greenberg 1990). Flaherty and Morell (1978; cited in Illback et al. 1990) refer to a number of factors that led to the increased concern for evaluating interventions, such as: guaranteeing that public funding would be distributed according to worthy criteria; researchers' increased concern for public matters; limited resources available for social sciences; and the need to improve methodologies available for evaluation itself. These factors combined have been contributing to an evolution in the way that planning and evaluation of interventions has been implemented over the last few decades.

Recognition of the importance of evaluation has been followed by the understanding that this effort should not focus on the *results* alone of intervention, but also on the process through which intervention implementation occurs (Illback, Kalafat & Sanders 1997). From here, consensus arose around the idea that programme evaluation should contribute in determining intervention efficacy and the efficiency of strategies used for programme implementation. The way to achieve this should be through the gathering of systematic information on a programme's activities, characteristics, and results (Almeida & Mourão 2010).

The purpose of evaluation should therefore be, on the one hand, to determine whether goals and expected results have been achieved, and on the other hand, to gain insight into how the programme could be improved (Almeida & Mourão 2010).

Regarding methodology for developing such evaluation, the literature suggests a combination of qualitative and quantitative approaches. There is, however, a growing trend to favour qualitative methodologies. In our own work we have been placing increasing emphasis on strategies such as observation, in-depth interviewing, focus-groups, and content analysis, since these methods seem to provide rich and detailed information concerning process and programme implementation (Illback et al. 1997).

The three main stages for evaluating an intervention programme consist of *Programme Planning*, *Process Evaluation*, and *Outcome Evaluation*. For each of these stages we will provide examples of our own approach employed in the evaluation of KosmiCare at the Boom Festival in 2010 (Carvalho et al. 2011). That evaluation will serve as an example to help you visualise each of the steps involved; however, it does not constitute a one-size-fits-all evaluation plan, as each evaluation effort must be designed according to a particular project's characteristics and context.

> *The purpose of evaluation should therefore be, on the one hand, to determine whether goals and expected results have been achieved, and on the other hand, to gain insight into how the programme could be improved.*

PROGRAMME PLANNING

Every programme should begin with thorough planning of the intervention being implemented. This means that the first task has to do with clearly stating intervention goals and strategies. However, these are not always easily definable; therefore, we suggest you reflect on what your intervention problem is, and who your target group is. We commonly refer to this stage as *evaluation of needs and available resources*.

At this stage you should consider who will conduct evaluation. There are two alternatives: evaluation conducted by an external agent, meaning a person who isn't involved in the intervention itself (as a care giver, for example); or evaluation conducted by a person who *is* responsible for some aspect of the intervention, and assumes an additional evaluation coordination role. The people responsible for evaluation will be in charge of collecting information alongside the team responsible for implementation (care givers) and the target group (guests). This can happen through in-depth interviewing, observation, questionnaires, checklists, written reports, or a combination of several strategies.

At our project we decided that evaluation was to be managed by a leadership team member. This person had the primary responsibility of organising the intervention team and care space. Occasionally this individual would also be involved in assistance with guests as needs required. This person supervised data collection, which was performed by a group of three research assistants, who took turns in eight-hour shifts. During this period they helped care givers collect information about guest identification, arrival details, intervention specifics, and departure. At the moment a guest was about to leave, and provided that informed consent had been granted, they would also conduct a small interview assessing guest satisfaction with the intervention. The research assistants had no involvement with actual intervention care. Additionally, a group of four external evaluators was present during all intervention stages, assisting in adjusting the process and making on-site decisions about evaluation methods. These consultants also had no involvement with intervention care. After the event, they produced a comprehensive report, which contained valuable insights about the care service's intervention.

Another requirement is that you *characterise your intervention problem* and *develop a conceptual framework*. This means you should describe the nature, scope, and localisation of the intervention problem you'll focus on (Kröger, Winter & Shaw 1998). National or local surveys and scientific publications are useful resources to consult when structuring your framework.

> *The research assistants had no involvement with actual intervention care. Additionally, a group of four external evaluators was present during all intervention stages, assisting in adjusting the process and making on-site decisions about evaluation methods.*

After clarifying this, succinctly present your ideas on the theories that support your opinions on causes, development, and control of the situation that requires intervention. Whilst doing this, clearly state why you set those *particular goals* to achieve, and the *methods* for achieving them (Kröger et al. 1998). Goals and methods are appropriately stated when they describe a clear picture of the expected effects that should be produced by the intervention and describe how those effects will be produced.

At our project we assumed our intervention problem concerned the potential risk for development of a mental health problem subsequent to an unresolved psychoactive substance-induced crisis in a recreational setting. Even though no epidemiological data of this particular problem was available for our intervention context, we counted on data from national and international surveys that showed increasing PAS use in recreational settings (EMCDDA 2006; EMCDDA 2009; Balsa 2008). We also counted on currently accepted interpretations of this trend that conceptualise it as a highly normalised behaviour, especially among youths' perceptions of their drug-using habits (Parker, Aldridge & Measham 1998; Parker, Williams & Aldridge 2002). Additionally, we could refer to crisis intervention models (Hoff & Adamowski 1998; Kanel 2003), the transpersonal psychology approach to psychedelic emergency (Grof 2008), and *harm reduction and risk minimisation* approaches to PAS use in recreational settings (Hedrich 2005; Marlatt 1998), as valuable contributions that helped us consolidate our programme's conceptual framework.

Carrying personal water bottles and protecting oneself from the sun is important during hot days at any summer festivals in order to stay hydrated and avoid heat stroke. Photo by Jon Hanna, 2010.

The care service project we were undertaking had occurred during number of previous editions at the specific event we attended. It was closely supported by that event's organisers, who actively promoted the project. It was the organisers' perception that such a service made sense at an event attended by tens of thousands of participants from all over the world who frequently chose to experience altered states of consciousness. We assumed that our project would contribute to the well-being of the participants, not only by diminishing the negative impact of unresolved difficult experiences with PAS, but also by taking the opportunity to encourage personal growth that might arise from such experiences.

With regard to *intervention methods*, reflect on whether the strategies you plan to use are the most appropriate for the attainment of your intervention goals. You can do this by considering aspects such as: Is there empirical evidence for the efficacy of these strategies? Or, is the intervention timeline appropriate for their implementation?

Another important task is to analyse, understand, and deliver what you need, in terms of *resources* for programme implementation. Aspects you should consider are: (1) A trained and skilled team; (2) Work schedule; (3) Budget; (4) Logistics (Where and how will the care space be settled? What materials do you need to assemble it and make it appropriate? What intervention equipment is required?).

At our project, intervention strategies were based on crisis intervention and psychedelic emergency principles, the most basic therapeutic technique consisting of *sitting* and *facilitating* the experience for the guest. The method for performing these techniques has been the subject of a considerable amount of literature, even though it is rare to find effectiveness reports of its use and impact. Programme coordinators tried to overcome this limitation through the recruitment of skilled and experienced staff, and by offering the team training that was conducted by experienced teachers. Despite the extended length of the festival, the care team was staffed to provide 100% coverage on every day of the event, which allowed us to maintain a positive therapeutic approach with the guests.

The planning stage was also fundamental for ensuring resources. Even though inevitable challenges arose in this area, with central elements sometimes failing and teams having to adjust to difficulties as they came up during intervention, we had several key items in our favour. The organisers supported us with the majority of our budget; we operated in partnership with a governmental agency that provided staff for implementation and consultancy; we had a university-provided budget and resources for evaluation and research;

and a number of non-governmental organisations assisted us with pro bono consultancy and harm reduction services that complimented and enhanced our interventions. With this support, the care team itself was able to concentrate on logistics, assembling the care space, and ensuring that it was ready on schedule for the event opening.

After you plan your intervention methods, we suggest you focus on your *target group*. Characterise the demographics of the target involved as thoroughly as you can. Think about the scope of the problem that involves them and what led you to choose that particular group or context. Think about the numbers you expect to cover; think about how you plan to contact, recruit, and motivate volunteers and other partners such as event organisers or public entities (Kröger et al. 1998). Also consider whether intervention has support from any potential intermediate or indirect target-groups; these are the groups or persons that, even though not directly served by intervention, may also benefit from it.

At our project we could predict the major demographics of our target group due to past similar interventions. In those previous events, even though no planned evaluation had been implemented, there were efforts to monitor and collect feedback about operations. That data proved valuable, as it allowed us to anticipate various factors such as age, gender, nationality, PAS-use patterns, and other considerations that influenced our intervention strategies (Nielsen & Bettencourt 2008; Ventura 2008). As the intervention unfolded, we noticed that our work wasn't solely benefiting guests in crisis, but also event staff members who became increasingly aware of PAS-related issues. They brought guests to our care service and wanted to know more about how to respond when finding someone in difficulty.

Keep in mind that *evaluation of needs* means that you are already aware of the dimension of your intervention problem and whether that dimension justifies the intervention and resources you plan to allocate to it. Consider such things as an estimation of how many people are affected, and present arguments in favour of your particular intervention to the relevant bodies. Questions you should be answering at this stage include: (1) How many people are affected by this problem? (2) How many new situations are expected and how frequently do they come up? (prevalence and survey data); (3) What is the result of the "status quo" of *not* providing any intervention? (4) How can the need for intervention be described? (5) Are there different opinions about the need for intervention? (6) How has the need for intervention been assessed? (7) Is there knowledge regarding other related interventions in the field? And if so, can benefit be obtained by following their efforts? (Kröger et al. 1998). The main points presented under "Programme Planning" above have been summarised in Figure 6, "Tasks for Programme Planning".

> *As the intervention unfolded we noticed that our work wasn't benefiting guests in crisis alone, but also event staff members who became more aware of PAS-related issues.*

PROGRAMME PLANNING CHECKLIST	
☐ 1. Characterise intervention problem	☐ 4. Decide on intervention methods
☐ 2. Clearly state goals and objectives	☐ 5. Characterise target-groups
☐ 3. Decide who does evaluation	☐ 6. Assess and guarantee resources

FIGURE 6:
Tasks for Programme Planning

At our process evaluation of a care service at a large scale event, we decided to gather information on our implementation through multiple approaches...

Process Evaluation

The central purpose of process evaluation is to determine whether intervention produced the expected results. Through this we promote process improvement, as areas in need of development are identified. Moreover, we can identify difficulties in procedures, and obstacles that emerged during programme implementation. We also document strengths and aspects in which the programme was effective. When we perform process evaluation, our trust in perceived benefits is increased because we are confident that results are directly associated with interventions that were implemented and not with random happenstance (Illback et al. 1997).

In developing process evaluation, one follows a planned methodology. This consists of obtaining answers to several questions: (1) Which variables and indicators will offer us useful information on intervention implementation? And what kind of information (qualitative and/or quantitative) do we intend to collect? (2) What methods and instruments will we use to collect that data (interviews, questionnaires, observation checklists, and so forth)? (3) Where, when, and for how long will we collect data regarding the intervention process? (4) Who will provide this data? (5) How will data be analysed?

These concerns strongly resemble the questions any scientist asks when planning a research project. What is particular here is that you will be planning research that has a specific intention: to know more about how intervention is occurring and how it can be improved in the future. Whilst scientific research has a global audience and community composed of every person studying the same problem or its analogue (academically or for intervention purposes), evaluation research is primarily aimed at a more restricted audience of programme coordinators, partners, and the team itself, as these stakeholders will benefit most from its results in the future.

At our process evaluation of a care service at a large-scale event, we decided to gather information on our implementation through multiple approaches, and through a combined use of qualitative and quantitative indicators. Observation checklists were created that allowed close monitoring of the intervention received by each guest. Even though it was the care givers' responsibility to provide this input, research assistants frequently assumed the lead in soliciting, documenting,

GUEST SATISFACTION QUESTIONNAIRE					
	Totally agree	Agree	Don't know / Can't tell	Disagree	Totally disagree
26. I consider I have been helped by the care services					
27. I consider the care space had all the appropriate conditions to satisfy my needs during my stay					
28. I consider the care services had well-prepared, efficient staff to help me deal with my situation					
29. I consider care givers were helpful, caring, and available to satisfy my needs during my stay					
30. Please feel free to comment below on any aspect(s) related to your experience at the care service					

FIGURE 7: Guest Satisfaction Questionnaire

and maintaining information for all guests at the care space. Additionally, our implementation was retrospectively evaluated through care team feedback subsequent to the interventions.

When you plan *process evaluation for implementation monitoring*, consider including information about indicators such as: (1) Intervention strategies; (2) The target group (how many and their demographics); (3) The target group's exposure to intervention (intervention duration and number of activities/interventions delivered) (Kröger et al. 1998). At our project, these indicators were approximately the same as we described above under "Feedback and Monitoring".

Process evaluation also contributes to *assessing programme efficacy*. This is obtained through the measurement (quantitative or qualitative) of the reaction of the subjects and their attitudes towards the programme: Did they accept intervention? Did they identify with the goals of the programme? Did they obtain benefit from intervention? These are just some examples of questions you can attempt to answer to help assess efficacy through process evaluation (Kröger et al. 1998). Consider what indicators you need in order to answer these questions, and how to collect this data.

> Did they accept intervention?
> Did they identify with the goals of the programme?
> Did they obtain benefit from intervention?

FIGURE 8: Care Giver's Assessment of Treatment Outcome

DEPARTURE					
31. Do you consider that this guest was helped by the care service?					
Yes, much	Yes, a little		Don't know / Can't tell	No, not much	No, not at all
32. Please include other comments below (for example, guest's verbalisations regarding his/her experience at the care service)					

> You must be ready to lose everything you take to BOOM. Especially yourself. Then you can find what you've always been looking for.

FIGURE 9:
Message left by a care service guest after an intervention in KosmiCare at Boom, 2010. Photo by Constance Rodrigues.

Our project included a guest satisfaction Likert-scale questionnaire for this purpose (Figure 7, "Guest Satisfaction Questionnaire"). Additionally, guests also expressed their view of the intervention's impact verbally and in writing, by responding to structured questionnaires we provided. Care givers also provided their perceptions regarding the degree of successful intervention for each guest (Figure 8, "Care Giver's Assessment of Treatment Outcome").

Process evaluation also includes data collection regarding team satisfaction and involvement, possible unexpected side-effects arising from intervention, and discrepancies between programme planning and programme implementation (Illback et al. 1997). You may choose to monitor these aspects through retrospective or through naturalistic methods. Retrospective monitoring occurs when data concerning implementation is collected through subjects and team members; naturalistic monitoring occurs when you directly observe and record the intervention process (Illback et al. 1997).

At our project, each care team member was invited to express their thoughts about the project by filling in a form that allowed for both "closed" (Figure 10) and "open" (Figure 11) responses. Closed items were "multiple choice" questions; care givers picked one answer from several possibilities presented. Open items required team members to express themselves in terms of SWOT Analysis, providing feedback regarding a project's Strengths, Weaknesses, Opportunities, and Threats (this data was later analysed through descriptive statistics and content analysis).

CARE TEAM SATISFACTION QUESTIONNAIRE					
	Totally agree	Agree	Don't know / Can't tell	Disagree	Totally disagree
1. Care service training was of an appropriate duration					
2. Care service training had well-prepared sessions					
3. Care service training content was relevant					
4. The content of the care service training contributed to my preparation for intervention					
5. Care service training was well organised					
6. Care service physical work conditions (lighting, temperature, comfort, etc.) were appropriate					
7. Guests' acceptance of intervention was positive					
8. Intervention met its purposes effectively					
9. Care givers' work was effective.					
10. Organisational support to the care service was effective.					
11. Care service implementation levels were high.					
12. The climate and cooperation in the care service team was very positive.					
13. Working conditions were appropriate.					
14. Care space capacity was appropriate for intervention's needs.					

FIGURE 10:
Care Team Satisfaction Questionnaire

At our project, each care team member was invited to express their thoughts about the project by filling in a form that allowed for both "closed" (Figure 10) and "open" (Figure 11) responses.

FIGURE 11:
Care Team Satisfaction through S.W.O.T. Analysis

CARE TEAM SATISFACTION / S.W.O.T. ANALYSIS					
Please fill in the following table referring to Strengths (S), Weaknesses (W), Opportunities (O), and Threats (T) of given topics.					
	Training	Team	Work conditions	Organisers	Implementation
Strengths					
Weaknesses					
Opportunities					
Threats					

PROCESS EVALUATION CHECKLIST	
☐ 1. Plan process evaluation (as you would prepare scientific research)	☐ 4. Include team satisfaction assessment
☐ 2. Include implementation monitoring indicators	☐ 5. Consider measuring side-effects and discrepancy
☐ 3. Include programme efficacy indicators	☐ 6. Discuss results

FIGURE 12:
Tasks for Process Evaluation

Figure 12, "Tasks for Process Evaluation" lists some of the main points discussed above under "Process Evaluation". To end, we suggest that when you report and discuss process evaluation results you focus on the following (Kröger et al. 1998):

- Compare intervention plan, intervention implementation, and evaluation results.

- Reflect on any discrepancies and their impact on the intervention.

- Identify the intervention's strengths and weaknesses and compare it with other interventions you have researched.

- Formulate suggestions for any future intervention and for future process evaluation approaches to the same intervention.

Outcome Evaluation

The central purpose of outcome evaluation is to determine to what level the original goals for intervention were attained. An essential requirement is to ensure that your goals and objectives have been stated clearly from the start of the programme. According to Illback, Kallafat, and Sanders (1997), however, the success of an intervention should be determined more by the subjects' perception of intervention efficacy than by the measurement of goals achieved. For this reason, it is also crucial to consider guest satisfaction for the purpose of outcome evaluation. We have presented a number of items above referring to guest satisfaction that may be used simultaneously as process and outcome measures.

Whilst *planning* for outcome evaluation, contemplate the following questions: (1) What do you consider to be the intervention's result indicators and how do you plan to measure them (through which instruments)? (2) What type of data (quantitative or qualitative, or both) do you intend to analyse? (3) What guarantees exist regarding the quality of those instruments (for example, if you use standardised instruments, are they objective, reliable, and trustworthy?) (4) Where, when, and how do you plan to collect those data? (5) How do you plan to analyse the results? (Kröger et al. 1998).

> *The central purpose of outcome evaluation is to determine to what level the original goals for intervention were attained. An essential requirement is to ensure that your goals and objectives have been stated clearly from the start of the programme.*

At our evaluation of a care service at a large-scale festival, we intended to measure if our goal of contributing to diminished mental health risk following a psychoactive substance-related crisis had been achieved. We determined that to accomplish this we could obtain a quantitative and standardised measure of guests' mental state through a symptom checklist on arrival at the care space and again on departure. Even though we had other more qualitative and indirect measures for intervention outcome (such as care giver perception and guest satisfaction, already presented above), we wanted to complement these with more direct and quantitative measures of our intervention.

Whilst performing a mental state exam (through instruments such as the *Mini-Mental State*,[1] for example) our attention should focus on the presence of symptoms and signs, and not so much on formally diagnosed "syndromes". Consequently, this exam consists of a discrete "instantaneous" assessment of an individual's operative functioning (Fugas 2011; Baños & Perpiñá 2002) which, unlike formally diagnosed "syndromes", might suffer alterations at any moment. Traditionally, a mental state exam is performed by a psychotherapist who observes a patient whilst conducting a clinical interview (Trzepacz & Baker 2001). But in our case, we had some challenges to overcome. Considering PAS produce modified states of mind that can have an impact on speech, data collection through an interview could be extremely challenging or not even possible. Another aspect was the immediate nature of the crisis intervention setting; this meant that all data had to be collected during the guests' time at the care space, as there was no expectation of further contact after their departure. Finally, we had to recognise that using standardised instruments was usually an impossible request for guests undergoing the often mentally distorting effects of PAS.

So we decided to build a new instrument—the *Mental State Exam Checklist* (MSEC) (Carvalho, Carvalho, Frango, Dias, Veríssimo, & Llandrich 2010)—consisting of 74 items that were evaluated by a trained observer (the care giver assigned to the guest). The 74 items were organised into eight sub-scales of dimensions: (1) Appearance, attitude; (2) Psychomotor behaviour; (3) Consciousness, alertness, attention, and orientation; (4) Language and speech; (5) Thought process; (6) Self-awareness; (7) Affect and emotions; (8) Physiological functioning. In this way we could ensure an unobtrusive

---

1 The *Mini-Mental State* exam was developed in 1975 (Folstein, Folstein & McHugh 1975), and it has been used as an auxiliary to the diagnosis of cognitive functioning problems. It consists of a series of requests and tasks that subjects must solve. Performance on these tasks can be quantified, yielding a final score.

description of the mental condition presented by a guest possibly under the influence of PAS. These results would be analysed later through descriptive statistics, allowing us to obtain the quantitative outcome indicator we were aiming for.

Creating a new checklist meant that we wouldn't be using a reliable and trustworthy data-collection instrument with proven results and quality standards. However, we could in this manner ensure maximum adjustment to our intervention programme's characteristics and contribute to a scientific research path that could be explored in the future.

If you intend to collect data through a standardised questionnaire that produces a quantitative measurement of a given outcome indicator, you must consider issues such as sample selection and sample demographics. Also consider the number of guests who may leave the intervention without completing their questionnaires.

Once sampling issues are solved, guarantee that your measures are suited to answer questions such as: (1) How did intervention affect the subject group's behaviour (directly and indirectly)? (2) Are there any specific sub-groups among your targets that intervention affected differently (for example, different age groups or genders)?

The main points discussed above for "Outcome Evaluation" are listed in Figure 13, "Tasks for Outcome Evaluation". Whilst discussing outcome evaluation results, we suggest you consider analysing a variety of aspects (Kröger et al. 1998), such as:

- Possible discrepancies between expected versus actual results, reasons for these discrepancies, and their impact on intervention.

- Compare results obtained with others from different studies and discuss their relevance and significance.

- Reflect on the degree to which your results are directly related to intervention and not to other random/indirect effects. (Can you find any other alternative explanations for your results other than the intervention?)

- Discuss how negative results can be explained.

- Formulate suggestions for future interventions and methods for developing outcome evaluations of similar programmes.

FIGURE 13:
Tasks for Outcome Evaluation

OUTCOME EVALUATION CHECKLIST	
☐ 1. Make sure you have clearly and concisely formulated intervention objectives	☐ 4. Chose measures, data collection instruments, type of data, and data analysis strategies
☐ 2. Include indicators related to target's perception of intervention efficacy (qualitative and/or quantitative)	☐ 5. Guarantee appropriate sampling
☐ 3. Include indicators that measure intervention effects on target groups' behaviour	☐ 6. Discuss outcome results

3. Research

Earlier in this chapter we described the demanding nature of scientific research. We also stated that monitoring/feedback, evaluation, and scientific research have different objectives, and that contribution for the sake of scientific research may be a lower priority, given the scope of implementing a care service for psychedelic emergencies. Reasons to consider undertaking scientific research—for those who have the appropriate skills and resources—were also mentioned.

We do not wish to gloss over the highly specific scientific research method steps that require lengthy and comprehensive training. We simply want to share how research opportunities might arise in this field of intervention, and describe how they were developed in our own case.

You might have noticed above how the same indicators and questions contribute towards distinguishable objectives. Basic data monitoring that concerns, for example, your subject demographics may also provide valuable input that allows you to better characterise the subject population for process evaluation. Indicators and questions may also serve as a starting point for developing a more in-depth research project. You may want to consider the feasibility of following up on people who attended the care service, and how they perceived the benefits, if any, from their interventions. You may want to take the opportunity to study these individuals' life-trajectories with biographic research into their life histories, including experiences with psychoactives and other aspects you deem relevant.

In our case, an opportunity arose that allowed us to develop the *Mental State Exam Checklist* we created for outcome evaluation. We have decided to research the instrument's validity and psychometric properties by replicating its use within a sample of controls who are not under the influence of PAS, and outside of a recreational setting (Fugas 2011).

We realise that our exposition of scientific evaluation may seem exceedingly academic or overwhelming to some readers. Nevertheless, we would like to encourage you to always develop at least some form of monitoring and evaluation of your work, regardless of the scope of your project. If you need to apply for public or private funding, it is likely that you will be asked to present this kind of data. Keep in mind that the principles of monitoring and evaluation are fundamental to the deliberate improvement of the quality of your work, as is open communication with others on the topic. We encourage you to incorporate monitoring and evaluation into your work to achieve better results for your project, your team members, your event, and ultimately, for your guests and the quality of care they receive.

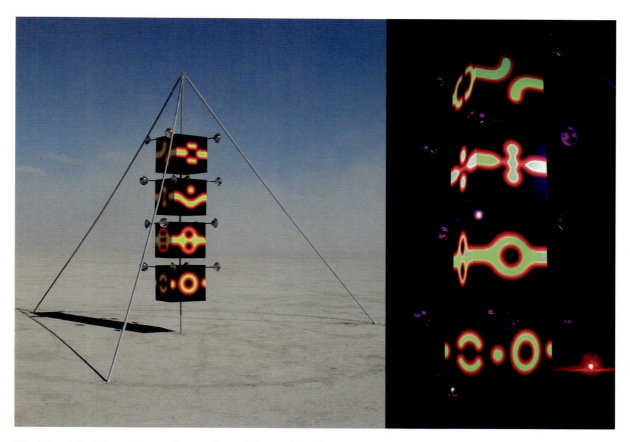

Wind Oracle by Vibrata Chromodoris and David Shamanik had four rotating cubes suspended by a fifteen-foot steel tripod. The cubes featured mystical symbols that aligned according to the wind patterns in order to answer one's questions. Photographed on the playa at the 2003 Burning Man Festival by Vibrata Chromodoris.

4. References

Almeida, D., and Mourão, B. (2010). "Avaliação de Programas de Prevenção das Toxicodependências" ["Evaluation of Addiction Prevention Programmes"]. *Revista Toxicodepend-ências* [*Addictions Magazine*] 16(3): 79–88. Accessed Nov. 20, 2014, from http://tinyurl.com/qjl7h66

Balsa, C. (2008). *Inquérito Nacional ao Consumo de Substâncias Psicoactivas na População Geral, Portugal 2007* [*National Survey on the Use of Psychoactive Substances in the General Population, Portugal 2007*]. Lisboa: Instituto da Droga e da Toxicodependência [Lisbon: Institute for Drugs and Drug Addiction]. Accessed Nov. 20, 2014, from http://tinyurl.com/njgztq3

Baños, R.M., and Perpiñá, C. (2002). *Exploración Psicopatológica* [*Psychopathological Examination*]. Madrid: Editorial Síntesis.

Carvalho, M.C., Carvalho, J., Frango, P., Dias, P., Veríssimo, L., and Llandrich, J. (2010). *Mental State Exam Checklist (MSEC)*. Porto: Faculdade de Educação e Psicologia da Universidade Católica Portuguesa, não publicado [Porto: Faculty of Education and Psychology, Catholic University of Portugal, unpublished].

Carvalho, M.C., Pinto de Sousa, M., Frango, P., Carvalho, J., Dias, P., and Veríssimo, L. (2011). *Crisis Intervention in Recreational Settings—Data From Kosmicare/Boom Festival 2010, Process Evaluation*. Porto: Faculdade de Educação e Psicologia da Universidade Católica Portuguesa [Porto: Faculty of Education and Psychology, Catholic University of Portugal]. Accessed Nov. 20, 2014, from http://tinyurl.com/khdhllp (see also http://tinyurl.com/lv3m6wj).

EMCDDA (2006). *Annual Report 2006, Selected Issues—Developments in Drug Use Within Recreational Settings*. European Monitoring Centre for Drugs and Drug Addiction. Accessed Nov. 20, 2014, from http://www.emcdda.europa.eu/html.cfm/index34883EN.html

EMCDDA (2009). *Selected Issues 2009—Polydrug Use: Patterns and Responses.* European Monitoring Centre for Drugs and Drug Addiction. Accessed Nov. 20, 2014, from http://www.emcdda.europa.eu/attachements.cfm/att_93217_EN_EMCDDA_SI09_poldrug%20use.pdf

Folstein, M.F., Folstein, S.E., and McHugh, P.R. (1975). "'Mini-Mental State': A Practical Method for Grading the Cognitive State of Patients for the Clinician". *Journal of Psychiatric Research* 12: 189–198. Accessed Nov. 20, 2014, from http://tinyurl.com/q45wpnv

Fugas, J.N. (2011). *Mental State Exam Checklist: Contributo para a Validação de um Instrumento de Avaliação do Estado Mental.* [*Mental State Exam Checklist: A Contribution for the Validation of a Mental State Evaluation Instrument*]. Porto: Faculdade de Educação e Psicologia da Universidade Católica Portuguesa, não publicado [Porto: Faculty of Education and Psychology, Catholic University of Portugal, unpublished Masters dissertation].

Grof, S. (2008). "Crisis Intervention in Situations Related to Unsupervised Use of Psychedelics". *LSD Psychotherapy*, fourth edition (pages 308–319). Santa Cruz, California: Multidisciplinary Association for Psychedelic Studies.

Hedrich, D. (2005). "...Putting Harm Reduction on the Map". Accessed Nov. 20, 2014, from http://tinyurl.com/p3tppl6

Hoff, L.A., and Adamowski, K. (1998). *Creating Excellence in Crisis Care: A Guide to Effective Training and Program Designs.* San Francisco, CA: Jossey-Bass Publishers.

Illback, R.J., Kalafat, J., and Sanders, D. (1997). "Evaluating Integrated Service Programs". In R.J. Illback, C.T. Cobb, and H.M. Joseph, *Integrated Services for Children and Families: Opportunities for Psychological Practice* (pages 323–346). Washington, DC: American Psychological Association.

Illback, R.J., Zins, J.E., Maher, C.A., and Greenberg, R. (1990). "An Overview of Principles and Procedures of Program Planning and Evaluation". In T.B. Gutkin and C.R. Reynolds *The Handbook of School Psychology*, second edition (pages 799–820). New York: Wiley.

Kanel, K. (2003). *Manual to Accompany A Guide to Crisis Intervention.* California: Brooks/Cole.

Kröger, C., Winter, H., and Shaw, R. (1998). *Guidelines for the Evaluation of Drug Prevention: A Manual for Programme-Planners and Evaluators.* European Monitoring Centre for Drugs and Drug Addiction. Accessed Nov. 20, 2014, from http://www.emcdda.europa.eu/attachements.cfm/att_78087_EN_manual1.pdf

Marlatt, G.A. (1998). *Harm Reduction: Pragmatic Strategies for Managing High-Risk Behaviors.* New York: Guilford Press.

Nielsen, S., and Bettencourt, C. (2008). "KosmiCare: Creating Safe Spaces for Difficult Psychedelic Experiences". *MAPS Bulletin* 18(3): 39–44. Nov. 20, 2014, from https://www.maps.org/news-letters/v18n3/v18n3-39to44.pdf

Parker, H.J., Aldridge, J., and Measham, F. (1998). *Illegal Leisure: The Normalization of Adolescent Recreational Drug Use.* London: Routledge.

Parker, H., Williams, L., and Aldridge, J. (2002). "The Normalization of 'Sensible' Recreational Drug Use: Further Evidence from the North West England Longitudinal Study". *Sociology* 36(4): 941–964. Accessed Nov. 20, 2014, from http://www.brown.uk.com/brownlibrary/parker.pdf

Trzepacz, P.T., and Baker, R.W. (2001). *Exame Psiquiátrico do Estado Mental* [*Psychiatric Mental State Examination*]. Lisboa: Climepsi Editores.

Ventura, M. (2008). "Energy Control: Harm Reduction with Drug Analysis at Boom Festival". *MAPS Bulletin* 18(3): 45–47. Nov. 20, 2014, from http://www.maps.org/news-letters/v18n3/v18n3-45to47.pdf

JON HANNA • *Sasha Presenting the Quantitative Scale of Potency, 2016* • digital (Adobe Photoshop)
http://www.mindstates.org

GUIDE TO DRUG EFFECTS AND INTERACTIONS

Timothy Bakas

Vince Cakic

Zevic Mishor

Christopher J. Ward

Gastone Zanette

Jon Hanna

This Guide summarises notable interactions that may be life-threatening or highly dangerous between different classes of psychoactive drugs. It also provides a quick reference index to those substances commonly encountered at music festivals and similar events. Although coverage of every drug used in these contexts is out of scope, we have included the major classes in such a way that the Guide should be able to provide a basic level of information regarding most substances.

For each chemical or botanical, the alphabetically ordered drug index entries include data on nomenclature, appearance, mechanism of action, psychoactive effects, pharmacokinetics, adverse reactions, contraindications, interactions, overdose, and harm minimisation. Where relevant, additional information on related compounds is included.

The information supplied in each entry is two-tiered. First, we present a practical overview regarding dose, duration, psychoactive effects, adverse effects, and harm reduction. Second, we provide technical data regarding relevant mechanisms, pharmacokinetics, and contraindications; this is information that medical staff working with a care service may find useful for their assessments. In addition to the practical and the technical, with each entry we have also included a bit of historical data and/or cultural context related to the featured drug.

Our research sources have been extensive, ranging from the latest studies published in medical journals, to first-hand accounts. Much of our information was obtained from standard texts and peer-reviewed sources. However, given the role of the Internet in disseminating information—and shaping drug trends themselves—several reliable online resources, including Erowid and Drugs-Forum, have been of invaluable assistance for preparing content, particularly with regard to subjective descriptions of the drugs' effects and with dose information.

The material contained in this Guide is intended to promote the reduction of suffering and the minimisation of harm in the context of drug usage in festival and other environments. Although keenly aware of the importance of accuracy to the integrity of this document, we also know that to err is to be human. In the same spirit of collaboration with which this Manual was written, we invite you to alert us to any errors or omissions that you may identify. Please contact the editors if you spot any mistakes.

While we have taken great care to provide accurate and relevant information, we do not accept liability for any errors or omissions; please refer to the disclaimer at the beginning of this Manual. One sentence from that disclaimer is reiterated here: *The editors and authors are not responsible for any specific health needs that may require medical supervision and shall not be held liable for any damages or negative consequences from any treatment, action, application, or preparation undertaken by and/or provided to any person reading or following the information in this book.*

This Guide aims to provide a rich source of information on many psychoactive agents, information rarely found in such a comprehensive yet concise format. We welcome you to use it to aid in providing assistance and information while working at a drug care service, as well as in any other setting for which it may prove valuable.

DRUG INTERACTIONS

Regardless of whether they are illegal, prescription, or over-the-counter (OTC), and whether used for medical, recreational, or spiritual/contemplative purposes, adverse drug reactions may arise from the combination of a variety of specific drugs. As such, a great number of possible drug interactions involving recreational (and other) drugs exist; covering every one of them is beyond the scope of this Guide.

Our focus is on dangerous and life-threatening interactions. These tend to be clustered around a particular few drug classes, namely CNS depressants (particularly alcohol and GHB) and monoamine oxidase inhibitors (MAOIs). Combinations of many recreational agents with these drugs may cause life-threatening or serious adverse consequences.

The Table of High-Risk Drug Interactions below summarises which common psychoactive drugs and other pharmaceutical drug classes constitute a potentially life-threatening interaction when mixed with alcohol, GHB, or MAOIs. In order to aid the reader in assessing for such interactions, also included is a list of the most commonly used medication names from within each pharmaceutical drug class as found in the table.

Further information on both harm minimisation and other potential drug interactions specific to many recreational agents can be found at the end of this Guide, in the Index of Drug Effects.

High-Risk Interactions

The three drugs/classes appearing at the top of the table—alcohol, GHB, and MAOIs—are those with potential for life-threatening interactions; the commonly found drugs that constitute such interactions are listed beneath each heading. Medical assistance should be sought immediately upon encountering adverse consequences from such combinations.

TABLE OF HIGH-RISK DRUG INTERACTIONS		
CNS DEPRESSANTS		**MAOIs**
ALCOHOL	**GHB**	
combined with:	*combined with:*	*combined with:*
First Generation Antihistamines	First Generation Antihistamines	2C-x
Barbiturates	Alcohol	Amphetamine
Benzodiazepines	Barbiturates	Antihistamines
GHB	Benzodiazepines	Cocaine
Heroin	Heroin	DOx
Ketamine		MDxx
		MDPV /α-PVP
		Mephedrone, etc.
		Methamphetamine
		SSRIs

Alcohol

Alcohol is a widely consumed agent that interacts with many other drugs and substances. As a general rule, CNS depressants should not be combined with one another. These depressants include alcohol, general anaesthetic agents, barbiturates, benzodiazepines, and GHB (γ-hydroxybutyrate). In addition, the concomitant use of these drugs with opiates/opioids, ketamine, nitrous oxide, or sedating antihistamines may result in serious adverse consequences. Symptoms of overdose include pronounced sedation, decreased heart rate and hypotension, motor incoordination, slurred speech, respiratory depression, coma, and death. Please see the Alcohol entry in the index below for further information.

GHB (γ-hydroxybutyrate)

GHB has synergistic effects with other CNS depressants such as alcohol, benzodiazepines, barbiturates, and opiates/opioids, and most GHB-related deaths have been associated with these sorfts of co-ingestions. GHB overdose can result in life-threatening CNS and respiratory depression, and requires immediate medical attention. Symptoms of overdose include drowsiness, respiratory depression, nausea, vomiting, confusion, tremors and twitching, rapid pulse, unconsciousness, and rarely, seizures. Please see the GHB entry in the index for further information.

Monoamine Oxidase Inhibitors (MAOIs)

Monoamine oxidase inhibitors (MAOIs) are a class of compounds, often used as antidepressants, which reduce the metabolising actions of the enzyme monoamine oxidase (MAO) on neurotransmitters, particularly serotonin and dopamine.

Consumption of recreational drugs that enhance the actions of monoamines, and concomitant use of MAOIs should therefore be strictly avoided. Monoamine-enhancing drugs include psychostimulants, such as amphetamines, cocaine, methamphetamine, and MDMA (and related compounds), as well as other antidepressants like SSRIs.

The risk of these interactions is serotonin toxicity (serotonin syndrome), a life-threatening condition characterised by excessive levels of serotonergic activation in neurons and muscles. Symptoms include agitation, sweating, tremors and hyperreflexia (overactive reflexes), muscle rigidity, twitching, and hyperthermia. Further, hypertensive symptoms may also arise, such as severe headache, rapid heart rate, and rises in blood pressure. Extreme symptoms include intracranial haemorrhage and acute cardiac failure.

MAOIs obtained from plant sources include Syrian rue (*Peganum harmala*), and the ayahuasca vine (*Banisteriopsis caapi*), both of which contain harmala alkaloids. In some instances, tryptamines such as DMT or psilocybin-containing mushrooms may be combined with these MAOIs to activate or potentiate the tryptamines' effects. These tryptamines have few direct actions on monoamine concentrations. As such, the risk of serotonin toxicity resulting from their concomitant use with reversible MAOIs (such as harmala alkaloids) is much lower than that seen between MAOIs and other psychoactive agents, for example stimulants such as the amphetamines or cocaine, empathogens such as MDMA or methylone, or psychedelic phenethylamines such as those in the DOx and 2C-x series of compounds, all of which should be strictly avoided with MAO inhibitors.

Identifying Prescription and Over-The-Counter Drugs with High-Risk Interactions

This section provides information to assist in determining which drug class a particular medication fits into. The drug classes that we have focused on are those with major interactions, as presented in the Table of High-Risk Drug Interactions above, such as: barbiturates, benzodiazepines, opiates/opioids, antihistamines, MAOIs, SSRIs, and stimulants.

In the listings below, the generic names (proprietary names in brackets) for the most commonly used drugs in each class are given. Some proprietary products may contain other drugs in addition to the main compound described by the generic name; in most cases we have not listed those other drugs. Please note that this list of drug names is far from complete, and does not identify many proprietary names. As such, additional resources may be required to identify particular prescription drugs, which class they belong to, and whether they possess potential for harmful interactions with particular commonly used recreational agents.

Use the lists below to determine the class—such as barbiturate, MAOI, and so forth—that the common prescription or OTC drug in question belongs to. Then use the Table of High-Risk Drug Interactions above to determine the potential consequences of drug combinations. Once again, the lists below are incomplete and provided for information purposes only. A medic should always be consulted when any dangerous drug combination is suspected.

Barbiturates
allobarbital (Cibalgine, Dial-Ciba); amobarbital (Amytal); aprobarbital/aprobarbitone (Allonal, Oramon, Somnifaine); barbital/barbitone (Medinal, Veronal); butalbital (Axocet, Axoxtal, Esgic, Fioricet, Fioricet#3 [with codeine]); mephobarbital (Mebaral); pentobarbital/pentobarbitone (Nembutal); phenobarbital/phentobarbitone (Luminal); secobarbital (Seconal); sodium thiopental/thiopental/thiopentone (Trapanal)

Benzodiazepines/Hypnotics
alprazolam (Xanax); chlordiazepoxide hydrochloride (Librium, Librax); clobazam (Onfi); clonazepam (Klonopin); chlorazepate (Tranxene); diazepam (Valium); estazolam (Prosom, Eurodin); lorazepam (Ativan); midazolam (Dormitol, Dormicum, Versed); oxazepam (Alepam, Bonare, Serax); temazepam (Restoril, Normison); triazolam (Halcion); zopiclone (Imovane, Zimovane), zolpidem (Ambien, Stilnox, Zolpimist)

Opiates/Opioids
buprenorphine (Buprenex, Butrans, Cizdol, Subutex, Temgesic); codeine (Paveral); diacetylmorphine/diamorphine (Heroin); ethylmorphine (Codethylene, Cosylan); fentanyl/fentanil (Actiq, Durogesic; Sublimaze); hydrocodone/dihydrocodeinone (Norco, Lortab, Vicodin, Vicoprofen); methadone (Dolophine); morphine (Avinza, Dolcontin, Kadian, MS Contin); oxycodone (OxyContin, Percocet, Percodan); oxymorphone (Opana, Numorphan, Numorphone); tramadol (Ultram, Zytram)

First Generation Antihistamines
bromopheniramine (Dimetapp); chlorphenamine/chloropheniramine (Allerest, Codral, Demazin); clemastine/meclastin (Tavist); cyclizine (Marezine); cyproheptadine (Peritol); dexbrompheniramine (Drixoral); dexchlorpheniramine (Polaramine); diphenhydramine (Benadryl, Dramamine, Sominex, Unisom SleepMelts, Unisom SleepGels); doxylamine (Dozile; Sleep Aid, Unisom SleepTabs); embramine (Mebryl); fexofenadine (Allegra, Mucinex); hydroxyzine (Vistaril); loratadine (Claritin); pheniramine (Avil); phenyltoloxamine (Duraxin); promethazine (Phenergan); rupatadine (Rupafin); triprolidine (Actifed, Zymine)

SSRIs/SNRIs
bupropion (Wellbutrin, Zyban); citalopram (Celexa); desvenlafaxine (Pristiq); duloxetine (Cymbalta); escitalopram (Lexapro); fluoxetine (Prozac); fluvoxamine (Luvox); levomilnacipran (Fetzima); milnacipran (Ixel, Savella); paroxetine (Paxil, Pexeva); sertraline (Zoloft); tofenacin (Elamol, Tofacine); vilazodone (Viibryd); venlafaxine (Effexor)

MAOIs
moclobemide (Aurorix, Manerix); bifemelane (Alnert); brofaramine (Consonar); toloxatone (Humoryl); harmaline; selegiline (Eldepryl, Zelapar); pargyline (Eutonyl); tranylcypromine (Parnate); phenelzine (Nardil); isocarboxazid (Marplan); procarbazine (Matulane, Natulan); St. John's wort (Hypericum perforatum) [Note: St. John's wort is an extremely weak MAOI, and no "adverse MAOI effects" have been reported that we're aware of. However, since it increases serotonin levels, it should not be taken with SSRIs or other drugs that strongly boost serotonin, like MDMA, MDA, etc. Additionally, St. John's wort contains compounds known to activate cytochrome P450 enzymes, which the body uses to metabolize many drugs; concurrent use may therefore reduce the effectiveness of whatever other drug has been taken if that drug is metabolized by CYP450.]

Prescription Psychostimulants
amphetamine/dextroamphetamine (Adderall, Dexedrine); fenfluramine (Adifax); methylphenidate (Ritalin, Concerta); methamphetamine (Desoxyn); lisdexamfetamine (Vyvanse); phentermine (Adipex-P, Duromine); phendimetrazine (Appecon, Bontril)

INDEX OF DRUG EFFECTS

Each drug entry in this index contains a brief introduction, relevant names, drug class, appearance, mechanisms of action, psychoactive effects, dosing approaches and the pharmacokinetics for different routes of administration, adverse reactions, contraindications, drug interactions, harm minimisation strategies, overdose descriptions, and related compounds.

DRUG NAME	PAGE
2C-B (2C-x, DOx)	336
Alcohol	338
Amphetamine (and Methamphetamine)	341
Cannabis	344
Cocaine	347
DMT (Dimethyltryptamine)	349
GHB (γ-hydroxybutryrate)	351
Heroin	353
Ketamine	355
LSD	357
MDMA (MDA and PMA)	359
MDPV	362
Mephedrone	364
25I-NBOMe (and other related compounds)	366
Nitrous Oxide	367
Psilocybin	369
Salvia divinorum	372
Scopolamine	375

2C-B

A psychedelic phenethylamine first synthesised by Alexander Shulgin in 1974. It possesses visionary and empathogenic properties, with putative aphrodisiac qualities, and has seen use as an adjunct to psychotherapy. 2C-B has a relatively shorter onset and duration than other hallucinogens. It gained popularity in the rave subculture in the late 1980s as a legal alternative to MDMA, later being scheduled by the United Nations' Convention on Psychotropic Substances in 2001.

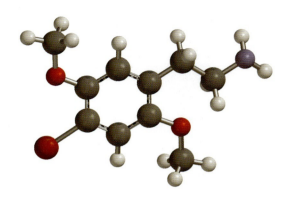

Chemical Name:
2-(4-bromo-2,5-dimethoxyphenyl)ethanamine;
- OR -
4-bromo-2,5-dimethoxyphenethylamine;
- OR -
2,5-dimethoxy-4-bromophenethylamine

Synonyms:
Nexus; B; bees; CB; bromo-mescaline; Venus; Erox; Ubalawu Nomothotholo

Class:
Serotonergic hallucinogen; psychedelic phenethylamine

Appearance:
Usually presents as a white powder, in gelatine capsules, or in tablet form.

Mechanism:
Partial serotonin agonist at $5\text{-}HT_{2A}$ and $5\text{-}HT_{2C}$ receptors. There is evidence of antagonism at $5HT_{2A}$ receptors. Additionally, affinity to various other serotonergic and adrenergic receptor subtypes has been shown.

Psychoactive Effects:
Characterised by visual effects akin to but milder than LSD, while also exhibiting empathogenic properties reminiscent of MDMA, with a lower propensity for stimulant effects. Alters perceptual processes, with visual patterning, auditory, olfactory, and tactile sensations reported. Changes in mental processes may include feelings of insight, closeness to self and others, emotional introspection, anxiety, and confusion. It is often described as possessing more euphoric effects than other psychedelic phenethylamines.

Pharmacokinetics:

Oral: 10–50 mg, with 15–30 mg as commonly used active doses. Onset 20–90 minutes, duration 3–5 hours, and after-effects lasting 2–4 hours.

Intranasal: 5–15 mg as commonly reported doses, and has a shorter onset and duration of action than oral ingestion. Disorientation following insufflation of higher doses is often self-reported. Increases in the prevalence and duration of side-effects have been self-reported with this administration route.

Rectal: 7–40 mg as commonly reported doses. Similar durations as per oral have been reported.

Injection: 1–3 mg reported doses, however this route of administration is rarely reported in surveys of users (<1%). It seems likely that the duration profile will be more rapid.

Note: A wide range of doses has been described for this drug, suggesting individual sensitivities to 2C-B.

Adverse Reactions:

Common: Decreased appetite; insomnia; increased blood pressure; increased heart rate; nausea.

Severe pain and irritation in the nasal cavity is often reported upon insufflation.

Less Common: Vomiting; anxiety; confusion; changes in body temperature; muscle twitches; excessive mucous production

Rare: Seizures

Life-threatening: None reported

Contraindications:
Psychiatric illness, particularly schizophrenia and related psychotic disorders; any medical condition where hypertension would be hazardous, for example cardiovascular disease.

Interactions:
None reported. Given that MAO-A and MAO-B are enzymes involved in the metabolism of 2C-B, the use of any MAO inhibitor may potentiate the risk of adverse effects including hypertensive crisis. With SSRIs, such risks are lower, where rather than a potentiation, additive effects have been noted with agents such as 2C-B. It is suspected that use with other stimulants will compound hypertensive effects. Co-usage of MDMA has been reported; information regarding potentially enhanced toxicity, however, is lacking. Synergistic effects have been reported with concomitant hallucinogen use.

Harm Minimisation:
Standard precautions as per all hallucinogens.

Overdose:
LD_{50} is unknown. Despite high oral doses of over 75 mg having been reported without harm, individual sensitivities to a wide range of doses have been reported, meaning that in some individuals, lower doses may carry greater risk.

Related Compounds:

2C-x

The halogen in 2C-B—namely the bromine moiety at the carbon 4-position—has been replaced with other halogens such as chlorine, fluorine, and iodine, to give rise to the compounds 2C-C, 2C-F, and 2C-I. In addition to halogen substitution, other substituents at this position include alkyl chains, O-methyl, and S-alkyl groups. Collectively these are often referred to as the "2C-x series", with over twenty-five different substances that have been synthesised. A few N-benzyl-oxy-methyl ("NBOMe") analogues of 2C-x compounds have also been synthesized and marketed, including 25B-NBOMe (or "25B"), 25C-NBOMe (or "25C"), 25D-NBOMe (or "25D"), and others. For more info on these, see the 25I-NBOMe listing.

It should be noted that these agents have extremely varied onsets, durations of action, and importantly varied intra-subjective effects. Some of the 2C-x series require over three hours before any initial effects are felt; because they take so long to come on, users anticipating an earlier onset may believe the agent that they took must have been adulterated, causing them to underdose. So they decide to "top up" and take more. This may lead to difficult experiences for some users. Potencies also vary substantially amongst the different 2C-x compounds; however, oral dosages are usually in the order of >10 mg, with the important exception of the extremely potent 25x-NBOMe (aka 2C-x-NBOMe) compounds, which are active at sub-milligram doses and sometimes sold on blotter paper misrepresented as LSD.

DOx

If there is an α-methyl substituent added to 2C-B then this will give rise to the amphetamine analogue DOB. Similar with the 2C-x series, subsequent alteration of the 4-bromo moiety gives rise to the DOx series. It includes DOB, DOI, DOM, and DOB-Dragonfly. Generally, these agents carry a greater risk for adverse sympathomimetic effects and are also noted to have very long durations, in some cases greater than thirty hours. The potency of these agents is also much greater than the 2C-x series, by about a factor of ten. With active doses ranging 1–3 mg, correct dosing can be difficult. In recent years, the challenge of properly measuring-out dose units has sometimes been addressed by soaking these compounds into perforated sheets of blotter paper.

For the four decades following the late 1960s, blotter paper was used almost exclusively as a delivery method to distribute a single drug: LSD. But in the mid-2000s, blotter began to increasingly appear that had been dosed with psychedelic compounds other than LSD. As vendors of research chemicals have expanded their offerings in the years since then, the trend of using blotter as distribution method for a widening variety of extremely potent drugs has increased. By 2017, the assortment of lysergamides, phenethylamines, tryptamines, and other compounds that have been distributed on blotter includes the drugs: 1P-LSD (1-propionyl-lysergic acid diethylamide), 5-MeO-αMT, 25I-NBF, 25I-NBOH, 25C-NBOH, 25B-NBOMe, 25C-NBOMe, 25I-NBOMe, 25N-NBOMe, AL-LAD (6-allyl-6-nor-lysergic acid diethylamide), bromo-dragonfly, 2C-C, 2C-E, 2C-I, DMA, DOB, DOC, DOI, DOM, lamid (methyl-isopropyllysergamide), LSZ (lysergic acid 2,4-dimethylazetide), along with the benzodiazapines etizolam, pyrazolam, diclazepam, and the powerful stimulant 3,4-dichloromethylphenidate.

Due to the popularity (and sometimes low availability) of LSD, and the high potency of these other "LSD-like" compounds, unscrupulous or uninformed dealers may misrepresent them as LSD. Some users who unknowingly take DOx or 25x-NBOMe instead of LSD, may experience anxiety from still being high for so long after they had anticipated the effects to subside. Additionally, while LSD is essentially non-toxic (overdose deaths due solely to adverse physiological responses are unheard of), a few fatalities have been associated with several of these other compounds.

Sasha Shulgin, pioneering creator of 2C-x and DOx compounds, held six psychedelic phenethylamines in such high regard that he referred to them as "the magical half-dozen". Joining the naturally inspiring compound mescaline, the five additional Shulgin synthetics he considered top shelf are: 2C-B, 2C-E, 2C-T-2, 2C-T-7, and DOM. It is therefore not surprising that these have been among the most commonly seen on the street.

ALCOHOL

Alcohol is a widely used intoxicant found in beer, wine, spirits, and other beverages, which has a long history of human use. The psychoactive effects of alcohol are generally biphasic, such that low doses tend to produce a disinhibited state, whilst depressant effects are seen with larger doses. Alcohol is commonly obtained via fermentation, a process where sugars undergo metabolism by yeasts.

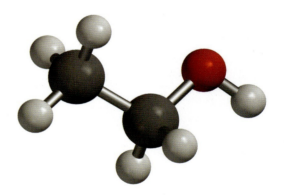

Chemical Names:
Ethanol;
- OR -
ethyl alcohol

Synonyms:
Grog; booze; liquor; alky; spirits; hooch

Class:
Depressant

Appearance:
A colourless volatile liquid

Mechanism:
Ethanol acts as a positive allosteric modulator of synaptic and extra synaptic $GABA_A$ receptors. At higher dosages, ethanol acts as a negative allosteric modulator at glutamatergic NMDA receptors. Ethanol also exerts actions upon other targets, including nicotinic receptors, AMPA and Kainate receptors, and L-type calcium channels, amongst others.

Psychoactive Effects:
Different concentrations of alcohol in the human

body have different effects on the consumer. The following table lists the common effects produced at increasing levels of blood alcohol content (BAC). Please note, however, that both tolerance and responses to alcohol can vary considerably between individuals.

BAC has traditionally been determined either as a percentage based on a mass of alcohol per *volume* of blood, or as percentage based on a mass of alcohol per *mass* of blood. BAC expressed in terms of weight-per-volume (% w/v) is not equivalent across-the-board to BAC expressed in terms of weight-per-weight (% w/w). For example, a BAC of 5.00 grams of alcohol per litre of blood is equivalent to a BAC of 4.71 grams of alcohol per kilogram of blood. Complicating things further, different countries employ varying units of measurement to report BAC: micrograms per litre (µg/litre), milligram per 100 millilitres (mg/100 ml), milligrams per decilitre (mg/dl), and grams per litre (g/l), are all in use. In the chart below, ranges are expressed using BAC (% w/v) figures.

BAC (% w/v) **0.03%–0.12%**	BAC (% w/v) **0.09%–0.25%**	BAC (% w/v) **0.18%–0.30%**	BAC (% w/v) **0.25%–0.40%**	BAC (% w/v) **0.35%–0.50%**
Elevated mood	Lethargy	Profound confusion	Stupor	Coma
Euphoria	Sedation	Emotional lability	Severe ataxia	Depressed reflexes (for example, pupillary responses to light)
Increased confidence	Impaired memory	Impaired sensory perception	Lapses of consciousness	Marked life-threatening respiratory depression
Enhanced sociability	Delayed reactions	Analgesia	Anterograde amnesia	Markedly decreased heart rate and hypotension
Decreased attention	Ataxia, or unbalanced walk	Advanced ataxia	Vomiting (death may occur due to inhalation of vomit while unconscious)	
Flushed appearance	Blurred vision	Impaired speech	Respiratory depression	
Impaired judgment	Other sensory impairments	Dizziness	Decreased heart rate	
Impaired fine muscle coordination		Nausea	Urinary incontinence	
		Vomiting		

Pharmacokinetics:
Ethanol is metabolised by the body, as an energy-providing nutrient, into acetyl coenzyme A (acetyl-CoA), an intermediate that can be used for energy in the citric acid cycle. Ethanol largely gets converted by liver enzymes into acetaldehyde, followed by acetic acid, which subsequently gets converted into acetyl-CoA. Those with acquired alcohol tolerance have a greater quantity of these enzymes, and metabolise ethanol more rapidly. Differences in the rates of alcohol-converting enzymes may produce a build-up of acetaldehyde and mild toxic effects in some individuals. Alcohol clearance follows zero-order kinetics and is excreted at a constant rate of approximately ten grams per hour, although this can vary between individuals.

Adverse Reactions:

Common: Sedation; loss of motor coordination; delayed reactions; impaired memory and comprehension; impaired speech; blurred vision; aggression; impulsivity. Hangover effects are characterised by intense headache, nausea, shakiness, and sometimes vomiting.

Less Common: Profound confusion; emotional lability; analgesia; dizziness; nausea; vomiting

Rare: Severe ataxia; loss of consciousness; anterograde amnesia; respiratory depression; decreased heart rate; urinary incontinence

Life-threatening: Unconsciousness; depressed reflexes; respiratory depression; bradycardia and hypotension; aspiration of vomit

Contraindications:
Severe mental disturbances; hepatic diseases

Interactions:
Alcohol interacts with many drugs and substances; as a general rule, all CNS depressants should be avoided. Drugs with actions on GABA receptors should be avoided, including: barbiturates, general anaesthetic agents, benzodiazepines, and GHB (γ-hydroxybutyrate). Opiates/opioids, ketamine, nitrous oxide, and antihistamines should also be avoided with alcohol. These interactions may enhance the dangerous effects of alcohol including, sedation, motor incoordination, unconsciousness, and respiratory depression. Mixing antibiotics and alcohol should be avoided, particularly metronidazole, tinidazole, and trimethoprim/sulfamethoxazole where disulfiram-like reactions of increased sensitivity to alcohol may occur and precipitate breathlessness, headaches, skin flushing, irregular heartbeat, light-headedness, and vomiting.

Harm Minimisation:
Alcoholism is a contributing factor to morbidity and mortality worldwide. In 2004, 3.8% of all global deaths were attributable to alcohol. Men are several times more likely to die from alcohol than women. Globally, the harmful use of alcohol is the leading risk factor for death in men aged 15–59 (WHO 2011). Alcohol is widely used in social contexts for its mood-enhancing, euphoric, and relaxant effects, and the maintenance of these effects requires a continuous consumption of the drug to be employed. The potential for harm in such cases may be minimised by monitoring levels of consumption and impairment to ensure an appropriate BAC. Some methods for modulating BAC include drinking water between alcoholic beverages and also eating food to delay absorption.

BAC of > 0.08% is associated with confusion and impaired senses, which enhance the propensity for risk-taking behaviours and poor judgement. Injury may result from impaired motor coordination. The active avoidance of potentially dangerous situations when inebriated is good practice. Driving whilst on alcohol is the largest criminal cause of death and injury in the Western world. As such, planning to not drive by designating a sober driver is the best practice. Whilst zero tolerance is practiced in some countries, most Western countries have legal limits of 0.02%–0.08% BAC.

Overdose:
Death is often due to coma and respiratory depression; however, overdose may lead to aspiration of vomit or severe bradycardia. Such effects may occur when the BAC is greater than 0.4%.

AMPHETAMINE

Amphetamine was first manufactured in 1887 by the Romanian chemist Lazar Edeleanu, who synthesised it from ephedrine, a naturally occurring compound within the Ma-Huang plant (*Ephedra sinica*). Amphetamine is a stimulant with euphoriant, anorectant, and sympathomimetic actions. It is a prototypic member and serves as a common structural template for other psychostimulants, but also for hallucinogens including the DOx and TMA series of amphetamines. It is used medically in the treatment of Attention Deficit Hyperactivity Disorder (ADHD), narcolepsy, and obesity.

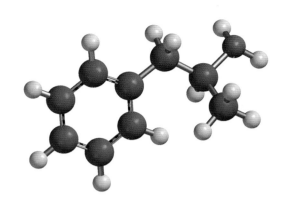

Nomenclature:
Alpha-methylphenethylamine (amphetamine); α-methylbenzeneethaneamine; 1-phenyl-2-aminopropane; phenylisopropylamine

Synonyms:
Hundreds of synonyms and proprietary names exist. Common proprietary names include: Adderall; Benzedrine; Dexedrine; Dextrostat; Evekeo and ProCentra. Street-names include: bennies; crank; dex; dexies; dexy; go-ey; speed; tweak.

Class:
Stimulant

Appearance:
Amphetamine usually presents as the salt form (often as the sulphate). Colour ranges from a white to brown powder sometimes with traces of grey, red, green, and other colours, which are often impurities remaining from its synthesis. As a pharmaceutical preparation, it comes as several different tablets and capsules; however, it is often encountered in various dosages (usually 5–30 mg) as small white tablets with a split in the middle.

Mechanism:
Amphetamine is an indirect sympathomimetic, with chemical structure similar to dopamine (DA), noradrenaline (NA), and also other endogenous trace amines. It essentially acts by releasing monoamines from within neurons into the synapse, particularly dopamine and noradrenaline. Specifically, amphetamine acts as a substrate for DA and NA reuptake transporters whereby it may be taken up into neurons. Within the neuron, amphetamine acts as a substrate for neuronal vesicle monoamine transporters (VMAT2), thus being taken up into vesicles and displacing monoamines and increasing cytosolic concentrations of DA and NA. Further actions include as a potent full agonist on trace amine receptors (TAAR1), which enables the efflux of dopamine and noradrenaline out of the cell and into the synapse.

Amphetamine is composed of two stereoisomers at the α–carbon, namely the *levo* and *dextro* forms. These isomers display similar actions but with different potencies on the varying sites they act upon. Dextroamphetamine is a more potent TAAR1 agonist and four-fold more potent at releasing DA, whilst the levo form is more potent as a releaser of NA. Moreover the dextro isomer has greater CNS psychostimulant effects, whilst the levo form is associated with greater cardiovascular and peripheral effects.

Psychoactive Effects:
Increased alertness; increased concentration and motivation; mood elevation; euphoria; emotional lability; heightened physical energy; prolonged stamina and reduced fatigue; enhanced tactility; aphrodisiac effects; decreased appetite

Pharmacokinetics:

Oral: 5–40 mg, with 5–30 mg as commonly reported active doses. Onset is typically 30–40 minutes, with a duration of 4–8 hours, and after-effects for 5–24 hours.

Intranasal: 5–30 mg, with 5–20 mg as commonly reported active doses. Onset is typically 1–5 minutes, with a duration of 3–6 hours, and after-effects for 5–24 hours. Insufflation of amphetamine tablets containing binders and fillers can be a very painful experience and is advised against.

Rectally: 5–30 mg as commonly reported active doses. Onset is typically 10–20 minutes, with a duration of 3–8 hours, and after-effects for 5–24 hours.

Intravenous: 2.5–30 mg as reported active doses. Onset is typically within seconds, with a duration of 3–6 hours, and after-effects for 5–24 hours. Amphetamine tablets contain both water-soluble and insoluble binders and fillers, whilst illicitly manufactured amphetamines regularly contain synthesis impurities and cutting compounds; for these reasons, the injection of amphetamine is strongly advised against.

Note: The dosages above are for pharmaceutical grade dexamphetamine in individuals with little to no tolerance. Tolerance develops rapidly to amphetamine, and dosages can be 2–3 times higher during periods of extended use. In people with diagnoses of narcolepsy, oral dosages are titrated up to a maximum of 60 mg/day over a number of weeks. Street speed is usually a mixture of 50% levo and 50% dextro isomers, and is commonly cut with glucose, other sugars, and caffeine. Because the purity varies, active dosages of street speed will vary from those presented above, requiring titration.

Adverse Reactions:

Common: Anxiety; grandiosity; restlessness; insomnia; agitation; increased body temperature; increased heart rate; increased blood pressure; bruxism (teeth grinding); heart palpitations; tremor; dry mouth; loss of appetite; temporary erectile dysfunction; hyperthermia; stereotypy (repeated behaviours such as grooming or scratching)

Less Common: Aggression; paranoia; panic attack; bruxism leading to damage to the teeth; difficulty urinating; tics; hyperthermia

Rare: Psychosis; mania; aggression; confusion and delirium in susceptible individuals or with prolonged usage

Life-threatening: Cardiac arrest or seizures; sudden death in individuals with structural heart defects and other serious heart problems; suicidal ideation in susceptible individuals; cerebral haemorrhage; rhabdomyolysis and kidney failure; sympathomimetic toxidrome; seizures

Contraindications:
Cardiac arrhythmia; history of symptomatic cardiovascular disease; arteriosclerosis; hypertension; hyperthyroidism; seizure disorders; glau-

coma; motor tics and Tourette syndrome; severe depression; anorexia nervosa; psychotic symptoms; suicidal tendencies; impaired renal function; psychotic disorders such as schizophrenia or bipolar disorder.

Interactions:
There are a great many agents with potential for drug-interactions with amphetamine. Whilst describing all these is beyond the scope of this Guide, important drug-interactions are described below. Under no circumstances should amphetamine be combined with a monoamine oxidase inhibitor (MAOI), as this can lead to serious hypertensive crises. Further, concomitant use of tricyclic antidepressants and amphetamine may also enhance the risk of hypertension. The concomitant use of amphetamine with other psychostimulants such as cathinones, MDxx, cocaine, as well as prescription stimulants including fenfluramine, phentermine, and methylphenidate may enhance the risk of dangerous hypertensive responses. Additionally, amphetamines may antagonize the hypotensive effects of antihypertensive medications. The effects and toxicity of amphetamines may be enhanced by CYP2D6 inhibitors; these include the SSRIs fluoxetine (Prozac) and paroxetine (Paxil), and also the antiretroviral protease inhibitor, ritonavir.

Harm Minimisation:
Amphetamine can be a highly habit-forming substance with repeated exposures. Insufflated and intravenous administration display an enhanced propensity for addiction, which has a characteristic withdrawal syndrome that increases in severity with both age and extent of usage. Repeated dosing with amphetamines results in greatly diminished psychoactive effects, requiring larger dosages with increases in adverse physiological effects and is advised against. Heavy comedown effects may ensue with such practices, which include cognitive fatigue, depression, anxiety, irritability, suppressed motivation, and sleep paralysis. Any individual intent on injecting drugs should be advised that even in clinical settings this form of administration carries inherent risks. Such discussion is beyond the scope of this Guide. However, users should be confident and aware of safe injecting practices, and know the risks involved from a lack of adherence to these.

Overdose:
Individual response to amphetamines varies widely. As such, doses of 30 mg can produce severe reactions; however, high dosages of over 300 mg are not necessarily fatal. Emergency medical treatment must be sought immediately if over-dosage is suspected. Monitoring of vitals and emergency stabilisation is required to manage those suffering seizure, cardiac arrest, or the acute consequences of arteriospasm or rupture such as stroke. It is extremely important to keep the individual hydrated. External cold packs may be applied to help bring the body temperature down and reduce sweating, in order to reduce hyperthermia, and the risks of rhabdomyolysis and kidney failure.

Related Compounds:
Below is a stub entry for methamphetamine, a structurally analogous and commonly encountered stimulant compound similar in effect to amphetamine. More importantly many of the mechanisms, effects, adverse reactions, risks, and harms as described above for amphetamine also apply to methamphetamine; as such, points of difference with other similar compounds are considered below.

METHAMPHETAMINE

Methamphetamine (MA) is a psychostimulant with euphoriant and aphrodisiac properties. Medical indications for MA (proprietary name: Desoxyn) include ADHD and obesity. It is commonly encountered as the hydrochloride salt, which can be smoked/vaporized without being converted to the freebase form first. (Many people incorrectly presume that smokable methamphetamine comes in freebase form due to this being the case with cocaine.) Slang names include: meth, crank, crystal, ice, shabs, tweak, and glass. MA crystals range from colourless to white in colour, with colourations indicating impurities. Dosages are similar to those reported for amphetamine. Like amphetamine, tolerance develops rapidly with repeated exposure, in these cases dosages may be higher than stated above. Insufflating MA results in great pain in the nasal cavity. When smoked or vaporised, amounts of 5–50 mg are commonly reported active doses. Onset is within minutes, with a duration of 1–4 hours, and after-effects for up to 24 hours. MA has a high addiction potential, particularly when smoked or injected. MA displays dopaminergic and serotonergic neurotoxicity in humans, which—with chronic use—is associated with post-acute withdrawals persisting for many months.

Other Analogues:
There are a great many analogues of amphetamine, with a variety of effects ranging from stimulant, to empathogenic/entactogenic, to psychedelic. Pharmacologically, these effects occur due to differences in the actions of the analogue at varying targets, which may result in different ratios and amounts of monoamines being released from presynaptic terminals, whilst psychedelic amphetamines usually exert additional direct effects on serotonin receptors. Always be aware of the active dose ranges, durations of action, and effects associated with such analogues.

Analogues of amphetamine used in medicine include fenfluramine (a weight loss agent); with substituent additions made to the 3-position on the phenyl ring and an ethyl group added to the amine of amphetamine, it acts as a stimulant at lower doses and a psychedelic when dosage is escalated. Phentermine is an appetite suppressant with stimulant effects; it has an additional methyl group added to the α-carbon of amphetamine and as such lacks the stereoisomers of amphetamine. Analogues of phentermine for medical use (containing chloro substituents added to varying positions of the phenyl ring), include 4-chloro-phentermine and 2-chloro-phentermine. Further addition of a keto group at the carbon gives rise to the cathinones (see the Mephedrone and MDPV index entries).

Other changes to amphetamine include halogens (bromo-, chloro-, iodo-) and methyl groups added to the 2-, 3-, or 4-position of the phenyl ring or combinations thereof; these generally appear to retain monoamine reuptake activity and have stimulant and anorectant properties. When 3,4-methylendioxy- substituents are added to amphetamine, serotonin release is enhanced and empathogenic effects are observed; these include MDxx compounds (see MDMA entry). Addition of a methoxy group to the 4-position gives rise to *para*-methoxy-amphetamine (PMA), a potent serotonin-releasing agent with a low therapeutic window for adverse effects. Further addition of three methoxy groups in varying combinations to the phenyl group gives rise to the trimethoxyamphetamines (TMAs), referred to as mescalamphetamine. Many compounds in this series have psychedelic properties. Further, the addition of halogens to the 4-position of the phenyl ring of 2,5-dimethoxy-amphetamine gives rise to a potent series of long-acting psychedelics, namely the DOx series developed by Sasha Shulgin, with actions as partial agonists at varying serotonin receptors (see 2C-B entry). As such amphetamine is a prototypic compound with many analogues in its class that produce a wide variety of psychoactive effects.

CANNABIS

Originating in Central Asia, cannabis is a plant with a long history of human use. Its stalks have been employed as a fibre source in textiles, candle wicks, rope, paper production, as a component in composite panels made for the automotive industry, and even used as insulation in home construction. Its nutritious seeds have been included in birdfeed and human food. They've been made into oil used in the production of paints and varnishes, incorporated into massage oils and various other body products, formed into biodegradable plastics, and used as a biofuel for

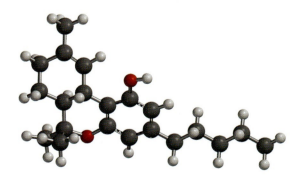

diesel engines. With the vast array of chemical compounds it produces (over a hundred cannabinoids have been isolated from the plant), it is not surprising that cannabis has been used medicinally for over 3,400 years, employed for wide diversity of therapeutic applications including the treatment of pain, nausea, insomnia, epileptic seizure, Parkinsonism, cancer, and many others. Archaeological finds of cannabis suggest that its ritual use as a spiritual sacrament goes back at least 2,500 years. Such entheogenic use continues today, sometimes comingling with less formal hedonistic–recreational approaches.

The twenty-first century has seen a shift in social and legal positions on cannabis, and a growing acceptance not only of the important medical applications of the plant, but also of the rights of individuals to consume it at their leisure without the threat of arrest and imprisonment looming as an ever-present concern.

Botanical Names:
Cannabis sativa; Cannabis indica; Cannabis ruderalis

Active Chemicals:
Δ-9-tetrahydrocannabinol (THC); cannabidiol (CBD); cannabichromene (CBC); tetrahydrocannabivarin (THCV); and numerous other cannabinoids

Synonyms:
Bhang; buds; charas; dabs: dagga; ganja; grass; hashish; hemp; kif; marijuana; Mary Jane; pot; shatter; weed; and many more. Often names are for specific commercially developed strains, such as AK-47, Blueberry, Bubblegum, Chocolope, Chronic, Dog Shit, Girl Scout Cookies, Granddaddy Purple, Green Crack, Neighbour Kid, Northern Lights, OG Kush, Sour Diesel, White Widow, etc.

Class:
Cannabinoid

Appearance:
Dried flowering tops or leaves (marijuana); solid, darkly coloured brown to black resin (hashish); solid, yellowish to dark amber-coloured butane- or CO_2-extracted resins (highly potent); edibles, such as cookies and cakes; oils and other extracts of varying consistency and colour.

Mechanism:
Over a hundred cannabinoids have been isolated from the cannabis plant, of which the major inebriating compound is Δ-9-tetrahydrocannabinol (THC). THC is a partial agonist of the cannabinoid receptors CB_1 and CB_2. Cannabidiol (CBD), a major non-psychoactive component of cannabis, is a neutralising modulator at cannabinoid receptors. In addition, CBD has a multitude of medicinal applications including as an antianxiety agent, a neuropathic pain reliever, an antipsychotic, and an antiepileptic. Recently, CBD been shown to act on ligand-gated ion channels including GABA and glycine receptors, as well as having actions on many other targets.

Psychoactive Effects:
Euphoria; modified body-feeling (heaviness or buzz); altered perception of time; increased associative thinking; increased creativity; psychological confusion; anxiety; paranoia; increased pulse rate; perceptive changes; dry mouth; red eyes; drowsiness. Larger doses may produce hilarity and laughter, visual and auditory hallucinations, and sedation.

Pharmacokinetics:
In the plant, THC is present as the non-inebriating THC acid, which requires heating in order to be decarboxylated into the psychoactive THC. For this reason, cannabis is usually smoked or cooked into edibles.

Smoking: Standard dose is 0.3 grams cannabis in a joint, and less, about 0.1 grams, in a water pipe. Depending on individual tolerance levels and other factors, acute effects may be experienced from a single inhalation. Onset is 20–90 seconds, duration lasts 2–4 hours, and after-effects may continue for another 2–4 hours.

Vaporisation: Similar effects, duration, and dosage as per smoking. Increasingly, purified gooey extracts of high THC content called "dabs" or "shatter" are vaporised in a process called "dabbing". Such extracts are very potent and should only be used by regular consumers of cannabis, otherwise adverse reactions may be experienced.

Oral: Onset of effects from edibles, such as cookies, cakes, etc., is 30–90 minutes. After onset, peak effects last for an hour, with a plateau phase of up to 5 hours. Comedown and hangover effects may extend to twelve hours or more after ingestion. When cannabis is used in edibles, often it has been pre-heated before being incorporated into the baked good, since such an approach helps maximize the decarboxylization of THC-acid into THC.

Adverse Reactions:

Common: Dry mouth; red eyes; increased pulse rate; lowered blood pressure

Less Common: Nausea; vomiting; dizziness; drowsiness

Rare: Severe adverse psychological reactions; sedation; vasodepressor syncope (fainting); risk of psychosis in susceptible individuals

Life-threatening: None reported

Contraindications:
Psychiatric illness, particularly schizophrenia and related psychotic disorders; cardiovascular diseases and arrhythmias.

Interactions:
No known dangerous interactions. Combining alcohol with cannabis may increase "negative" effects, including nausea, vomiting, drowsiness, anterograde amnesia, and reduction of psychophysical performance. In an individual who is already moderately intoxicated with alcohol (for example), smoking a joint is likely to elicit predictably adverse effects, including nausea, vomiting, dizziness, general weakness, and a disturbed psychological state.

Harm Minimisation:
While having the potential to cause an adverse psychological experience (particularly in the naïve user), the ingestion of cannabis—even in high doses—very rarely presents any physiological danger.

Overdose:
None reported. The LD_{50} of cannabis is given by some sources as being in the order of 20,000 to 40,000 times the amount contained in a single average-sized joint.

Related Compounds:
Most synthetic cannabimimetics are unrelated structurally to the phyto-cannabinoids. Being structurally novel, the cannabimimetics may exert actions at a vast array of additional physiological targets alongside actions at cannabinoid receptors. Adverse reactions that may result from use of synthetic cannabimimetics include seizures, severe withdrawals, and other mentally and physically unpleasant effects. As there is no way for the average consumer to be certain of the identity of the synthetic cannabimimetic(s) in most products on the market, such products are best avoided.

COCAINE

A psychostimulant and local anaesthetic obtained from the *Erythroxylum coca* plant. The drug was first isolated in 1859 by the German chemist Albert Niemann. Modern recreational use was popularised in the 1970s, although its consumption through the chewing of coca leaf is a practice that is thought to date back thousands of years. In its salt form cocaine is typically consumed intranasally, while its freebase preparation, crack cocaine, is more readily smoked. Cocaine possesses considerable addiction liability, particularly in smoked form.

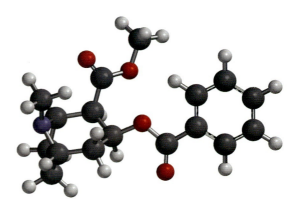

Chemical Name:
Ecgonine methyl ester benzoate;
- OR -
benzoylmethylecgonine

Synonyms:
Coke; blow; Charlie; C; crack; big C; biscuits; caine; chalk; coca; snow; yayo; and numerous others

Class:
Stimulant; tropane alkaloid

Appearance:
In its hydrochloride salt form, cocaine usually presents as a white or off-white powder. In its freebase form the drug may appear as a white, yellowish-white, or light brown powder or in larger crystals ("rocks"), often composed of varying textures.

Mechanism:
Cocaine acts on monoamine reuptake transporters to inhibit the reuptake of dopamine, serotonin, and noradrenaline, resulting in increased synaptic concentrations and enhanced monoamine neurotransmission. Additionally, cocaine acts as a non-selective monoamine oxidase (MAO) inhibitor, a sigma-1 (σ_1) non-opioid receptor agonist and upon serotonin-2 and -3 receptor subtypes. Local anaesthesia is mediated via the blockade of sodium (Na^+) on cell membranes, preventing the conduction of nerve impulses (that is, action potentials).

Psychoactive Effects:
Cocaine acts as an indirect sympathomimetic, producing stimulant, euphoriant, and anorectic effects. Typical dose-dependent effects may include increased alertness; mood elevation; euphoria; emotional lability; reduced fatigue; sexual arousal; decreased appetite; irritability; insomnia; and restlessness. Cocaine carries a high potential for addiction.

Pharmacokinetics:

Oral: 50–200 mg as commonly used active dosages. Onset is within 30–40 minutes, with a duration of 60 minutes, and peak subjective effects 20 minutes after onset.

Intranasal: 30–100 mg as commonly used active dosages. Onset is within minutes or even faster, with a duration of 40–60 minutes, and peak subjective effects 15 minutes after onset.

Rectal: 20–100 mg as commonly reported doses. Onset is within 10 minutes; otherwise similar durations as per oral have been reported.

Injection: 10–25 mg as commonly reported active dosages. Onset is within seconds, with a duration of 5–10 minutes, and peak subjective effects 3 minutes after onset.

Inhalational: 15–30 mg as commonly reported active dosages. Onset is within seconds, with a duration of 5–15 minutes, and peak subjective effects are within 2 minutes of onset.

Note: Significant tolerance to the psychostimulant effects of cocaine occurs with chronic use and active doses may be greater in certain users.

Adverse Reactions:

Common: Anxiety; agitation; paranoia and fear; headache

Less Common: Hypertension; tremors; gastrointestinal complications such as abdominal pain and nausea

Rare: Acute psychosis; rapid breathing; hyperthermia; hyperreflexia; chest pain

Life-threatening: Cardiac arrhythmia; heart attack; respiratory failure; stroke; convulsions

Contraindications:
History of cardiac disease; acute myocardial infarction; coronary artery disease; cardiac arrhythmias; hypertension; seizure disorder; hyperthyroidism; Tourette syndrome; cerebrovascular disease; pregnancy

Interactions:
Additive effects and increased toxicity may be observed when cocaine is combined with other stimulants. Cannabis may have additive effects on hypertension, tachycardia, and possibly cardiotoxicity. Alcohol consumption will result in the formation of cocaethylene, a metabolite more toxic than cocaine. MAO inhibitors and tricyclic antidepressants enhance the risk of hypertension with cocaine. Citalopram (SSRI) and cocaine may enhance the risk of a subarachnoid haemorrhage (bleeding in brain). Cardiac glycosides, for example digoxin, enhance the risk of cardiac arrhythmias, increased heart rate, and hypertension. Medications that decrease the seizure threshold are contraindicated, for example tramadol (opioid analgesic) and bupropion (noradrenaline–dopamine reuptake inhibitors). Co-administration of cocaine and opiates/opioids increases the risk of both nonfatal and fatal overdose.

Harm Minimisation:
Cocaine has a short half-life, commonly leading to repeated dosing in order to maintain effects. Such consumption patterns enhance the risk for potentially dangerous dose escalations to occur. When the effective dose is escalated, greater euphoria may result; however the incidence of toxic and unpleasant effects rises as well. Avoidance of "binge" consumption is recommended, and taking care to note both cumulative dosage and time between administrations is a good practice to minimise these risks. Whilst dosage levels may vary depending on administration method, one should be confident that the psychoactive effects of previous administrations have largely subsided before re-dosing.

The use of alcohol and cocaine results in the formation of the cocaethylene, a metabolite with significant cardiotoxicity. The co-administration of both alcohol and cocaine is associated with a more than twenty-fold increase in the risk of fatal overdose. Cocaine is commonly of low purity with adulterants added, including other local anaesthetics, ephedrine, and other stimulants. In recent years, levamisole has often been used as a cutting agent; it has been reported as a component in over 80% of cocaine seizures. Levamisole suppresses the immune system and can greatly increase the risk of infection, as well as being associated with autoimmune disorders such as vasculitis.

Physical side-effects specific to the route of administration include nosebleeds and intranasal perforations from insufflation, as well as coughs, laboured breathing, and sore throat from smoking freebase cocaine. Importantly, if taken via injection, the harm-minimisation practice of employing standard safe needle protocols should always be maintained. Cocaine possesses a large addiction liability and chronic usage is associated with many long-term adverse effects. These range from persisting neurological effects, such as motivational and other psychiatric disorders, cognitive deficits, cardiovascular toxicity, haemorrhages, and blood clots.

Overdose:
Cocaine is associated with a large number of overdoses worldwide. Toxicity is characterised by hyperthermia, hypertension, chest pain, anxiety, and agitation. Whilst the majority of cocaine-induced deaths are due to hyperthermia, overdose may manifest as hypertension, convulsions, stroke, cardiac arrhythmias or ischemia, respiratory failure, and muscle overactivity leading to rhabdomyolysis and subsequent kidney dysfunction.

Related Compounds:
Compounds that act as serotonin–noradrenaline–dopamine reuptake inhibitors (SNDRIs) include other stimulants such as methylphenidate (Ritalin). Many analogues of cocaine exist, having been designed in an attempt to isolate/modify actions on sodium channel blockade or on dopamine reuptake inhibition. Some of these analogues include troparil, 2'-hydroxycocaine, and cocaethylene.

DMT

DMT is a powerful psychedelic tryptamine found in many plants, and contained endogenously in all mammals studied to date. DMT is naturally present in the human body. When DMT is consumed (for example, by smoking), radical changes in consciousness are experienced. Some indigenous groups in South America make use of various DMT-containing preparations. For such groups, the visionary experience is usually situated at the heart of their cosmology and cultural practices. The ayahuasca brew represents a remarkable technology, wherein, out of many thousands of available plant species, a precise concoction was found that combined leaves from a DMT-containing plant (such as *Psychotria viridis*) with a monoamine oxidase inhibitor–containing species (such as the *Banisteriopsis caapi* vine), thereby rendering the DMT orally active.

Chemical Name:
N,N-dimethyltryptamine

Synonyms:
D; Dimitri; elf spice; spice; ayahuasca and changa (when DMT is used with a monoamine oxidase inhibitor)

Class:
Serotonergic hallucinogen

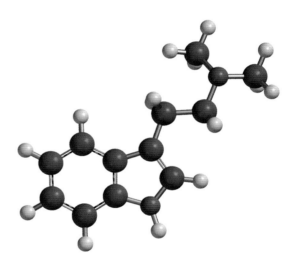

Appearance:
Pure DMT is a white crystalline solid, and is usually in the freebase form to facilitate smoking. Crystalline DMT extracted from plants may have different colours and textures, often in yellow/orange/red tones, depending on impurities present.

Mechanism:
Similarly to other classic hallucinogens, DMT is a serotonin receptor agonist, considered to primarily act on the 5-HT$_{2A}$ receptor, but it has also been found act as an agonist on 5-HT$_{2C}$, 5-HT$_{1A}$, 5-HT$_{1D}$, and 5-HT$_7$ receptors. Other, non-serotonergic activity for DMT has also been demonstrated, as

an agonist at G protein-coupled trace amine (TA) receptors, and as a possible endogenous agonist for the sigma-1 receptor.

Psychoactive Effects:

The experience of injected or smoked DMT has been described as a radical shift in the user's reality. The drug facilitates powerful changes in awareness, perceptions, emotions, and cognition. At appropriate doses these changes manifest as visionary experiences, often featuring distinct phenomena arising in open- and closed-eye visuals. These visual may consist of phosphenes, form constants, animated geometries and folding manifolds, through to complex immersive experiences of imagery and scenes, strange creatures, foreign otherworldly environments, and humanoid entities in various forms. As the phenomenology of DMT can be overwhelming, rapid, alien and intense, deep fear may arise, sometimes resulting in difficult experiences.

Pharmacokinetics:

Inhalational: Active at doses of 5–50 mg, with commonly used dosages of 15–30 mg. Onset of effects within 5–30 seconds, with a duration of 3–15 minutes, and come down around 5 minutes. Total duration of effects is up to 20 minutes.

Intranasal: Active at doses of 5–50 mg. Onset of effects within 5 minutes, with a duration of 15–30 minutes, and come down around 10 minutes. Total duration of effects lasts up to 45 minutes.

Injection: For intravenous injection, 0.2 mg drug/kg of bodyweight typically marks the psychedelic threshold, while 0.4 mg/kg and above may be considered a "high" dose. Time of onset is seconds, peaking at 2–5 minutes. Intramuscular injections take 2–3 minutes for onset, peaking in 10 minutes, and are over in under an hour.

Oral: DMT is inactive when consumed orally unless a MAOI is taken concurrently. Ayahuasca made from the Amazonian DMT-containing plant *Psychotria viridis* and the MAOI-containing vine *Banisteriopsis caapi* is a traditional orally active preparation. But ayahuasca analogues, or anahuasca, can be brewed from non-Amazonian plants, such as certain DMT-containing *Acacia* species or *Mimosa tenuiflora* and the MAOI-containing plant *Peganum harmala* (Syrian rue). And some folks prefer to take their oral DMT via a pharmahuasca preparation that combines pure DMT with a pharmaceutical MAOI such as moclobimide. An approximate per person dose for ayahuasca includes 50–100 grams of *B. caapi* vine with 50–100 grams of *P. viridis* leaves, prepared in water as a tea and cooked for many hours. If *P. harmala* is used as the MAOI source instead of *B. caapi*, only 3–4 grams of ground seeds are needed. Alternatively, active doses of purified plant extracts have been reported from the combination of 35–150 mg of DMT, with 35–50 mg being an oft-recommended range, taken with 100–250 mg of harmala alkaloids. Onset is usually 20–60 minutes, with a plateau phase of 1–3 hours, and after-effects that may continue for up to eight hours.

Adverse Reactions:

Common: Anxiety; the sensation that the user is no longer breathing or is dying; dilated pupils; heightened blood pressure; increased pulse; hyperthermia

Less Common: Overwhelming fear; nausea; vomiting (usually associated with high doses); lung irritation; diarrhoea; highly disorientating experiences (usually associated with high doses)

Rare: Psychosis in susceptible individuals

Life-threatening: None reported

Contraindications:
Mental illness, particularly schizophrenia and other disorders characterised by periods of psychosis; hypertension; cardiovascular disease

Interactions:
None reported for DMT. Using DMT in combination with other hallucinogens may increase the effects and the likelihood of adverse reactions. If taken orally with a MAOI, standard precautions for consumption of a MAOI should be followed (see beginning of this Guide).

Harm Minimisation:
Standard precautions as per all hallucinogens. Guests are highly unlikely to present to a care service whilst undergoing a DMT experience, unless it is in the form of an ayahuasca trip. Guests may seek assistance after a DMT experience; this will usually involve debriefing, discussion, and psychological support.

Overdose:
No known fatal overdose has been reported solely from DMT consumption.

Related Compounds:
5-methoxy-N,N-dimethyltryptamine (5-MeO-DMT) is also found in a wide variety of plant species and in the Sonoran Desert toad, *Incilius alvarius* (*Bufo alvarius*). It is more potent than DMT and may have a slightly longer duration in some users. When vaporized, a 5–20 mg dose range is commonly used. Although the effects produced by 5-MeO-DMT are similar in some ways to those produced by DMT, there are some notable differences. Whilst fractalesque, kaleidoscopic imagery may be experienced at the onset of the 5-MeO-DMT experience, it is generally less visual and less colourful than DMT. Powerful and often difficult experiences—characterised by ego-dissolution and what is described as "merging with light"—have been reported by 5-MeO-DMT users. Many people have little desire to repeat the experience once they've taken an immersive dose of 5-MeO-DMT. Some users will combine DMT with 5-MeO-DMT at a ratio of around 5:1 (due to the higher potency of the later), in order to achieve an experience that blends the effects of both compounds; this combination has been referred to by the name "the Mayan twins".

GHB

GHB, or gamma-hydroxybutyrate is a CNS depressant commonly consumed as a recreational drug or as a sleep aid. Its effects most closely resemble those of alcohol and its steep dose–response curve and synergistic effect with other depressants significantly increases risks of overdose. Found endogenously, research into GHB commenced in the 1960s and its role in growth-hormone production made it popular amongst bodybuilders in the 1980s. Increased recreational use and its characterisation as a date-rape drug by the media ultimately prompted prohibition worldwide by the early 2000s. Under the name sodium oxybate, GHB is approved for prescription use treating the sleep-related disorder narcolepsy.

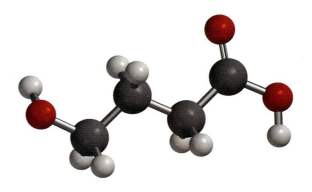

Chemical Name:
γ-hydroxybutyrate;
- OR -
sodium oxybate;
- OR -
sodium 4-hydroxybutyrate;
- OR -
4-hydroxybutanoic acid

Synonyms:
Liquid E; fantasy; G; GBH; liquid X, Xyrem®

Class:
Depressant

Appearance:
Generally presents as a clear, odourless salty-tasting liquid, or less commonly as a white powder.

Mechanism:
Full agonist of the GHB receptor, weak partial agonist of the $GABA_B$ receptor, and an agonist of extrasynaptic $GABA_A$ receptors.

Psychoactive Effects:
The effects of GHB are reminiscent of alcohol. Users report that it induces a pleasant state of relaxation and tranquillity, and at higher doses it can be helpful as a sleep aid.

Pharmacokinetics:

Oral: Moderate dose is 2–3 grams (28–43 mg/kg in a 70-kg person). Onset within 10–20 minutes, with a duration of 1–3 hours, and after-effects lasting 2–4 hours. Absorption is reduced and delayed by food; metabolism is delayed by liver impairment.

Adverse Reactions:

Common: Headache; nausea; vomiting; dizziness; unconsciousness

Less common: Confusion; irrational behaviour; slurred speech; urinary incontinence

Rare: Very low breathing; twitching or convulsions; slowed heart rate; fixed pupils; sleepwalking

Life-threatening: Higher doses of GHB may cause both unconsciousness and vomiting, which can lead to aspiration of vomit and damage to the lungs or suffocation.

Contraindications:
Compromised liver function, e.g., cirrhosis; impaired respiratory drive, e.g., sleep apnoea; depression or suicidal ideation; succinic semialdehyde dehydrogenase deficiency (SSADHD)

Interactions:
Cumulative effects observed when mixed with other depressants as well as an increase in negative side-effects. Mixing GHB with alcohol causes cumulative depressive effects as well as increased nausea and vomiting. Avoid mixing with alcohol, opiates/opioids, ketamine, or other depressants.

Harm Minimisation:
Given its steep dose–response curve, individuals usually start with a low dose, and increase the dose incrementally, especially with a batch of unknown concentration. Accidental or surreptitious administration of GHB may be prevented by dying preparations with blue food colouring. Mixing with alcohol or other depressants is extremely dangerous and implicated in over one-third of GHB-related deaths. Whenever reasonably possible, GHB users should inform others about what they have taken. There are numerous stories of GHB users who have woken up in a hospital, having been taken there by friends or strangers who were concerned because they had become unconscious and were unrousable.

Overdose:
Oral doses of 50 to 63 mg/kg are associated with loss of consciousness and profound coma. Until they regain consciousness, persons who are unconscious should be turned on their side in the recovery position—particularly if they are actively vomiting—so that their airway is kept clear and they don't aspirate or choke on vomit. The oral LD_{50} in rats is 9,690 mg/kg.

Related Compounds:
Gamma-butyrlactone (GBL) and 1,4-butanediol (1,4-B) are both pro-drugs of GHB, and are converted to GHB in vivo. Although it can be somewhat difficult to readily distinguish GBL from GHB, 1,4-B has a freezing point of 20.1°C and in its pure form will solidify at around room temperature (or if refrigerated).

HEROIN

Heroin is a semi-synthetic opiate derived from morphine, which is present in the opium poppy. It was first synthesized in 1874 by the English chemist C.R. Adler Wright. It was rediscovered by the German pharmaceutical company Bayer in 1897, and by 1898 Bayer was marketing it to physicians under the name of Heroin. Described as "the sedative for coughs", it was purported to be a non-addictive alternative to morphine. Its addictive properties became readily apparent in the years to follow, and in 1913 Bayer decided to cease production. The addition of two acetyl groups to morphine forms heroin, or diacetylmorphine. Heroin crosses the blood–brain barrier readily, where it is metabolised to morphine before exerting actions on opioid receptors. Heroin's effects are characterised by euphoric indifference, relaxation, sedation, and analgesia. Heroin possesses a high potential for addiction, and is associated with significant morbidity and mortality, particularly when injected intravenously.

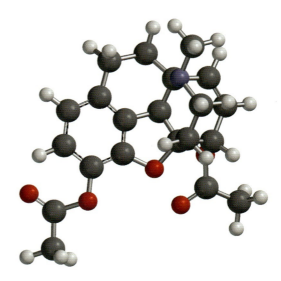

Chemical Name:
3,6-diacetylmorphine;
- OR -
diamorphine

Synonyms:
Dragon; gear; H; Harry; horse; junk; scag; smack

Class:
Opiate

Appearance:
Heroin may present as a freebase or salt form, and usually ranges from a crushed powder or granules through to crystalline rocks of varying composition. Colours of crystallised heroin include white to off-white, beige, tan, brown and even black. Unrefined black or brown heroin may indicate the presence of mono-acetylated morphine derivatives.

Mechanism:
The primary mechanism of action is as a μ-opioid receptor agonist. Heroin acts as a pro-drug of morphine; the presence of the two acetyl groups make heroin more lipophilic than morphine, allowing it to more readily cross the blood–brain barrier. Once in the brain, heroin undergoes additional metabolism and is de-acetylated into morphine, which has actions as an agonist at μ_1- and μ_2-opioid receptors. Further, a major active metabolite of morphine, morphine-6-glucoronide, by adopting a unique folded conformation, also crosses the blood–brain barrier with surprising efficiency, where it significantly contributes to the analgesic effects by virtue of its activity at μ-opioid receptors. This G protein–coupled receptor system undergoes pronounced regulatory changes upon repeated exposure to opiates/opioids, and tolerance can develop. These mechanisms are also associated with withdrawal phenomena.

Psychoactive Effects:
Administration by intravenous injection is typically characterised by a rapid onset of euphoria and causes a "rush" phenomena lasting for a few minutes, followed by sedation lasting a few hours. When injected intramuscularly or snorted, there is a slower onset and less intense effects. The effects of heroin are dependent on the dose administered and vary based on the quality of material, the route of administration, and the set and setting. These effects include feelings of euphoria, well-being, ataraxia, relaxation, sedation, and analgesia.

Pharmacokinetics:

Oral: Approximately 50–70 mg. Onset of 20 minutes, peak with 30 minutes, total duration of 5 hours or more. Heroin possesses considerably better bioavailability than orally administered morphine.

Intranasal: Approximately 5–40 mg. Onset of minutes, peak within 10 to 20 minutes, with a peak duration of up to 15 minutes, and a total duration of 3 hours.

Smoked: Approximately 15–25 mg. Onset of 10 seconds, peak onset within 10 minutes, with a peak duration of 5 minutes, and a total duration of 3–4 hours.

Injection: Approximately 5–10 mg intravenous for non-tolerant user. Onset is within 15 seconds, and a duration of 4–5 hours.

Adverse Reactions:

Common: Nausea and vomiting; constipation; pruritus (itching) due to histamine release; tolerance; addiction

Less Common: Loss of consciousness may occur with higher doses.

Rare: Anaphylaxis

Life-threatening: Fatal respiratory depression

Contraindications:
Hypersensitivity to morphine or other opiates/opioids; acute respiratory depression

Interactions:
Combined use with other drugs, especially CNS depressants such as alcohol and benzodiazepines, is significant, and is a strong risk factor in both fatal and non-fatal heroin overdoses. Post-mortem studies typically implicate depressants in approximately 40% of all heroin-related deaths. Respiratory drive is mediated by the brainstem, and densely innervated by μ-opioid receptors. As such, the inhibitory actions of heroin on respiratory drive are potentiated by the concomitant use of alcohol or benzodiazepines, and these combinations are a major cause of fatalities.

Harm Minimisation:
Heroin overdose is potentially life-threatening but easily managed with prompt care. If accessible, the overdose may be rapidly and reliably reversed by intramuscular administration of the opioid antagonist naloxone. There are also naloxone nasal sprays that can be used to similar effect. Although not ubiquitous, peer-based access to naloxone is legal in a number of countries worldwide, including much of North America, Europe, and Australia. Harm-minimisation policies, including ready access to naloxone, have been shown to reduce the risk of death from aspiration of vomit.

The prevalence of blood-borne viruses, particularly Hepatitis C, is exceptionally high among intravenous drug using populations. In countries where needle exchange programs are widespread, for example Australia, rates of infection are approximately 50%, while rates of 90% are seen in many parts of the United States and Europe. Under no circumstances should needles or other injecting paraphernalia (such as tourniquets or spoons) be shared or re-used.

Any individual intent on administering drugs intravenously should be advised that even in clinical settings this form of administration carries inherent risks. Such discussion is beyond the scope of this Guide; however, users should be aware of safe injecting practices, and know the risks involved from a lack of adherence to such practices. Whenever possible, heroin should not be consumed alone, nor should its purity be assumed based on prior purchases. Analysis of drug seizures indicates considerable variability in heroin purity, including unanticipated increases in purity, which can contribute to the likelihood of an overdose.

Overdose:
Despite possessing linear dose-dependent effects, heroin poses considerable risk of overdose, particularly when used intravenously. Furthermore,

tolerance develops with repeated administrations, and tolerant users may inject doses up to twice the amounts reported above. Changes in a particular intravenous drug user's tolerance to heroin following abstinence, and/or increases in anticipated purity based on prior purchases, are major contributing factors in fatal and non-fatal overdoses.

Related Compounds:
There are several structurally related analogues of morphine that are effective analgesics when used in the clinical management of pain. Prescription opioids include oxycodone (Oxycontin; Endone), hydrocodone (Vicodin, Norco), fentanyl (Duragesic), and several others. These drugs are widely abused, with significant morbidity. They vary in potencies, active doses, durations, effects profiles, therapeutic windows, and propensities for overdose. While the inclusion of detailed specifics for each of the available prescription opioids is beyond the scope of this Guide, much of the information provided above for heroin is generally applicable to any opiate/opioid drug.

KETAMINE

A dissociative used primarily in anaesthesiology, with psychedelic effects at sub-anaesthetic doses. Ketamine has also shown promise in the treatment of depression and alcoholism. Effects from sub-anaesthetic doses include sensory distortions, confusion, motor incoordination, hallucinations, and deeply dissociated states, often referred to by recreational ketamine users as a "K-holes".

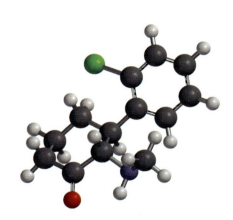

Chemical Name:
2-(2-chlorophenyl)-2-(methylamino)cyclohexanone

Synonyms:
K; Ketalar; Ketaset; Ketavet; kit-kat; special K; vitamin K

Class:
Dissociative hallucinogen; arylcyclohexylamine

Appearance:
Sometimes diverted from veterinary settings and may present in its original vial as a solution for injection. However, ketamine is more commonly encountered in powder or tablet form.

Mechanism:
Ketamine's dissociative properties are primarily exerted via NMDA receptor antagonism. Ketamine has a complex pharmacology, however, and acts upon numerous targets in the central nervous system.

Psychoactive Effects:
Dissociation characterised by loss of pain sensation, motor incoordination, and feelings of detachment from the external world. When sufficiently high doses are administered, a state referred to as the "K-hole" is reached, whose phenomenology may be reminiscent of out-of-body experiences (OBEs), near-death experiences (NDEs), and lucid dreaming.

Pharmacokinetics:

Oral: Active doses range 0.5–8 mg/kg, with approximately 6–8 mg/kg required to reach the K-hole. Onset up to 20 minutes, with a duration of 90 minutes, and hangover effects lasting 4–8 hours.

Intranasal: Active doses range 0.2–2 mg/kg, with approximately 2 mg/kg required to reach the K-hole. Onset within 5–15 minutes, with a duration of 45–60 minutes, and hangover effects lasting 1–3 hours.

Rectal: Active doses range 0.5–5 mg/kg, with approximately 6–8 mg/kg required to reach the K-hole. Onset within 5–10 minutes, with a duration of 2–3 hours, and hangover effects lasting 4–8 hours.

Injection: Active doses taken intramuscularly range 0.2–1.5 mg/kg, with approximately 1.5 mg/kg required to reach the K-hole. Onset within 5 minutes, with a duration of 30–60 minutes, and hangover effects lasting 2–4 hours. Non-medical intravenous use is uncommon.

Adverse Reactions:

Common: Loss of motor coordination; nausea; hypertension; increased heart rate; double vision

Less Common: Muscle stiffness and jerking movements sometimes resembling a seizure; hypotension; reduced heart rate; ketamine-associated ulcerative cyctitis and other lower urinary tract symptoms (LUTS)

Rare: Psychosis in susceptible individuals

Life-threatening: Anaphylaxis; severe respiratory depression with high doses

Contraindications:
Psychiatric illness, particularly schizophrenia and related psychotic disorders; history of seizures; glaucoma; any medical condition where hypertension would be hazardous (for example cardiovascular disease)

Interactions:
Use of depressants such as alcohol and GHB can result in increased CNS and respiratory depression. Benzodiazepines, for example diazepam, may prolong the half-life of ketamine. Ketamine is largely metabolised by the CYP3A4 enzyme and use of CYP3A4 inhibitors (like ketoconazole, for example) may also prolong its half-life.

Harm Minimisation:
Standard precautions as per all hallucinogens; however, there is a greater risk for psychosis and delusional ideation in susceptible individuals. Injury from loss of motor coordination is possible. Importantly, if taken via injection, the harm-minimisation practice of employing standard safe needle protocols should always be maintained. Chronic use is associated with cognitive deficits; and unlike other hallucinogens, ketamine is considered to have the potential to be psychologically addictive.

Overdose:
LD_{50} is approximately 100-fold greater than doses typically used in recreational settings. Overdose of ketamine can result in severe respiratory depression requiring medical treatment.

Related Compounds:
Other arylcyclohexylamines include methoxetamine (MXE); phencyclidine (PCP, Sernyl); eticyclidine (PCE); tiletamine (Telazol [with zolazepam]). Please be aware these agents have greatly varying durations of effects and dosages.

Additional Comments:
Although commonly used in veterinary medicine, ketamine's branding as a horse tranquilliser is a misnomer.

LSD

Lysergic acid diethylamide (LSD) is arguably the most iconic psychedelic drug. Some have described it as the "fuel" that enabled the 1960s countercultural movement. LSD is derived from alkaloids found in the ergot fungus, *Claviceps purpurea* (whose accidental ingestion was historically referred to as St. Anthony's fire). The drug was first synthesised by Albert Hofmann in 1938 at Sandoz Laboratories in Basel, Switzerland. Its psychedelic effects were discovered by Hofmann five years later following an accidental exposure, inspiring an intentional bioassay on 19 April 1943. As the LSD began to affect Hofmann, he left the lab and struggled to ride his bicycle home. Reflecting on that fateful day, Hofmann remarked: "I suddenly became strangely inebriated. The external world became changed as in a dream..."

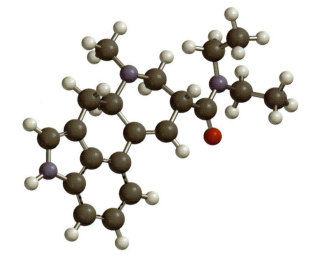

Chemical Name:
d-lysergic acid diethylamide;
- OR -
LSD-25 (being the 25th compound in a series of modified lysergamides that Hofmann synthesised to be investigated for potential therapeutic uses)

Synonyms:
Acid; Alice; blotter; Delysid®; doses; fry; gel; hits; L; Lucy; tabs; trips; uncle Sid

Class:
Serotonergic hallucinogen

Appearance:
A crystalline salt, often found as the tartrate. The drug is extremely potent, and in order to enable accurate dosing is commonly soaked into blotter paper that has been perforated into small squares ("tab"). It is also made available as a liquid, prepared by dissolving the crystal into ethanol. Other forms include pills, gelatine, and liquid dropped onto sugar cubes. LSD possesses a somewhat unstable structure, which degrades when exposed to UV light, high temperature, moisture, or chlorine.

Mechanism:
The primary mechanism associated with the psychedelic effects of LSD is its action as a partial agonist at $5\text{-}HT_{2A}$ receptors. In addition, LSD acts upon $5\text{-}HT_{1A}$, $5\text{-}HT_{2B}$, $5\text{-}HT_{2C}$, $5\text{-}HT_{5A}$, and $5\text{-}HT_{6}$ receptors. Further, LSD acts upon a large number of other G protein–coupled receptors, including dopamine and adrenergic subtypes.

Psychoactive Effects:
LSD is a classic/prototypic psychedelic; it could be said to define "psychedelic" as a descriptive class. LSD's effects include alterations to sensory- and thought-processing, resulting in powerful changes in consciousness. These changes may manifest in associative thinking, in auditory and visual perception, as closed- and open-eye visuals, states of deep psychological reflection and introspection, spiritual experiences, mood shifts, laughter, feelings of connectedness, anomalous perception of time, synaesthesia, and unusual thoughts and speech. The LSD "trip" also has potential to produce temporary anxiety, paranoia, panic, and overwhelming feelings. These may culminate into a very difficult experience, with adverse psychological effects occasionally persisting after the acute effects of the drug have worn off, sometimes for days, or weeks, or even months longer.

Pharmacokinetics:
LSD has a wide active dose range. It is most often administered orally or sublingually. Threshold ef-

fects are felt with as low as 25 μg, with moderate effects at 75–125 μg and pronounced psychedelic effects at 150–400 μg. Higher doses have been reported; however, larger amounts can be very difficult to handle, particularly in festival environments. Onset is within 20–60 minutes, with a plateau of 3–6 hours, and a total duration of approximately 6–12 hours. Acute administration of LSD results in rapid onset of tolerance to the drug and cross-tolerance to most other serotonergic hallucinogens (for example, psilocybin), lasting approximately 3–7 days.

Adverse Reactions:

Common: Anxiety; jaw tension; increased salivation and mucous production; overwhelming feelings; insomnia; difficulty regulating body temperature; slight increase in heart rate; difficulty focusing

Less Common: Nausea; dizziness; confusion; paranoia, fear or panic; tremors; increased blood pressure

Rare: Hyperreflexia; exacerbation of latent or existing mental disorders; flashbacks; and Hallucinogen Persisting Perception Disorder (HPPD), characterised by an ongoing awareness of sensory alterations reminiscent of those produced by LSD administration. It is a very rare condition, reported by individuals with previous exposures to hallucinogens.

Life-threatening: None reported

Contraindications:
Psychiatric illness, particularly schizophrenia and related psychotic disorders

Interactions:
Use of certain antidepressants such as lithium and tricyclic antidepressants may trigger a dissociative fugue state. There are anecdotal reports that lithium and LSD may be associated with enhanced risk of seizures. Use of SSRI antidepressants, for example fluoxetine, has been shown to reduce the subjective effects of several serotonergic hallucinogens, including LSD.

Harm Minimisation:
Standard precautions as per all hallucinogens. Use of vehicles and other heavy machinery must be avoided.

Overdose:
No well-documented cases of pharmacologically induced deaths from overdose on LSD have been reported, and none of the scant few LSD-related deaths described in the medical literature can be unquestionably stated as having been solely caused by LSD. In rare cases, LSD may have played a role in some suicides. And some behavioural fatalities—accidental deaths related to erratic and/or incautious behaviour—may have occurred. In one instance of non-fatal LSD overdose in eight patients who were seen 15 minutes after having snorted massive doses of LSD (having mistaken it for cocaine), "Emesis and collapse occurred along with [signs] of sympathetic overactivity, hyperthermia, coma, and respiratory arrest. Mild generalized bleeding occurred in several patients and evidence of platelet dysfunction was present in all. [...] With supportive care, all patients recovered." In recent years, with an increasing assortment of psychedelic "research chemicals" being sold on blotter (sometimes misrepresented as LSD, sometimes mistaken for LSD), there has been an increase in media reports of "LSD overdoses", which are highly likely to have involved something *other than* LSD.

Related Compounds:
There are a number of compounds related to LSD—lysergamides, both natural and semi-synthetic—with psychedelic effects similar to LSD. Compared to LSD, some of these compounds may have enhanced risk for vasoconstriction, restricting oxygen flow to tissues and muscle. Lysergamide (aka LSA, or ergine) is a naturally occurring psychedelic found in ololiuhqui (*Turbina corymbosa*), baby Hawaiian woodrose (*Argyreia nervosa*), and morning glories (*Ipomoea tricolor*). LSA is less potent than LSD, with an active dose in the range of 0.5–2 mg. Semi-synthetic derivatives include ALD-52, AL-LAD, ETH-LAD, LSM-775, LSZ, 1P-LSD, PRO-LAD, and others. The doses of most

of these agents are roughly comparable to that of LSD, with LSZ and ETH-LAD (doses to 150 μg reported) being slightly more potent, whilst LSM-775 is less potent (doses up to 750 μg reported). Differences in the active dose range and duration of effects of these analogues should be noted. Further, these compounds have not been extensively used by, nor studied in humans, and data regarding toxicity and long-term effects is limited or non-existent. Sold as "research chemicals", some of these compounds are marketed directly by the vendor having been placed onto blotter paper, and at other times they are purchased in powder form and then placed onto blotter by the customer (who may go on to misbrand the material as "LSD" in order to increase sales and/or charge more for it).

MDMA

MDMA is a stimulant with empathogenic and euphoriant properties. The drug was first synthesised by Merck pharmaceuticals in 1912 as an intermediate in the production of hydrastinine; MDMA, however, was not assessed for activity until many years later. In 1976, Alexander Shulgin initiated some of the earliest MDMA studies in humans; two years later he co-authored a journal article with David Nichols reporting on its chemistry, dosage, and effects. By the late 1970s and early 1980s MDMA, had been brought into use as an adjunct to psychotherapy. However, its growing popularity in recreational settings led to it being scheduled in the United States in 1985. Recent research argues strongly for the utility of MDMA-assisted psychotherapy in the treatment of severe posttraumatic stress disorder.

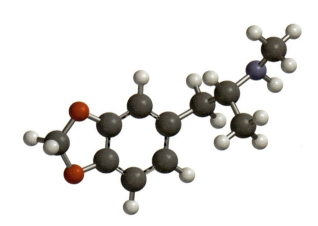

Chemical Name:
3,4-methylenedioxymethamphetamine

Synonyms:
Adam; E; disco biscuits; ecstasy; Mandy; Molly; pingers; X; XTC. Names often also reflect the large range of imprinted logos found on tablets.

Class:
Stimulant; empathogen

Appearance:
MDMA may present as a crushed powder or crystal of varying textures and colours. Colours of crystalline or powdered MDMA may include off-white, beige, yellow, pink, brown, and may be due to the presence of non-psychoactive contaminants from its synthesis. MDMA is also commonly found in pressed pill form, exhibiting various colours and logos.

Mechanism:
MDMA acts as a releasing agent of the monoamines, namely: serotonin, noradrenaline, and dopamine. Specifically, MDMA is a substrate for monoamine reuptake transporters, and has greatest affinity for serotonin transporters, through which it may be taken up into the neuron. Once in the neuron MDMA can act upon vesicular monoamine transporter-2 (VMAT2), limiting uptake of monoamines into vesicles, and increasing monoamine concentrations in the cytosol. Further actions of MDMA cause reversal of the monoamine transporters, resulting in large effluxes of serotonin (and also dopamine and noradrenaline) into the synapse, where they can act on post-synaptic receptor densities.

MDMA also has inhibitory effects on tryptophan hydroxylase and monoamine oxidase (MAO). MDMA appears to be associated with enhanced blood oxytocin concentrations, which may be involved in its pro-social effects.

Psychoactive Effects:
Euphoria; increased desire to communicate; feelings of comfort and relaxation; belonging, closeness, and bonding with others; increased awareness of senses; heightened sensuality and/or sexuality; body "buzz"; altered sense of time; difficulty concentrating; decreased hunger

Pharmacokinetics:

Oral: 50–150 mg, depending on size and sensitivity; however, 80–125 mg as commonly used active doses. Onset is within 20–60 minutes, peak effects at 75–120 minutes, duration 3–5 hours, and after-effects for up to 24 hours.

Intranasal: 30–70 mg as commonly used active doses. Onset is 10–30 minutes, with peak effects at 45–70 minutes, a duration of 3–4 hours, and after-effects for up to 24 hours. Severe pain and irritation in the nasal cavity is often reported upon insufflation (note that oral dosing is the most common route of administration for MDMA). With insufflation, the effects generally come on somewhat quicker and also subside a little earlier. However, more intense peak effects are elicited and may result in uncomfortable experiences.

Rectal: 50–120 mg, depending on size and sensitivity; however, 70–100 mg as common active doses. Onset is within 20–40 minutes, peak effects at 60–120 minutes, duration 3–5 hours, and after-effects for up to 24 hours.

Injection: Intravenous administration of MDMA is uncommon and it is advised against due to the potential for hypertensive effects and serotonin toxicity.

Adverse Reactions:

Common: Short-term memory loss; difficulty concentrating; jaw clenching; grinding of teeth; insomnia; lack of appetite; rapid heartbeat; hot and cold flashes; nausea; vomiting; dizziness; anorgasmia; dilated pupils; eye-wiggle; fatigue and depression for a few days afterwards (referred to as the "Tuesday blues" following weekend use)

Less Common: Anxiety; blurred vision; faintness; overheating (especially combined with physical activity without sufficient hydration)

Rare: Bouts of dizziness or vertigo after frequent or heavy use

Life-threatening: Dehydration; hyperthermia; hyponatremia (through overhydration); serotonin toxicity, resulting in agitation, tremors, muscle rigidity, hyperthermia, and seizures; acute hypertensive symptoms culminating in intracranial haemorrhage or acute cardiac failure

Contraindications:
Serious heart condition or hypertension; aneurysm or stroke; glaucoma; liver and kidney disorders; hypoglycaemia

Interactions:
Use of MAOIs in conjunction with MDMA may result in serotonin syndrome, overdose, and death (see the Drug Interactions section at the front of this Guide). St. John's wort (*Hypericum perforatum*) taken in combination with drugs that strongly boost serotonin (like MDMA, MDA, etc.) may

also present a risk of inducing serotonin syndrome. Use of SSRI antidepressants is associated with blunted subjective effects from MDMA. It has been speculated that poor cytochrome P450 2D6 (CYP2D6) metabolisers, which comprise approximately 7% of Caucasians, might be more susceptible to adverse reactions. If this is the case, then poor CYP2D6 metabolisers who are also taking CYP2D6-inhibiting drugs—such the antiretroviral protease inhibitor, ritonavir (Norvir)—could be at even greater risk. Indeed, there has been at least one fatality involving the consumption of ritonavir and MDMA. Other commonly used CYP2D6 inhibitors include fluoxetine (Prozac) and paroxetine (Paxil). Concomitant use of psychostimulants, such as amphetamine and cocaine, may enhance the risk of dangerous hypertensive responses. MDMA has immunosuppressive effects, and co-usage with immunosuppressants including methotrexate and corticosteroids such as prednisone may result in an immune-compromised state.

Harm Minimisation:
Some users double-dose to enhance or prolong MDMA's effects. Unfortunately, this often results in uncomfortable experiences, whilst increasing the risk of adverse effects. Additionally, re-dosing when the initial effects are subsiding may lead to blunted experiences due to serotonin depletion. Many users who double-dose also report experiencing more severe hangover effects afterwards. Without testing, dosage in tablets cannot be known.

It is important to stay hydrated, particularly if dancing within a crowded, hot nightclub. However, sometimes users who feel dehydrated and drink a lot of water, end up over-hydrating. Drinking far too much water without adequate electrolytes can cause a condition called hyponatremia. Whilst good hydration is recommended, drinking excessive amounts of water has led to fatal outcomes.

Increases in temperature have also been implicated in MDMA toxicity, suggesting that one should avoid using a hot tub while on the drug. Experiments performed on rats have shown that MDMA neurotoxicity can be prevented and tolerance between doses can be lowered via the prophylactic use of antioxidant supplements such as vitamins C, E, beta-carotene, and selenium. Some MDMA users who incorporate a nutritional approach toward minimising harm have reported fewer unwanted side-effects and less or no hangover after they began to regularly consume doses of particular vitamins or other powerful antioxidants, such as BHT, along with their MDMA.

Overdose:
Large ingestions of MDMA (>0.5g) have been reported. In many cases, minimal to moderate signs of toxicity were experienced, which included confusion, hallucinations, tachycardia, and hypertension, without hyperthermia or hyponatremia. However, severe cases of overdose can lead to coma, cerebral edema, malignant hyperthermia, seizures, serotonin syndrome, and death.

Related Compounds:
Below is a stub entry for MDA, a commonly encountered empathogenic compound similar in structure and effect to MDMA. The risks and harms as described above for MDMA also apply to compounds such as MDA; as such, it is the points of difference from MDMA that we consider below.

MDA

MDA is slightly less potent than MDMA with active dosages ranging from 50–180 mg. Onset is within 30–90 minutes, with a duration of 5–8 hours. The psychoactive effects experienced on MDA are similar to MDMA with euphoria, empathy, openness, and pleasant physical sensations experienced. However, some users describe MDA as being somewhat more psychedelic than MDMA.

This claim is seemingly verified twofold. Firstly, pharmacological studies confirm that the S-isomer of MDA (S-MDA) has appreciable affinity for serotonin receptors, including the $5HT_{2A}$ subtype commonly affected by psychedelics. Secondly, phenomenological studies describing psychedelic visual effects from S-MDA have also been reported. Additionally, MDA may pose greater risk of neurotoxicity than MDMA, due to enhanced dopamine release. Human fatalities have occurred at very high dosages of 800 mg; symptoms of overdose resemble acute amphetamine overdose and include: profuse sweating; hyperthermia; violent, irrational or stereotypically compulsive behaviour (picking at skin, etc.); seizure; and coma. If a combination of the above effects occurs, seek medical attention.

Other Analogues:
There are a great many MDMA analogues and each of them has different active dose ranges. It is important to avoid taking an excessive dose of any of them, in order to minimise adverse responses.

MDMA is a substituted amphetamine, with a methylenedioxy group attached to the 3,4-position of its phenyl ring. Other 3,4-substituted amphetamines may exhibit empathogenic effects similar to MDMA. These include 3,4-methylenedioxyethylamphetamine (MDEA) and 3,4-methylenedioxyamphetamine (MDA). Other serotonin-releasing agents with empathogenic properties, including a few developed by David E. Nichols for research purposes, have been found in recreational markets. These include 5-methoxy-6-methyl-2-aminoindane (MMAI), 5,6-methylenedioxy-2-aminoindane (MDAI), and 1,3-benzodioxolylmethylbutanamine (MBDB).

Some MDMA analogues have small therapeutic windows, which means that the risk of adverse effects is enhanced with slight increases in dose. If these are mistaken for MDMA, due to either an unscrupulous or uninformed dealer, this danger may not be appreciated and overdoses may occur. Such compounds include *para*-methoxyamphetamine (PMA), 4-ethoxyamphetamine (4-ETA), *para*-methoxy-N-ethylamphetamine (PMEA), *para*-methoxy-N-methylamphetamine (PMMA). These compounds have a much higher propensity for producing serotonin syndrome with dose escalations.

MDPV

MDPV is a relatively uncommon synthetic cathinone-based stimulant that may be euphemistically sold as "bath salts" in a marketing strategy akin to the sale of synthetic cannabinoids as "incense". Despite having been developed by the international pharmaceutical corporation Boehringer Ingelheim in 1969, reports of recreational use first emerged for MDPV in the mid-2000s. The drug's stimulant effects are reminiscent of both amphetamine and cocaine. Use may be characterised by compulsive re-dosing, and following a rise of MDPV-related fatal and non-fatal overdoses across Europe and the United States circa 2011, by 2012 MDPV became scheduled throughout much of the world.

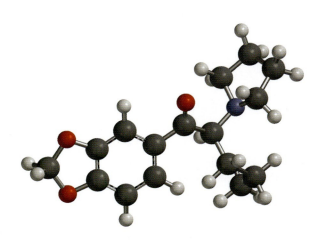

Chemical Name:
3,4-methylenedioxypyrovalerone

Synonyms:
MDPV; NRG-1; bath salts

Class:
Stimulant; synthetic cathinone

Appearance:
Hydrochloride salt presents as fine hygroscopic powder with a tendency to clump. Colour may range from white to yellow-tan with a fishy or bromine-like odour that increases with degradation.

Mechanism:
Predominant action is as a noradrenaline–dopamine reuptake inhibitor (NDRI), with limited activity on the serotonin transporter (SERT). Compared with cocaine, MDPV is 50-times more potent as an uptake blocker at the dopamine transporter (DAT) and 10-times more potent at the norepinephrine transporter (NET).

Psychoactive Effects:
At low doses, MDPV possesses stimulant effects that have been likened to methylphenidate (Ritalin), whilst at higher doses to agents such as

cocaine and amphetamine. Although described anecdotally as possessing aphrodisiac properties, MDPV does not appear to elicit empathogenic/entactogenic effects.

Pharmacokinetics:

Oral: Approximately 5–20 mg. Common active doses range 5–15 mg. Onset up to 15–30 minutes, with a duration of 2–7 hours, and hangover effects lasting 2–48 hours.

Intranasal: Approximately 2–15 mg. Common active doses range 2–10 mg. Onset up to 5–20 minutes, with a duration of 2–3.5 hours, and hangover effects lasting 2–48 hours.

Rectal: Approximately 4–18 mg. Common active doses range 4–12 mg. Onset up to 10–30 minutes, with a duration of 2–7 hours, and hangover effects lasting 2–48 hours.

Adverse Reactions:
Limited data is available. However as MDPV inhibits reuptake of dopamine and noradrenaline, hypertensive consequences may arise with dose escalations. The following adverse reactions have been reported anecdotally and clinically, although the frequency with which they may occur is unknown: increased heart rate; palpitations; hypertension; anxiety; acute kidney failure; tremor; agitation; aggression; insomnia; abdominal pain; rhabdomyolysis; panic reaction; self-harm; psychosis.

Contraindications:
Likely as per all other stimulants, including any medical condition where hypertension would be hazardous, for example cardiovascular disease, psychiatric illness, seizure disorders, and/or history of aneurysm or stroke. Further, given the higher risk of rhabdomyolysis from cathinone derivatives, greater caution should be exercised by with pre-existing renal impairment. Poor metabolisers of MDPV would be at enhanced risk of toxicity; these include those with altered CYP2C19 and CYP2D6 expression.

Interactions:
The concomitant use of agents, which like MDPV have effects on catecholamines, may enhance their effects and toxicity, and should be avoided. These range from psychostimulants such as cocaine and amphetamines through to pharmaceutical agents such as buproprion. Serious risks of death from combined use with monoamine oxidase inhibitors MAOIs. Furthermore, hepatic metabolism of MDPV is largely via CYP2C19, but also CYP2D6, and CYP1A2. Agents that inhibit CYP2C19 enzymes and may increase the effects and toxicity of MDPV include some SSRI antidepressants, and HIV antiretrovirals.

Harm Minimisation:
Given its potency, doses of MDPV should be measured using an accurate scale. Reports suggest MDPV is strongly habituating, and may be characterised by compulsive re-dosing. Dosing should be closely monitored to prevent cumulative toxicity resulting from prolonged use. Toxicity is exacerbated in hyperthermic conditions and high temperature environments. Given a number of fatal and non-fatal overdoses resulting from acute administration, and the absence of long-term toxicological data, abstinence from MDPV and related synthetic cathinones is strongly advised.

Overdose:
Data is scant. Several hospital admissions and deaths associated with MDPV use have been reported in the recent literature. Adverse effects typically involve cardiovascular and psychiatric symptoms. Refer to Adverse Reactions above.

Related Compounds:
MDPV is a cathinone with a pyrrolidino substitution at the amine. Related compounds include α-pyrrolidino-pentiophenone (α-PVP; Flakka; Gravel), 4-methyl–α-pyrrolidino-propiophenone (4-MePPP, MPPP), and α-pyrrolidino-propiophenone (α-PPP). Further substitutions made include the familiar methylenedioxy moiety of MDMA, at the 3,4-position of the phenyl group, and include MDPV itself, but also 3,4-methylenedioxy-α-pyrrolidinopropiophenone (MDPPP). Please note deaths have been associated with these related compounds. Further, each compound may have unique active dosages, onsets, durations, and propensities for serious adverse reactions.

MEPHEDRONE

Mephedrone is a synthetic cathinone. Cathinones, or keto-amphetamines, are a class of monoamine reuptake inhibitors based on cathinone (or α-amino-propiophenone), which is a naturally occurring stimulant present in the African shrub qat or khat (*Catha edulis*) with a history of use in the Arab Peninsula and Eastern Africa. Mephedrone possesses stimulant properties that are likened to that of cocaine and amphetamine, with additional empathogenic effects reminiscent of MDMA. Use of mephedrone gained prominence from 2007 onwards and from 2009–2013 it was implicated in fatalities in the United Kingdom and other countries. Although little is known regarding toxicity, compulsive re-dosing is commonly reported among users.

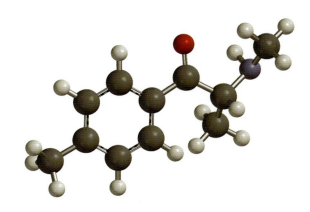

Chemical Name:
4-methyl-*N*-methylcathinone;
- OR -
2-methylamino-1-*p*-tolylpropan-1-one

Synonyms:
4-MMC; meow meow; M-CAT; MC; white magic; drone

Class:
Stimulant; synthetic cathinone

Appearance:
Most commonly presents as white powder or crystals, or less commonly in pill form. Possesses a distinctive odour that some describe as fish-like.

Mechanism:
Mephedrone (4-MMC) acts as a substrate for monoamine reuptake transporters, thereby inhibiting monoamine reuptake. 4-MMC and MDMA are equipotent in inhibiting noradrenaline reuptake. However, 4-MMC differs from MDMA in that greater potency is seen at dopamine transporters (DAT) than at serotonin transporters (SERT). Additionally, it has been suggested that 4-MMC is more potent than cathinone and methamphetamine at SERTs. Further, 4-MMC likely promotes the release of monoamines from the presynaptic terminal into the synapse; however, in terms of dopamine release, actions at vesicular monoamine transporters (VMAT) exhibit lower potency as compared with MDMA.

Psychoactive Effects:
Stimulation; euphoria; feelings of openness; enhanced mood; mild aphrodisiac effects. Produces mild perceptual changes but not hallucinations. Consumption, especially intranasally, appears to exhibit a bingeing tendency similar to that observed with cocaine use.

Pharmacokinetics:

Oral: Approximately 100–200 mg. Onset is within 30–45 minutes, with a duration of 2–5 hours, and after-effects lasting 2–4 hours.

Intranasal: Approximately 20–80 mg. Onset is within 15 minutes, with a duration of 2–4 hours, and after-effects lasting 2–4 hours.

Note: Intravenous injection of 4-MMC is extremely dangerous, with enhanced potential for serious dangerous adverse reactions. Further, the compulsion for re-dosing with mephedrone, could lead to dangerous dose escalations with this route of administration.

Adverse Reactions:

Common: Insomnia; hyperthermia; teeth-clenching

Less common: Nausea; dizziness; heart palpitations; racing heart; increased blood pressure; agitation

Rare: Rhabdomyolysis; hyponatraemia

Life-threatening: Cardiovascular problems and hyperthermia

Contraindications:
Likely as per all other stimulants. These include any medical condition where hypertension would be hazardous (for example, cardiovascular disease); psychiatric illness; seizure disorders; and/or history of aneurysm or stroke. As with other cathinone derivatives, higher risks of mephedrone-induced rhabdomyolysis may pose additional dangers to those with pre-existing renal impairment.

Interactions:
Likely as per other stimulants. Serious risk of death from combined MAOI use. The concomitant use of agents that have effects on catecholamines may enhance the effects and toxicity of 4-MMC and should be avoided. These include cocaine, amphetamines, MDMA, and other similar compounds. Further, it seems likely that CYP2D6 inhibitors will increase the effects and toxicity of 4-MMC; these inhibitors include antiretroviral protease inhibitors and some SSRIs.

Harm Minimisation:
As per all stimulants. Compulsive re-dosing of mephedrone is commonly reported. Dosing should be closely monitored to prevent cumulative toxicity resulting from prolonged use. There is evidence to suggest that mephedrone itself is not neurotoxic, but that it can potentiate the neurotoxic effects of other stimulants, such as amphetamine, methamphetamine, and MDMA.

Overdose:
Overdose most commonly presents with tachycardia, hypertension, agitation, and psychosis, and is most usually treated with fluids, benzodiazepines, or antipsychotics. Mephedrone has been implicated in fatal overdoses.

Related Compounds:
N-methylcathinone was synthesized in 1928 and was used as an antidepressant in the Soviet Union during the 1930s. Further methylation of the 4-position of the phenyl group gives rise to 4-methyl-N-methylcathinone, or mephedrone, which was first synthesized in 1929 but re-emerged as a legal psychoactive in early the 2000s.

Many substituted cathinones have since been developed in clandestine labs attempting to produce novel stimulant compounds in order to circumvent current drug legislation. Common substitutions to cathinone include methyl and ethyl groups, and/or halogens at the 2,3,4-positions on the phenyl ring, or combinations thereof. In addition, extensions on both the amine group and to the methyl group of cathinone have also been produced. As such, there is potential for a great many variants on cathinone that will likely retain substantial stimulant activity.

Some 4-substituted cathinones include the N-demethylated variant, 4-methyl-cathinone (4-MC), and also 4-methylpentedrone (4-MPD). Methylone is a cathinone analogue of MDMA, the 3,4-methylenedioxy analogue of methyl-cathinone. However, methylone possesses significantly lower affinity for vesicle transporters, likely to be the reason why its effects were reported by the late Alexander Shulgin as lacking "the unique magic of MDMA".

25I-NBOMe

25I-NBOMe is an *N*-benzyl derivative of the psychedelic phenethylamine 2C-I. It was developed in 2003 as a molecular probe of the serotonergic system. Like the other classic psychedelics and with a potency approaching that of LSD, 25I-NBOMe acts on 5-HT$_{2A}$ receptors, although unlike classic psychedelics, it acts as a *full* agonist. Troublingly, its safety profile appears less forgiving than LSD, with reports of fatal and non-fatal overdoses emerging from around 2012 and onwards. These fatalities are largely a result of 25I-NBOMe's small therapeutic window in combination with it being sold on blotter and misrepresented as LSD, one of the safest of psychoactive drugs. Hence the recent emergence of the expression, "If it's bitter it's a spitter", referring to the more strongly bitter taste of 25I-NBOMe on blotter paper (as compared to LSD), and the advice to spit the hit out.

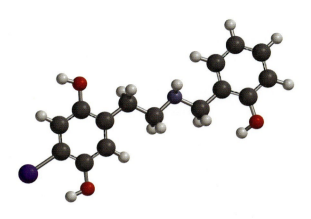

Chemical Name:
4-iodo-2,5-dimethoxy-*N*-(2-methoxybenzyl) phenethylamine

Synonyms:
25I; 2C-I-NBOMe; N-bomb; smiles; wizard

Class:
Serotonergic hallucinogen

Appearance:
White powder soluble in water

Mechanism:
25I-NBOMe acts as a full serotonin 5-HT$_{2A}$ receptor agonist with picomolar potency. It is some 500-fold less potent on its other targets. Those targets include 5-HT$_{1A}$, 5-HT$_{1D}$, 5-HT$_{1E}$, 5-HT$_{2C}$, 5-HT$_{5A}$, dopamine D$_3$ and D$_4$ receptors, α_{2C} adrenoceptor, and serotonin transporter (SERT).

Psychoactive Effects:
Characterised by visual effects akin to LSD, 25I-NBOMe alters perceptual processes, with visual patterning, auditory, olfactory, and tactile sensations reported. Changes in mental processes may include feelings of insight, emotional introspection, and altered perception of time, but also, anxiety and confusion, emotional lability, paranoia, panic, and overwhelming feelings.

Pharmacokinetics:

Sublingual/ Buccal: Active doses range 200–1000 µg, with common active doses of 500–800 µg. Onset of effects within 15–120 minutes, with peak effects for 4–6 hours, and a total duration of 6–10 hours. Hangover effects may last 24 hours or more.

Intranasal: Active doses range 200–1000 µg, with commonly consumed doses of 500–800 µg. Onset of effects within 5–10 minutes, with peak effects for 2–4 hours, and a total duration of 4–6 hours, with hangover effects lasting 24 hours or more.

Adverse Reactions:
Data regarding the frequency of adverse reactions is limited. However adverse reactions

appear to range from tachycardia, agitation, profuse sweating, and hyperthermia, to cardiac ischemia, vasoconstrictive effects, hypertension, and seizures.

Contraindications:
Psychiatric illness, particularly schizophrenia and related psychotic disorders. Due to reports of vasoconstriction in toxicology reports, any medical condition where hypertension would be hazardous, for example, cardiovascular disease.

Interactions:
No data available. In the absence of a clear understanding of its mechanism of action and toxicity, the use of others agents—recreational, therapeutic, or herbal (particularly with serotonergic activity)—is ill advised. Combined use of a monoamine oxidase inhibitor (MAOI) may be fatal.

Harm Minimisation:
The potency of 25I-NBOMe approaches that of LSD, and dosing to any safe level of precision is not possible without an analytical scale. A number of fatalities involving 25I-NBOMe are attributable to its behavioural effect (for example, lack of coordination resulting in falls), reiterating the importance of having a sober sitter present and available.

Overdose:
Overdose is characterised by severe agitation, confusion, and a significant stimulant effect, speculated to be a manifestation of serotonin syndrome.

Related Compounds:
As alluded to above, 25I-NBOMe is an *N*-benzyl derivative of 2C-I, with some 16-fold greater potency. Interestingly, the *N*-benzyl derivative of DOI lacks any such activity.

Other analogues include halogen substitutions made at the 4-position of the phenyl group in the phenethylamine backbone, which gives rise to the 25x-NBOMe compounds and includes bromine, and chlorine. Additional similar analogues include NBOMe-mescaline and 2C-B-Fly-NBOMe, amongst others. All of these compounds are likely to have unique active dosages, onsets, durations, and propensities for serious adverse reactions. See additional discussion under Related Compounds within the 2C-B entry above.

NITROUS OXIDE

An inhalational anaesthetic used in general and dental medicine for its anxiolytic, sedative, analgesic, and anaesthetic effects. Nitrous oxide is also used in: the production of sodium azide, which is employed as the explosive agent that inflates automotive airbags; it is used to enhance engine performance within the racing industry; and it acts as the lipophilic preservative and propellant that keeps whipped cream fresh and makes it fluffy. Commonly called laughing gas, nitrous was famously employed by William James, a turn-of-the-century Harvard professor of psychology and philosophy, considered to be one of the greatest of American thinkers. James (who in some circles became known as the "Nitrous Philosopher") would inhale the gas to induce mystical experi-

ences, and subsequently pursue philosophical ponderings and writings.

Chemical Name:
Nitrous oxide (N_2O);
- OR -
dinitrogen monoxide

Synonyms:
Bulbs; hippy crack; laughing gas; nitrous; nos; nangs; Whip-it!

Class:
Dissociative anaesthetic

Appearance:
At room temperature nitrous oxide is a colourless non-flammable gas with a slightly sweet odour and taste. It is commonly distributed in two forms, either in a large metal pressurised-gas tank for medical or racing industry use, or it can be found in small steel "bulbs" or "chargers" (about 7 cm in length) that are used for pressurizing whipped cream dispensers. Because the whipped cream chargers are easier to obtain, they are likely the main source for nitrous oxide that is inhaled recreationally.

Mechanism:
NMDA receptor antagonism is presumed to be the primary mechanism of action for both euphoric and dissociative effects. However, nitrous oxide also interacts with a number of other ionotropic targets, acting as an antagonist on nicotinic and 5-HT_3 receptors. In contrast, nitrous oxide has enhancing effects at $GABA_A$ and glycine receptors. The analgesic effects of the drug have not been fully explained, but are thought to involve the endogenous opioid system.

Psychoactive Effects:
Anxiolysis; analgesia; anaesthesia; euphoria; laughter; perceptual changes including sound distortions; hallucinations; feelings of detachment; dream-like state; motor incoordination; tingling sensations

Pharmacokinetics:
Unlike other drugs, gaseous agents distribute in the body according to pressure gradients between alveoli, blood, and tissues. As nitrous oxide may only be administered via inhalation, dose is usually expressed in terms of a percentage, often in terms of minimum alveolar concentrations. A 50% nitrous mix delivered via a dental gas mask usually equates to less than 10% in plasma. However, one whipped cream bulb containing approximately 8 grams of nitrous oxide is sufficient to produce immediate effects that may last for up to several minutes. Concerned about potentially serious brain damage that could be caused from hypoxia resulting from the inhalation of straight nitrous oxide, some users obtain oxygen tanks in order to blend the two gases into the safer combination preferred by dentists and anaesthesiologists.

Adverse Reactions:

Common: Loss of motor control; short-term impairment in mental performance

Less Common: Nausea; vomiting; diarrhoea; headache; amnesia; depression; fatigue; shortness of breath

Rare: Numbness in extremities with high dosages; long-term use of nitrous oxide may lead to permanent nerve damage, heart damage, and brain injury, and it can interfere with DNA synthesis. The mechanism for some such toxicity is likely due to an interaction between nitrous oxide and vitamin B_{12} synthesis, which leads to reductions in the activity of the B_{12}-dependant essential enzyme methionine synthase.

Life-threatening: At high dosages or pure concentrations, as may occur when inhaled through a mask or in an enclosed breathing space (such as a paper bag), life-threatening loss of consciousness may ensue. An airway obstructed by vomiting adds an additional level of risk.

Contraindications:
Psychotic disorders such as schizophrenia or bipolar disorder; vitamin B_{12} deficiency; middle ear pathologies; bowel obstruction; pneumothorax; immunosuppressed individuals; history of hypotension

Interactions:
Nitrous oxide has a reputation for combining well with other psychoactive drugs. Its co-administration with hallucinogens, cannabis, and *Salvia divinorum* may lead to very intense experiences, and care should be taken in regards to set and setting with such administrations. CNS depressants such as alcohol, barbiturates, benzodiazepines, opiates/opioids, ketamine, and dextromethorphan should be avoided, as the user may experience

severe adverse reactions including respiratory depression and asphyxiation.

Harm Minimisation:
Inhalation of nitrous oxide at > 50% concentrations results in a rapid loss of motor control. As such, do not inhale nitrous oxide while standing. Never use a mask or any other delivery mechanism for nitrous oxide that does not readily fall away, unless under medical supervision. Deaths are commonly associated with garbage bags falling over somebody's head, a mask that stays attached to the face, and other delivery methods that cause hypoxia/suffocation. Death usually occurs when users, attempting to achieve increasingly higher states of euphoria, breathe pure nitrous oxide in a confined space (such as a small room or a sealed automobile) or by placing their head inside a plastic bag. As a means toward mitigating possible nerve damage, before an extended nitrous oxide session some partake in the potentially prophylactic practice of pre-loading with 4–8 grams of methionine (sold by nutritional supplement vendors), along with some vitamin B_{12}, and folic acid. Because normal enzyme activity takes a while to fully recover following the consumption of nitrous oxide, limiting one's sessions and spacing them out by a couple of weeks may also be prudent.

Overdose:
As discussed throughout this entry, incorrect use of nitrous oxide can result in hypoxia and death in a very short space of time. Nitrous oxide concentrations greater than 50% impose the risk of loss of consciousness and respiratory depression.

Additional Comments:
The compulsive use of nitrous oxide may lead to psychological addiction in some users. Perhaps due to nitrous oxide's short, yet intriguing and pleasurable effects, "bingeing" in the course of a single session is a common practice. For this reason the gas is sometimes referred to as "hippy crack".

PSILOCYBIN

Psilocybin is a naturally occurring tryptamine hallucinogen present in over 200 mushroom species, predominantly of the *Psilocybe* genus. Hallucinogenic mushrooms have a rich history of use, dating back thousands of years with evidence from cave paintings in Northern Algeria through to ancient temples depicting mushroom gods in Central America. In 1955, their existence and use in shamanic rituals was "rediscovered" in Mexico by the banker and amateur ethnomycologist R. Gordon Wasson.

The effects of psilocybin are prototypic of other serotonergic psychedelics, with characteristic changes in consciousness and perception. Psilocybin has been shown to reliably produce mystical and spiritual experiences. Recently, these effects have been explored for utility in treating depression and anxiety (in palliative/end-of-life scenarios), where they appear to have provided positive and sustained outcomes.

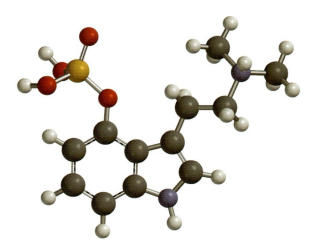

Experiments using psilocybin as an adjunct to treatment for tobacco and alcohol addiction have also shown promising results. Other recent studies have shown that psilocybin can occasion meaningful mystical experiences that result in substantial and sustained life improvement through an increase in well-being and/or life satisfaction.

Chemical Name:
[3-[2-(dimethylamino)ethyl]-1H-indol-4-yl] dihydrogen phosphate;
- OR -
4-phosphoryloxy-N,N-dimethyltryptamine;
- OR -
O-phosphoryl-4-hydroxy-N,N-dimethytryptamine;
- OR -
4-HO-DMT phosphate ester

Synonyms:
CY-39; Indocybin®; psilocibin, psilocin phosphate ester; PSOP; psilocybine / cubes; hongos; magic mushrooms; mushies; mushrooms; teonanácatl; shrooms

Class:
Serotonergic hallucinogen

Appearance:
Most commonly presents as psilocybin-containing mushrooms, either fresh or dried. May be prepared as a tea, toasted and ground-up and mixed into honey or chocolate, or packed into capsules.

Mechanism:
Psilocybin itself is not psychoactive; rather, it acts as a pro-drug, which the body metabolizes by dephosphorylating it into psilocin. It is psilocin that subsequently acts as a classic hallucinogen. Psilocin (4-hydroxy-N,N-dimethyltryptamine) acts as a partial agonist to several receptors involved with the neurotransmission of serotonin, most notably the $5HT_{2A}$ receptor, but also $5\text{-}HT_{2C}$, and $5\text{-}HT_{1A}$.

Psychoactive Effects:
As per all serotonergic hallucinogens, psilocybin's effects include alterations to sensory- and thought-processing, resulting in powerful changes to consciousness. These changes may manifest in associative thinking, deep psychological reflection and introspection, spiritual and mystical experiences, mood shifts, laughter, insights, and feelings of closeness to one's self and others. At high dosages, visual patterning is characterised by phosphenes and form constants; other auditory, olfactory, and tactile changes; anomalous perception of time; synaesthesia; yawning and sleepiness. Psilocybin also has potential to produce temporary anxiety, paranoia, panic, and overwhelming feelings.

Pharmacokinetics:
As a pure compound, active psilocybin doses range from 5–50 mg. A recent landmark study looking at psilocybin-induced mystical experiences used a high but safe dose of 30 mg psilocybin/70 kg person. The highest dose on record having been given to a human was 120 mg, and a "maximum safe dose" has been estimated at 150 mg. Pure psilocybin is virtually non-existent on the black market. For this reason, psilocybin is most often taken in the form of dried mushrooms or sclerotia (truffles).

Mushrooms of any kind should not be eaten raw. Mushrooms have very tough cell walls composed of chitin, making them practically indigestible if they are not cooked first. Employing short cooking times for fresh psilocybin-containing mushrooms or preparing dried mushrooms as a hot tea does not noticeably lower their potency, and heating the mushrooms in such manners may help prevent nausea and indigestion that raw mushrooms are more likely to produce.

The psilocybin (and psilocin) content of mushrooms varies widely depending on species, but also within species. Intraspecies variation in potency is common with natural products. For example, an analysis of fifteen specimens of cultivated *P. cubensis* showed them to contain 5.0–14.3 mg of combined psilocybin/psilocin alkaloids per gram of dried mushrooms. Generally "wood loving" mushrooms are more potent; *P. azurescens, P. cyanescens,* and *P. subaeruginosa* can be 2–3 times as potent as *P. cubensis* species (although exceptions exist). The more potent species require about half the doses presented below for *P. cubensis*. Mushrooms exhibit "maximum shelf life" and retain their potency for the longest time when they are kept whole, well dried, and stored in a moisture-free, cool or cold dark place. However, even when stored impeccably, mushrooms tend to drop in potency over time.

Dosages presented refer to *dried* mushrooms; as a rule of thumb, a dose of the same weight of the fresh fungus will contain ten times *less* psilocybin (although this figure can vary widely in each instance). This should be kept in mind regarding ingestion information that may be obtained from a guest in the course of a drug care scenario.

Active doses for dried *P. cubensis* range from 0.5 grams to doses of greater than 5 grams, with commonly used doses of 1–2.5 grams. Strong doses range 3–5 grams, and heavy visionary doses are greater than 5 grams. Onset in 15–60 minutes, with a duration of 3–6 hours, and afterglow effects lasting 1–3 hours.

Truffle dosages range from 10–25 grams fresh weight, depending on potency.

Adverse Reactions:

Common: Anxiety; fear; overwhelming feelings; nausea; gastrointestinal discomfort

Less Common: Dizziness; confusion; paranoia

Rare: Working memory disruption; light-headedness or fainting (in cases of lowered blood pressure); exacerbation of latent or existing mental disorders

Life-threatening: None reported

Contraindications:
Psychiatric illness, particularly schizophrenia and related psychotic disorders

Interactions:
The concomitant use of a number of SSRI antidepressants has been reported to blunt the subjective effects of psilocybin. In contrast, the use of monoamine oxidase inhibitors (MAOIs) has been said to increase their effects significantly. MAOIs obtained from plant sources such as Syrian rue have been combined with mushrooms for a potentiation of their effects. Such a combination has been called "psilohuasca" or "shroomahuasca". A common dose is approximately 3 grams of ground Syrian rue seeds, which effectively halves the amount of mushrooms required per dose; however, the propensity for nausea is increased. The psychoactive effects of mushrooms in combination with MAOIs have generally been reported to produce a more visual and "deeper" experience. Please be aware of the potential for dangerous adverse reactions that can result from the combination of MAOIs with some other drugs; these are summarised at the beginning of this Guide.

Harm Minimisation:
Standard precautions as per all hallucinogens. If picked from the wild, mushrooms should not be consumed unless they have been positively identified. A number of fungi are toxic, and although infrequent, deaths from the consumption of misidentified mushrooms do occur.

Overdose:
A single case appears in the medical literature where the immediate cause of death was listed as "severe pulmonary congestion" due to or as a consequence of "suspected drug intoxication (psilocin)"; this fairly well-known case documents the death of John Griggs who founded the Brotherhood of Eternal Love. Griggs appears to have consumed an unknown but presumably large amount of pure psilocybin, was having a bad reaction but refused to go to the hospital out of fear of being busted. Eventually his wife persuaded him to go, but he died just after arrival. It seems possible that the pulmonary congestion resulted from his having aspirated vomit. The lethal dose of psilocybin is unknown in humans; however, is likely to be at least several hundred-fold the active dose range. Based on LD_{50} data for rats (280 mg/kg, intravenously), it has been estimated that for an individual who weighs 80 kilograms, 22 grams of pure psilocybin might be lethal. Such a therapeutic window would require the ingestion of an impractical amount of mushrooms: 3.5 kilos dried, or 17 kilos fresh, has been given by one estimation, or "more than a person could physically eat, even if using the most potent species known" by another individual who pointed out that an oral LD_{50} would undoubtedly require more material than one based on intravenous administration.

Related Compounds:
Additional synthetic 4-substituted tryptamines include: 4-AcO-DMT, 4-AcO-DET, 4-OH-DALT, 4-OH-DET, 4-OH-DIPT, 4-OH-DPT, 4-OH-MIPT, amongst others. Each of these compounds has particular active dose ranges, durations, and varied subjective phenomena, which should be taken into account in a drug care scenario.

Additional Comments:
Alkaloids found in psychedelic mushrooms primarily include psilocybin and psilocin, but some species also contain other psychoactive N-demethylated derivatives, including baeocystin (4-phosphoryloxy-N-methyltryptamine) and norbaeocystin (4-phosphoryloxytryptamine). These minor components are likely to be cleaved into their 4-hydroxy analogues within the body before exerting effects, in the same way that psilocybin is metabolized into the active compound psilocin. The tryptamines derived from the fruiting bodies of these fungi are all substituted at the 4-position of the phenyl group, which is unusual in nature. Most naturally occurring substituted tryptamines in both the plant and animal kingdoms occur at the 5-position, like serotonin (5-hydroxytryptamine), bufotenin (5-hydroxy-N,N-dimethyltryptamine), and 5-MeO-DMT (5-methoxy-N,N-dimethyltryptamine).

SALVIA DIVINORUM

Salvia divinorum is a plant-based dissociative/psychedelic, whose primary psychoactive constituent salvinorin A is an atypical and potent hallucinogenic terpenoid. Although usually smoked in dried or fortified leaf preparations, the active ingredient may also be absorbed buccally. As such, effective administrations include "quidding" by slowly chewing a wad of leaves that is retained in the mouth, or by holding a high-proof ethanol tincture in the mouth. Salvia can produce a short-lasting dissociative-like state, accompanied by unusual and intense somatic and visionary experiences. Traditionally used as a sacrament by the Mazatecs of Oaxaca, Mexico, *Salvia divinorum* was first collected by R. Gordon Wasson and Albert Hofmann in 1962, and identified as a new species by Carl Epling and Carlos D. Játiva-M the same year.

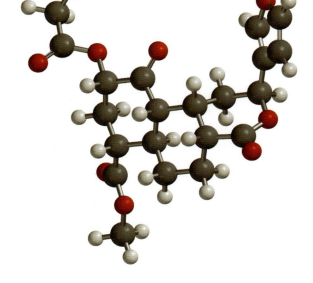

Botanical Name:
Salvia divinorum

Chemical Name:
(2S,4aR,6aR,7R,9S,10aS,10bR)-9-(acetyloxy)-2-(3-furanyl)dodecahydro-6a,10b-dimethyl-4,10-dioxo-2H-naphtho[2,1-c]pyran-7-carboxylic acid methyl ester;
- OR -
salvinorin A
- OR -
divinorin A

Synonyms:
Diviner's sage; ska María Pastora; shepherd's herbs; sadi; Sally; Sally D

Class: Dissociative hallucinogen

Appearance:
The plant usually presents as dried leaf, or as leaf fortified with extracted salvinorin A redeposited onto dried leaf to increase the material's potency. Salvinorin A is rarely encountered in its pure crystalline form.

Mechanism:

The main psychoactive component is salvinorin A, which acts as a potent non-nitrogenous agonist of the κ-opioid receptor (KOR). In addition, salvinorin A acts as a partial dopamine agonist at the D_2 receptor. Salvinorin A elicits physiological and psychological effects at doses as low as 200 μg, making it one of the most potent naturally occurring psychoactive drugs. With vaporized salvinorin A, maximum plasma concentrations are reached at 1 and 2 minutes after dosing. Vaporised salvinorin A severely reduces external sensory perception while inducing strong alterations in audio-visual perception; it increases systolic blood pressure, as well as increasing the release of cortisol, prolactin, and—to a lesser extent—growth hormone. These perceptual, cardiovascular, and neuroendocrine effects are blocked by pre-treatment with the nonspecific opioid receptor antagonist naltrexone, with the KOR partial agonist nalmefene, or the with the opioid antagonist quadazocine. As would be expected based on its binding profile, salvinorin A's effects are *not* blocked from pre-treatment with the selective 5-HT_{2A} receptor antagonist ketanserin, nor with the cannabinoid antagonist rimonibant.

Psychoactive Effects:

At high doses the effects of *Salvia divinorum* are unpredictable; whilst it can facilitate transcendent psychedelic experiences, very difficult hellish experiences have also been reported. Unlike the largely positive descriptions of effects produced by the classic hallucinogens, the subjective effects of *S. divinorum* are more often described as unpleasant. This is potentially due to its action at the κ-opioid receptor, which is implicated in dysphoric states.

The *Salvia divinorum* Information and Research Center categorises the plant's effects into six possible dose-dependant levels in its SALVIA Experiential Rating Scale. We have adapted the scale to provide a concise version here:

S — SUBTLE EFFECTS:
Mild feelings of relaxation and sensual appreciation

A — ALTERED PERCEPTION:
Colours and textures are more pronounced; altered depth perception; short-term memory difficulties; music enhancement; no visuals yet

L — LIGHT VISIONARY STATE:
Closed-eye visuals composed of clear imagery; fractal patterns; vine-like and 2-D geometric patterns; visions of objects; hypnagogic-like phenomena

V — VIVID VISIONARY STATE:
Complex fantasies and three-dimensional realistic scenes; voices may be heard; encounters with other beings, and entities, sometimes involving travels to other times and places

I — IMMATERIAL EXISTENCE:
Deep dissociation; loss of contact with consensual reality; experiences of merging with god, mind, universal consciousness; bizarre fusions/mergings with objects

A — AMNESIC EFFECTS:
Unconsciousness; complete memory loss during experience; somnambulism

Pharmacokinetics:

Inhalational: 0.25–0.75 grams of leaf as commonly reported doses. Onset is 30–180 seconds, with a typical duration of 2–20 minutes.

Buccal: *Salvia divinorum* may be consumed buccally (administered via the mucosal membranes of the cheek), by means of packing quids of the plant into the mouth. Users slowly chew these quids over a 15–20 minute period, in order to aid release of the active ingredient. A light effect may be obtained from 2 grams of dried leaf (or 10 grams of fresh leaves), a heavy experience from 10 grams of dried leaf (or 50 grams of fresh leaf). Onset is 10–20 minutes, and usually lasts for up to an hour-and-a-half.

Note: The doses listed above are for unenhanced leaf. In commercially marketed products, which are generally sold for smoking rather than for oral consumption, leaf is often fortified. The amount that it has been enhanced by is usually expressed as a figure-multiple displayed prominently upon the packaging. For example, a gram bag of a product sold as "5X" is presenting itself as having the salvinorin A content of five grams of leaf contained in one gram; a "10X" has ten grams' worth of salvinorin A per gram of material, and so on. Historically, there have been relatively few products marketed that actually set a standard concentration of salvinorin A per gram of leaf. Doing so requires a manufacturer to make a purified extraction of salvinorin A and then redeposit a specific amount onto leaf that has previously had the salvinorin A extracted from it. Producing pure salvinorin A in order to standardize potency is more labour intensive and time consuming than simply soaking a crude extraction from four-parts of leaf material onto one part of unextracted material to create a "5X" product. Because *Salvia divinorum*, like most natural products, is highly variable with regard to potency, a non-standardized "5X" could be less potent than non-enhanced leaf in one batch, and more potent than "10X" enhanced leaf in another batch, from the same manufacturer. Therefore, unless one is using a standardized extract, knowing what an appropriate dose is can be difficult. New batches of material should be tested by using small amounts at first and working up stepwise. If using an enhanced extract buccally, remember that the above-noted doses would need to be divided and reduced by whatever the product's "X" number is (so if you have a 10X, you would use one-tenth as much material as suggested). In recent years, standardized extracts have become more available, although non-standardized extracts still dominate the market.

Adverse Reactions:

Common: Loss of motor coordination and balance; dysphoria; itching; changes in one's sense of body, space, and physical balance

Less Common: Disturbed ambulatory behaviour at higher doses; headache

Rare: Psychosis in susceptible individuals. There has been one reported suicide with a perceived connection to *Salvia divinorum* use, although it would be difficult to say for certain that this drug was a primary causal factor in the death.

Life-threatening: None reported

Contraindications:
Psychiatric illness, particularly schizophrenia and related psychotic disorders

Interactions:
None reported; difficult experiences may ensue if combined with other hallucinogens

Harm Minimisation:
Standard precautions as per all hallucinogens. Salvia should be consumed whilst seated or lying down, to prevent injury from loss of motor coordination. Due to the drug's effects on balance and motor control, and potential for producing a sort of drug-induced somnambulism, a sober sitter is strongly advised, and more thought should be given to the safety of any given setting (i.e., ground floor, away from swimming pools and busy street traffic, etc.).

Overdose:
There are no known cases of Salvia overdose resulting in death. An adverse reaction is likely to predominantly be psychological in nature, requiring debrief and counselling.

Related Compounds:
A few semi-synthetic spin-offs from the salvinorin A molecule have been made for use as scientific research tools within investigations of the opioid receptor system. RB-64 or 22-thiocyanatosalvinorin A is a κ-opioid receptor agonist that exhibits biased agonism (or "functional selectivity") in signal transduction in favour of G protein versus β-arrestin-2, and it produces a long-lasting analgesia-like effect without producing as many of the prototypical side-effects associated with unbiased KOR agents. Herkinorin is an opioid analgesic analogue of salvinorin A that was discovered in 2005; and while salvinorin A is a selective κ-opioid agonist with no significant μ-opioid receptor affinity, herkinorin is a μ-opioid agonist with over 100 times higher μ-opioid affinity and a 50 times lower κ-opioid agonist affinity compared to salvinorin A. Another salvinorin A analogue is salvinorin B methoxymethyl ether, which is about five times the potency of salvinorin A and has a longer duration of 2–3 hours. But an additional analogue, salvinorin B ethoxymethyl ether, which has been given the common name "Symmetry", is even more potent! One of the pioneering individuals who first bioassayed this compound felt an "alert" of effects from 10 μg, and several experimentalists reported undeniable psychoactive effects at the 50 μg level.

SCOPOLAMINE

Scopolamine is a plant-based tropane alkaloid derived from members of the Solanaceae family, for example, *Brugmansia* and *Datura* species. Other such naturally occurring tropanes include atropine and hyoscyamine. Use of these agents may induce delirium, a severely confused state characterised by hallucinatory disturbances, delusions, incoherent speech, and amnesia. Anticholinergic tropanes, as found in mandrake, henbane, and nightshade, have a long history of magico-religious use in the "Old World" of Europe and Asia, and were traditionally associated with witches and faerie tales, as well as used as deadly poisons. Today, the consumption of anticholinergic tropanes often results in emergency room admissions, and overdose on these agents can be lethal.

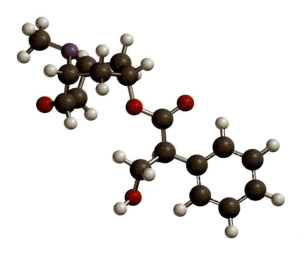

Chemical Name:
Scopolamine; 6,7-epoxytropine-tropate; Hyosol®

Synonyms:
burundunga; devil's breath; the devil's plant; hyoscine; scop; zombie drug; scop

Class:
Tropane alkaloid; deliriant

Appearance:
May appear as white tablets, often in over-the-counter travel sickness medications; found in many Solanaceous plants, including *Brugmansia* and *Datura* species.

Mechanism:
Scopolamine, atropine, and hyoscyamine are all muscarinic–acetylcholine (mACh) receptor antagonists (anticholinergic agents).

Psychoactive Effects:
Delirium; hallucinations; extreme disorientation; amnesia. Scopolamine and related tropanes are "true deliriants", in that they may induce experiences and fantasies quite removed from consensus reality, yet experienced as absolutely real by the intoxicated individual.

Pharmacokinetics:
There is no way to accurately gauge a safe dose from plant sources. This is because tropane concentrations vary widely between different individual plants of the same species and within any single individual plant at different stages of the plant's development. Since the potency of the plant material is highly variable, and considering the small therapeutic window between an active dose and a lethal one, ingestion of plants containing anticholinergics is strongly discouraged. It should be noted, however, that small amounts of tropane-containing Solanaceous species are sometimes included within indigenous preparations of ayahuasca in South America.

Travel sickness tablets commonly contain 0.3–0.4 mg of scopolamine hydrobromide, with active dosages of 0.6–0.8 mg, and toxic effects reported with dosages as little as 2 mg. Effects consist of an onset of 20–120 minutes, with a duration of up to 15 hours, and after-effects of up to a day. As such, the total duration of effects may be nearly two days. This extended timeframe can be somewhat attributed to delayed absorption, due to reduced gastrointestinal immobility.

Adverse Reactions:

Common: Mydriasis (pupil dilation); dry mouth; delirium; flushed dry skin; dizziness; incoordination of movement; tachycardia; urinary retention; cycloplegia (paralysis of the ciliary muscle of the eye, disrupting focus on near objects); gastrointestinal immobility

Less Common: Hyperthermia; myclonus (muscle jerking); respiratory depression

Rare: Seizures (increased risk in combination with other anticholinergics, tricyclic antidepressants, and antihistamines)

Life-threatening: Coma; respiratory failure; cardiovascular collapse

Contraindications:
Mechanical stenoses of the gastrointestinal tract; achalasia; paralytic ileus; intestinal atony; prostatic hypertrophy with urinary retention; myasthenia gravis; glaucoma; pathological tachyarrhythmias; megacolon

Interactions:
Scopolamine has interactions with drugs that possess anticholinergic properties, such as tricyclic antidepressants, MAO inhibitors, and antihistamines. Antipsychotics may also potentiate the effects of scopolamine. Enhanced cardiovascular effects, such as increased heart rate, may result from the use of sympathomimetic drugs, including stimulants such as amphetamine or prescription drugs such as salbutamol, in combination with tropane alkaloids. Additive sedative effects are elicited when combined with CNS depressants.

Harm Minimisation:
The use of scopolamine and related plants should be actively discouraged; a person received by drug care facilities under the effects of tropanes must have their vital signs monitored at all times, whilst emergency medical intervention is sought. If the person's behaviour is presenting a risk of harm to themselves or to others, some form of physical restraint should be employed in an appropriate manner. Seeking immediate emergency medical intervention is the recommended course of action, since absorption is so unreliable and toxic effects may not present until well after the individual was initially intoxicated. Any dose presenting as severe intoxication should be treated as an overdose.

Overdose:
Overdose symptoms will include disorientation and delirium. Dilated pupils along with flushed skin, fever and an absence of sweating may indicate that an individual has consumed tropanes, although these are signs common to many other psychoactive states as well. Overdose on anticholinergic tropane alkaloids is life threatening.

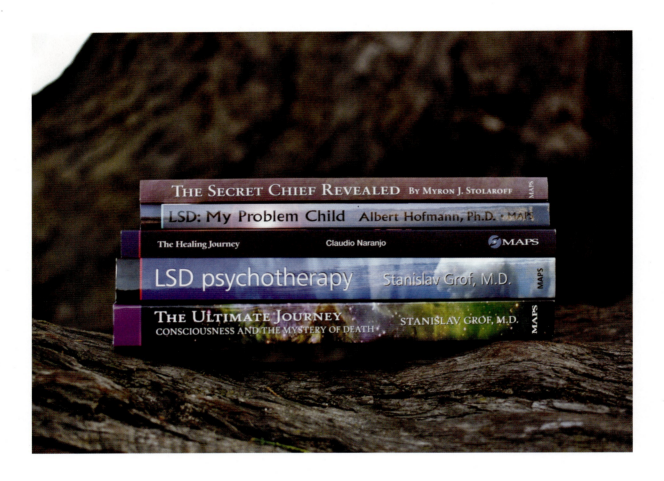

ABOUT THE PUBLISHER

Founded in 1986, the Multidisciplinary Association for Psychedelic Studies (MAPS) is a 501(c)(3) non-profit research and educational organisation. Since our founding in 1986, MAPS has raised over $36 million to develop psychedelics and marijuana into prescription medicines and to educate the public honestly about the risks and benefits of these substances.

Learn more about our work at maps.org.

MAPS works to create medical, legal, and cultural contexts for people to benefit from the careful uses of psychedelics and marijuana. MAPS furthers its mission by:

- Developing psychedelics and marijuana into prescription medicines
- Training therapists and working to establish a network of treatment centres
- Supporting scientific research into spirituality, creativity, and neuroscience
- Educating the public honestly about the risks and benefits of psychedelics and marijuana.

Our top priority is developing MDMA-assisted psychotherapy into an approved treatment for posttraumatic stress disorder (PTSD). MAPS has completed six Phase 2 clinical trials into the safety and efficacy of MDMA-assisted psychotherapy for PTSD, and is beginning Phase 3 clinical trials in 2017. Data from Phase 3 clinical trials will be submitted to the U.S. Food and Drug Administration (FDA) and European regulatory agencies, with approval anticipated as soon as 2021. With promising results and growing support from medical and therapeutic professionals, the main challenge is to raise the funds necessary to support this vital research.

For more about how you can help make psychedelic therapy a legal treatment, visit maps.org.

At the time of this publication, there is no funding available for these studies from pharmaceutical companies or major foundations. This means that—at least for now—the future of psychedelic and medical marijuana research rests in the hands of individual donors.

Please join MAPS in advancing the expansion of scientific knowledge in the promising area of psychedelic research. Progress is only possible with the support of those who care enough to take individual and collective action.

Learn more and sign up for our monthly newsletter at **maps.org**, or write to us at **askMAPS@maps.org**.

Why Give?

maps.org/donate

Your donation will help create a world where psychedelics and marijuana are available by prescription for medical uses, and where they can safely and legally be used for personal growth, creativity, and spirituality.

Every dollar we spend on this work has come from visionary individuals committed to our mission. For-profit drug companies don't invest because there is no economic incentive to develop these drugs; these compounds cannot be patented and are taken only a few times. We're encouraging government agencies and major public foundations to support our research. For now, however, it's up to individuals like you to support the future of psychedelic medicine.

To thank you for your contribution to MAPS, we offer these benefits:

> **Give $50 or more** ($60 for international donors): Receive the tri-annual MAPS *Bulletin*
>
> **Give $100 or more** ($120 for international donors): Receive a free MAPS-published book
>
> **Give $250 or more:** Receive a copy of *Modern Consciousness Research and the Understanding of Art* by Stanislav Grof, or another MAPS-published book. We'll also send a one-year *Bulletin* subscription to a friend or colleague.
>
> **Give $1,000 or more:** Receive invitations to attend special interactive webinars with MAPS' executive staff, and a silver MAPS logo pendant.
>
> *Each giving level includes the benefits for the levels listed above.*

Donations are tax-deductible as allowed by law, and may be made by credit card, or by personal cheque made out to MAPS. Gifts of stock are also welcome, and we encourage supporters to include MAPS in their will or estate plans.

maps.org/bequests

MAPS takes your privacy seriously. The MAPS email list is strictly confidential and will not be shared with other organizations. The MAPS *Bulletin* is mailed in a plain white envelope.

Sign up for our monthly email newsletter at **maps.org**.

MAPS

PO Box 8423, Santa Cruz, CA, 95061 USA

Phone: 831-429-MDMA (6362) • Fax: 831-429-6370

E-mail: askmaps@maps.org

Web: **maps.org** | **psychedelicscience.org**

More Books Published by MAPS

maps.org/store

Ayahuasca Religions:
A Comprehensive Bibliography & Critical Essays

by Beatriz Caiuby Labate, Isabel Santana de Rose, and Rafael Guimarães dos Santos

translated by Matthew Meyer

ISBN: 978-0-9798622-1-2 $11.95

The last few decades have seen a broad expansion of the ayahuasca religions, and (especially since the millennium) an explosion of studies into the spiritual uses of ayahuasca. *Ayahuasca Religions* grew out of the need for a catalogue of the large and growing list of titles related to this subject, and offers a map of the global literature. Three researchers located in different cities (Beatriz Caiuby Labate in São Paulo, Rafael Guimarães dos Santos in Barcelona, and Isabel Santana de Rose in Florianópolis, Brazil) worked in a virtual research group for a year to compile a list of bibliographical references on Santo Daime, Barquinha, the União do Vegetal (UDV), and urban ayahuasqueiros. The review includes specialised academic literature as well as esoteric and experiential writings produced by participants of ayahuasca churches.

Drawing it Out: Befriending the Unconscious
by Sherana Harriette Frances
ISBN: 0-9669919-5-8 $19.95

Artist Sherana Frances' fascinating exploration of her LSD psychotherapy experience contains a series of 61 black-and white illustrations along with accompanying text. The book documents the author's journey through a symbolic death and rebirth, with powerful surrealist self-portraits of her psyche undergoing transformation. Frances' images unearth universal experiences of facing the unconscious as they reflect her personal struggle towards healing. An 8.5-by-11 inch paperback with an introduction by Stanislav Grof, this makes an excellent coffee table book.

Healing with Entactogens: Therapist and Patient Perspectives on MDMA-Assisted Group Psychotherapy
by Torsten Passie, M.D.; foreword by Ralph Metzner, Ph.D.
ISBN: 0-9798622-7-2 $12.95

In this booklet, Torsten Passie, M.D., a leading European authority on psychedelic compounds, explores MDMA and other entactogens as pharmacological adjuncts to group psychotherapy. He presents intimate insights into entactogenic experiences from first-hand accounts of clients who participated in group therapy sessions, and crucial background on the neurobiological and psychospiritual components of those experiences. The word "entactogen" refers to compounds that "produce a touching within," and is derived from the roots *en* (Greek: within), *tact's* (Latin: touch), and *gen* (Greek: produce). Entactogen is used to describe a class of psychoactive substances that decrease anxiety; increase trust, self-acceptance, and openness; and allow easier access to memories, providing fertile ground for transformative healing.

Honor Thy Daughter: A Family's Search for Hope and Healing
by Marilyn Howell, Ed.D.
ISBN: 0-9798622-6-4 $16.95

This is an intimate true story by Marilyn Howell, Ed.D., about her family's search for physical, emotional, and spiritual healing as her daughter struggles with terminal cancer. The family's journey takes them through the darkest corners of corporate medicine, the jungles of Brazil, the pallid hallways of countless hospitals, and ultimately into the hands of an anonymous therapist who offers the family hope and healing through MDMA-assisted psychotherapy. The story was originally featured in a 2006 Boston Globe article entitled "A Good Death" in which Howell's identity was concealed. With psychedelic medicine increasingly a part of the mainstream vocabulary, in this poignant new book Howell comes out of the closet and shares with us how psychedelic therapy helped heal the bonds ripped apart by illness.

Ketamine: Dreams and Realities (out of print)
by Karl Jansen, M.D., Ph.D.
ISBN: 0-9660019-7-4 $14.95

London researcher Dr. Karl Jansen has studied ketamine at every level, from photographing the receptors to which ketamine binds in the human brain to observing the similarities between the psychoactive effects of the drug and near-death experiences. He writes about ketamine's potential as an adjunct to psychotherapy, as well as about its addictive nature and methods of treating addiction. Jansen is the world's foremost expert on ketamine, and this is a great resource for anyone who wishes to understand ketamine's effects, risks, and potential.

LSD: My Problem Child
by Albert Hofmann, Ph.D. (4th English edition, paperback)
ISBN: 978-0-9798622-2-9 $15.95

This is the story of LSD told by a concerned yet hopeful father. Organic chemist Albert Hofmann traces LSD's path from a promising psychiatric research medicine to a recreational drug sparking hysteria and prohibition. We follow Hofmann's trek across Mexico to discover sacred plants related to LSD and listen as he corresponds with other notable figures about his remarkable discovery. Underlying it all is Dr. Hofmann's powerful conclusion that mystical experience may be our planet's best hope for survival. Whether induced by LSD, meditation, or arising spontaneously, such experiences help us to comprehend "the wonder, the mystery of the divine in the microcosm of the atom, in the macrocosm of the spiral nebula, in the seeds of plants, in the body and soul of people." Nearly eighty years after the birth of Albert Hofmann's "problem child," his vision of its true potential is more relevant—and more needed—than ever. The eulogy that Dr. Hofmann wrote himself and was read by his children at his funeral is the foreword to the 4th edition.

LSD Psychotherapy
by Stanislav Grof, M.D. (4th Edition, Paperback)
ISBN: 0-9798622-0-5 $19.95

LSD Psychotherapy is a complete study of the use of LSD in clinical therapeutic practice, written by the world's foremost LSD psychotherapist. The text was written as a medical manual and as a historical record portraying a broad therapeutic vision. It is a valuable source of information for anyone wishing to learn more about LSD. The therapeutic model also extends to other substances: the MAPS research team used *LSD Psychotherapy* as a key reference for its first MDMA/PTSD study. Originally published in 1980, this 2008 paperback 4th edition has a new introduction by Albert Hofmann, Ph.D., a foreword by Andrew Weil, M.D., and colour illustrations.

Modern Consciousness Research and the Understanding of Art; including the Visionary World of H.R. Giger

by Stanislav Grof, M.D.

ISBN: 0-9798622-9-9 $29.95

In 200 spellbinding pages—including over 100 large, full-colour illustrations—*Modern Consciousness Research and the Understanding of Art* takes readers on an enchanting tour of the human psyche and a visual tour of the artwork of H.R. Giger. In this book, Grof illuminates themes related to dreams, trauma, sexuality, birth, and death, by applying his penetrating analysis to the work of Giger and other visionary artists.

The Ketamine Papers

edited by Phil Wolfson, M.D., and Glenn Hartelius, Ph.D.

ISBN: 0-9982765-0-2 $24.95

The Ketamine Papers opens the door to a broad understanding of this medicine's growing use in psychiatry and its decades of history providing transformative personal experiences. Now gaining increasing recognition as a promising approach to the treatment of depression, posttraumatic stress disorder (PTSD), and other psychological conditions, ketamine therapies offer new hope for patients and clinicians alike. With multiple routes of administration and practices ranging from anesthesia to psychotherapy, ketamine medicine is a diverse and rapidly growing field. *The Ketamine Papers* clarifies the issues and is an inspiring introduction to this powerful tool for healing and transformation—from its early use in the 1960s to its emerging role in the treatment of depression, suicidality, and other conditions. This comprehensive volume is the ideal introduction for patients and clinicians alike, and for anyone interested in the therapeutic and transformative healing power of this revolutionary medicine.

The Secret Chief Revealed

by Myron Stolaroff

ISBN: 0-9660019-6-6 $12.95

The second edition of *The Secret Chief* is a collection of interviews with "Jacob," the underground psychedelic therapist who is revealed years after his death as psychologist Leo Zeff. Before his death in 1988, Zeff provided psychedelic therapy to over 3,000 people. As "Jacob," he relates the origins of his early interest in psychedelics, how he chose his clients, and what he did to prepare them. He discusses the dynamics of the individual and group trip, the characteristics and appropriate dosages of various drugs, and the range of problems that people worked through. Stanislav Grof, Ann and Alexander Shulgin, and Albert Hofmann each contribute writings about the importance of Leo's work. In this new edition, Leo's family and former clients also write about their experiences with him. This book is an easy-to-read introduction to the techniques and potential of psychedelic therapy.

The Ultimate Journey: Consciousness and the Mystery of Death
by Stanislav Grof, M.D., Ph.D. (2nd edition)
ISBN: 0-9660019-9-0 $19.95

Dr. Stanislav Grof, author of *LSD Psychotherapy* and originator of Holotropic Breathwork, offers a wealth of perspectives on how we can enrich and transform the experience of dying in our culture. This 360-page book features 50 pages of images (24 in colour) and a foreword by Huston Smith. Grof discusses his own patients' experiences of death and rebirth in psychedelic therapy, investigates cross-cultural beliefs and paranormal and near-death research, and argues that—contrary to the predominant Western perspective—death is not necessarily the end of consciousness. Grof is a psychiatrist with over sixty years of experience with research into non-ordinary states of consciousness and one of the founders of transpersonal psychology. He is the founder of the International Transpersonal Association, and has published over 140 articles in professional journals. The latest edition of *The Ultimate Journey* includes a new foreword by David Jay Brown, M.A., and Peter Gasser, M.D.

Shipping and Handling

Shipping varies by weight of books.

Bulk orders are welcome. Please contact MAPS for details.

Books can be purchased online by visiting **maps.org** (credit card or Paypal), over the phone by calling +1 831-429-MDMA (6362), or through your favorite local bookstore.

You may also send orders by mail to:

MAPS

P.O. Box 8423

Santa Cruz, CA, 95061

Phone: +1 831-429-MDMA (6362)

Fax: +1 831-429-6370

E-mail: **orders@maps.org**

Web: **maps.org**
      mdmaptsd.org
      psychedelicscience.org